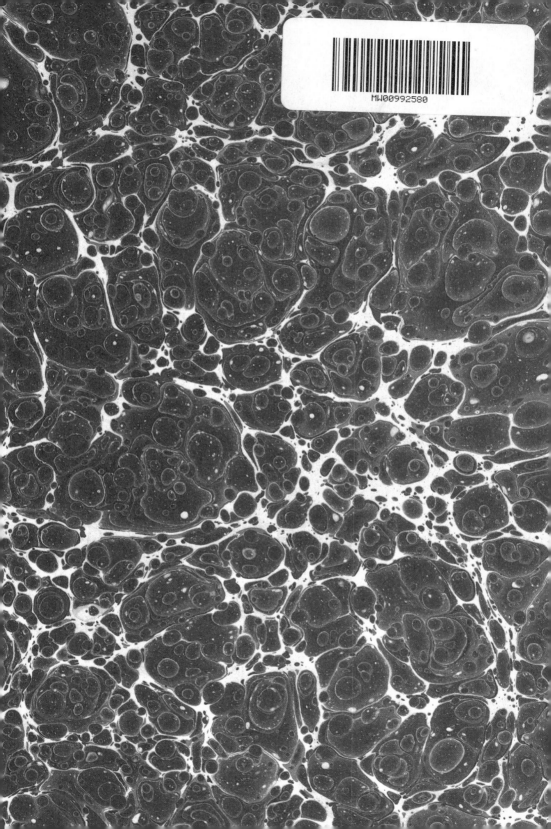

OSTFRONT 1944
Alex Buchner

Also by Alex Buchner
The German Infantry Handbook • 1939-1945

OSTFRONT 1944

The German Defensive Battles on the Russian Front 1944

Alex Buchner

Translated from the German by David Johnston

Schiffer Military/Aviation History
Atglen, PA

Translated from the German by David Johnston.
Cover photo courtesy of Ullstein Verlag.

Book Design by Robert Biondi

Printed in the United States of America.
ISBN: 0-88740-282-8

This book was originally published under the title,
Ostfront 1944,
© 1988, by Podzun-Pallas Verlag.

We are interested in hearing from authors with book ideas on related topics.

Published by Schiffer Publishing Ltd.
4880 Lower Valley Road
Atglen, PA 19310
Phone: (610) 593-1777
FAX: (610) 593-2002
E-mail: Schifferbk@aol.com.
Visit our web site at: www.schifferbooks.com
Please write for a free catalog.
This book may be purchased from the publisher.
Please include $3.95 postage.
Try your bookstore first.

In Europe, Schiffer books are distributed by:
Bushwood Books
6 Marksbury Road
Kew Gardens
Surrey TW9 4JF
England
Phone: 44 (0)181 392-8585
FAX: 44 (0)181 392-9876
E-mail: Bushwd@aol.com.

Try your bookstore first.

Foreword

The fate of the German Sixth Army surrounded in Stalingrad was decided in early 1943, marking the turning point in the eastern campaign. From then on the German forces were steadily on the retreat in the face of continual Soviet offensives. As 1944 began, the superiority of the Red Army had become so crushing, aided by the obstinacy at the highest levels of German command, that the German Eastern Front, which was under heavy pressure everywhere, suffered a number of disasters which cost the eastern armies alone more than half a million German soldiers killed, missing and wounded.

It began with the Cherkassy Pocket, where two corps were smashed. Then followed the end of the German forces defending Ternopol, the belated evacuation of the Crimea, the destruction of Army Group Center, the failed breakout of an entire army corps from the encirclement near Brody and the collapse of the entire Army Group South-Ukraine in Rumania. The hundreds of thousands of German soldiers who had to endure this fate were symbols of distress, suffering, sacrifice and death, of fulfillment of duty, courage and comradeship, as well as of fear, desperation and self-sacrifice. It borders on the miraculous that the German soldier continued to stand and hold out despite these bitter setbacks of such enormous proportions.

Cherkassy and Ternopol, Crimea and Sevastopol, Vitebsk, Bobruisk and Minsk, Brody, Jassy and Vutcani entered the history of the Second World War as beacons in a pitiless struggle with tragic results.

These truly dramatic events, concealed at the time and until now the subject of only a very few essays, are not well known. They are brought together in this volume for the first time. In addition to purely military history, individual divisions and former combatants have been given their say in order to better illustrate the nature of the inferno of those days and weeks.

This is a book which shows what German fighting men, officers as well as common soldiers, had to endure at a time when the war was already lost.

This is a book that had to be written, because never again should such a thing be allowed to happen.

Dillishausen, Summer 1988   Alex Buchner

CONTENTS

Photo Section Follows Page 160

Introduction

Adolf Hitler was legally named Chancellor of the German Reich on January 30, 1933 by the then Reichspräsident von Hindenburg. Strengthened by domestic and foreign political successes, he quickly became the all-powerful dictator of Germany. Hitler was leader of the political party he had built, the National Socialist German Workers Party, with all of its ubiquitous sub-organizations. He became head of state, Reichskanzler and Reichspräsident in one, and from 1938 was also Commander-in-Chief of all the German Armed Forces. To the German people he remained simply *der Führer*.

In 1939 Hitler launched the campaign against Poland, which widened into the Second World War. Following the subsequent victorious campaigns in Holland, Belgium, France, Norway, Yugoslavia, Greece, Crete and North Africa he was hailed by German propaganda as the "greatest strategist of all time." By the beginning of the Russian Campaign Hitler had lost sight of what could be realistically expected from the armed forces which he commanded, subordinating such considerations to his political and economic interests, as well as to thoughts of his own prestige. His unlimited self-overestimation was summed up in one sentence when he took over command of the army during the Winter of 1941: "The little matter of operational command on the Eastern Front is something anyone can do."

At the latest, Hitler's unsuccessful conduct of the war became apparent with the destruction of the Sixth Army at Stalingrad in the Winter of 1942/43 and the final abortive German offensive near Belgorod-Orel in the summer of 1943. From then on the growing Soviet forces launched one offensive after another along the entire front, from Finland to the Black Sea, while the ever more depleted German divisions were constantly on the retreat. The result for the German Army was heavy defeats and disasters which could no longer be made good. Hitler's estimation of the Soviets was such that he always believed they were just about finished. This was wishful thinking, because exactly the opposite was true. His whole strategy in the face of the continual enemy advances exhausted itself in obstinacy: no surrender of a single square meter of captured ground [1], a defense at any price, which made the change to a flexible conduct of the war impossible and denied an elastic defence. Frederick the Great had said: "He who wants to defend everything, defends nothing." With Hitler, on the other hand, unwilling to listen to reason, the watchwords were: hold! – stay put! – not one step back! The bridgeheads, "fortified locations", great advances of the front, and so on, which he demanded, underline this obstinate and stubborn thinking. On the situation maps he saw only the many pencilled-in German divisions and corps without considering that these had long since ceased to possess capabilities equivalent to their designations, and often possessed only half their authorized strengths.

Hitler considered the senior commanders at the front, themselves Field Marshals and commanders of armies, as mere takers of orders whom he replaced at will, and who often enough were made scapegoats for his own command errors. Their freedom of decision was so restricted that any withdrawal or the smallest realignment of the front, even the deployment of a single division, had to be approved by Hitler from his distant headquarters in Rastenburg, East Prussia, or from his home in Berchtesgaden. Two examples should illustrate just how vigorously this policy was enforced: When, in the winter of 1941, *General* Sponeck dared to withdraw his corps (which consisted of only a single division) from the Crimea on his own initiative because it was in danger of being cut off, he was brought before a court martial on Hitler's orders, sentenced to death and later shot. In early 1944 Hitler declared Rovno in the Ukraine a "fortified location" with a garrison of 600 men. The enemy had already entered the city and there were no reserves available. *Generalleutnant* Koch therefore ordered his forces to pull back to positions just southwest of Rovno. For this independent order he was sentenced to death by a court martial on Hitler's orders for "reckless disobedience." Massive protests by the army group and army led to Koch's return. Demoted to the rank of *Major*, he was sent back to the front to "prove himself."

To sum up, Hitler saw things as he wished them to be, refusing to admit the facts. The reality was very, very different.

•

By far the strongest branch of the German Armed Forces, or Wehrmacht, the Army, which by the beginning of 1944 had been forced to wage a more than four-year-long war, had already suffered heavy losses, with about 1.6 million dead, including 33,700 officers. These losses weighed especially heavy, because in the face of personnel and materiel shortages they could no longer be replaced. During the almost ceaseless battles of defence and withdrawal on the Eastern Front since mid-1943 the German divisions had literally been burned out, their strength exhausted. Divisions were now more or less large battle groups. Regiments, battalions and companies, as well as independent battalions and batteries, had sunk to far below their authorized strengths, a large percentage of weapons and equipment had been lost, the units in many cases lacked mobility due to missing equipment, and the men were exhausted as a result of the continuous strain without adequate time to rest and recover. The inadequate numbers of young and inexperienced replacements which reached the front could not make good or replace the heavy losses in experienced soldiers, NCOs and officers, no matter how willing to fight they were.

In the field of armaments the most acute shortages were in artillery, assault guns, prime movers, self-propelled weapons, anti-aircraft guns and heavy anti-tank guns. The one-man anti-tank weapon which had been urgently demanded for so long was only just entering service (the *Panzerfaust*). As a result, the Soviet tank remained the greatest threat to the German infantryman.

In the panzer force, which had made possible the spectacular "lightning victories" of the early war years – when tanks were employed for strategic purposes for the first time – the divisions had virtually all been reduced to the status of battle groups, and there was a shortage of armored vehicles. Commanders now employed panzer divisions only for local, limited counterattacks and thus they were used up and frittered away.

Then there was the defensive system, which due to the shortage of forces scarcely warranted the title. It always consisted of a linear disposition of divisions, one unit beside the other, without any great depth. The line consisted of simple earthworks reinforced by wooden beams, which offered no protection against a direct hit by a heavy artillery shell or a bomb. These shelters, which also served as the soldiers' quarters, were designated as bunkers.[2] The most forward part of the system of positions formed the Main Line of Resistance (HKL, or *Hauptkampflinie*), which consisted of a few trenches, infantry positions and earth bunkers, with barbed-wire and mine obstacles in front. Then there was the Main Defensive Position (HKF, or *Hauptkampffeld*) which was about four or five kilometers in depth. Within this zone were located the positions of the heavy weapons (heavy machine-guns, heavy mortars, anti-tank guns, light and heavy infantry guns), command posts and – when these had made their way up – a limited number of reserves. Behind these were the artillery positions and the supply train areas with their billets – and then the end of the defensive line. Still farther to the rear there were usually well-built blocking, intermediate and rear defence positions, but these were unmanned and therefore worthless.

Once the limited depth of the HKL and the HKF had been pierced and the troops manning the defensive line were under constant pressure from the enemy, it was virtually impossible for them to regroup and settle down again in the rear positions. Hitler placed no value in such positions in the rear areas and was often against them. ("They encourage the Generals to have an eye to the rear," he once observed.) As a rule, the available reserves were one division for each army, one battalion for each division and one company for each regiment – a laughable number.

It was obvious that any major Soviet offensive must lead to the immediate penetration and breakthrough of such a defence, with all of the unavoidable consequences.[3]

The Luftwaffe still had moderate resources available in early 1944 and provided valuable support. However, following the invasion in the West and the increasingly heavy bombing raids on Germany that summer, its presence diminished. The long-time German command of the air over the Eastern Front was lost.

Contrary to what Hitler had so often prophesied, the Russian colossus was not on the verge of collapse. On the contrary, The Red Army had recovered surprisingly quickly from the many defeats of 1941 and 1942, and had become more powerful than ever thanks to the tremendous reserves of man-power in the East, an immense armaments production and the deliveries of materiel from the Allies.

Stalin, dictator of the Soviet Union and Hitler's opposite number, had taken a decisive step when he called not for the defence of the Soviet state, which was loved by few Russians, but appealed to Russian patriotism and proclaimed the "Great Patriotic War." Every Russian understood and approved of the defence of "Mother Russia." A new group of military commanders had replaced the old, which had often failed. They had learned enough of the German principles of command: breakthroughs and subsequent advances without regard to lengthening, open flanks; quick, sweeping movements by tanks and motorized units; pincer operations and double-sided envelopments; encirclement of the enemy with following infantry armies, and so on. Offensives by the individual large formations (Fronts[4,] Armies) were always closely coordinated by the senior operations staffs.

The Russian infantry had not become better than the German, but their shattered and decimated units were rebuilt in quick time from the Soviet Union and the recaptured territories, while their vast resources allowed them to form new, fresh and powerful front-line units. Outfitting of the troops with automatic weapons was good, and plenty of anti-tank weapons were on hand. Mobility was increased through growing motorization and the unique Soviet style of infantry riding into battle aboard tanks.

Soviet tank units, initially parcelled out in brigades and battalions to support the infantry, had now been concentrated in tank armies and corps.[5] These represented extremely mobile operational units possessing considerable striking power. Already streaming from the Soviet tank factories was the proven T-34, supplemented towards the end of the war by the super-heavy "Stalin" tank and large numbers of assault guns. The total production of the Soviet tank industry was enormous. Stalin himself had declared that artillery was "the God of War." In addition to the lavish numbers of artillery pieces (some of which were quite outstanding, especially the 7.62-cm multi-purpose gun, the much-feared "*Ratschbum*") supplied to individual divisions, there were independent mortar regiments, artillery divisions and even artillery corps. The concentrations of artillery and the preparatory bombardment before a Soviet offensive were always overwhelming.

The greatest surprise in 1944 was the Soviet Air Force, which appeared to have been almost destroyed after the first years of the war, but which now intervened in every battle with tremendous numbers of new bombers and close-support aircraft.

In addition to the Soviet arms industry, which in contrast to Germany's was not threatened by enemy air attack and therefore could produce on a tremendous scale, the Red Army was also strengthened by the unhindered deliveries of tanks, aircraft, motor vehicles, weapons and military equipment of every description from the Allies, which reached their peak in 1944.

Thus in a few sentences the question is answered as to why the Soviets could destroy so many still effective German Eastern Front divisions, often within a brief period of time. In addition to the completely misguided senior German command and the steadily decreasing strength of the German Army, it was the tremendous numerical superiority of the Red Army in soldiers, tanks, artillery and aircraft, in addition to the improved morale brought about by its successes, that had transformed it into an overpowering opponent.[6]

Germany's military situation at the beginning of 1944 was as follows: The setbacks on the Eastern Front had begun with three major Soviet offensives in the South between November 1942 and January 1943, which had led to the collapse of the entire southern sector. The Sixth Army had been lost at Stalingrad and Army Group A was forced to evacuate the Caucasus. Not until mid-March 1943 was the

Soviet offensive brought to a halt near Kharkov.

Germany's attempt to regain the initiative through Operation *"Zitadelle"* failed when the Red Army succeeded in breaking into the flank and rear of the German Army Group Center near Orel.

The Soviet general offensive broke out on July 17, beginning on the Donets. Russian forces, far superior in men and materiel, recaptured the entire area between the Sea of Azov and the Upper Dniepr, cutting off the German-occupied Crimea. On January 4, 1944, Soviet divisions crossed the former Russian-Polish border at Wolhynien.

As on all other fronts, the military initiative in the East had passed to the enemy. The battle in North Africa had ended on May 13, 1943, with the surrender of Army Group Afrika in Tunis, and it was only two months later that Allied forces landed in Sicily. Germany's Italian allies could take no more and concluded a cease-fire with the enemy. Encouraged, the Allies landed in southern Italy a few days later. A new third front had been created, after the battle against the growing strength of the Greek and Yugoslavian partisans had become the second front. And finally, with the landing of the Allies in Normandy on June 6, 1944, there was added a fourth front in the West. The battle by German U-Boats in the Atlantic had been lost and Germany lay increasingly helpless under the bombing attacks of the Allied air forces. The "Battle for Europe", a catch-phrase which originated at that time, had begun.

At the beginning of this catastrophic year German divisions in the East were still deep inside Russia in the Crimea, the lower Dniepr and before Leningrad; by the end of the year they had been pushed back to Budapest, the Vistula and as far as East Prussia. Of four German Army Groups, two had been lost, of eleven Armies, six had been destroyed and five badly battered. In the six Eastern Front battles described herein, over 600,000 German soldiers were killed, posted missing or taken prisoner.

A withdrawal of the entire Eastern Front behind an "East Wall" at the beginning of 1944 could have helped avoid these tremendous losses and protected Germany's frontiers in the East.

Notes:

[1] His dictum: "Where he has once set his foot, the German soldier will never retreat."

[2] The expression "bunker" originates from the First World War, and refers to block-shaped concrete structures, which were employed mainly in the shell-torn terrain of Flanders.

[3] An example of a Soviet defensive system is the one constructed by them in the summer of 1943, when they were expecting a German attack in the Belgorod-Orel area. The entire Kursk salient, which featured three continuous lines each separated by ten to twenty kilometers, was occupied by troops, anti-tank guns, artillery and tanks. Behind these were three further unoccupied systems of positions forty to eighty kilometers apart.

More than 300,000 people from the civilian population were employed in the digging of field positions alone.
[4] A Soviet "front" was roughly equivalent to a German army group.
[5] At the beginning of 1944, for example, the normal disposition of a Soviet tank army at full authorized strength consisted of two tank corps, a motorized-mechanized corps, units of other arms and supply services. Its strength was 46-48,000 men, 620 tanks and 190 assault guns.
[6] This was obvious from the ever-decreasing numbers of deserters – in contrast to the first years of the war.

I

Cherkassy:
XI and XXXXII Army Corps

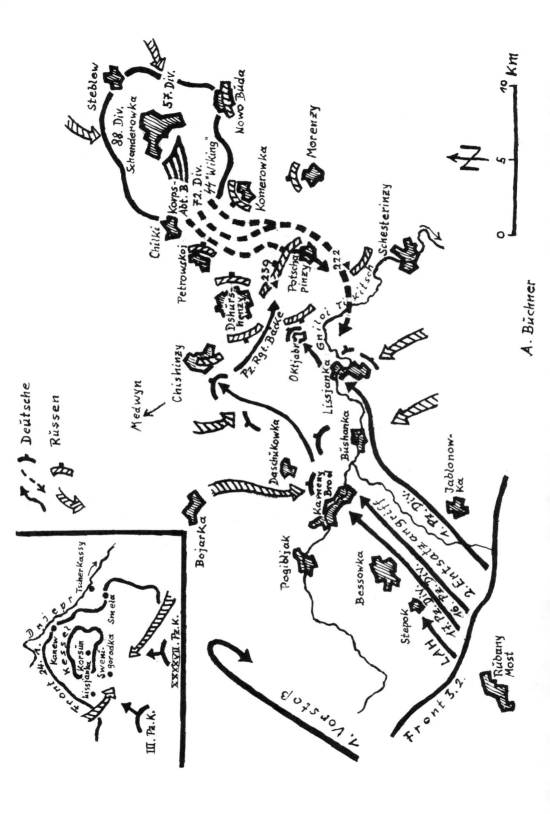

Cherkassy: XI and XXXXII Army Corps

Winter Drama on the Gniloy Tikich

The Ukraine – the fertile Russian land of black earth between the Dniepr and the southern Bug – a vast, open, rolling country, wooded in places, interspersed with deep clefts (*balkas*). Towns and farm villages lay in valleys and sometimes on the low hills, linked by unpaved roads and paths. In summer giant, almost endless, fields of corn and sunflowers stretched across the countryside. Winter brought bitter cold and deep snow; it was the time when Russian farm families huddled around the large clay ovens in their houses and cottages. And then, in the spring and autumn, there was the *rasputitsa*, the period of absolute immobility. Under the influx of the autumn rains or the spring thaw, the hard earth was transformed overnight into knee-deep mud which dissolved roads and pathways, bringing large-scale movement to a halt or at least reducing it to a tiresome struggle on the few, poor roads.

This then was the stage on which the following dramatic events were to take place.

Two Army Corps Surrounded

During their winter offensive of 1943/44, the Soviets had succeeded in bringing about the collapse of the German defenses on the middle Dniepr, crossed the river and advanced westward. The only German force still holding a front along the river was the Eighth Army, with XI and XXXXII Army Corps, which held a sector approximately 100 kilometers long between Kanev and Cherkassy. This sector extended much further to the east than the remainder of the German front. The German units there had held their positions throughout January 1944.

Feldmarschall von Manstein, Commander-in-Chief of Army Group South, had been unable to move Hitler to give up this bulge in the front. They must fight for time until the situation was clarified by the expected invasion in the West, and therefore must hold out where they were, was Hitler's argument. He therefore refused to order a withdrawal of the front – until it was too late.

At the beginning of January 1944 the Soviets launched an offensive thrust in the direction of Uman and Vinnitsa with the First Ukrainian Front. This was halted and thrown back after heavy fighting. Uman, the supply base for Army Group South, was saved. Following this setback the Soviets turned to the bulge in the German front near Cherkassy. A major offensive followed on January 24. The Fifth Guards Tank Army of the Second Ukrainian Front under Army General Konev attacked from the east to the northwest against the German XI Corps while, following a violent artillery bombardment, Army General Vatutin's First Ukrainian Front resumed its breakthrough attempt, this time attacking from the northwest to the southeast against XXXXII Corps. In the east the Soviets succeeded in breaking through Eighth Army's front near Schpola and in the west against the First Panzer Army in the area of Biala Zerkov. Streaming through the gaps in the German front behind the tanks, in spite the defensive fire, were dense masses of infantry and entire cavalry units.

The spearheads of the First and Second Ukrainian Fronts[1] met on January 28 northeast of Uman near Svenigorodka. The German salient containing XI and XXXXII Army Corps had been cut off from all contact with the rear. Despite all countermeasures, two German corps had been encircled in five days.

Something had to happen, and quickly, if a second Stalingrad was to be avoided. The most rational solution would have been to give the order to both corps for an immediate breakout to the southwest to reestablish contact with the German front and help close the enormous gap which had arisen between First Panzer Army and Eighth Army. Initially, all that could be done was to insert two infantry divisions into the gap in an effort to provide at least a makeshift defence there. However, the most senior level of the German command not only forbade a breakout from the pocket which was forming, but proposed that the Russian forces which had broken through be encircled. Hitler was still planning large-scale operations, and an offensive was to be carried out, which incorporated the territory still held by the two corps around Kanev-Korsun. In his opinion the Soviet divisions had been exhausted and bled to death (once again) during the heavy fighting of the past winter. A powerful German thrust was to be carried out along the Dniepr to Kiev, cutting off everything Russian that had advanced across the river to the West. It was to be a repetition of one of the great battles of encirclement of 1941/42, which would deliver a death blow to the Russian colossus before the beginning of the invasion in the West. The plan would have been good if it had corresponded to reality and to the facts, but these looked quite different at the front than in Führer Headquarters 1,000 kilometers away.

The First Tank Attack – The Shot Misses

Army Group South was not disinclined toward the first part of Hitler's plan, to encircle the Soviet pincers around the two German corps. Nine panzer divisions were to be committed. The orders were as follows:

> To the First Panzer Army: It was to bring the battle against the Soviet First Tank Army east of Vinnitsa to a conclusion and disengage III Panzer Corps as quickly as possible. The corps was to transfer the 16th and 17th Panzer Divisions and the SS-Panzer Division "LAH"[2], as well as Heavy Panzer Regiment Böke to the right wing of the army in the area of Uman and assemble it there as the northern attack group. The 1st Panzer Division was to follow as soon as possible.
>
> To the Eighth Army: It was to disengage XXXXVII Panzer Corps, with the 3rd, 11th, 13th and 14th Panzer Divisions, from the front and assemble them behind its left wing before Svenigorodka as the southern attack group. The 24th Panzer Division was to be sent in later.

But what kind of shape were the nine Panzer Divisions really in?
On February 3, First Panzer Army had only the 16th and 17th Panzer Divisions ready for action. Both divisions were battle-weary and had received barely two days rest since their transfer from the previous area of operations. The other two panzer divisions had not yet arrived. The Eighth Army, separated from the First Panzer Army by a large gap and itself hard pressed by the Soviets, could provide little in the way of help. The 24th Panzer Division, which was at full strength, was ordered by Hitler to the Nikopol bridgehead where fighting had flared up once again.

In vain the Commander-in-Chief of the Eighth Army, *General* Wöhler, pointed out that the forces available for the planned counter-blow would not be strong enough, and that in regard to his two corps within the pocket there was no time for large-scale operations. He also made a futile request that III Panzer Corps not be committed to the encirclement of the Russians as planned, but rather that it establish contact with XXXXVII Panzer Corps as quickly as possible for a joint advance directly at the pocket, as otherwise the two corps would succumb to the growing enemy pressure from all sides. Army Group South, however, stuck with Hitler's plan. On February 1 the Eighth Army attacked from the south with the 11th and 13th Panzer Divisions. With the weak forces available the attack failed to reach the pocket. As ordered, the First Panzer Army assembled General Breith's III Panzer Corps as the northern attack group for the northward thrust. It was to veer to the east in the vicinity of Medwyn, surround and destroy the Soviet forces between it and the pocket and at the same time free the encircled corps.

Early on the morning of February 4 *General* Breith launched the attack with the 16th and 17th Panzer Divisions –including the Heavy Panzer Regiment under *Oberstleutnant* Dr. Böke with thirty-four Tiger and forty-seven Panther tanks, a considerable force. The attack had scarcely got under way when the weather god intervened. As the winter of 1941/42 had been the coldest and had seen the most snow in 140 years, so now the winter of 1943/44 in the southern sector of the Eastern Front was the shortest and mildest in human memory. Up until February 5 the Ukraine had lain under about 60 centimeters of snow and temperatures of minus 15 degrees. The next day saw a sudden influx of warm air. Sun, rain and a warm wind combined to create a powerful, very early thaw, which brought on the dreaded *rasputitsa*, the rapid transformation of the entire region into a sea of mud. The Ukrainian soil was turned into a deep, thick, viscous brew which froze solid during the colder nighttime hours. The panzer and motorized units became stuck in the bottomless morass of this unexpected muddy period on the third day. The attack as a whole gained ground to the north in the face of great difficulties with the terrain and heavy fighting, until all movement finally succumbed to the deep mud and stiffening Russian resistance. On February 7 the entire counteroffensive ground to a halt. III Panzer Corps jutted northwards like the point of a wedge, extending thirty kilometers into enemy territory. Thirty kilometers still separated it from the pocket to the east, which had meanwhile become the scene of heavy fighting. There was no doubt that the thrust by the northern attack group had failed – it had neither surrounded the Russians nor freed the encircled corps. The southern attack group, XXXXVII Panzer Corps, had scarcely deployed its weak panzer divisions when it was pushed back and forced onto the defensive by the Russians. Hitler's great plan had come to nothing right at the outset. At least the two advances had forced the enemy to form a double ring around the pocket – one to encircle the surrounded German corps, and the other to defend against further relief attacks.

But five days had been lost by these first unsuccessful advances, days in which the enemy, making use of the railway lines in the Cherkassy area, moved in further substantial forces and large amounts of materiel.

Emergency in the Pocket

As already stated, the German VI and XXXXII Army Corps had been surrounded in an initially huge pocket, whose northern front was still on the Dniepr. The encircled units consisted of the 57th Infantry Division (with attached elements of the 389th Division), the 72nd and 88th Infantry Divisions, *Korpsabteilung* B[3], the 5th SS-Panzergrenadier Division *Wiking* (with the attached Assault Brigade *Wallonie*)[4], with corps units, supply services, Russian auxiliary volunteers ("*Hiwis*"), and so on, according to an Eighth Army daily report a total of about 56,000 men. From the time of the encirclement the two corps, under the command of the Commanding General of XXXXII Corps, were designated "*Gruppe Stemmermann*."

The commanders in the pocket were aware that only quick and decisive action on their part would lead to their rescue. First of all they had to establish new fronts at the breakthrough points, especially in the south. As there were no reserves available, elements had to be taken from both corps in battalion strength, which led to a great intermixing of units. The major enemy penetrations against XXXXII Corps accelerated the withdrawal of the front in the north, in the course of which the Dniepr positions were abandoned. In the southeast, XI Corps withdrew from one intermediate position to the next. By February 6, contrary to expectations, the German forces had succeeded in establishing a continuous, temporary pocket front of 150 kilometers. The focal point was the large town of Korsun[5] with the pocket's lone airfield, through which supplies were at first flown in, the sole direct contact with the outside world. Otherwise the only communication was by radio. The pulling-back of the front freed some units which could be used as vitally needed reinforcements and as a limited reserve; however, the pocket had to be kept at a reasonable size for the forces available. It could not be allowed to become too narrow, otherwise the necessary freedom of movement within the pocket would be lost and the forces inside would become too vulnerable to enemy artillery fire.

At first the soldiers knew nothing of these important and necessary command measures, but they felt the effects of them every day. There were no longer any fortified positions, bunkers or billets. With the move to new positions the pocket was constantly changing form, and this meant not only fighting day and night, but also marching, wading through knee-deep muck and digging new, meager shelters. The infantry lay in the open fields without cover, their uniforms were soaked daily by the rain and froze to their bodies during the night.

The following are some notes from the pocket:

"February 1:

The positions on the Dniepr have been abandoned. – Fighting in deep mud, filth and water.

February 3:

Enemy attacks in the south and southwest are intensifying, pushing the surrounded units further back towards the north in order to further distance them from their own front outside the pocket.

February 4-6:

The road from Gorodische in the southeast to Korsun is jammed with giant columns. Thousands of vehicles of every type, often three abreast, are crawling along a 20-kilometer stretch of road through muck and holes, offering the enemy air force targets which could scarcely be better. The Russian machines buzz like angry wasps and dive on the columns mired in the mud every ten minutes. Trucks are burning everywhere. The chewed-up, softened earth is deep and clinging, making any progress impossible. All that is left for the endless columns of the supply trains and rear units is to use the section of road between Gorodische and Korsun. By night the way to Korsun is marked by the flames from a hundred burning vehicles.

February 7:

In spite of everything, order and discipline reign in the pocket. All movements are carried out calmly and according to plan. Rearguard and flanking cover fight almost to the precise moment of the next withdrawal. Gaps in the front are closed.

February 8:

The enemy is attempting to reduce the pocket from all sides.

February 9:

Our withdrawals are considerable. The surrounded divisions give up more ground in the southeast, east, north and northeast. The pocket has already shrunk considerably.

February 10:

Rescue appears ever more questionable. The surrounded units are nearing the end of their strength. There is little ammunition and no regular rations. The men are dead tired and have been completely soaked for days. Even by the most optimistic view the collapse is only a few days away.

February 10/11:

The night again passes with numerous, difficult battles, rain and deep, clinging mud.

February 11:

At 1100 two very correct Russian officers appear in front of our sector carrying a message from the Soviet High Command to the commander of the surrounded German units. The message is a final ultimatum – either we surrender or the final measures to destroy the pocket will begin at 1300. A prime-mover takes the officers through the mud back to the Russian lines.

In the afternoon the enemy attacks from all sides. We must get out of the pocket. When will the order come to break out?

February 12:

Despite all their efforts of the last 14 days the Russians have had no success, now they want to accelerate the finishing of the pocket. After their ultimatum is rejected out of hand begins the assault on all sectors.

Once again heavy rain, mud, wet, filth, trenches and holes filled with water.

The pocket has become extremely small, territory will definitely have to be won in the south and southwest in the direction of the planned breakout.

Superhuman efforts are demanded of the troops. Every few minutes the enemy breaks through the positions somewhere, counterattacks have to be carried out and enemy penetrations sealed off.

The field bakeries in Korsun bake the last bran-bread. Together with the small packets of concentrated chocolate dropped with the supply canisters it is the only rations issued after February 13 . . ."

The days and weeks passed in hard, back-and-forth, strength-draining battles in an unimaginable sea of mud. The Soviets gained ground slowly, but only by constantly throwing in fresh units[6], while the German troops, who had been in battle for months without relief, fought doggedly to beat off the enemy attacks. The more the Soviets pushed the German units together, the harder they fought to achieve their destruction. In contrast to the Luftwaffe, which was able to provide only limited support for the ground battle, the Soviet close-support units were constantly in action in growing numbers.

Not only did the Soviets employ air and ground attacks, artillery fire, rockets, and aerial bombs and cannon fire in their efforts to destroy the German forces within the pocket, they also employed every available psychological means to break down resistance. Loudspeakers droned day and night over the front lines, urging the soldiers to desert, employing a mixture of promises and threats. So-called passes, which promised every deserter on presentation good treatment in Russian captivity and an early return home after the war, fluttered down in their thousands from Soviet aircraft. Leaflets containing a map illustrating the desperate situation in the pocket were also dropped. Arriving daily by the same route were photos of German soldiers already taken prisoner by the Soviets, sitting at fully spread tables. Individual captured German soldiers were sent back with chocolate and cigarettes in their pockets, telling of the extremely comradely reception they had received at the hands of the Russians. A continuous series of messages was sent to all German radio stations with the same promises. Captured German Generals sent personal letters to division commanders they knew inside the pocket. And then, on February 8, there appeared a Russian General Staff Colonel, duly accompanied by a bugler and a white flag, with an official surrender offer from

Marshall Zhukov, demanding that the German forces lay down their weapons. The offer would expire at 1430 the same day. The parlementaire was escorted back and the offer was not answered. The same went on elsewhere – Soviet parlementaires appeared at division command posts offering separate surrender negotiations or making threats. On February 10 *General* Seydlitz, who had been taken prisoner at Stalingrad and was now president of the League of German Officers established in the Soviet Union, spoke over the transmitter of the likewise Soviet-established National Committee for a Free Germany to the German soldiers in the pocket. He, too, urged them to surrender and promised good rations and accommodations, complete security, and so on.

No answer came from the pocket and there were very few desertions. The German soldier had long known what awaited him in Soviet captivity – a pitiful life of hunger, degradation and forced labor. And this was no propaganda slogan.

On February 7 the changing pocket still had a diameter of 45 kilometers from northwest to southeast. No rescue was to be expected from XXXXVII Panzer Corps in the southeast, all hopes were now pinned on III Panzer Corps in the southwest. The latter was to strike towards the pocket, and therefore it was necessary to change the shape of the pocket fronts while holding on to Korsun airfield as long as possible. That day the Eighth Army radioed the following orders: "Gruppe Stemmermann is to shorten its front lines and move with the entire pocket, attacking in the direction of Shenderovka, so as to be in position to advance toward the relieving armored forces at the designated time."

General Stemmermann now set about the difficult task of "wandering" with the pocket. In the east the *Wiking* Division gave up the village of Gorodische, while in the north the 88th Division evacuated the Janovka area. Korsun and its airfield became the pivotal point for the new movements, which were to extend the pocket in a southwesterly direction. XI Army Corps therefore gave up additional territory in the east, and following an extremely difficult march over muddy roads, attacked in a southwesterly direction. Daily losses were running at 300 men. There were 4,000 wounded who could not be evacuated. The supply trains had long since been disbanded except for a few vitally-needed horse-drawn units. Like the staff units which were no longer needed, they were incorporated into the combat units.

The New Relief Attempt Bogs Down

While conditions inside the pocket were growing worse daily, III Panzer Corps was preparing to launch another relief attempt directly toward the pocket. This attack was to be carried out by four panzer divisions and was to be launched from the Vinograd area (Rubanny Most) northeast through Bushanka, Lysyanka, Chishintsy and Dzhurzhentsy – the shortest route to the pocket. In the meantime the 1st Panzer Division and the "LAH" SS-Panzer Division had arrived, but regrouping cost two valuable days. Vehicles sank to their axles in the mud and a march of 15 to 20 kilometers was the most which could be achieved in one day. Even this required a maximum effort, and often all movement was impossible.

In spite of all the difficulties with the muddy terrain the attack divisions managed to assemble by the specified deadline. In the center the 16th and 17th Panzer Divisions formed the spearhead of the attack, while the "LAH" SS-Panzer Division and the 1st Panzer Division covered the northern and southern flanks, respectively.

The attack began on February 11. The day began hopefully, with the 1st Panzer Division pushing far ahead and capturing Bushanka on the Gniloy-Tikich, while the 16th and 17th Panzer Divisions crossed the river to its left and established small bridgeheads. This effort exhausted the force of the attack, however. Misty, foggy weather hampered German air support. For the same reasons the flow of supplies, especially fuel, to the attack forces backed up. Virtually the only supplies to get through were air-dropped and these were insufficient to meet the requirements of the units. The enemy and the terrain combined to prevent a quick advance, and many tanks became stuck in the muck and filth. The wheeled vehicles became hopelessly bogged down, while the clinging mud pulled the narrow tracks off the armored personnel carriers. Most of the artillery's gun tractors were useless. Only the heavy tractors and tanks were capable of dragging the guns through the mud, and then only at a speed of 4 to 5 kph with very high consumption of fuel and increased wear and tear on the vehicles. During the cold nights the ground, which had been transformed into bogs and pools of standing water, froze, so that vehicles often had to be chipped out of the frozen ground with pickaxes and their motors warmed by fires and blow-torches before they could be started.

And then there was the enemy, who defended desperately and launched repeated counterattacks. Admittedly he, too, had to contend with the same difficulties presented by the weather and terrain, but in addition to better roads the Soviets had several decisive advantages: they were already in position around the pocket, while the German panzer divisions had to drive forward to reach it. On the first day major German supply dumps, including vast quantities of fuel, had fallen into Soviet hands. With their great numbers of soldiers, some could be employed to deliver supplies. Hundreds of Red Army soldiers maintained a shuttle service, carrying ammunition and fuel canisters for kilometers through the mud to the front.

Ammunition and fuel – those were the most important things to the Soviets. Only after these had been secured did they worry about their meager rations, and then nothing more.

On February 12 the main body of the "LAH" SS-Panzer Division was involved in heavy defensive fighting near Vinograd, as was the 16th Panzer Division on the road from Medwyn. Further west the 17th Panzer Division was battling Soviet tanks. The 1st Panzer Division, which in spite of its flanking role had pushed far ahead, continued to attack toward Lysyanka.

February 13 and 14 brought no decisive success for the attackers. On the left wing the Soviet Sixteenth Tank Corps drove into the rear of the 16th Panzer Division from Bojarka, forcing it to divert a significant part of its forces to the west and north. In vain the 17th Panzer Division attempted to facilitate 1st Panzer Division's advance by attacking on its right wing, driving south from the area east of Dashudovka. On February 12 the 1st Panzer Division's *Panzerkampfgruppe* Frank (reinforced 1st Panzer Regiment) had taken Lysyanka-West and cleared the village after heavy fighting with enemy units. At noon on the 13th the division sent tanks and a company of the 113th Panzergrenadier Regiment cross the Gniloy-Tikich, and from the 14th held a bridgehead in the eastern part of Lysyanka against powerful Soviet counterattacks. However, it lacked the forces to do any more.

The attack by III Panzer Corps had become a narrow corridor, whose ever-lengthening flanks had to be protected against the continual Soviet attacks by the "LAH" SS-Panzer Division and elements of the 1st Panzer Division on the left and elements of the 1st Panzer Division on the right.

Despite all the efforts of the tank crews, panzergrenadiers, artillerymen, combat engineers, signals men, drivers and all the other soldiers, the relief attempt was halted 15 to 20 kilometers from the extreme southern edge of the pocket. It could simply go no further. Only *Oberstleutnant* Dr. Bäke and his heavy panzer regiment, which was under the command of the 16th Panzer Regiment, managed to get any closer. On February 14 he drove into Chishintsy, barely 10 kilometers from the pocket. However, his tanks alone could not hold the village against the concentric attacks of the Soviet Fifth Guards Tank Corps and were forced to withdraw to the west.

The relief force could simply go no further.

The 16th Panzer Division reported on the relief attack:[7]

> "On February 11 the Bäke Heavy Panzer Regiment, the 506th Tiger Battalion, elements of the 2nd Panzer Regiment with 2nd Battalion/64th Panzer Grenadier Regiment, and behind it *Kampfgruppe Blömecke* with the rest of the 2nd Panzer Regiment, 1st Battalion/64th Regiment, the

16th Artillery Regiment and 3rd Company/16th Pionier Battalion, set off to free the 50,000 with the panzergrenadiers riding on the tanks. Dive-bombers and close-support aircraft accompanied the attack, and sunshine and spring warmth covered the land.

Under heavy fire from the left flank, the division drove through the lines of the 198th Infantry Division, rolled in a broad front across the railway embankment 5 kilometers northeast of Rubanny-Most and reached Point 239.1. On the left the 17th Panzer Division took Stepok in the initial assault, while the 16th Panzer Division broke through three enemy positions and reached Frankovka at 1030. So great was the enemy's surprise, and such was the force of the advance, effectively supported by the Luftwaffe thanks to the sunny weather, that the bridge over the Gniloy-Tikich near Kamenny, which had been prepared for demolition, fell into our hands undamaged. Bushanka, southeast of Frankovka, fell to the 1st Panzer Division, and small bridgeheads were established across the river's western course.

Kampfgruppe Blömecke, which was following the panzers, took Vishnevka and then secured the main road against powerful armored attacks from the northwest. During the night the infantry climbed aboard the tanks, drove to Frankovka and took over security in the bridgehead, where the armored battle group had established an all-round defensive position. Despite the once more deteriorating road conditions, in a twenty-four-hour battle with the mud the men of the supply units managed to bring forward adequate quantities of ammunition and fuel. The attack could continue.

On February 12 the armored wedge set out to expand the bridgehead. This time, however, thick fog grounded the Luftwaffe. The grenadiers with their wheeled vehicles bogged down in the mud and were unable to clear the territory won by the tanks. Pockets of resistance flared up in the rear, and deliveries of ammunition and fuel from the air were impossible. The Russians sent in fresh forces from their Fifth Guards Tank Corps to meet the German armored spearhead.

The enemy's 16th Tank Corps launched an energetic drive southward from Bojarka into the rear of the advancing 16th and 17th Panzer Divisions. The "LAH" gave way, so that elements of the assault force (17th Panzer Division) had to be diverted to the left flank. The attempt to expand the bridgehead failed.

On February 13 the corps ordered contact established with the surrounded units at all costs.

Battle Groups Blömecke and Schiller (16th Armored Reconnaissance Battalion) launched an attack in the direction of Dashudovka at 0725. The Russians defended from well-fortified blocking positions. Sixteen tanks, fifteen assault guns and twenty anti-tank guns were destroyed in intense firefights. The 64th Regiment cleared Dashudovka and took up security positions at the edge of the village. It was later relieved by the 79th Panzergrenadier Regiment, while the tanks, with the 16th Reconnaissance Battalion and the armored 2nd Battalion, 64th Regiment, captured Chessnovka at 1120 and pushed on in the direction of the main road. The road was reached at 1300 and barricaded near Point 239.8. Following heavy fighting, the battle group reached the western edge of Chishintsy. Only ten kilometers now separated the relief force from their surrounded comrades. However, the armored units alone could not hold the position against the concentric attacks of the Russian Fifth Guards Tank Corps and were forced to withdraw to the west . . ."

Thus this attempt to rescue the surrounded forces had also failed. The Eighth Army as well tried everything to come to the aid of the surrounded corps. On February 10, XXXXVII Panzer Corps set out once again with the 11th and 13th Panzer Divisions against the gap separating it from the First Army to the west. It was unable to close the gap, however, and was diverted northward, reaching the hill just south of Svenigorodka on the 12th, still more than 30 kilometers from the southern edge of the pocket and 25 kilometers from III Panzer Corps. These efforts, which had failed to achieve a linkup with III Panzer Corps or open the pocket, had completely expended the strength of the weak panzer divisions.

The Breakout Area Must Be Captured

The dramatic events increased from day to day, while the distress inside the pocket grew by the hour. *General* Stemmermann began to steadily reduce the pocket and alter its shape toward the southwest, from which direction the relief attack by the German armored forces was expected. In order to create a favorable base from which to launch the breakout attack, territory occupied by the Russian encircling forces had to be recaptured and various villages taken from the enemy. Further regrouping took place between February 11 and 13. On the 10th and 11th the 72nd Division's veteran 105th Infantry Regiment was pulled out of the punishing defensive battles on the pocket's eastern front. It was given the job of expanding the pocket to the southwest. Its first objective was to capture the area around Novo Buda. The men of the regiment, which like all the others had been severely weakened, and which now consisted of a single rifle battalion, were soon to show what they were capable of.

The regiment attacked during the night of February 11/12. The village of Novo

Buda was captured, 200 prisoners taken and an enemy company with trucks and rocket launchers shot to pieces. The following morning the regiment repulsed powerful counterattacks launched from the area north of Orentsy against the southern part of Novo Buda. An enemy penetration was sealed off and two Russian tanks destroyed from close range. The regiment was then relieved by the *Wallonie* SS-Brigade, which continued to hold desperately onto Novo Buda but suffered heavy casualties in the process. It lost more than 200 killed, including the brigade's commander, *Oberstleutnant* Lippert. On the other hand, all attacks against Shenderovka by the neighboring 5th SS-Division *Wiking* were repulsed. On February 13 and 14 the 105th Regiment was involved in heavy fighting for Komarovka. During the night of February 12/13 the regiment stormed the village, supported by the last three assault guns detached by division. However, the enemy then began a series of almost uninterrupted day and night attacks in an attempt to recapture Komarovka. In the course of the battles for Komarovka the 105th Regiment destroyed 21 tanks and took 240 prisoners. Its own losses were heavy, with one-third of the regiment's soldiers becoming casualties. In addition, two assault guns, one self-propelled 20mm anti-aircraft gun and two attached guns from the 72nd Artillery Regiment were total losses. Shenderovka was taken on the afternoon of February 13 following heavy fighting with a Soviet machine gun battalion. With the capture of Novo Buda, Komarovka and Shenderovka, the planned breakout area had been secured. The 105th Regiment's next objective was the equally important small village of Chilki. Once again the regiment launched a night attack. During the night of February 14/15 it stormed Chilki and cleared it of enemy forces. A subsequent Soviet counterattack was beaten off with heavy losses to the attackers. Nevertheless, as dawn broke on the 15th the enemy broke into the southwestern part of the village with six tanks and mounted infantry. Four of the tanks were destroyed, but the last assault gun and the last self-propelled 20mm anti-aircraft gun were lost. The remaining Soviet forces were eliminated in close-quarters fighting.

At the same time fighting was going on all along the pocket front.

•

Korsun was abandoned on February 13. Three-thousand wounded, who could not be evacuated, had to be left behind for handover to the Russians. Nothing is known of their subsequent fate. In preparation for the breakout *General* Stemmermann now concentrated the main body of his forces in the direction of the area of captured terrain in the south in a small, but dangerously narrow, pocket north of

Shenderovka. Pressed into an area seven by eight kilometers, approximately 50,000 men waited for the order to break out and for the final, decisive thrust by the relief forces.

The following are several more diary entries:

"February 13:

A several-kilometer-long lake southeast of Korsun ends in a tremendous dam. The troops evacuating Korsun have to cross the lake over an almost kilometer-long wooden bridge which the pioniers have built along the top of the dam. Everything is going smoothly despite the giant chain of men and vehicles. The cold has set in again and the mud has frozen. Everywhere people are trying to get vehicles going or are pushing them to the side so as not to block the road and hinder the panje wagons which, pulled by small horses and oxen, can get through more easily.

February 14:

The news of our relief advance is totally inaccurate. In the north of the pocket we are withdrawing alarmingly, but scarcely advancing in the south. The Russians, who are staying on the heels of the rearguard, pushed into Korsun early this morning. The village of Novo Buda in the south must be held no matter what, it forms the left pillar of the break-out area. If the enemy takes back Novo Buda he will only have to advance 6 kilometers to the west to cut off everyone near Shenderovka.

The men in their dirty, mud-covered winter uniforms are totally exhausted. There is almost nothing to eat and only dirty water from the sides of the road to drink. The only heat for warming and drying out comes from meager fires made from corn husks. Added to this is the mental strain.

The weather has changed, the rain has stopped. The wind whistles and the onset of the cold brings snow.

February 15:

Shenderovka, the breakout gate, has finally been taken following three days and two nights of fighting. In our rear, on the other hand, the Russians have pushed far beyond Korsun.

The worst thing is the rations. We have no more, nothing at all. The last supplies were issued in Korsun. The men, without sleep and shivering from the cold, have received nothing, hot or cold, for three days, and are living off what they have with them.

A collective farm which has been transformed into a field hospital is hit by fire from a Stalin Organ. Dozens of wounded create a bloody shambles. More than 1,200 wounded have already spent several days and nights in the open in straw-filled, light panje wagons requisitioned from villages in the pocket. After the rain of the previous weeks they have become soaked to the skin; now they must face the biting cold and lie half-frozen beneath their snow-covered blankets. One scarcely hears any moaning or groaning; many have given up, and no longer ask for anything. As soon as one dies he is laid beside the wagon by the Russian volunteers detailed as drivers and his place is taken by a new casualty. There are no more medicines and dressings are in short supply. The doctors do all that is within their power, but they cannot help many. They do it to satisfy their consciences.

In the north the enemy continues to press and is already three kilometers from Shenderovka . . ."

The decision was made on this February 15. Since timely relief by III Panzer Corps could no longer be expected, the Commander-in-Chief of Army Group South, *Feldmarschall* von Manstein, decided to give the order for a breakout. He did so without checking with Führer Headquarters, so as to avoid any objections. That same day Eighth Army passed on von Manstein's order and at 1105 radioed to the pocket: "Capabilities of III Panzer Corps reduced by weather and supply problems. Gruppe Stemmermann must carry out decisive breakthrough to Dzhurzhentsy–Hill 239, two kilometers to the south, with its own forces. Link up there with III Panzer Corps."

This was a clear order. However, it already contained the seed of the coming drama. Inside the pocket *General* Stemermann assumed that the commanding hills with Point 239 had already been taken by the relief forces – which was not the case.

The hopes of the men surrounded in the pocket rose once again. The decisive order had finally been given; the unshaven, dirty, mud-smeared faces brightened. They had been surrounded for three weeks now, enduring the tough defensive battles in rain and blowing snow, persevering in spite of inadequate supplies. Now the hour of liberation was to come. What they did not know was that the armored forces coming to free them had already bogged down in the face of the mud and the enemy, their strength spent.

Operations by the Luftwaffe

The Luftwaffe, whose capabilities at that time were somewhat limited, tried to intervene in the land battle as best it could. It had two tasks to perform – maintain an adequate level of supply to the divisions surrounded in the pocket, and take over the job of supplying the relief groups, whose own supply routes were strained by the prevailing poor weather and terrain conditions. In addition, the Luftwaffe was to support the ground forces wherever possible.

These tasks were taken on by VIII *Fliegerkorps* under *Generalleutnant* Seidemann through the Knapp Operations Staff in Uman. Even if all the demands could not be met on account of the many obstacles, the operations staff, as well as the flying and ground personnel, worked tirelessly to do as much as they could. In the period from January 28 to February 20, 1,536 aircraft were employed in the air transport and escort roles. This number consisted of 832 Ju 52s, 478 He 111s, 58 Fw 190s and 168 Bf 109 fighters.

One advantage was the relatively short (100 km) distance from Uman airfield to the pocket. The disadvantages were far greater, however. These began with the difficulties encountered by the aircraft when taking off or landing from unpaved airfields whose surfaces had been softened by the thaw. On many days there was such thick fog and heavy icing that all aircraft were grounded. Flying resumed whenever the icy fog lifted and gaps appeared in the low cloud, or when the night cold hardened the ground, and supplies were dropped to the surrounded units and the advancing armored spearheads coming to their aid. The transport units which had been moved into the area braved the curtain of anti-aircraft fire the Soviets threw up around the pocket without regard to losses. During the first days of the supply effort the aircraft landed at the several useable airfields within the pocket, bringing out wounded on the return flight.

In spite of all efforts the air supply situation worsened from day to day. Only a fraction of the 150 tons required daily could be delivered. Like Uman, the makeshift airfield at Korsun was often closed by bad weather. After a week of warm weather the airfield was completely flooded. Engineers worked to drain off the water and shore up the airfield. The last arriving aircraft turned over on landing in the almost meter-deep mud. From February 10 no more aircraft were able to land or take off. Ammunition, fuel and food had to be dropped, often directly from the aircraft due a shortage of supply containers.

A total of 2,026.6 tons of supplies was landed or air dropped into the pocket. This total comprised 1,247 tons of ammunition, 45.4 tons of food, 38.3 tons of equipment and medical supplies and 695 cubic meters of fuel. 121 soldiers were also flown into the pocket.

Flown out of the pocket were: 2,188 wounded, of these 637 non-ambulatory (severely wounded), 2.1 tons of equipment (mostly special signals equipment) and 101 soldiers (specialists and the crews of shot-down or crashed transport aircraft).

Total losses following the cessation of fighting were: 32 Ju 52s, 13 He 111s and 5 Bf 109s. 113 Ju 52s and He 111s and 47 fighters were damaged.

Twenty-two Luftwaffe personnel were killed during air supply missions, 56 were listed as missing and many wounded.

Fifty-eight enemy aircraft were shot down in air combat or by anti-aircraft fire.

III Panzer Corps – One Last Effort

Outside the pocket another rescue attempt was about to get under way. On February 16, III Panzer Corps set out on a final attempt to break through. While the 16th Panzer Division protected their rear and northern flank, the 17th and 1st Panzer Divisions were to drive from Lysyanka toward the commanding Hill 239, south of Dzhurzhentsy, and Heavy Panzer Regiment Bäke was to set out through Chishintsy toward Komarovka in the direction of the pocket.

Once again the German tank crews and panzergrenadiers were expecting extremely heavy fighting. The 16th Panzer Division screened to the north and east with 2nd Battalion, 64th Panzergrenadier Regiment and its armored battle group, holding its positions against all attacks and covering the flanks of the other two panzer divisions. The 64th Panzergrenadier Regiment's 1st Battalion even launched an attack from its line of security against the commanding village heights north of Chessnovka in the east. Seven Soviet T-34 tanks and twelve assault guns were destroyed. Following the bitter fighting the bodies of 400 Russian soldiers littered the battlefield. However, the battered units of the 17th Panzer Division were unable to go any further, and the drive by the 1st Panzer Division, which had been halted near the bridge over the Gniloy-Tikich in Lysyanka, was unable to get going again. In the face of enemy counterattacks the third relief attempt never had a chance to fully unfold and ground to a halt. On the evening of February 16 the most forward elements of III Panzer Corps were bogged down in a line Lysyanka-Oktyabr-Chishintsy. Covering the final 10 to 15 kilometers was beyond human ability. The men of the relief force had willingly given their all for the men in the pocket, but they had been completely overtaxed, their resources were spent.

Help for the pocket had come too late and had been too little. The climax of the catastrophe was near.

The fighting during the last day of the third relief attempt is described in the history of the 1st Panzer Division (shortened extracts):[8]

> "On Wednesday, February 16, Lysyanka again lay under heavy enemy fire. Construction work at the collapsed bridge over the Gniloy Tikich also suffered from the considerable enemy activity. But it was the enemy aircraft, which attacked the bridge every ten minutes when the visibility was good, that made the work of the armored engineers so difficult and also hit the bridge several times. Nevertheless, following

unspeakable struggle and difficulties it was ready that day and was kept open for traffic.

Late in the morning supplies arrived. This time, finally, the air-dropped supplies were adequate. The Ju 52s dropped 200-liter drums of fuel and canisters containing artillery ammunition and rations from altitudes of 30 to 40 meters. Even though a number of containers burst, there was enough for Armored Battle Group Frank to look forward to the coming battles with confidence.

At the same time elements of the Soviet Fifth Guards Tank Corps again tried a counterattack with more than twenty T-34s from the direction of Hill 239 through Oktyabr toward Lysyanka-East. The enemy advance collapsed at the edge of the village under the destructive fire of the 73rd Armored Artillery Regiment, and the T-34s were forced to turn back. The rest of 1st Battalion, 1st Panzer Regiment under the command of *Hauptmann* Cramer immediately attacked northeastward toward Oktyabr. This frontal attack soon stalled in front of a strong Russian anti-tank front.

At about the same time the enemy again attacked Lysyanka-East. This time the strong enemy attack with tank support came from the southeast, from the direction of Hill 222.5. *Hauptmann* Cramer sent *Oberfeldwebel* Strippel to the threatened position on the right flank. The *Oberfeldwebel* and his seven Panthers destroyed 27 T-34s from the attacking force of 30 tanks, while losing only one of their own.

Since late afternoon the German screening force in Lysyanka-South had also been involved in heavy fighting, repelling Soviet attacks from the south against the right flank of Armored Battle Group Franck.

The weather was a great hindrance to the tanks and panzergrenadiers. It grew cold again, and the terrain and frequent storms made great demands of the soldiers. Unserviceable tanks were prepared for demolition as a precaution.

The attack was resumed in the afternoon and once again there was bitter fighting. The 2nd Battalion of the 113th Panzergrenadier Regiment, which meant the battalion's last 50 to 60 panzergrenadiers, reinforced by men of 2nd Battalion, 1st Panzergrenadier Regiment under the command of *Hauptmann* Ebeling, advanced across an open, coverless slope toward the small village of Oktyabr. The panzergrenadiers stormed forward under the covering fire of four Panthers of 1st Company, 1st Panzer Regiment. With the last of their strength, and at the cost of heavy casualties, they managed to take a ravine west of Oktyabr, which provided good cover. For the time being the tanks were left far behind; they had stumbled into in a snow-covered swamp and become stuck. At the same time the Panther tanks of 2nd Company, 1st Panzer

Regiment under *Hauptmann* Cramer were pushing the enemy back on both sides of the road to Oktyabr.

Meanwhile, further north the Tiger tanks of the 503rd Heavy Panzer Battalion intervened in the battle for Oktyabr. The Tigers belonged to Heavy Panzer Regiment Bäke, which had set out to support the attack to the southeast and in doing so brought considerable relief to the attack on Oktyabr. Taking advantage of this, *Hauptmann* Ebeling moved forward again with his thrown-together "battalion." After four T-34s had been destroyed by 1st Company, 1st Panzer Regiment and others driven off, Oktyabr was taken by storm and cleared of enemy troops after a brief period of intense house-to-house fighting. The last company commander and almost all the platoon leaders were killed or wounded in this action. Nevertheless, a line of security was immediately established around Oktyabr and soon afterward the grenadiers had to withstand the first enemy counterattack. The 1st Panzer Regiment's 2nd Company, which attacked frontally toward the north, also suffered bitter losses against the in-depth Russian anti-tank defenses. Among those killed was *Hauptmann* Cramer.

The Russian counterattacks went on. Several waves of Stuka divebomber attacks finally managed to pin down the enemy. Oktyabr was held . . ."

Shenderovka – "Hell's Gate"

Once again inside the pocket. The situation of the surrounded troops was coming to a head; events were beginning to overtake them.

While the troops battled the Russians in the rain, mud and filth, the command staffs squatted in pitiful peasant cottages under enemy artillery fire. Under the light of flickering candles and tiny Hindenburg lamps they went about their work, planning, calculating, organizing, taking reports, issuing orders, directing and controlling. Finally, *General* Stemmermann's staff came up with a plan to break out of the pocket. The plan was as follows: the breakout was to take place under the cover of darkness on February 16 with three spearheads. The attack was to begin without artillery preparation. The forward troops were to work their way forward quietly, launch a surprise attack against the enemy with fixed bayonets and overrun him, forcing gaps in the enemy encircling ring and opening the way for the remaining forces to reach the anticipated positions of the German relief force.

The three spearheads each consisted of a division, which was to be assembled in three waves:

1st Wave – infantry with fixed bayonets.

2nd Wave – heavy weapons, such as infantry guns, anti-tank guns, mortars, etc.

3rd Wave – artillery and trains.

The divisions were assigned the following assembly and attack areas:

Right: *Korpsabteilung B* in Chilki with line of attack across the high ground south of Petrovskoye - Dzhurzhentsy South.

Center: 72nd Infantry Division in the valley 1.5 kilometers southeast of Chilki toward Dzhurzhentsy Forest – north of Hill 239 - Oktyabr.

Left: 5th SS-Panzergrenadier Division *Wiking* with SS-Brigade *Wallonie* in Komarovka, with line of attack parallel to the 72nd Division south past Hill 239.

The total force was not quite 40,000 men.

The 57th and 88th Infantry Divisions formed the rearguard. Positioned in a shallow arc around Shenderovka they were to guard the rear of the breakout units and then fall back on receiving a code-word by radio. Then the 57th Division, which still had a strength of about 3,500 men, including splinter units from other divisions, was to move into the area behind the *Wiking* Division, while the somewhat weaker 88th Division followed into the breakout area behind the 72nd Division. The entire rearguard consisted of 6,500 men, as the trains and other rear echelon elements of those units were already with the breakout divisions.

All serviceable guns, tanks, assault guns and self-propelled guns were to accompany and support the break-out; all unnecessary vehicles, equipment, even private luggage, were to be destroyed. Each man was to take only his weapon and as much ammunition as he could carry.

1,450 non-ambulatory wounded were to be left behind in Shenderovka with their doctors and care personnel and handed over to the Russians, as taking them along seemed impossible. Nevertheless, many units tried to take their wounded comrades with them in panje wagons and gun tractors.

On the morning of the breakout VIII *Fliegerkorps* was to screen the flanks of the breakout zone by launching air attacks on the enemy, while outside the pocket attacks by German relief forces were to engage and tie down the Russian forces, drawing them away from the area of the breakout.

Time was pressing, and every hour was precious. However, the implementation of the plan on February 15 and 16 encountered one difficulty after another. These began with the conveyance of the orders themselves. The field telephone lines had long since been destroyed by shellfire, and the radio equipment, which had been moved onto *panje* wagons, did not work all the time and was subject to frequent failures.

Preparations for the breakout went on through both days. There were fires everywhere as everything which could not be taken along was burned. Vehicles, guns which were no longer usable and other war materiel were blown up to prevent them falling into enemy hands. All the time the enemy attacks and artillery fire on the entire pocket went on. The pocket had become so small, now only 3.5 kilometers in diameter, that it could be brought under fire from all sides. Shenderovka, which had only been taken a few hours before, and in which the dead of friend and foe still lay in the streets, became the focal point of the entire breakout operation. Streets, gardens and farm cottages were crammed with command posts, guns, damaged tanks, vehicles and horse-drawn carts, as well as the arriving, assembling and waiting units.

On the evening of February 15 *General* Stemmermann demanded further air drops of ammunition for the breakout and sent the following message to the Eighth Army: "Gruppe Stemmermann can break through the enemy facing its front (inner encircling ring), but will be unable to force a second breakthrough through the enemy (outer ring)."

Army Group South radioed back: "Watchword freedom, objective Lysyanka. Set out at 23.00 on the 16th."

Wednesday, February 16:

Shenderovka had become a gate to hell. The way to the assembly areas led every unit through the village with its one through-road, the sole approach road for the first three divisions, all of the train units and the rear-echelon services of both corps. Movement was slow and laborious over the muddy, rutted and worn surface. The endless columns of marching men and motor and horse-drawn vehicles became wedged together, resulting in a tremendous traffic jam. Since the Russians had a clear view into the pocket and the movements inside could not be concealed, directed artillery fire, as well as fire from heavy mortars and Stalin Organs[9], fell continuously among the halted and slow-moving masses, inflicting further heavy casualties. Shells and howling rocket projectiles impacted everywhere. The single road was soon blocked by shattered vehicles, dead horses, exploding munitions vehicles, burning trucks, heaps of dead and wounded, shattered remains of walls and burning wooden houses. It was a hellish scene filled with bursting shells, smoke and dust, the cries and moans of the severely wounded, and the roar of German artillery as it fired its last rounds before spiking its guns. Anti-aircraft guns roared as enemy aircraft strafed and bombed the columns. And all the time fresh units continued to move into Shenderovka from the north, east and west. There was no way around the town and the only chance for freedom lay to the southwest.

Low-flying He 111s dropped canisters containing rifle and machine-gun ammunition and shells. These landed among the columns.

At 15.00 the last radio message arrived from III Panzer Corps: "Oktyabr taken!" – This gave some encouragement.

Unfavorable reports were coming in from the rear areas of the pocket. Near Steblev in the northeast the Russian armored forces broke into the withdrawal movements of the 57th and 88th Divisions. Only with great difficulty was the attack halted and this dangerous penetration sealed off. Nevertheless the enemy's front line had been pushed forward to within a few kilometers of Shenderovka. There was also renewed fighting over the assembly areas which had been captured in the southwest. Late in the morning, Komarovka, where the *Wiking* SS-Division was fighting, changed hands for the fourth time. There was also renewed fighting for Novo Buda which pushed the German front lines back as much as three kilometers toward Shenderovka.

General Stemmermann's command post was located near Chilki. Command was now almost impossible. Messengers and aides tried to deliver orders in the hellish confusion and often failed to return. In front of the door of the corps headquarters lay the body of an officer whose head had been torn off by a shell fragment.

The entire shrunken pocket was under great pressure. A penetration by the enemy would bring panic and chaos, the catastrophe would be upon them.

It scarcely seems possible, but despite the enemy fire and chaotic conditions, the units forced their way through the mud into their assigned assembly areas.

Dusk began to fall at about 16.00. As it grew dark the Russian artillery fire gradually abated and the situation in the pocket became calmer.

There were now no more instructions to issue; everything would have to take place as planned. There was only one order left to give: "Break out as ordered! – Watchword freedom!"

Tremendous tension gripped the thousands of men who were now to set out on the last, but probably the most difficult, leg of their journey into freedom. Everyone was hopeful – it must and would succeed. The tanks of the German relief forces were near, still eight, perhaps ten kilometers away. The early nightfall, accompanied by frost and snow flurries, had come at the right time. The worse the weather, the better the chances of surprising the enemy and breaking through. The Russians were not supermen and in this weather they would be seeking warmth and protection in the village huts and in their positions and foxholes. The enemy seemed unaware of the planned breakout.

The three spearheads reported preparations complete. It was after 2300. The breakout began. The attacking spearheads of the first wave set out, without artillery preparation as planned, their rifles unloaded and with fixed bayonets. *Korpsabteilung* B was organized with the 258th Regiment Group forward on the right, in the center the 72nd Division led by the 125th Regiment, and in front of the *Wiking* Division on the left was the 5th Armored Reconnaissance Battalion. The units disappeared without a sound into the dark, moonless night. An icy wind was blowing out of the northeast, driving light snow flurries before it. The troops advanced straight across the open terrain, with its large valleys, ridges and deep ravines. They walked over the frozen mud and the thin, crusty covering of snow.

Shortly after midnight *General* Lieb, the Commanding General of XI Army Corps, who was in command of the first wave, moved into his command post on the western edge of Chilki. His initial concern was not for the first wave, because the Russians were now exerting heavy pressure from the flank against Chilki and had driven from the west almost to the edge of the village. The Russians had also again broken into Komarovka and the southern part of the village had been lost. Both villages were important as they formed the right and left pillars of the breakout area. In Chilki the Russians were halted by an artillery commander and 100 men, while in Komarovka men of the *Wiking* Division were forced to intervene and throw the Russians out of the village. The men of the next units to move out strained to hear any indication of fighting by the first wave. The only sounds they heard were the occasional "hurray," which soon ebbed slowly away.

The experiences of the 105th Infantry Regiment were typical of those of the units in the first wave. The enemy was taken completely by surprise and the soldiers broke through the first enemy positions employing bayonets and all available automatic weapons. A second Russian position was also overrun. Brief, but heavy firefights broke out when the advancing troops came upon two battery positions and took them in close-quarters fighting. The regiment continued to advance toward the southwest. At about 0330 it reached the deep valley terrain southeast of Dzhurzhentsy. Ahead, however, enemy tanks and vehicles were in position on the road between Dzhurzhentsy and Potshapintsy where it led over a line of hills (Point 239). The regiment was able to cross the road through a gap, unnoticed by the enemy. Two-hundred meters to the west the regiment's leading elements suddenly came upon enemy positions which were facing southwest. These formed the last outer ring against the relief forces. The Russians were asleep in their foxholes. The regiment broke into the positions, resulting in a brief close-quarters engagement, which at first was fought mainly with pistols and bayonets. However, a firefight became unavoidable. In this situation the tanks on the road turned on their headlights and spotted the following elements, which were in the process of crossing the road. The regiment and other scattered elements still managed to reach the first German tanks southeast of Chihintsy and at about 0400 reached the lines of the relief forces.

The 105th Infantry Regiment was, with the *Wallonie* Brigade, the only German unit which succeeded in breaking out as a unit with its small arms. Its strength in Lysyanka consisted of 3 officers, 1 doctor and 216 men. These were all that remained of the 27 officers and 1,082 men the regiment had on strength three weeks before, at the time it was encircled.

And now the calamity began . . .

•

The Soviets were now awake and on the alert; the attackers had failed to achieve general surprise. More searchlights were switched on, signal flares were fired and wild firing began. Suddenly there was fighting everywhere. The Soviets spotted the main body of the 72nd Infantry Division, which was following close behind the 105th Regiment. It became involved in a hopeless battle against the Russian defenses on the open fields in front of Dzhurzhentsy. Soon the division was forced to ground by the heavy defensive fire and later had to turn back. Things were not going much better for *Korpsabteilung* B. Leading the way, the 112th Division Group had overrun the first enemy security outposts without firing a shot. But then the *Korpsabteilung* was spotted. It advanced further to the southwest, where it ran into the main body of the 72nd Division and was forced southward. The commander of the *Korpsabteilung*, *Oberst* Fouquet, was seriously wounded in an attack on an anti-tank position. He later died in Soviet captivity.

The *Wiking* SS-Division's 5th Armored Reconnaissance Battalion likewise covered the first leg of the breakout relatively quickly. The first enemy encircling ring was broken, machine-gun and anti-tank positions overrun and the first hill positions at Potshapintsy taken. The reconnaissance battalion then came upon the heavily-manned Russian positions at the road close to the commanding Hill 239 at about the same time as the 105th Regiment. The battalion attacked at about 0430, but the first assault was halted below the hill. Flanking fire raked the battalion and the *Wallonie* Brigade which was following close behind. The reconnaissance battalion, which had one Panzer III left, tried again, but in vain. The fire from the now wide awake Russian defenders was too strong.

In the meantime the main body of the *Wiking* Division arrived. The breakout waves from the 72nd Division which had failed to cross the road further north pushed forward. The units became mixed together. In the darkness and enemy fire command was no longer possible. The first wave was unable to get through.

In the meantime the second wave arrived and ran into the first. Confusion and disorder grew. To the rear in Shenderovka increasing numbers of rear-echelon units and their vehicles struggled through the confusion of the burning village, which was once again under fire. The Russians had broken through to the edge of the village. Once again they were turned back by the *Wiking* Division's 5th Panzer Regiment in a wild tank battle which saw both sides suffer heavy losses. Thirty-two Russian tanks were destroyed; not a single one of the 5th Panzer Regiment's tanks returned. This sacrifice did, however, save the 57th and 88th Infantry Divisions which, as rearguard, were fighting bitterly and holding on.

The elements of the third wave that made it through the hell of Shenderovka fanned out on the far side of the village and marched, drove and rode across the broad, snow-covered, undulating fields. Unaware of events, they continued on and then ran into the second wave in the darkness.

General Stemmermann and an escorting officer were killed shortly after the beginning of the breakout as a result of a direct hit by an enemy anti-tank gun during a change of command posts. *General* Lieb assumed overall command.

Sometimes wading through the deep snow which had accumulated in the gullies and ravines, and all pressing together toward the southwest in the direction of Hill 239 where the relief forces were expected to be, the thrown-together units tried to fight their way forward led by their commanders, determined officers and NCOs.

If Shenderovka was the gate to hell, then the night of February 16/17, which was filled with bursting shells, streams of tracer and signal flares of all colors, was hell's vestibule.

But on February 17 this hell became even worse . . .

The Desperate Break for Freedom

When morning dawned the men of the break-out force realized to their bitter disappointment, and even horror and dismay, that it was not the tanks of the German relief force which were waiting for them on both sides of Hill 239, but a fully alerted enemy. Russian tanks, anti-tank guns and artillery fired into the already confused and exhausted elements of the first wave and the steadily growing stream of approaching columns from the second and third waves. Everything became inextricably entangled, was seized by an unholy disorder and began to disintegrate. Any semblance of command ceased to exist. Horse-drawn vehicles were smashed, horses ran away and bogged-down vehicles went up in smoke and flames. Men ran about seeking cover in the mostly open terrain. Clusters of men ran forward with loud shouts, trying to get through, while others sought refuge in the deep, snow-covered ravines or in clumps of trees. Increasingly heavy fire smashed into the dense masses, which at first stayed put as if stunned and apathetic. Many grenadiers tried to fight back. Apart from *Panzerfaust* rocket launchers, however, they had no effective weapons against the enemy tanks which appeared everywhere. Despite their teams of eight and ten horses the German anti-tank and light field guns had been left behind on the smooth, icy slopes or had become bogged down. Some Russian tanks were destroyed by the *Panzerfaust* anti-tank rockets. Two men of the 389th Anti-tank Battalion, which had long since been without guns, disabled five tanks. The others turned away. However, more tanks appeared and the enemy fire became ever heavier. Until now the troops had dragged all of their heavy weapons along with them, but now they were left behind, light and heavy field guns, as well as mortars and machine-guns. The fate of the wounded in the *panje* wagons was also decided here; they, too, had to be left behind. And the enemy knew no pity. *Oberst* Franz, Chief-of-Staff of XXXXII Corps, saw about 15 Russian tanks roll through a ravine in which a column of *panje* wagons carrying wounded had stopped. The Russians shot the horses with machine-guns and crushed the wagons beneath the tracks of their tanks. Of these 130 seriously-wounded men of the *Wiking* Division Dr. Thon was able to rescue perhaps a bare dozen. Approximately 140 other seriously-wounded men had been taken along in the division's tracked vehicles. These were shot up by Soviet tanks west of Shenderovka. Doctor Isselstein was killed by fire from a T-34. A column carrying wounded from the *Wallonie* Brigade also failed to get through, as did several others.

And this hellish day was far from over.

The sound of battle seemed weaker to the southeast. The only choice for the German troops was to evade the enemy fire and make their way in that direction. Beginning with individuals, then in whole squads and sections, the masses of German troops rose, on their own and desperate, in an effort to find a way out of the chaos. Hundreds, thousands of soldiers from every unit and arm of the service struggled in that direction, sometimes under the command of the highest ranking officer available. In the face of this wild rush the Russians evacuated the eastern part of Potshapintsy. Russian infantry was swept away and individual tanks even turned away from this human wave. Nevertheless, bursts of machine-gun fire and shells from artillery, anti-tank guns and tank cannon continued to smash into the uncoordinated and vulnerable mass of men, inflicting further casualties. Only when losses again became unbearable did the troops try to evade the Russian fire. Their only thoughts were to walk and run, just to get out of this constant fire and toward the German armored units, which must be somewhere. On foot, on horses which had been released from their harnesses, and in the last few cross-country vehicles, the mass finally crossed over and around both sides of Hill 222.5 before veering back toward the southwest. The Russian positions there were less heavily manned then expected, enabling the German troops to break through. But the anticipated few kilometers had become a death march of twenty to thirty kilometers lasting hours.

Finally, it appeared that they had broken through the enemy's encircling ring.

But there was still one terrible obstacle – the Gniloy Tikich. In summer it would have been little more than a large brook, but after the previous three weeks of warm weather it had become a rushing torrent, twenty to thirty meters wide and more than two meters deep. The cold of the past few days had not been enough to freeze it over again. The edges of the stream were ice covered, but it was open in the center and ice floes were being driven along by the current. The area of the stream bank was marshy, the banks themselves about two meters high, steep and ice-covered.

There was no bridge, and there were no boats to be seen anywhere.

In the course of less than half an hour about 20,000 men had assembled at the bank. They had no idea where the leading elements of the relief force were, they were unaware that *Oberstleutnant* Dr. Bäke and his heavy panzer regiment had set out again that morning to relieve the pocket and in the course of the day even reached the fateful Hill 239 south of Dzhurzhentsy[10], they did not know that German panzergrenadiers were holding Oktyabr to cover their withdrawal[11], and they did not know that only three kilometers upstream lay Lysyanka, in which the 1st Panzer Division had built a bridge and a footbridge for them. They had gone further south then the defenders of the Lysyanka bridgehead could have expected.

It was about eleven in the morning. Everyone was deliberating how to cross the stream. Generals Lieb and Gille and *Oberst* Dr. Hohm arrived and attempted to establish a semblance of order and organize a crossing. A heavy tractor was driven into the river to serve as the basis for a crossing. It was rolled away by the current, however, and other pieces of equipment which had been pushed in behind it were also swept away. The men formed teams of swimmers and non-swimmers, but the non-swimmers were pulled away by the current and went under. Many tried to ride across on horses and were swept downstream, others crawled out onto the ice and went through. Still others took off their uniforms, bundled them up and threw them across to the other side and then tried to swim across, usually in vain.

The temperature at the time was minus five degrees and the area was being swept by an icy wind.

Then the pursuing Soviet tanks reached the area of the river. The first four T-34s drove to within a few hundred meters and began firing into the masses of men with machine-guns and high-explosive shells. There was no stopping now – they had to get to the other side where the Russians could not follow. Once again the result was a terrifying scene. In groups of thirty to forty, the frozen, half-starved soldiers plunged into the ice-cold water and tried to fight their way through the rushing torrent. Heads and arms poked up between the ice floes, cries for help rang out, bodies of horses and men floated and sank in the current. The Generals, too, were swimming. *Oberst* Dr. Hohn, the commander of the 72nd Infantry Division, waited completely soaked in the freezing cold on the far bank until the last of his men arrived. Still on the other side, however, were the wounded, who could not cross. The entire bank was littered with discarded small arms, items of equipment and parts of uniforms.

For those who were fortunate enough to make it across, as soon as they emerged from the water the uniforms froze to their bodies. And they had still not reached safety. The long, open line of hills south of Lysyanka lay under artillery and tank fire. Under enemy fire, thousands of men, some in frozen uniforms, some half dressed and some completely naked, ran through the snow toward the distant houses of Lysyanka-East.

Hundreds of German soldiers who had previously escaped death lost their lives at the Gniloy Tikich, a few hundred meters from the forward outposts of the 1st Panzer Division. They died with freedom in sight, the freedom of which they had been dreaming for weeks and for which they had held on.

When the 1st Panzer Division learned of the dreadful situation on the river side of the bridgehead from the first half-dead survivors in their frozen uniforms, it immediately dispatched a party of panzergrenadiers with a platoon of tanks. Parties of guides tried to direct the still arriving and swelling masses of men along the riverbank toward the bridges at Lysyanka; however, the reigning atmosphere of panic prevented an orderly evacuation. Under the covering fire of two Panther tanks, which drove away the Soviet T-34s, the armored engineers threw makeshift bridges across the river at various locations for those units still on the other side as well as for stragglers to cross.

The following are descriptions by men who survived those terrible hours of February 16 and 17:

The Signals Officer of XXXXII Army Corps:

"February 16, 44: Shenderovka. We are going to break out! The door out of the pocket will be opened at midnight. We can no longer expect relief. All of our armored forces are bogged down in the mud and can move no further. Their foremost spearheads have fought their way to within ten kilometers of the southwest corner of the pocket. It is said that 'their further freedom of action is limited by weather and supply conditions.' The enemy encircling ring must be broken from within. Therefore we will have to force our way through to the bogged-down relief forces on our own. Those are the orders.

The watchword is 'freedom.' The power of this word is enough to transform danger and uncertainty into confidence and expectation. We're breaking out! The feeling drives us all toward the point of freedom... Just before the decisive attack all paralyzing fears have been banished.

We're breaking out! I hear the words from the mouth of the Chief-of-Staff. The words have a carefully-considered and cool ring to them. The chief reads the brief breakout order once more. Matter-of-factly it states that the enemy is trying to reduce the pocket through concentric attacks. In this respect the relatively strong encircling ring might be easily broken by a quick surprise attack.

The breakout plan is clear and simple. Three powerful spearheads will throw themselves against the enemy with cold steel. Heavy weapons, artillery and train units will follow close behind, ready for battle. The rearguard will hold out until it is time for them to withdraw.

Success will be certain. Shenderovka shows a friendly face in spite of the sad winter landscape, where the frost cannot master the deep mud and morass, but the icy wind bites razor-sharp at the face. Restlessly men and vehicles stream from the north into the village and then south into the assembly areas. The difficult task of regrouping in preparation for the attack must be completed by late evening. A masterpiece of orders unfolds. The question of whether or not all of the deadlines can be met remains open. There are many gaps in the lines of communication, the distances are great, the roads terrible, able to support only one-way traffic for motor vehicles, namely through the village.

The enemy gives us no respite. All around his harassing fire is quite lively. Strong attacks with tank support on our left flank during the preceding night were beaten off with some difficulty. Continuous attacks throughout the entire morning finally force us back from this planned assembly area. Six enemy tanks are smoldering, but nevertheless the attack forces have to be shifted further to the west. There is also enemy activity in our rear. One thousand Russians break in with tanks. The main line of resistance has to be pulled back, the enemy thrust is parried to a certain extent.

I go into the southwest section of the village. Almost in the middle of the crossroads an abandoned enemy gun points its long barrel toward the sky. Behind it one of our heavy batteries is firing. It has gone into position among the pitiful huts. In the bushes near the next house is a former Russian machine-gun nest. Shards of metal, bullets in a mud-smeared hemp belt. Electrical wire, the barrel of a Maxim machine-gun, beneath it only half the carriage. Then dead Soviets. Further to the right another former strongpoint with recesses for ammunition and rations, in the same condition as the last. Here there are more dead, scattered about by a direct hit, a rickety barricade. A large quantity of telephone wire, ammunition and hand grenades lies nearby. Then another firing nest, at the end a small heap of dirt, in the houses firing embrasures and observation slits, beams and heavy machine-guns.

Slowly I recognize the enemy's defensive system in which a machine-gun battalion had hung on and defended tenaciously under a clever commander for two days. Following careful fire preparation this place, far to the rear of our advancing troops, was eliminated in hand-to-hand fighting. Few escaped.

The enemy fliers are again in the air, and the village is under constant attack. Their cannon force us to take cover. Then, in the midst of our rattling defensive fire, a pair of bombs explode. A last burst from their cannon and the ponderous, black-grey aircraft with the red Soviet star disappear behind the next hill. Behind them they leave smoke, cries, shattered houses and smashed vehicles.

Shenderovka is burning, swaths of dense smoke whirl upwards and bright flames lick skyward.

All horse-drawn and motor vehicles that cannot be used to transport munitions and wounded or for command purposes during the breakout have to be destroyed. Not a document, not one immobilized weapon is to be allowed to fall into the hands of the enemy. At first the destruction of our own equipment is difficult. We begin somewhat sadly and hesitantly, but the second and third times there is less hesitation.

This great baggage lightening for the breakout extends down to the last man. This time no one can escape. I feel the effects of it myself. All personal effects are to be burned. I have already lost everything I own several times. Having learned from this I pull on two pairs of socks, two pairs of underwear, two shirts, my best uniform and best boots. My remaining precious everyday things, along with my few well-worn books and small mementoes, are gone forever. Outside alert units are being formed from stenographers, drivers, signals men and personnel from the baggage and supply trains. I can hear running and shouting. The sound of enemy artillery impacting in the village fades . . .

There are still five hours to go before the attack begins. Several times I inspect my submachine-gun and its six clips of ammunition.

17 February: Two hours before midnight I arrive at the new corps command post. It consists of two four-wheel-drive vehicles. In one of them sits the Chief-of-Staff with two field telephones. The *Kübelwagen* have been driven into a small valley. All around stand slender saplings, and 500 meters to the south the first clay huts of Chilki rise out of the ground. The right spearhead will advance from this village.

In the rear Shenderovka is glowing in several places. Does the terrible congestion still reign there? I had lost contact with my men on departure. It was impossible to get past the stopped columns which were completely blocking the road.

Near Shenderovka's western exit the road leads through a narrow defile toward a short bridge. The only bridge. Throughout the entire day it has been used to assemble the three attack spearheads. The enemy appears to have recognized this bottleneck. It comes under heavy fire, resulting in congestion, tumult and confusion, with the strongest pushing their way through. Later it was to become calmer. At last I make contact with my men. Plenty of questions, but no one knows anything.

I am forced to think that so far everything has gone our way, except in confused and congested Shenderovka. In the meantime the commanders there have been unable to have any effect on the congested mass.

Our ten-thousand men, still with much heavy equipment and numerous vehicles, are now pressed into a broad circle barely seven kilometers wide. This unusual, tremendous gathering makes the task of the commanders much more difficult. Actually one would expect the opposite. But everywhere the field telephone cables have been shot up or broken, even though they were laid in open fields. Also the change from motor vehicles to panje wagons has not been kind to the radio equipment. Some sets have broken down. Staff officers need time, however, and are just about at their wits end with the congestion. Therefore our fanatic will and our determination to reach freedom may be the only things keeping the attack plan going and will have to carry us to the objective. It might not be possible to parry every unforeseen obstacle thrown up by the enemy in time. Perhaps this thought has also occurred to the General and the Chief-of-Staff in addition to their many concerns. Their faces do not betray their inner turmoil.

An hour before midnight. The 'breakout at any cost' must now begin. There are no longer any communications with the individual divisions and the attached neighboring corps. Intermittent sounds of battle. The enemy artillery fires sporadic harassing fire, a rocket launcher adds its weight.

An hour later there is still no clear picture of the attack. There are no reports. Weak rifle fire from the direction of the attack spearhead and somewhat livelier artillery fire on our former assembly areas. A short firefight flares up on the right flank. Otherwise nothing. What could be going on up front? This question is asked again and again.

On the road between the trees the vehicles have begun to move. From now on everything flows forward. The attack must have gained ground. The Chief-of-Staff calls for me. Order: establish contact with the neighboring corps at once and report the situation. The corps is supposed to be in Chilki.

0300: I limit myself to what is absolutely necessary: submachine-gun, pocket map and binoculars, and I take a *Wachtmeister* with me, a resourceful man. Slipping and stumbling we press through the columns into the village. I can't understand where the vehicles are coming from. A large number have already been destroyed, and apart from those which are indispensable the rest were to have been destroyed as well. Most of the numerous *panje* wagons are carrying ammunition. Several are empty, though, and one is already carrying wounded. Contrary to orders, out of comradeship, they have been taken along by the troops. With heavy hearts we have had to leave more than 1,000 seriously wounded to the enemy as per international law. Medical personnel remain behind with them. For the corps medical officer the decision was the hardest of his life. Everything humanly possible has been done to save the lives of the wounded. We take our leave of them with the weariness of hope.

Nothing is to be found of the corps command post we are seeking. We ask around, but get no information. Heavy artillery fire is falling on the western section of the village. The main street remains blocked. A load voice roars in the midst of this confusion. Everything begins to move, pushed along from the rear. A column of twelve artillery pieces is wedged in the mass. A *Leutnant* on horseback calls for the 1st Battery. All of its guns are to be blown up at once. I can't understand the reason why, and I also do not know where his battery is. He tells me that he has seen several officers of the corps headquarters I am seeking.

For the second time I go into several packed houses. I am met by surly replies. Outside I stop briefly and peer into the darkness. There is an atmosphere of disaster hanging over everything . . .

There is a large bend in the road just beyond the southern exit from Chilki. Just before it I recognize the imposing figure of the corps chief on a horse. I make my report. The new command post of XI Corps has been moved forward two kilometers. The state of the attack is unclear. Soon afterward *General* Lieb comes on foot, accompanied by the adjutant and his aide. He walks calmly and somewhat tiredly. His old head wound appears to be causing him pain. He issues an instruction to a column vehicle.

The road widens on the hill. The stream of men and horses leaving the village can split up here, it flows apart. Suddenly firing from the right. Bullets whistle past our heads. Cries of: 'The Russians are coming!' Several are working their way forward in a narrow ravine, there can't be many. In any case a machine-gun is brought into position. More Soviets follow the first group. The firefight begins. Our *General* Stemmermann stands upright and blazes away with a submachine-gun. In an instant our march column on the road is scattered. The majority stream toward the opposite side. Only a few stop and join in the fire. The Reds have lost their courage. Soon there is only scattered firing. A small *Kübelwagen* drives past. It is stopped and the *General* and his aides climb in. It is the last time I see him . . .

My *Wachtmeister* has become separated and I go on alone. The column has reassembled and marches on. More seem to follow from Chilki, the column becomes denser. Along the road signs of battle. Shot-up wagons, a shattered Russian anti-tank gun. And dead – German and Russian.

0630: Morning twilight has disappeared. Visibility is not particularly good. Mist on the horizon. One cannot see far, as the entire terrain consists of hills and valleys and the view extends only as far as the next hill. The maps did not show such carved up terrain. In particular there is no suggestion of the clay soil in every valley and deep ravine, whose yellow-brown morass has no bottom and which is impervious even to the frost.

Guns thunder in the distance to the east and west. There is also rifle fire directly to the right. I run down a long slope. At the bottom a wide clay swamp. A clump of vehicles is stuck there. Tractors, radio vehicles, three trucks, a dozen *panje* wagons and one artillery piece. A truck burns under a dense cloud of smoke. I have to make my way over the bloody remains of horses, stumble to the left. There is a cry from somewhere. I can see clearly the muzzle flashes of the Russian anti-tank gun which is firing from the hill in front of me. The gun is 1,000 meters along the valley to the east.

The Russians assemble as it becomes light. They have awakened from their surprise and are looking about to see what has happened. The number of impacting shells from anti-tank guns and light artillery grows from minute to minute. Fragments whistle singing through the air, interspersed with the rattle of machine-gun fire. There are also detonations to the right and left of me in the valley. Black columns of smoke rise and expand. The relatively orderly march groups have become a swarm of ants. Even an approaching aircraft cannot disperse the thousands of dots, all striving southward. 'Breakout at any cost!' Behind streams an ever-increasing flow of men and vehicles. There is no move to seek an area where the fire is not so heavy. Everyone begins running after the man in front. It is a frightful scene when all order breaks down.

The reception positions of our relief forces must be somewhere close by, why then have we not reached them? Ahead faster!

The momentum of the mass grows rapidly, irresistibly gaining control. There is no leadership. It's no longer possible to direct this storm under enemy fire according to any sort of plan. The units on foot, on horseback, with panje wagons, the guns and motor vehicles which have managed to get this far, are all interspersed among the artillery, anti-tank and mortar fire of the enemy on the bare hills. They pour into the valleys and up the shallow slopes, spurred on by the thought that they must soon meet German tanks and their own troops. There is no stopping.

I also hurry up the slope. Several times I throw myself down to rest. Just in front of me there is a flash in the midst of a group of men. Pieces of bodies whirl through the air. I manage to get through and reach the crest of the hill. Above is an abandoned vehicle, the horses slit open – direct hit. Baggage strewn about. I can only console the wounded man and help him into the vehicle. He has bandaged his leg himself.

There are brief snow flurries and a cold wind. A Soviet close-support aircraft roars in at low altitude. There is no cover at all in this open terrain. But he does not fire, unsure of who is friend or foe.

Fire from an anti-tank gun strikes the hill from the west. After the first shellbursts I veer to the left. It is difficult to get away from the masses. My compass points to the east. It's not long before everyone is streaming in that direction. What good are rifles and submachine-guns when one is being pursued across the broad slopes by heavy fire and has no enemy infantry in front of him. Heavy snow lies on the ground, knee-deep in some places. Often there is blood on the snow.

One vehicle after another has become stuck in the clay soil of a small valley. A tractor comes down the slope at full speed. As if blind, the driver heads straight into the worst part of the morass. Several panje wagons manage to cross successfully.

The fire must be coming from a new Russian blocking position. Over to the left is a forest. The Russian artillery is firing into it. I want to swing out to the west, but am forced back by machine-gun fire. One of our assault guns appears over the nearest hill, however it does not fire. Mortar rounds explode near the forest's edge. I walk parallel to it along the middle slope. A shell bursts nearby.

Plodding through the snow is extremely fatiguing. One must lift one's feet high. The point of the forest ends at a narrow, very deep valley. A number of stuck vehicles rest inside. Probably the last remaining ones.

In a wood there is a steep slope. Vehicles have gathered in front of it. Carrying wounded from the earlier fighting they climb the slope slowly, meter by meter. Laboriously I clamber up between the tree trunks. I want to save my strength and follow my compass. Several shells burst with a crash among the branches. This must be undirected fire, I think to myself. As I turn to the right I am met by infantry fire. I can't move up, because scarcely anyone comes with me. I must go back into the forest. Tanks fire nearby. The short, dull, double crack of their guns is unmistakable.

The forest thins out, suddenly houses in front of me – a village (Potshapintsy). A few Russians run toward me along the main street. Everyone immediately turns away in the direction of the forest. But a few determined soldiers fight back, shouting loudly. Hurray! Those next to them join in. The shouting continues, growing louder and louder. There must be a tremendous number of our people in the forest. The Russians disappear again.

At a road crossing there is a bloody mixup of horses and wrecked wagons. Some wounded lean against the small steps of a brick house. The result of tank gunfire. I move on through hedges, along a ravine and then a road between two small lakes and up a long slope to the right. The whole field is being swept continuously by machine-gun fire. Now and then an anti-tank gun fires. Then high-explosive shells. Enemy fire from three sides, it's a wild turmoil.

There is a direct hit on a mass of men ahead of me to the right. The smoke clears quickly. Several men whimper and moan. The panje vehicle right behind is struck by a shell and is blasted a meter into the air. The Russians dig in in front of us.

The blast from a shell bursting nearby takes my breath away. As I'm lying on the ground, however, I only take a few thick lumps of earth off my back. Thirstily I suck on the snow. It's terrible to lie on this bare slope under machine-gun fire with no cover; I force myself to get up. Many others stagger and totter forward in an upright position. Whether or not they are killed makes no difference to them.

At the edge of a village (part of Potshapintsy) it becomes quieter. Suddenly a Soviet tank roars along the street. It does not fire, instead rolls over everything in its path. I crawl through a fruit garden and over a frozen ploughed field toward a small wood. There are weapons lying about everywhere, thrown away by exhausted men. At the edge of the forest I assemble a group of men from all arms. Now they have all become infantrymen.

I take time to orientate myself precisely with the compass and map. We have strayed too far to the southeast. As a result I decide to proceed across the next large valley in a westerly direction. The lowland is in sight when riders appear out of the mist. Many, there must be more than a hundred. Russian cavalry? It's possible. Should we take cover? First we move closer. Even through my binoculars I can't make them out clearly, they're moving across out path. A few shots are fired. Several riders turn toward us, they're mounted German artillerymen.

Stragglers assemble in the large valley. There's no sign of the expected reception position, but Lysyanka can't be more than five kilometers away. Surely the village is occupied by our people.

Visibility becomes poorer. Ahead one can hear scattered rifle fire. The shooting becomes heavier, until we finally realize that we've been firing at each other. Fresh groups of stragglers join us. The stream of men becomes wider and heavier.

Behind some torn-up bushes begins an area of knee-deep, gray mud. A jumble of men are struggling to get through the morass. Several thousand I estimate. Enemy tanks are firing into the crowd. Machine-guns rattle from the right. The mass halts before a river. It is about twenty meters wide with a strong current carrying along chunks of ice (Gniloy Tikich).

Everyone wants to get across to save himself from the enemy fire. The leading horsemen leap into the water in waves. A number drown. On the far side large numbers of those who have already crossed are running up the bank. The picture becomes more awful. Dead horses spin awkwardly in the current. A few trucks which have been driven into the river disappear in its depths, only their rear ends still showing. There is no ford through which to wade across. At one place several soldiers try to crawl across a thin sheet of ice. I watch as two break through and disappear beneath the shards of ice. Others strip the clothing from their bodies, try to throw their weapons to the far side, mostly in vain, and jump into the water. Those who make it keep going. The enemy fire intensifies. There is also now the crack of rifle fire from the left. Wounded cry and plead to be taken along. Organizing a foot-bridge is impossible in this tumult.

I try to get away from the mass. Just in front of me a direct hit blows men and boards into the air. The enemy tanks cannot be far away. But between the mud and the clumps of willows I can't see them. I decide to swim the river. I hang my submachine-gun around my neck and shove my packet of maps down the back of my shirt. I spot a good area of bushes on the far side where I can climb out, estimate the drift, walk several steps upstream and then slide slowly into the ice-cold water because of the load I am carrying. After several short strokes I am at the other side. Behind me there is a gurgling sound. Others have followed me, but, being poor swimmers, they are beginning to go under. There is nothing I can do to help.

On the other side I pass through a narrow band of trees across a bare slope, which is being raked by enemy machine-gun fire. Many are hit here. I must harden my heart, because I cannot help the wounded alone. Consolation is so empty . . .

The wind blows strongly from behind, occasionally driving snow before it. A soldier who has collapsed from exhaustion lies on his back, his eyes glazed. His raised left forearm falls slowly. Camouflage suits discarded by those who have swum across flutter in the wind, frozen stiff like paper. My coat, too, is like a board and clatters with each step. The ice water squelches in my boots. I am terribly cold, but I must go on and dare not stop.

The sound of fighting dies away. Finally houses appear – Lysyanka. I skirt along a stream and a few marshy areas. Ahead of me a pair of soldiers support an older comrade, pale and yellow from exhaustion. A soldier from one of the relief units helps them across a trench. Then we are in the village.

Many are happy, but there is no celebration. They simply say: 'we have made it," and think of their comrades, whose fate is unknown.

Shivering and shaking I walk into a command post. There is no news of my headquarters staff. Then I let the warmth from a large stove envelop me.

Slowly the survivors gather. Ahead there is still a tiring march through storm, cold and much snow before we reach the reception area for the fighters of the Cherkassy pocket. Long columns move past. Many men have been able to fight their way through, but many are missing."

A member of the SS-Panzergrenadier Division *Wiking* recalled:

"Pressed into a small area, we waited for the order to break out of the pocket.

February 16: The snow lies over the countryside like an endless, dirty shroud . . . At about noon we learn that the breakout is to begin tonight at 2300.

Our mood is subdued. Each is lost in his own thoughts . . . All conversations turn to the breakout. Will it succeed? Pauli, our jokester, rouses himself for a forced joke: 'Off we go – we'll want to make out our wills.

In the evening suddenly the sound of aircraft – but they do not sound like the usual Russian 'coffee grinders' or 'sewing machines.' Then one dives toward us: 'German fliers! They're dropping supply canisters!' Suddenly we don't feel so abandoned and realize that we haven't been completely written off. Outside the machines roar over us at low altitude, their searchlight beams flitting over the dark, snow-covered village like ghosts. Gradually it becomes quiet again and then comes the long-awaited order: 'Mount up!' (on artillery tractors).

There is a brief halt at the 7th Battery's firing position.

The night is bitterly cold. The frost bites more sharply from hour to hour. The leather of my boots squeaks with every movement. It is unlikely that I'll get away without suffering frostbite. Ahead a tank has broken through a bridge, blocking the road. The advance comes to a halt. We take shelter temporarily in a large stable and curl up in a corner to get some sleep. But it is too cold to sleep. Now and then one of Ivan's[12] shells bursts outside.

February 17: At about 0200 the word is given again: 'Mount up!' Slowly our vehicles toward the main road. It is already the scene of a giant mixup. In spite of strict orders to take along only those vehicles capable of negotiating difficult terrain or those which are indispensable, the road is jammed with horse-drawn wagons, buses, cars, tractors and *Kübelwagen*. We have to forcibly make our way into the column. Bumper to bumper, the vehicles move forward a few meters at a time. The road is so clogged that one can make significantly faster progress on foot. We therefore go on ahead to check out the situation up front. There is much grumbling and complaining, but it does little good. I return to my vehicle and take my seat, which is surrounded by boxes and crates. Exhausted, I fall half asleep and doze, oblivious to what is going on around me. The buzzing of the 'sewing machines' above us also fails to bother me, until suddenly I am awakened by two tremendous explosions. Muck and stones hail down on the top of the truck and rattle off its sides. This was followed shortly by another crash. We have had a close shave; the bombs fell in front of and behind us, destroying a panje wagon. The horses wallow about on the ground, covered in blood. A car and a tractor have also been hit. Medics take the wounded into a house, where their wounds are dressed. Finally the wounded are put into a truck. The cold gets worse from hour to hour.

By dawn we have scarcely gone a kilometer. At first light two Russian reconnaissance aircraft appear. We make our way on foot past several of the stalled vehicles until we can see all of the extended valley through which the road leads. Before us in the valley lies a damaged bridge, over which vehicles are slowly passing one by one. But this is taking far too long for everyone to be able get across. Beyond the bridge on the gentle slope, two endless columns are attempting to reach the crest under heavy artillery fire. If only we were the first over there!

In order to escape the enemy fire on the bridge we veer off to the left of the road and trudge across the open field through the snow toward an area of the stream which is not yet under fire. Scarcely have we left the bridge 200 meters behind us when shells begin to burst there too. We head toward the slope at a trot, which is probably about two kilometers away. I no longer know how many times we have pressed ourselves into the snow when shells burst nearby. Finally we are on the high ground and breathe a little easier. Behind us a long column is winding its way along the road.

A village appears ahead, according to the map it must be Chilki. The enemy ring around the pocket is supposed to be four kilometers deep, therefore we should meet the first of our relief forces just beyond Chilki . . .

To the right a narrow footpath dips down into a valley, at the bottom of which we can see a firm road. Numerous tire tracks show that many others have already gone before us. In order to avoid likely Russian bombardments of the main road, we turn off to the right. After about 100 meters, however, I and another comrade are struck by the thought that this path seems too peaceful and quiet. Following a brief palaver – the others want to continue in this direction – the two of us turn back toward the main road. There is no trace of the others to this day.

Finally we reach Chilki. The air here is damned metallic tasting, and no one knows where it comes from. Shells burst here and there, but there is nothing to be seen of the Russians. The last of our tanks and vehicles are stripped, blown up and set on fire. Ahead, beyond a flat hill, the advance falters again. We stop for a moment to gather our strength. Suddenly, a burst of machine-gun fire slams into the body of a horse just in front of us and we throw ourselves flat onto the snow. Making use of the cover provided by a shallow depression, we crawl forward as quickly as possible. Something is wrong up ahead – more and more men are pressing ahead from behind, but no one dares cross the hill. We are filled with a tremendous uneasiness.

Cautiously we make our way to the crest of the hill . . . there! Two T-34s are sitting on the road and are blocking the way – the way to freedom! Finally a wounded *Obersturmführer* from the *Wiking* panzers seizes the initiative. Everyone gathers round him, and under his leadership we begin to charge up the hill toward the tanks brandishing our rifles and shouting hurray! The cannon and machine-guns of the T-34s inflict carnage in our ranks, but desperation drives us on. As we are running and during the pauses as we take cover, I see that the two Russian tank commanders are standing upright in their turrets issuing orders. However, no one shoots at them, no one takes the time to, everyone wants to get away as quickly as possible – to freedom.

We are now within 100 meters of the tanks, and still the Russians pour round after round into our advancing column. All of a sudden we cannot believe our eyes. The two Russian commanders suddenly disappear into their turrets, the engines roar and, tracks rattling, they begin to move.

The T-34s are rolling away!

Relieved, the shouts of hurray, which before had been so grim, swell – the way is free! Apparently, the desperate charge by our mass of troops frightened the Russians, although we had no weapons other than pistols and rifles.

However, our long-awaited freedom does not last long – again there is the sound of a tank engine – a third T-34, which was previously hidden by the mist, rolls straight towards us. Everyone hurries on to escape its field of fire . . . About 200 meters behind us it breaks into the column, crushing everything in its path.

We struggle on through seemingly endless snowdrifts and storm past old positions and many dead Russians from earlier battles.

Our column stretches as far as the eye can see – a chain of dark figures, without a beginning or ending, in the midst of a desolate, icy snow desert.

More Russian tanks appear, this time there are six. We spread out to offer them a less tempting target. In long strides we try to reach the protection of a hill, but we have to throw ourselves into the snow many times before we reach it. To our right shells burst among a group of soldiers.

We carry on. Now and then several men stop to rest and try to quench their thirst by eating snow. True to our principle of staying away from large groups, we once again strike off to the side into a ravine. It is very narrow and we have little fear of being ambushed. Exhaustion now begins to make itself noticeable. Cramps in my thighs and calves paralyze my legs for a while and prevent me from going on. A young *Gefreiter* has joined up with me. 'Herr *Feldwebel*, shall we go on together?' Why not? This and that comrade passes me by. 'Man, don't stay sitting here!' 'You won't get away if you wait!' . . . "No, go on,' I wave them all away, 'we'll get going again in a moment, we're just taking a short rest.'

And then we move on. The short rest has done us good. In the ravine the long-scattered column is pressed close together, a mixture of troops from all arms. Then everything is once again an impetuous rush forward. At every shot from a hidden Russian position everyone breaks out in wild shouts of hurray as if to give themselves courage. In this case, however, it's a mistake; we would be better off not to betray our position to the Russians. The results are not long in coming. In a small wood we come under fire from machine-guns and Stalin Organs. It is so heavy that we dare not raise our heads from the snow. And once again this shout of hurray . . .

With great difficulty I succeed in escaping this witch's cauldron. I press on, uphill, downhill, across country, always west. And still there is nothing to be seen of our relief forces. Gradually it becomes quieter, and only occasionally do the Russian machine-guns send a burst in our direction.

Then, suddenly, we see a wide, open stream ahead. There are no bridges far and wide. There are many shell holes on both banks, dead soldiers and dead and wounded horses. The many abandoned panje wagons, some shot up some driven part way into the water, show that the area had been under enemy artillery fire and that it could get hot again here at any moment. Should we jump into the stream and swim across? But how would we ever dry out our clothes on the other side, they would freeze to our bodies. Others jump in without thinking. We, however, walk a distance along the bank in hopes of finding a crossing some-where. Just as we are about to give up and climb into the water, we finally discover a footbridge. Here, too, are shell holes, dead men and horses and shot-up vehicles. Balancing ourselves we cross cautiously one after another. A lone canteen cup hangs beside the footbridge. Each man takes the cup, scoops up some water from the stream, quenches his thirst and carefully returns the cup to its place for the next man. I, too, help myself, undeterred by the blood on the water. Just don't quit now! The worst must be behind us.

Suddenly, two dark points appear on the horizon far in the distance, moving back and forth. They must be forward sentries of the relief forces. We scarcely dare to hope.

As we move on my gaze falls on a wounded soldier lying at the side of the path. 'Come on, you can't stay here, you must go on,' I say to him. His face is smeared with blood. 'I'm just going to rest a moment,' he groans. But a rest so close to the objective could easily become an eternal rest. The man must come with us or he is lost. I call to the next man behind me: 'Come, take hold of him. We can't leave him here after he's come this far!' Without a word the other takes hold of the wounded man with me. Our pace will now be very slow, but our wounded comrade must be taken along no matter what the cost. Now and again he moans: 'Leave me, I can't go on.' The man doesn't want to hold us up. But with some encouragement he summons his strength. A rider appears ahead of us as if by providence. It is a *Hiwi*[13], who is likewise trying to save himself, and who obligingly dismounts and continues on foot. We place the wounded man on the horse and take the reins, which increases our pace noticeably. Luckily the wounded man is able to hold firmly onto the horse's mane. After several kilometers we meet a group of soldiers standing around a *Feldwebel*. He is lying in the snow, wounded badly in the thigh and buttocks. The men are uncertain as to how to move him. Then our wounded man, who can barely hold himself upright, says: 'I'm alright now. I'll climb down and we can put the *Feldwebel* on the horse.' With this he slid laboriously out of the saddle.

And then we reached our lines! Our assumption had been correct, the two 'figures on the horizon' were in fact forward sentries of the relief force. The supposed four kilometers which we were to cross had in fact become 25 to 30, but we had made it anyway. We all breathe a great sigh of relief. Even though our trials and exertions are not over, we have escaped the enemy.

Ahead of us in the sun and snow lies Lysyanka. A steady stream of Junkers 52 ambulance aircraft lands there, evacuating the seriously wounded. After dropping off our two wounded at one of the advance dressing stations, we allow ourselves a short rest in Lysyanka. As we are walking up to one of the miserable mud huts, another group comes out. Breadcrumbs lie on the table, there are puddles of water on the floor and it is terribly cold. We pick out the larger crumbs, and then I take a can of fish from my field bag and open it slowly and deliberately. The fish is frozen, but to us it tastes better than ever before, even if each us gets only a few bites.

We have been under way for eight hours now, but we have not yet reached our objective. Thousands of men are coming from the pocket, and where are they all to stay in this small place? The wounded can only be given first aid. We get to our feet and make our way to the next village seven kilometers away. It is dark when we finally arrive. All of the accommodations are so crowded that there is not room for a single man. What now? Go on? The we discover a rickety shack at the edge of the village. It is already crowded and the wind whistles through the cracks – but it's still better than standing outside in the snow. So in we go!

Now for the first time we realize how tired we are. We simply let ourselves drop and wriggle in amongst the others in spite of loud protests.

Finally at rest, my feet and legs begin to pain, until I fall into a half-sleep from exhaustion, from which I am now an again awakened by the pain . . ."

Léon Degrelle, the new commander of the SS-Sturmbrigade *Wallonie*, wrote[14]:

"I was summoned to *General* Gille[15] (February 16). All of the senior officers from the Shenderovka sector were there. There was no long discussion. 'Only a desperate effort can save us. Further waiting is useless. At five in the morning tomorrow the 50,000 men of the pocket will go to the attack to the southwest against any resistance. Break-through or death. There is no other solution. Troop movements begin this evening at 2300.' That was his address.

The two army corps Generals and *General* Gille very carefully avoided describing the true situation. By their account only five-and-a-half kilometers separated us from the relief forces. These had, they said, had been making progress since the day before. Tomorrow they would come further toward us. If we set out at the same time with 50,000 men we must overrun the enemy.

The nerves of all the officers and men were on edge. A wave of hope surged through us. We returned to our people to bring to them our enthusiasm over the upcoming attack.

The orders which the *Wallonie* Assault Brigade had received were not easy to carry out. As rearguard, we had to hold out near Novo-Buda until the last moment. At 2300 all of the less seriously wounded, those who could walk, were to set out to the southwest. At 0100 the brigade's Wallonian infantry began to withdraw from east to west, but the positions near Novo-Buda were to be held until 0400 on the morning of the 17th at all costs. By that time the 10,000 who had pressed together in the valley would be three kilometers southwest of Shenderovka. Not until then could our rearguard fall back, while they deceived the enemy by keeping up their heavy fire until the last moment. – The brigade would form up again on the move and place itself at the head of the column, joining the advance guard of the breakthrough forces.

In our situation anything was better than doing nothing. The men knew they were lost if they stayed where they were. They simply could do no more. They were suffering from hunger, staggering from exhaustion and shaking with fear. – The news that we were going to break out the next morning gave everyone a tremendous lift. Even the weakest felt a new hope for life. The same words were repeated often: 'Tomorrow we'll be free! Be free! Be free!' One way or another the Cherkassy Pocket was coming to an end.

As soon as darkness fell in the valley the German columns began to move toward the southwest. The way led through the village of Shenderovka and then over a bridge. Beyond the bridge the steppe extended to two villages, which lay a good three kilometers apart to the south and west. These two villages had been taken after heavy fighting. Before day broke all of the vehicles would have to be in the two villages.

From 2100 in the evening the confusion in Shenderovka was unimaginable. During this time I had to direct my brigade's withdrawal to Novo-Buda according to plan, in stages and sector by sector. If anything happened in our rearguard positions the entire operation in Shenderovka would collapse.

The fires of battle blazed on the hills.

At 2300 I tried to pass through Shenderovka to facilitate the evacuation of my brigade's wounded and to see for myself that the necessary measures had been taken for our people for daybreak. After fifty meters I had to abandon our last four-wheel-drive vehicle. A huge column was pouring through the defile and the village. Trucks and vehicles of all kinds tried desperately to get through four or five at a time. I ran to every panje wagon carrying our Wallonian wounded and urged all those whose legs were still sound, with one last effort, as bad as their wounds and pain were, to try their luck on foot. In this way I collected about fifty men together and worked my way through between the horse-drawn vehicles and trucks.

A frightful spectacle awaited us.

The enemy was pressing from the north, and his tanks and artillery had already reached the vicinity of Shenderovka. Since ten in the evening the Soviet batteries had been laying down fire on the center of the village. Houses were in flames, lighting the ongoing troop move-ments as bright as day. From there the Soviet gunners had an easy game of it. Their shells smashed into the huge column accurately and pitilessly. Stalin Organs poured their rockets into the stream of vehicles of every type. Fuel trucks caught fire. Vehicles burned along the entire length of the

narrow road. Repeatedly we threw ourselves into the snow to protect ourselves from the shells. Between the dozens of burning vehicles horses gasped in the snow, convulsing terribly. With them lay clusters of wounded, lying on their backs and stomachs, illuminated by the glow of the fires. Some tried to crawl, others wandered helplessly in terrible pain.

The burning vehicles between the precipitous slopes made any further progress almost impossible. The infantry fought their way forward through the enemy fire only with great difficulty, moving past fiercely-burning vehicles and dead and dying horses. In vain the drivers of still-intact wagons tried to urge their teams on. Only a few heavy trucks got through, crushing the groaning horses

fighting the flames. All of these desperate efforts had the same result. The confusion became even greater, shrouded by the sound of engines, the impacting shells, the cries and calls for help.

Finally we discovered the reason for this hellish traffic jam. Everything from Shenderovka had to cross a wooden bridge to get out of the valley. A German heavy tank had broken through the bridge, demolishing it in the process and halting all traffic to the southwest. When we saw this monster amid the tangle of beams and boards we thought all was lost. The banks of the river were steep and completely unnegotiable. The bridge had been blown by the Russians two days before when they were driven out of Shenderovka, and had been hastily rebuilt by our people. The light tanks had come from Shenderovka and crossed the bridge. Then a heavy tank had driven across without incident. The second had destroyed everything. In one minute this steel giant of 40,000 kilograms, which was now stuck in the bridge like a post, had destroyed two days' work.

It was light as day. Infantry and wounded slipped past the unlucky tank as best they could. From the heights above the valley one could see Shenderovka, red in the glistening white snow. Wild cries came from countless throats . . .

After our wounded had crossed the bridge I placed them in the hands of one of our medical officers with orders to join the forces three kilometers further forward, which were advancing for the attack. They moved across the steppe, where the darkness was not lit by the burning trucks.

In this atmosphere of ruin, after two hours of unspeakable exertion, our pioneers succeeded in causing the tank to plunge into the water and then laid heavy beams across the gaping hole. Traffic began to move again under ever heavier enemy fire.

The soldiers walked over the dead and dying. But they were walking. They had to trample down everything to advance. They wanted to live.

Far to the northwest on the icy hills of Novo-Buda the Wallonians of our brigade, true to their orders, continued to resist and shoot back. They saw the fires from the stalled and crushed column in Shenderovka. They could hear the terrible cries of thousands of men pressing forward through shells and fire.

Between 0100 and 0500 during the early morning of February 17 the platoons of our brigade withdrew one after another. Softly they slid through the snow. The ground was hard. They came to a gully in the southeast, where they assembled. Now they had three kilometers to go to Shenderovka. They didn't need to look for the way. The glowing red torches from the fires stood out above the brightly-lit village. The men made their way past burning vehicles, dead horses and dead men in contorted positions.

The whole night through small, fast groups of Wallonians passed through the village.

Our rearguard remained unshakably at their posts in Novo-Buda. The kept up a steady fire on the Russians, pinning them down on the hill. At five in the morning they disappeared in carrying out the final part of the plan and linked up at once with the last blocking position of the *Wiking* Division at the northern exit from Shenderovka. Then they crossed over the patched-together bridge behind the last vehicles.

A column of trucks and panje wagons, almost two kilometers long and fifty meters wide, moved up close to the battle lines. I had swung toward a load of ammunition and from there assembled my Wallonians, who remained irrepressible in spite of everything.

The jumble of units and vehicles was unimaginable. The new day had been shining on this tangle of tanks, motor vehicles, horse-drawn vehicles, mixed battalions, Ukrainian civilians and Soviet prisoners of war for a few moments. Suddenly, a shell fell in the midst of the multitude. Then ten shells. Then even more. The enemy tanks and guns had reached the Shenderovka hills opposite us. We offered an excellent target.

The last twenty German tanks left the column en masse and drove to a ravine, crushing everything in their path. Truck and team drivers scattered to the four winds. Horses ran away wildly. Others, whose hooves had been crushed by the tanks, neighed loudly. Shell fragments tossed snow and earth into the air . . .

The *Wallonien* Sturmbrigade received orders to make its way to the head of the column by daybreak, in order to take part in the ultimate breakthrough attack.

Salvation or destruction!

Moving quickly, we drove southwest through the disarray the Soviets had caused among the last thousand German vehicles. Behind us the noise was ear-shattering. Shenderovka had not held out longer than an hour, the Russians were already on their way out of the village behind us. Their tanks rolled toward us for the ultimate confrontation. Our remaining tanks were sacrificed in a counterattack . . . They rolled off on their tracks through the snow and the confusion of the retreat. None of them came back – not a man, not a tank. The panzer soldiers died to a man south of Shenderovka on the morning of February 17 to gain an hour's time, an hour which might allow ten-thousand soldiers to be saved. Under the protection of the tank attack everything else stormed toward the southwest. It was snowing in huge flakes. The heavy snow meant salvation, as it limited visibility. In clear weather the enemy air force would have destroyed us all. Under the dense flakes we ran as fast as we could. The enemy-free area was very narrow. The lane cleared by the troops ahead of us was only several hundred meters wide. The terrain was hilly. We advanced from one hill to the next. In the hollows was a terrible jumble of destroyed vehicles and dozens of dead soldiers lay in the red snow. Enemy guns kept the open spaces under heavy fire. We stumbled over the bleeding wounded and took cover among the dead.

Scarcely were we out of a hollow when we came under fire from both sides from enemy sharpshooters. Men cried out and fell to their knees in the snow, clutching their stomachs. The snow soon covered the dying. Five minutes later all one could see were faces and strands of hair. After another ten minutes they were nothing more than white humps in the snow, over which the others stumbled.

Nevertheless, all in all the column had retained a certain order. At that moment a wave of Soviet tanks drove past the last vehicles. They set upon more than half the horse-drawn vehicles, crushing the wagons with their tracks, running over them one after another, killing the drivers, wounded and horses. As fast as we could we herded the wounded to the front and covered the escape of the remaining panje wagons which had escaped the tanks as best we could.

We found a moment of peace when the Russian tanks, which had become bogged down in a hollow, tried to get out of the field of wreckage from the vehicles they had crushed.

We passed a wood and came to another valley. Scarcely had we reached the next rise, when we saw several hundred riders racing down from a hill to the southwest. I took out my glasses and from their uniforms determined that the riders were cossacks. In a wild charge they fell upon our rearguard. – We were stunned. The Soviet infantry were firing at us, Russian tanks were chasing us, and now the Cossacks, too, had taken up the chase. When would they come, when would the tanks of the relief forces arrive which were supposed to be driving toward us from the southwest . . .

We had already walked more than ten kilometers and still there was nothing to be seen. But we had to press onward, always onward.

In the maelstrom of the breakout and the fighting we were lucky to reach a wood in time, through which we planned to travel to the vicinity of Lysyanka after dark.

Three-hundred meters ahead of us on the road to Lysyanka the guns of the enemy tanks were still pointing to the northwest, where the second major breakout point lay. There, too, the advance had been massive. For several hours it drew the Soviet tanks and infantry towards it. This distraction saved us.

Night fell. The snow fell slowly in large flakes. From the distant steppe we could hear the desperate, heart-rending cries of the wounded. Their calls and cries remained unanswered . . .

While we waited for total darkness the 3,000 survivors, who lay strewn about our wood, had been grouped according to rank. Every branch of the service was represented. There were also many Ukrainian civilians, fleeing the Red Army. Without food or drink we had survived since morning on a few handfuls of snow. But the snow only made us thirstier. Our wounded shook with fever. We pressed together as best we could to warm ourselves a little. Filled with wasting impatience and fear we waited for the end of this frightful day. Not until the enemy tanks on the hills and the road to Lysyanka could no longer see our movements did we dare leave the protection of the wood.

At thirty minutes past five we set out in strict order. From the hills which had been barricaded by the Soviet tanks, from the slopes and from the valleys which we had crossed in the morning, rang endless cries for help. We could hear them very clearly in the cold, snowy night . . . We closed our hearts to this terrible sound and moved on toward liberation. A narrow path led us along the edge of the forest. The night became brighter. The entire column moved silently. From these 3,000 men, including the last 632 Wallonians of my brigade, there was not a voice, not a whisper.

Led by scouts, we walked two kilometers along a path which led through swamps; the mud was up to our knees. None of the Russians noticed us.

We climbed a snow-covered hill. On the other side a waterway glistened in the moonlight. One after another we crossed over a heavy, swaying, slippery beam. We moved on another fifty meters. Then there was wild excitement. Three shadows with steel helmets suddenly appeared before us. They were the first forward sentries of the relief forces near Lysyanka-North.

The pocket was now only a frightful dream. We had been saved, yes, we had really been saved.

We spent the rest of the night as best we could in nearby houses and huts. We were still quite close to the Russians, but where were we to go in the middle of the night in the blowing snow? . . .

I woke up at five in the morning. We tramped through the deep snow and moved along the road. Orders were to leave Lysyanka at once and march on as far and as long as possible . . ."

During the night of February 16/17 the 57th and 88th Divisions had held the pocket's northern front in heavy fighting, including Hill 192, covering the rear of the withdrawal. Throughout the 17th they continued to hang on, holding off the pursuing enemy. When the agreed upon radio code word was not issued, both division commanders agreed to disengage from the enemy during the course of the 17th and break out. Splitting up into small groups, the two units were able to work their way through the Russian blocking units with comparatively light casualties, reaching the river by about midnight on the 17th. Taking advantage of the crossings which had been built, they were thus spared the task of swimming the ice-cold Gniloy-Tikich.

The 1st Executive Officer of the 57th Infantry Division wrote:

"February 17: The pause between the departure of the three waves on the 16th at 2300 and the planned withdrawal of the rearguard at 0500 on the 17th was too great and thus disastrous. By 0600 the order to follow had not yet arrived, and the rearguard remained in their positions. The two division commanders decided to withdraw on their own. When the division's units had assembled once again at the west end of Shenderovka, a battalion commander reported to the division commander that his battalion's fighting strength was three officers and eleven NCOs and men. By this time the breakout divisions had long since arrived in Lysyanka. The enemy had used the pause to reduce the approximately three-kilometer-wide breakout lane from both sides.

Following their departure the masses of troops, which were now hurrying southwest, came under heavy fire from both sides. One cannot describe the scenes witnesses during this flight. *General* Trowitz was deeply moved when he came upon a large number of panje wagons in a wood. The division medical officers had placed their wounded in these in hopes of keeping them out of the hands of the Russians, from whom they could expect little mercy. In fact, about 250 of the division's wounded were brought out of the pocket.

As a result of continued enemy action the breakout groups were scattered. The survivors formed new groups. Within the approximately fifty-man-strong group led by the division commander, for example, there were members of every unit of the 57th Infantry Division. The group escaped enemy tank fire by taking to narrow ravines. The men made their way through thick thorn hedges. As darkness fell the enemy fire ceased. They slipped past stationary Russian tanks, maintaining a compass reading of twenty-three. Burning buildings in Lysyanka showed the way over the last kilometers. As a result, the group veered southeast and avoided the swollen Gniloy Tikich, which had already swallowed up hundreds of exhausted soldiers.

The troops slipped past the Russian foxholes in the dark and snow, without a shot being fired by either side. The division commander's small group arrived in Lysyanka at 2400. When they reached the Gniloy Tikich, which ran through the town, pioneers began to build a footbridge. The last soldiers of the rearguard arrived by morning.

February 18: After a few hours sleep the march continued. At about 1000 *General* Trowitz reported to III Panzer Corps by telephone. From the commander of the 16th Panzer Division Trowitz learned that the division had only two serviceable tanks left.

The remains of the 57th Infantry Division assembled in Moledetskoye. Among the many missing was the Ia of the division, General Staff *Oberstleutnant* Heidenreich . . ."

For the soldiers escaping from the pocket, reaching the 1st Panzer Division's bridgehead did not mean an end to their flight. Lysyanka could not be held. There was time for a little sleep before the exhausted and worn-out men set out the next day to march the many kilometers to the actual German front and the first rations distribution centers and, finally, the planned reception area. In long columns, half frozen, tired and hungry, but lucky to have escaped the pocket, they withdrew through the barely 600-meter-wide "corridor" along the road from Lysyanka, threatened from both sides and under fire from Soviet artillery. German tanks covered the flanks.

After a number of the seriously wounded had been flown out in transport aircraft, late in the evening of February 18 more than 1,500 sick and wounded set out in horse-drawn columns from Lysyanka-South toward the rear through Bushanka, likewise under the protection of German tanks. There *Stabsarzt* Dr. Königshauser and his assistants worked at an aid station until the last casualty had been tended to and evacuated.

The German panzer divisions, which in spite of the great difficulties, all their efforts and heavy losses had not come any closer to the pocket, held their positions for another two days in order to wait for the last of the rearguard. For the 1st Panzer Division, in whose battle zone the breakout had taken place, the 18th of February passed relatively quietly, as the enemy, too, had to wait for supplies, assemble and regroup. Courageous Ju 52 crews landed near Lysyanka on hastily-fashioned landing strips, which resembled ploughed fields more than runways, often under artillery fire, to evacuate numbers of sick and seriously wounded soldiers. Individual groups escaping from the pocket continued to arrive near Oktyabr and Lysyanka until evening.

Oktyabr had to abandoned for good at 1900; it was not expected that anyone else would come out of the pocket and the enemy pressure was increasing. The bridgehead around Lysyanka was still being held by twelve Panzer IVs and Vs and a few damaged tanks dug in as anti-tank guns. As well there were about eighty panzergrenadiers, three squads of armored pioneers and a forward observation section from the artillery – that was all.

Following the reception and evacuation of the troops from the pocket, it was concluded that the last men had been picked up and that the Russians were preparing a new attack with the forces freed from the encircling ring. As a result the four German panzer divisions had to pull back. At about 0530 on the morning of February 19 the rearguard of the 1st Panzer Division began withdrawing from Lysyanka, after repelling an enemy tank attack. It was high time too – the withdrawal route already lay under heavy enemy fire.

The bitterness of the fighting was reflected in the total of 140 enemy tanks and about 70 heavy anti-tank guns destroyed by the 1st Panzer Division.

But many members of the panzer divisions had paid for the relief effort with their lives. Armored Battle Group Frank of the 1st Panzer Division had three to five tanks left as well as about seventy-five men of the 113th Panzergrenadier

Regiment's 1st Battalion and the attached unit of the "LAH," plus a few pioneers. The other panzer divisions were not much better off. 1st Battalion, 64th Panzergrenadier Regiment of the 16th Panzer Division had left two officers and twenty-eight men – from an entire battalion!

About 25,000 to 30,000 survivors from the pocket were assembled in prepared reception camps north of Uman – from the approximately 56,000 who had been trapped in the pocket. There are no exact figures, and various sources do not agree. After their victory near Korsun the Soviets reported 11,000 German troops killed and 18,000 captured, which contrary to the usual Soviet exaggerations may have been close to the truth.

It had not become a second Stalingrad, but two German army corps had ceased to exist and the better part of six divisions, which were soon to be bitterly needed, had been destroyed. Having escaped a twenty-one day battle of encirclement, the ten-thousand German soldiers were not fit for action for some time, and their faith in the highest levels of German command had been severely shaken. The two corps had also lost their entire complement of armaments, equipment, vehicles and horses.

Hitler's totally absurd plan for a German offensive toward Kiev had failed at the outset, and his authorization for a breakout from the pocket had been given far too late. The enemy could no longer be stopped. The Soviet flood broke loose again, overwhelming the entire Ukraine, and soon reached the Dnestr.

Extracts from Wehrmacht Communiques:

February 18:
. . . After fighting off heavy enemy counterattacks, contact was reestablished with powerful German battle groups cut off for a week in the area west of Cherkassy, which had fought their way through to the panzer units coming to their relief . . .

February 19:
. . . West of Cherkassy contact was made with further elements of the freed battle group, in spite of numerous enemy counterattacks, which were repulsed, and extremely difficult terrain conditions . . .

February 20:
. . . Further to the February 18 report of the freeing of the German battle group surrounded west of Cherkassy, the Wehrmacht High Command announces that:

"The recovery of the freed divisions is complete. The troops of the Army and Waffen-SS under the command of *General der Artillerie* Stemmermann and *Generalleutnant* Lieb, surrounded since January 28, held fast against an assault by far superior enemy forces in a heroic defensive battle, and then in bitter fighting broke through the enemy's encircling ring."

Disposition

Surrounded Forces (Gruppe Stemmermann)
XI Army Corps (*Generalleutnant* Lieb)
XXXXII Army Corps (*General der Artillerie* Stemmermann)
57th Infantry Division (*Generalmajor* Trowitz)
72nd Infantry Division (*Oberst* Dr. Hohn)
88th Infantry Division (*Generalmajor* Graf Rittberg)
Korpsabteilung B (*Oberst* Fouquet) with the 112th, 255th and 332nd Division Groups (the remains of these shattered divisions, now in regiment strength)
Minor elements of the 167th, 168th and 389th Infantry Divisions, 213th Security Division, 14th Panzer Division
5th SS-Panzergrenadier Division *Wiking* (Gene*ralleutnant* Gille)
SS-Volunteer Sturmbrigade *Wallonie* (*Oberstleutnant* Lippert, then *Hauptmann* Degrelle).

Relief Forces (First Panzer Army):

III Panzer Corps (*General* Breith) with:
1st Panzer Division (*General* Koll)
16th Panzer Division (*Generalmajor* Back/Hillebrand)
17th Panzer Division (*Generalmajor* von Meden)
SS-Panzer Division *Leibstandarte Adolf Hitler* (*SS-Gruppenführer* and *Generalleutnant* Wisch)
Heavy Panzer Regiment Bäke (*Oberstleutnant* Dr. Bäke) with 2nd Battalion, 23rd Panzer Regiment and the 503rd Heavy Panzer Battalion.

Notes:
[1] Consisting of the Fourth Guards Army, the Twenty-seventh, Fifty-second and Fifty-third Armies, the Fifth Guards Tank Army and the Sixth Tank Army.
[2] Commonly used abbreviation for *Leibstandarte Adolf Hitler*.
[3] *Korpsabteilung*: During the retreat to the Dniepr in the summer of 1943 the German front-line divisions suffered losses which could not be made good. Numerically, their combat strengths stood in an unfavorable

ratio to the trains, supply services, etc, which had suffered less. The Army High Command (OKH) therefore decided to concentrate three weakened infantry divisions each into a so-called *Korpsabteilung*.

A *Korpsabteilung* was equivalent to an infantry division and consisted of three division groups (equivalent to three infantry regiments) each with two regiment groups (equivalent to two battalions).

[4] A unit of Belgian volunteers.

[5] Cherkassy Pocket was a German designation; the Russians more accurately called it the Korsun Pocket.

[6] Around the entire pocket the enemy's superiority was 10:1 in infantry, 8:1 in artillery and 30:1 in tanks.

[7] Excerpt from: W. Werthen: *Geschichte der 16. Panzerdivision.*

[8] Stoves: *1. Panzerdivision.*

[9] Russian multiple rocket launcher.

[10] The panzer regiment with which Dr. Bäke launched his attack to the southeast from the area southwest of Chishintsy consisted of only six Tiger tanks and a few Panthers. It did in fact reach the area north of Hill 239, but was unable to do any more than tie down strong enemy forces. Unaware of this, the majority of the escaping troops had already fled to the south and southeast. Dr. Bäke was likewise unaware of this development.

[11] On this day Oktyabr changed hands several times, but ended up in German possession.

[12] A common soldier's expression for the Russians.

[13] Soldier's term for Russian auxiliary volunteers in German service.

[14] Excerpt from Degrelle: *Die verlorene Legion.*

[15] Commander of the SS-Division *Wiking.*

II

Ternopol:
Fortress Garrison

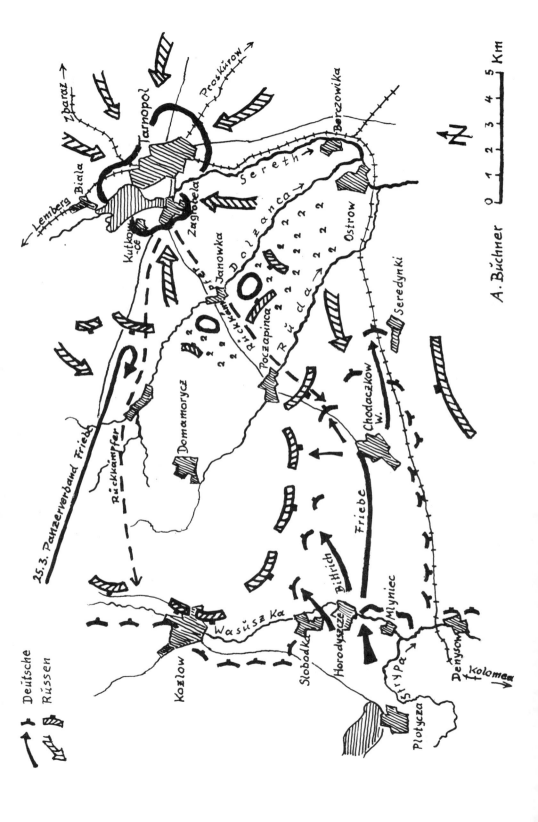

Deütsche
Rüssen

25.3. Panzerverband Friebe

Rückkämpfer

Lemberg
Biala
Zbaraz
Tarnopol
Proskurow
Berezowika
Sereth
Zagrobela
Kutkow-ce
Janowka
Dolzanca
Rückkämpfer
Ruda
Poczapinca
Ostrow
Seredynki
Domamorycz
Chodaczkow W.
Friebe
Bittrich
Kozlow
Wasiuszka
Slobodka
Horodyszcze
Mlyniec
Strypa
Denysow
Kolomea
Plotycza

A. Büchner

N

0 1 2 3 4 5 Km

Ternopol: Fortress Garrison[1]

Of 4,600 Soldiers 55 Came Back

The next scene of action was located in what had formerly been the Podolien District of Southern Poland. This was a largely flat area, with scattered low hills and small woods, and villages with – for the Germans – almost unpronounceable names. The Seret River and its tributaries ran through the region, and located on the east bank of the river, forty kilometers from the former Polish-Russian border, was the city of Ternopol. At the point where the Seret flowed out of a marsh-bordered lake a dam and bridge led across the river to the two small, rural suburbs of Zagrobela and Kukowce. With its extensive metropolitan area surrounded by outlying settlements and its 35,000 inhabitants, Ternopol was certainly a significant city – as the provincial capital and a major trading center with industrial facilities, but above all as a transportation center with rail lines running north, south, east and west. With its network of streets, stone houses, municipal administration, churches, large railroad station, main post office, business, trading and market activity, it offered a typical picture of a medium-size Eastern European city.

In spite of its importance as a transportation center, Ternopol had never played a military role. It was a garrison city, but without any actual fortifications. Before World War One it had belonged to the Austro-Hungarian monarchy; after 1918 it became part of the newly-created Polish state. At the outbreak of war in 1939 it was occupied by the Soviets and was captured by the Germans in 1941. Now the Russians were coming again.

In early 1944 the Soviets continued their offensive against the entire German Southern Front (Army Groups South and A) despite the onset of the muddy period. The Soviets attacked in several directions and by mid-April had pushed the German front back to Galicia, the edge of the Carpathians and the Dnestr River. The dramatic struggle for Ternopol was part of this ongoing heavy fighting.

Ternopol: "Fortified Place"

After pausing to regroup and prepare for its next move, the Soviet First Ukrainian Front under Marshal Zhukov resumed its offensive. On March 4 it advanced west of Shepetovka, and after two days of heavy fighting had smashed deep into the front held by the German Fourth Panzer Army (*General der Panzertruppen* Raus). Near Jampol these penetrations were soon expanded into a forty-kilometer-wide breakthrough. If the Russians reached Ternopol or Proskurov, the last major rail line east of the Carpathians from Lemberg (Lvov) to Odessa would be cut and the Germans would be forced to supply both army groups via the long route through Rumania.

While the main Russian offensive continued to grind its way southward, a secondary operation saw Soviet troops advance west and southwest. In the period March 5-12 they pushed the right wing of the Fourth Panzer Army back to the Seret. With great difficulty XXXXVIII Panzer Corps, reinforced by three infantry divisions which had been rushed to the scene, was able to establish a new front. During the fighting the Soviets drove past Ternopol on two sides, and the city was threatened with encirclement. Zbaraz, not 20 kilometers away, was occupied on the evening of March 3. The same day Hitler unconditionally ordered Ternopol held, even at the threat of encirclement. After this things moved quickly. At noon on March 7 the enemy was already on the east bank of the Seret, on the 8th Ternopol was partly encircled from the east, and at first light the following day the Soviets broke into the city. Ternopol was surrounded for the first time. Soviet tanks drove through the streets firing wildly and confident Russian infantry felt sure they would have an easy time of it. The available German garrison, which was quickly reinforced, began to offer determined resistance and soon heavy fighting had broken out in the city. For many rear-echelon units and part of the civilian population the arrival of the enemy was the signal for the start of a disorderly flight to the west. The headlong flight of the medical officer responsible for Ternopol was to have especially grave consequences later on. He and most of his personnel "withdrew," taking with them most of the medical stores.

After heavy fighting, which saw anti-tank units and assault guns sent in to support the garrison, the Russians were thrown out of the city again. By March 11 Ternopol had been cleared of Russian forces, but from then on lay under continuous artillery bombardment.

At this point in time Hitler had another of his "inspired" ideas, a new means by which he thought he could bring to a halt the steady Soviet advance on all fronts.

The concept was defined in *Führer* Directive No. 11 of March 8, 1944, in which he established "fortified places." The idea was first implemented at Ternopol, and despite its negative consequences Hitler made further use of it in the future. The order prudently avoided the use of the term "fortress," even though the objectives of a "fortified place" as laid down by Hitler were very similar. Larger towns and cities which had a certain significance, or which achieved such in the course of combat operations, were to consciously allow themselves to be surrounded with their garrisons. Acting as "breakwaters," they were to halt or delay the enemy's advance, splitting his forces and compelling him to tie up major units to lay siege to the surrounded cities. The idea was not new, and it had proved its effectiveness in the previous century, most recently in World War One (at Verdun in the West and Przemysl in the East, for example). During the four and a half years of the Second World War, however, even the most modern fortresses had fallen quickly (Eben Emael and the Maginot Line in 1940, the Metaxas Line in 1941, and Sevastopol in 1942, for example). "Fortified places" were therefore nothing more than great traps – Ternopol and all the others which were to follow. Quite apart from the fact that fortifications had not been built and the necessary strong garrisons were absent, the Soviets had men and materiel enough to surround and reduce the "fortified places" and still continue their offensives at full strength. – Ternopol was be an especially sad example of this.

On March 10 Hitler issued a *"Führerbefehl"* declaring Ternopol a "fortified place."

There could be no talk of construction of fortifications, or even of fortified sectors, however. An inner and outer ring of fortifications with forts and individual works, with broad fields of obstacles and anti-tank ditches, with concrete, bullet-proof bunkers supported by deep trenches and field positions, and a central fortress with a citadel and bomb-proof casemates, quarters and hospital: all of this was missing, as were magazines filled with ammunition, stores and rations, heavy fortress artillery, an airfield, and so on. As well, Ternopol lacked a cohesive, powerful and well-armed garrison.

Ternopol's defenses consisted of a thin ring of field positions within a two to three kilometer radius of the city center. The troops manning this system of trenches and strongpoints lacked sufficient ammunition, especially for the light artillery and heavy weapons, first-aid supplies, artillery and anti-aircraft guns; there was not even a landing strip for aircraft. Then there was the makeshift garrison, comprising units of varying strength and effectiveness. There were barely-trained eighteen-year-old soldiers alongside older militiamen, Waffen-SS men alongside career soldiers, troops of the 8th Panzer Division alongside

Fusiliers from the Demba Training Grounds, as well as German and Galician volunteers. The garrison was also short on firepower. Other than light and heavy machine-guns, mortars and light artillery, there were only a few assault guns, tanks and self-propelled guns available, as well as fifteen anti-tank guns (including some of the long-obsolete 37mm versions). For anti-aircraft defence there was only three light 20mm and four heavy 88mm guns, while the artillery had only three light 105mm and eight heavy 150mm pieces, most of which lacked ammunition. This was all that the "fortified place" Ternopol had. In the period March 13-20, XXXXVIII Panzer Corps, strengthened by the arrival of two fresh infantry divisions, attacked southeast of Ternopol and succeeded in driving back the Soviet forces, closing the gap to the neighboring First Panzer Army and freeing Ternopol. Then, however, Marshal Zhukov resumed his offensive in the contested area between Ternopol and Proskurov with fresh, powerful forces. The new offensive was launched on March 21 in cooperation with the Second Ukrainian Front. By the third day the Soviets had broken through south between the Fourth and First Panzer Armies, which led to the latter being surrounded with about 200,000 men. First Panzer Army managed to escape destruction by becoming a "wandering pocket," which eventually succeeded in restoring contact with German forces. A further Soviet thrust to the west (Soviet Sixtieth Army with 11 rifle divisions, 1 artillery division and IV Guards Tank Corps) between March 21 and 24 drove XXXXVIII Panzer Corps back once again, this time as far as the Wosuzka River.

As of the afternoon of March 23 the "fortified place" Ternopol was cut off once again and this time – about twenty kilometers from the new German front – was encircled for good. If the Ternopol garrison, which had fought well, believed that the city would be abandoned as the German front fell back in the face of the overpowering Soviet advance, it had deceived itself. The city's new commandant, *Generalmajor* von Neindorf, realized that the city could not be held for long for the reasons outlined earlier. Von Neindorf pointed out several times that Ternopol had not been fortified for defence, had a weak garrison and was short on supplies; nevertheless, the *Führerbefehl* stood: the "fortified place" was to be defended and was to hold out to the last man! The defenders therefore prepared to defend the city, which was divided into North, South, East and West Sectors, that on the west bank of the Seret encompassing the two suburbs of Kutkowce and Zagrobela. The troops began to dig defensive positions, the heavy weapons were brought into position, observation posts were set up and the few guns moved into positions from which they could fire in all directions, while the small force of assault guns was held in reserve for counterattacks. The garrison headquarters set to work organizing the distribution of rations[2] and ammunition, laying down lines of communication and setting up assembly points for the wounded, as well as forming alert companies and limited reserves. The only contact with the "outside" was by radio.

There was not much time left – on March 23, even before the city was completely encircled, the Soviets resumed their attacks on Ternopol on a larger scale. These tank-supported attacks from the north, east and south were beaten off, however. On March 24 the Soviets launched repeated attacks in the west on the far side of the Seret against Kutkowce and Zagrobela. The suburb of Kutkowce was lost, but Zagrobela, which changed hands several times during the day, was firmly in the hands of the defenders when night fell. At the same time the defenders were forced to deal with renewed assaults from the north and south on the east side of the river. For the first time a Russian parlementaire appeared, proposing the surrender of the city and its defenders. The offer was rejected. By the evening of that day four Soviet rifle divisions, reinforced by tanks, artillery and batteries of rocket launchers, had completely surrounded the "fortified place" Ternopol.

The First Pointless Armored Advance

Something incomprehensible now took place on the German side. In an effort to replenish the city's inadequate stockpile of ammunition and medical supplies as quickly as possible, a supply convoy carrying 40 tons of ammunition was assembled in Lemberg, about 120 kilometers away, and on March 25 was sent from the northwest through enemy-held territory toward Ternopol. The convoy was to be accompanied by an armored battle group from the 8th Panzer Division under *Oberst* Friebe, who had recently created some "breathing room" for the hard-pressed XIII Army Corps in the Brody area. The battle group's task was to smash the enemy forces west of Ternopol and ensure safe passage for the convoy. Such an operation would have been understandable and militarily justifiable; however, in spite of the urgency of the situation, the convoy with its fifteen trucks and five ambulances had not arrived when the appointed time came for the attack to begin. In spite of this the Fourth Panzer Army ordered *Kampfgruppe* Friebe to set out (the convoy was presumably to be sent on afterward) and break through to Ternopol. However the armored unit was neither to remain and reinforce the "fortified place" nor evacuate the garrison, rather it was to return to its own lines that same night. This was totally incomprehensible, because such an advance could provide the surrounded defenders a brief respite at best. According to the *Führerbefehl* the "fortified place" was to continue to hold out.

Orders are orders, so at 0430 on the morning of March 25 *Oberst* Friebe set out to break through to Ternopol with his tanks and panzergrenadiers, who had scarcely had time to rest since arriving from Brody. His force consisted of the 2nd and 10th Panzer Regiments, with the Panther battalion leading the way, followed by 1st Battalion, 8th Panzergrenadier Regiment and 1st Battalion, 74th Panzergrenadier Regiment in their half-tracked armored personnel carriers. Initially the advance met no resistance, and Friebe's forces soon crossed the narrow Dolzanca River. Artillery fire then became noticeable on the northern flank, and it was discovered that the road had been heavily mined. As a result the vehicles were forced to continue the advance in the muddy, difficult terrain on both sides of the road. An increasing number of tanks and armored personnel carriers became stuck and broke down trying to free themselves from the mud. The battle group had to cross three diagonal lines of hills on which the Soviets had dug in, with their positions protected by anti-tank guns. When the leading tanks were disabled by mines or knocked out by Soviet fire, the panzergrenadiers were forced to dismount and attack on foot. Within a short time they broke through three such enemy positions, destroying about twenty-five Soviet anti-tank guns. Soviet resistance became even greater as Friebe's battle group approached Ternopol. Artillery and anti-tank guns fired on the armored force from the north as it advanced closer to the city. The threat became so great that several units had to be sent north of the road to provide flanking protection. By late afternoon the advance had reached the edge of the forest four kilometers west of Zagrobela. There the battle group ran into the last, but strongest, outer defensive position of the Soviet ring around Ternopol. Red Army troops with anti-tank rifles lurked in the woods, and tanks and anti-tank guns fired from concealed positions. Mortar rounds poured down and artillery thundered and crashed from three directions. Then Soviet aircraft appeared, wave after wave of them. There was no hope of breaking through here. *Oberst* Friebe therefore decided to regroup and withdraw for a further advance to the southeast.

As the commander of the 8th Panzergrenadier Regiment was conferring with his officers Soviet close-support aircraft dove on the command post, dropping bombs and strafing. Killed in the attack were the regimental commander, both battalion commanders and a number of other officers. The radio station was also knocked out, and the panzergrenadiers were rendered virtually leaderless. The entire regrouping was delayed and was not completed until about 1200. Since reconnaissance had revealed that the battle group could expect to encounter further well-built defensive positions in its new direction of attack, and in view of the fact that increased enemy activity had been detected north and even southwest of the road, and no air support could be expected, it was clear that the final breakthrough to Ternopol would be possible only at the cost of further heavy losses and considerable time. Many tanks and armored personnel carriers were already stranded in the mud and ammunition and fuel were running low. As the supply convoy had not followed – fortunately, as it would probably have been destroyed by the enemy guns – and the garrison of Ternopol was not to be relieved, an hour later *Oberst* Friebe decided to break off the operation and pull back to the German lines as ordered, taking the wounded and all recoverable armored vehicles with him. The remaining serviceable tanks laid down smoke to cover the withdrawal.

The garrison of the "fortified place" had listened to the approaching noise of battle with growing anticipation; however, as the sound of fighting gradually faded, all hope for quick relief disappeared. No panzers had come to take them to freedom, and no ammunition, which the defenders so desperately needed, had arrived (delivery by air was now promised).

The advance by *Kampfgruppe* Friebe, which was made at such cost in men and materiel, had been for nothing. Soon after its return, the battle group was sent back to XIII Army Corps in the Brody area as a mobile "fire-brigade."

The "Fortified Place" Becomes a Pile of Rubble – and Holds On

With the futile sortie by *Kampfgruppe* Friebe the fate awaiting the "fortified place" and its garrison began to loom on the horizon. At the time of the second encirclement of Ternopol the city's garrison consisted of about 4,600 men: one *General* as commandant[3], one *Oberst* as deputy commandant, 101 other officers and officials and 4,499 others – infantry, the crews of the infantry and anti-tank guns, artillerymen, the crews of the assault guns and self-propelled guns, the commandant's soldiers, and members of the supply, medical and first-aid units. From now on they would be forced to fight a hopeless battle to the bitter end.

There was no question of the armored sortie having provided any kind of relief. In fact the opposite was true: a Soviet regiment attacked the "fortified place" from the east while *Kampfgruppe* Friebe was still advancing toward the city. The Soviet unit achieved a deep penetration into the German lines, which was not cleared up until a counterattack was launched with much heavy fighting. On the evening of that same March 25 the defenders had to fight off an attack against the northern sector by seventeen tanks with escorting infantry. At the same time the suburb of Zagrobela was attacked by overwhelming forces which crushed the German positions west of the Seret. The latter attack in particular was carried out with great ferocity. Moreover, it was determined that a steady flow of Russian units was moving into every sector of the front around Ternopol, especially west of the city, as it was there that the Soviets were expecting a new German advance or a breakthrough to rescue the garrison, something they definitely wished to prevent.

The Soviets kept up the pressure on the defenders day after day and night after night. The defensive sectors and the entire city lay under constant mortar and artillery fire. The defending German troops could see with their naked eyes how the Soviet units approached, dug in and prepared for their next attack, and how their batteries and rocket launchers drove onto the surrounding hills and took up firing positions openly and virtually unmolested. There was little hope of engaging them, as artillery ammunition was running low. Every round had to be saved for an actual attack. Minor enemy advances, which were obviously reconnaissance missions, and frequent increases in the intensity of the constant harassing fire by the Soviet artillery suggested that a major attack was not far off. This began on March 28 following a two-hour barrage by guns of every caliber. A rifle division, supported by tanks and aircraft, stormed the southeast sector of the defensive ring. After bitter fighting the attackers broke into the German positions. The defensive strength of the young soldiers of 2nd Battalion, 949th Grenadier Regiment seemed to disappear; the battalion was partly destroyed in the fighting. A counterattack failed in the face of strong resistance. Efforts to seal off the penetration the next day also failed, and the main line of resistance had to be pulled back to the edge of the city. On March 29 the Soviets achieved another major penetration along Access Road IV. Once again the soldiers of the 949th Grenadier Regiment failed. No matter how determined, the eighteen-year-old soldiers, who had been thrown into the front after cursory training and had ended up in a major battle in Ternopol, were not equal to such a test physically or mentally. It also appeared that the older militiamen were suffering badly from the effects of prolonged periods under fire. Afterward, as expected, they all fought with greater toughness and endurance.

The steadfastness of his soldiers was only one of the many concerns facing the commandant. As at Cherkassy, the Soviets employed psychological means in an effort to wear down the morale of the defenders. On March 25, for example, groups of German prisoners were sent back (a total of 32) with flyers exhorting the defenders to desert. Surrender ultimatums were also delivered to the commandant. But everyone knew – and this was no German propaganda fairy tale – what could be expected from surrender and Soviet captivity, so the young and old soldiers rallied to stand together with the veterans until they were relieved from this "fortified place" and set free.

While the inhabitants of Ternopol who had not already fled to the west or to outlying villages sought cover in their cellars, the increasingly bitter battle continued. On March 30 the Soviets closed in from all sides, indicating that another major attack was at hand. The expected assault began on March 31 following a several-hour artillery bombardment. Supported by close-support aircraft, numerically superior Soviet forces launched another attack in the east between the two rail lines. They broke through the German positions and advanced to the rail station, which was occupied. Because of the heavy losses suffered and the lack of reserves, recapture of the former main line of resistance was no longer possible. Under intense enemy pressure, the northern and southern sectors also had to be withdrawn to the city's edge, where new positions were occupied. The dwindling garrison thus found itself penned into the actual city area on the east bank of the Seret, an area of approximately one by one-and-a-half kilometers. Confused fighting was also raging in the west, where the Soviets had managed to penetrate the positions around Zagrobela. The territory available to the defenders was shrinking steadily, and since the hills were already in enemy hands, the Soviet tanks, anti-tank guns and artillery could fire into the city as they liked, because the German artillery lacked the ammunition to respond.

Ammunition – this was one of the greatest worries of the commandant and his staff, alongside the shocking increase in casualties and destroyed war materiel. Without ammunition the defence of the city would collapse; they must have ammunition, especially for the few artillery pieces and heavy weapons. First-aid supplies were also in desperately short supply. Once again the Luftwaffe was called upon. As there was no landing strip in Ternopol, the only possibility was to drop the supplies to the defenders. This was made all the more difficult by the powerful Soviet air defenses, which forced the transport aircraft to fly their missions at night, and the ever smaller area, which allowed no room for error. An April 1 radio message from the commandant reported that of the 90 supply containers dropped the previous night, only 5 had arrived. Some of the containers, which were dropped by parachute, fell in enemy territory, while others were blown into the lake or the swamps or were scattered over the entire city area where they were not found among the remains of the houses. The requested first-aid materials also failed to arrive, and none of the severely-wounded could be evacuated due to the lack of an airfield.

Other radio messages reached the commanding XXXXVIII Panzer Corps on April 1, including a report on equipment losses. For the three day period beginning March 30 these losses totalled thirty machine-guns, twelve heavy mortars, one light and one heavy infantry gun, one anti-tank gun and one anti-aircraft gun – a considerable loss of heavy weapons which could not be replaced.

The utter hopelessness of the situation became clear to *Generalmajor* von Neindorff, who had questioned the suitability of Ternopol as a "fortified place" from the beginning. He radioed: "Despite bitter resistance unable to hold on any longer. Request Führer's permission for a breakout attempt."

Hitler's answer was not long in coming. That same day he decided that the "fortified place" was to continue to be held until it was possible to restore contact. But Ternopol had never been a "fortified place," and had now become a pocket.

The following day *Generalfeldmarschall* Model replaced *Generalfeldmarschall* von Manstein as Commander-in-Chief of Army Group South, which was renamed "Army Group North Ukraine."[4] This move was of no help to the doomed defenders of Ternopol. The city was surrounded by four enemy divisions and under constant attack. The fighting went on with undiminished ferocity. Zagrobela was the scene of especially heavy fighting. Because of its position it was especially important to the defenders as the only exit for a breakout to the west, and the Soviets were well aware of this. Holding Zagrobela was the veteran Demba Fusilier Battalion. It was able to clear the enemy penetration of April 1 by launching a counterattack the next day, and smashed two further Soviet attacks supported by tanks. Following the loss of Kutkowce during the first days of the battle, the main line of resistance had to be withdrawn to the limits of the village, so that for all practical purposes Zagrobela was the entire western sector.

The Soviets continued to attack with tanks and superior numbers of infantry. After they had pushed the front back to the city limits in the north, east and south, the Soviets attempted to split the German defensive zone within the city itself. They drove back the east and southeast wings, and the defenders were forced to pull back to a new line to prevent the entire defensive front from being over-whelmed. A Soviet thrust toward the city center was repulsed, but only by committing the last of the reserves. Ten Soviet tanks were destroyed by the defending German troops. But what good were these costly successes if the defenders were being squeezed into an ever smaller perimeter?

On April 2 the commandant signalled: "Continued resistance in confined area in the face of enemy pressure is only a question of time." The question of time was left open by *Generalmajor* von Neindorff; however, the situation was growing more critical by the day, and the corps, army and army group were all well aware of this fact.

The situation in Ternopol was bad enough already, but it was to become even more frightful from now on. The Soviet attempts to break into the new defensive front on April 3 failed, and their advances were repulsed almost everywhere, but once again at great cost to the defenders. As before, a lack of ammunition prevented the German artillery from effectively engaging the Soviet tanks and artillery. The defenders of Ternopol did receive some relief from the air. Acting as "flying artillery," Stuka dive-bombers made effective attacks on enemy troop concentrations and assembly areas. Successful as they were, these attacks had little effect on the mass of Soviet forces. On April 4 they again attacked the city from all sides, forcing the defenders to once more shorten their front. In the west the Soviets initially held back their forces on the far side of the Seret near Zagrobela, intending to first capture the city on the east bank of the river. Continuous heavy fire resulted in the destruction of a large part of the city, preventing all movement, destroying communications centers and making command more difficult.

The Soviets wanted to put an end to the Ternopol chapter.

On April 5 the Soviets blanketed the city with fire from heavy batteries and aircraft showered the defenders with bombs. Nevertheless, the infantry assault which followed the bombardment was stopped. Afterward the Soviet infantry pulled back again, allowing their artillery to resume its bombardment of the city. The tightly-stretched German defensive ring held out against several subsequent attacks. This day was the most difficult so far in the fourteen-day siege, and German casualties were very high. Probably as a result of the astonishing German resistance, the next day did not see a resumption by the Soviets of their concentric attacks.

Nonetheless, Ternopol and its garrison were heading toward inevitable defeat unless something decisive happened.

•

A murderous struggle had begun, in which every officer and man was in the front lines. Soldiers young and old fought with the courage of desperation. Elements of the 949th Grenadier Regiment, which had failed several days earlier, were now fighting well, and received the full recognition of the commandant.[5] Over the city itself hung a black, brown and gray cloud deck. Fiery flashes shot from the fountains of smoke and dust which marked the points of impact of incoming artillery rounds. The air was filled with thundering, crashing and roaring sounds. Flames leapt high into the air, houses collapsed and walls crashed to the ground. Projectiles howled and whistled in from all sides from Soviet heavy mortars, from 76.2mm "*Ratschbum*" all-purpose guns, 122mm and 172mm heavy guns and from "Stalin Organ" rocket launchers. Street and house fighting raged in every corner and end of the city. Troops of the Red Army, clad in their earth-brown uniforms, charged with shouts of "*Urray!*", firing their submachine-guns, rapid-firing rifles, anti-tank rifles and light machine-guns and throwing hand grenades. They worked their way forward over piles of rubble and through tangled beams, many of them falling under the hammering defensive fire. Ever-smaller groups of German defenders held on bitterly, fighting for every street, every block of houses and every shattered building. The infantry barricaded themselves in the stout stone buildings, firing from windows, cellars and holes in the roofs. German anti-tank guns dug into the rubble fired until they had no more ammunition. The few assault guns and self-propelled guns still left rumbled through the rubble-filled, deserted streets, responding to enemy breakthroughs with immediate counterattacks. Groups of Russians which succeeded in infiltrating the German lines were flushed out and driven back with hand grenades and small arms. Some barricaded themselves inside houses, which were blown up. But the Russians kept coming, smoking out the German nests of resistance with incendiary shells and flame throwers.

Conditions were especially bad for the wounded, who either dragged themselves to the makeshift cellar aid stations or were carried there. There was no field hospital. The few medical officers attached to individual units did their best, but there was little they could do to cope with the tremendous amount of suffering. Since there had been no deliveries of medical supplies, everything was in short supply – bandages, medicines, ether, tetanus serum, and so on. A radio message sent on April 4 reported 850 severely wounded, remarking that the situation was becoming catastrophic.

The nightly air drops of supplies continued, but the greatly reduced area held by the defenders had made the task even more difficult, and only a small proportion of the supply canisters landed on target. The Luftwaffe made one last effort to help. Beginning on April 8, courageous pilots flew cargo gliders into the city, making extremely difficult pinpoint landings under enemy fire. There was no escape for the glider pilots, of course, and the supplies they brought were a mere drop in the bucket.

Then there was the constant enemy propaganda. During pauses in the fighting Soviet loudspeakers broadcast German melodies. Along with the music came requests for the garrison to surrender as the situation was hopeless. Then the enemy fire began again, heavier than ever. It was clear to the city commandant that the situation was becoming ever more hopeless. His requests for relief became more urgent, as a planned breakout now seemed impossible.

On April 6 and 7 the attackers were less active, and instead attempted to systematically smash the defenders' ability to resist through small patrol-size raids and the increased use of their heavy weapons. Major Soviet troop movements were observed, indicating that another major attack was in the offing. These suspicions were heightened on April 8 by the increasing number of air raids on the city and the growing intensity of the artillery barrage. The next day, following an hours-long bombardment, the troops of four Soviet divisions attacked the city from all sides. By now fire, shelling and demolitions had reduced the city to a pile of rubble. The Soviets managed to break into the city in several places in the east and south, but were repulsed in the north and west. The houses comprising the eastern defensive ring were shelled and most set afire. The weakened German units abandoned the burning houses and occupied a makeshift defensive line. In the south the defenders once again succeeded in sealing off the enemy penetrations and restored their battered line. The defenders had once again beaten off a numerically far superior attacker at great cost, and despite the most difficult conditions held on amid the burning rubble.

The Soviets continued their attack the following day. Once again enemy infantry were able to infiltrate the area. They systematically destroyed nests of resistance and houses converted into strongpoints – as well as the soldiers manning them – with direct fire from anti-tank guns and light artillery.

On April 10 *Generalmajor* von Neindorff sent repeated messages informing his superiors that, due to a shortage of forces and the decreasing effectiveness of his weapons, necessary measures against the attackers were no longer possible, and his soldiers were not in a position to hold out any longer. A further message reported the garrison's losses: from March 23 (the first day of the encirclement) until April 8 these totalled 16 officers and 1,471 NCOs and men killed or wounded and unable to fight.

The commandant also received a significant signal that day. It was an order from the Fourth Panzer Army, which wiped away the despondency and depression of the surrounded men in one blow, and caused a resurgence in hope of rescue and freedom. The message read (excerpt): Relief attack under the direction of XXXXVIII Panzer Corps will begin on March 11. Prepare to break out taking all weapons and equipment, destroy all equipment which will not be taken on a timely basis. Prepare wounded for evacuation. Group by ambulatory and non-ambulatory. Report numbers by radio. Form a strong battle group to act as rearguard during the breakout. Breakout to begin only on radioed orders from the panzer corps. Password: No soldier better than we!

The Second Relief Attack – Far Too Late

The senior commanders in the headquarters right up to the army group had also long since regarded the situation at Ternopol as extremely threatening, but until now had taken no action beyond issuing orders and exhortations to hold out. The only question now was how long the pocket could hold – at most another few days. Something had to be done. Nothing had been heard from the Führer Headquarters and Hitler, who had given the order for the "fortified place" to hold out, – they had other worries. Therefore the army group, having stabilized Fourth Panzer Army's front somewhat, finally decided to act. A new relief attack, this time right through to Ternopol, would have to be mounted to free the city's defenders. However, a breakout by the garrison and an attack toward the relief force, which would have been possible during the first relief attempt, was now out of the question. The enemy forces west of the city were too strong, and the garrison no longer possessed the necessary strength.

Many clarifying discussions had to take place between army group, army and corps, before it came to a relief attack at all. Proposals had to be evaluated, plans made, preparations initiated and the necessary troops moved into position. This time the attack was to be made from the southwest, and chosen once again to take part was *Panzerverband Friebe*[6], which had been engaged in heavy fighting in the Brody area. Also brought in to add weight to the attack force was the 9th SS-Panzer Division *Hohenstaufen*. Starting positions were to be in the area around Horodyszcze, but this area, as well as the crossings over the Wosuszka and Strypa had to be won first. Weather conditions permitting, all available units of VIII *Fliegerkorps* were to support the relief attack.

The Fourth Panzer Army's order of April 10 read (excerpt): Since April 10 the enemy has resumed his attacks on the "fortified place" of Ternopol with superior forces. The garrison has repulsed the enemy attacks in extremely heavy street fighting and awaits Day 1 of our relief attack.

To this end, at first light on Day 1, following a brief artillery bombardment, XXXXVIII Panzer Corps will move forward through our main line of resistance in the Horosdyczcze-Kozlov sector with 9th SS-Panzer Division *Hohenstaufen* and *Panzerverband* Friebe, force crossings of the Strypa and Wosuszka and drive through to Ternopol by the shortest route while providing adequate protection to the spearhead's flanks. The so-called "Day 1" has been fixed as April 11.

Everything may have been well planned, prepared and ordered, but all did not go as it was supposed to. There were ill omens right from the start. To begin with, the weather almost brought the entire operation to a halt. A deluge lasting several hours transformed the ground into a morass which made any movement extremely difficult. Even the tracked vehicles became hopelessly bogged down. In the north, Panzerverband Friebe set out near Kozlov in the early morning hours of April 11 in spite of extremely difficult terrain conditions and the fact that many of its half-tracks, heavy weapons and other vehicles were stuck in the mud. The advance soon bogged down in the face of heavy defensive fire, and following three unsuccessful attempts to force a crossing the unit had to be diverted south into the Horodyszcze area.

There the attack's other armored spearhead, the 9th SS-Panzer Division *Hohenstaufen*, had taken the village and sent two platoons of pioniers across the blown bridge. These established a bridgehead on the far side of the Wosuszka. Further south two battalions crossed the river near Mlynice in assault boats and captured a larger bridgehead. It was there that the engineers were to throw a bridge across the Wosuszka; however, the heavy bridging equipment could not be brought up due to difficulties with the terrain. It was decided that the small bridgehead near Horodyszcze would be expanded the next day and a bridge thrown across the river there. It turned out, however, that this bridgehead no longer existed, as the pioniers had been forced to withdraw.

A bridge had to be thrown across the river no matter what the cost. The entire relief attack depended on it; how else were the tanks and other vehicles supposed to get across the river? More valuable time was lost. Finally, the army pionier commander himself was able to find a location southwest of Horodyszcze where a bridge could be built into the Mlynice bridgehead. The engineers worked day and night digging away the banks, constructing the approaches and the building the 135-meter-long log road, but the bridge was not ready until the early morning of April 14.

In the meantime Hitler had become involved again and on April 12 ordered: The garrison of Ternopol is to be gotten out in spite of all difficulties. He personally had a message sent to the commandant: Hold on at any price, the order for your liberation has been given.

But it was too late – already far too late.

•

In Ternopol the final battle had begun. The Soviets, who now intended to take the entire city, attacked on April 11 with the same ferocity as before, achieving several penetrations into the German defensive positions. Although the outlook for a breakout to the west to meet the German panzer divisions which were expected to arrive soon was worsening, the garrison carried out all the necessary preparations as ordered with order and discipline. During the night of April 11/12 the Soviets launched another assault with massive artillery support, making further penetrations which the defenders were no longer able to drive back or seal off. After a terrible three-week struggle the garrison's strength was beginning to sink more and more. Under enemy fire day and night and continuously in combat, the men simply could do no more. *Generalmajor* von Neindorff still firmly believed that the relief attack was well under way, but his radio messages requesting help and information as to the progress of the attack were becoming ever more desperate.

These messages are typical:

> April 12, 2125: Situation extremely desperate, penetrations can no longer be cleared up, contact lost between units. Serious consequences to be expected from further enemy pressure. Relief imperative before it is too late.

> April 13, 0650: All sectors under heavy pressure through the entire night. New penetration northern wing. Hemmed in further in west, pressure from north toward the bridge.

> At 0905: Garrison under pounding in ruins since 0700. Enemy tanks and anti-tank guns in the streets, as well preparatory artillery and mortar fire.

> At 1255: Heavy barrages on entire defensive perimeter since 1000. Infantry attacks in the south. Critical situation urgently requires relief.

> At 1520: House-to-house fighting in the south and east. Ammunition running low. Where is relief?

By April 13 it was perfectly clear that the garrison was lost unless relief came soon. Every day counted.

A Soviet assault from the south succeeded in splitting the pocket into two parts, the remaining German-held areas of the city on the east bank and the suburb of Zagrobela on the west bank of the Seret. The only link between the two parts of the garrison was the dam over which the road led, and this was already under observer-directed enemy fire.

The relief attack finally got under way from the Mlynice pocket on April 14 following a considerable improvement in the weather – three days late. At 0600 the first panzers crossed the completed pioneer bridge to the other side of the Wosuszka. The infantry forces of the 9th SS-Panzer Division *Hohenstaufen* were assigned to provide flanking protection to the northeast as Battle Group Bittrich.[7] At noon, following a heavy preparatory artillery barrage, *Oberst* Friebe set out with all the available tanks (including those of *Hohenstaufen*) directly toward

Ternopol, at the same time deploying a screening force to the southeast. His force consisted of 71 tanks and 27 assault guns. In the afternoon the armored spearhead reached the Chodaczkow Wielki area, where it was halted by determined enemy resistance. The advance could not be resumed until the early morning of the 15th, after additional forces had arrived. It was no longer a question of days, but hours – the situation was approaching its dramatic climax.

Radio message from the commandant on April 14, 0800: Enemy attack imminent. Ammunition low. Where is relief? And at 1100: Relief, ammunition urgent. However, the order to break out, which *Generalmajor* von Neindorff expected hourly, did not come.

Even the exhortations of the commanders could not help the relief forces. XXXXVIII Panzer Corps: Attack day and night, situation in Ternopol permits no hesitation. Forward – no delay is acceptable. Fourth Panzer Army: Situation in Ternopol permits no rest. Onward at once. Every minute is vital!

Even the Commander-in-Chief of Army Group North Ukraine, *Feldmarschall* Model, appeared at the headquarters of XXXXVIII Panzer Corps, but he too was unable to change the situation.

Not until the evening of April 15 was Chodaczow Wielki taken. A planned night attack had to be postponed, because the Luftwaffe could not drop the necessary fuel and ammunition for the panzers until daybreak on the 16th. *Kampfgruppe* Friebe was unable to resume its advance until the morning of that day.

The relief force had covered about nine kilometers since setting out from Horodyszcze. It was another eleven kilometers to Ternopol – eleven kilometers which would not be covered, even with support from the Luftwaffe. Everywhere the Soviets defended bitterly and even launched powerful counterattacks.

Then something unexpected happened. Numbers of shabby, dirty men, scarcely recognizable as German soldiers, appeared before the leading tanks on the hills east of Chodaczow Wielki, beaming and overjoyed to have met up with the German armored forces. They were the first ten men from the Ternopol Pocket. The garrison had broken out and soon the rest would appear, thought the panzer crews. Thirty-three more members of the Ternopol garrison reached Chodaczow Wielki – then no more came.

The Last Radio Message from Ternopol: Commandant Fallen – Then Nothing More

In the end *Generalmajor* von Neindorff's greatest concern was that he might be completely cut off from the single avenue of retreat across the dam to the planned breakout area in Zagrobela. That was where he wanted to assemble the remaining elements of the garrison. Furthermore, further air drops of supplies were only possible in Zagrobela, as the area still being defended in Ternopol had become too small. During the night of March 13/14, therefore, the bulk of the defenders, still more than 1,300 men, moved across to Zagrobela. The wounded who could walk or hobble, or who were carried by their comrades, went too. The remaining heavy weapons were one tank, two assault guns, two self-propelled guns, one anti-tank gun and two light infantry guns. Smaller elements remained in the city on the east bank of the Seret. Their job was to hold off the Soviets until those who could not walk and the seriously wounded were evacuated across the river. The seriously wounded had to be carried on stretchers, as there were no vehicles available. Constant pressure from the Soviets forced the evacuation of the last German-held area of Ternopol on the night of March 14/15. Seven-hundred seriously wounded men had to be left behind.

At noon on March 15 came the last radio message from the Zagrobela pocket. It reported the death of the commandant. *Generalmajor* von Neindorff had fallen in close-quarters fighting.

A reconstruction of the final terrible events revealed the follows.

Following the death of *Generalmajor* von Neindorff, *Oberst* von Schönfeld assumed command of the remains of the garrison now squeezed into Zagrobela. There were about 1,500 men, but the situation in Zagrobela was hopeless from the beginning. It was a pocket about 1,000 meters in diameter in an area surrounding the open, village-like residential area. There was next to no cover available, and the area was under constant bombardment from Soviet heavy weapons and was subjected to waves of bombing and strafing attacks from the air. Since most of the houses there were made of clay or wood with no cellars, losses mounted extremely quickly. The wounded were placed in the few available cellars. For the worn-out, exhausted, battered German soldiers, with their bearded, smoke-blackened, emaciated faces, and their sad eyes, the situation in the coverless terrain was catastrophic. Rations, which had been relatively plentiful in Ternopol, now began to run short, as only the most vital things had been brought over from the city. Worst of all, there was scarcely any water. The single well was under enemy fire day and night until it was completely destroyed. The troops suffered from the shortage of drinking water, the wounded worst of all. All that could be done was to wet their lips with vodka; there was no way to get water for the new wounded. Moreover, ammunition was running out and the last radio had been put out of action.

The surrounded garrison of Ternopol fought with the courage of desperation right to the end. They tried to hold out in preparation for their rescue. Day by day, and finally hour by hour, they waited for the arrival of the German tanks – they did not come. At the end there was widespread hopelessness, despondency and bitterness. They could not remain in Zagrobela any longer, or they would be wiped out to the last man. Therefore, at 2200 on March 15 *Oberst* von Schönfeld called a meeting of all remaining officers and gave the order for a breakout no matter what the cost. The order was made known only to the officers, none of whom managed to reach the German lines. It is therefore not known how the breakout took place and exactly what transpired. Descriptions from the few men who did make their way back revealed the following:

The breakout by those members of the garrison still able to fight and all ambulatory wounded took place at about 0200 on March 16. Two groups were formed of about 700 men each, under the command of the officers. The two groups set off in different directions. Starting out together, both groups managed to pierce the inner encircling ring around Zagrobela relatively easily, apparently having taken the Russians by surprise. While one group now set off in a westerly direction, the other, under the command of *Oberst* von Neindorff, set out to the southwest. Still together, and with negligible casualties, the group made its way across the hills southwest of Zagrobela, past the village of Janovka and into the forest south of the village, where it came upon Soviet anti-tank gun and artillery positions. Some of the guns crews were killed or scattered, but then the group was attacked from the sides and rear and slowly pushed out of the forest into an open field to the west, where it was completely scattered. Losses were heavy and all the officers were killed, including the *Oberst*. The survivors formed small groups which continued to try and reach the German lines, suffering further losses. Most of these small groups were completely wiped out. Only forty-three men managed to get as far as the area north of Chodaczow, where they met up with the German armored spearhead.

Of the western group nothing is known except for one especially tragic incident. By the early morning of April 16 about fifty men had managed get to within shouting distance of the positions of the 357th Infantry Division north of Kozlov. They were unable to reach these positions, however, as the enemy was in control of the commanding high ground and poured heavy fire on any movement. Communicating by shouting, the men identified themselves as survivors from the Ternopol garrison, but they could scarcely raise their heads without drawing fire from the Russians. All attempts to rescue the men failed. That evening five members of the group managed to run to the safety of the positions of the 357th Infantry Division. The German infantry could only watch as the rest were driven into a house, which was then destroyed by artillery fire.

Two more soldiers turned up on April 18. They had fought their way through to Jezierna, six kilometers north of Kozlov. As well that day, five other men who had been captured by the Soviets and held in Zbaraz for three days were sent back with propaganda material. Of the 4,600 soldiers in the "fortified place" of Ternopol only fifty-five had returned – nothing more was heard of the remainder. In a sheer superhuman performance amid terrible suffering, the surrounded garrison had held out in Ternopol for three weeks on Hitler's orders – in vain.

Kampfgruppe Friebe resumed its advance toward Ternopol on April 17, but made no progress in the face of mounting Soviet counterattacks. Like Battle Group Bittrich, it was forced to go over to the defensive and fight for its own survival. Since it was unlikely that any further members of the Ternopol garrison would be able to reach the German lines, on April 18 the second relief attack was broken off and the forces involved returned to their starting positions. The Soviets immediately followed up, harassing the withdrawal. On their arrival both German units were immediately sent elsewhere.

In the period April 15-17 the two battle groups (Bittrich and Friebe) had inflicted heavy losses on the Soviets, destroying 74 tanks, 24 anti-tank guns and 84 artillery pieces. Their own losses had been 1,200 killed, wounded and missing and 18 tanks.

Even this sacrifice had not been enough to save the Ternopol garrison. The "fortified place" of Ternopol existed no more.

Excerpts from Wehrmacht Communiques:

April 17:
... Following heavy fighting near Ternopol our troops broke into enemy artillery positions from the west and picked up part of the courageously-fighting garrison, which had carried out a planned breakout toward the west ...

April 18:
... Near Ternopol further elements off the garrison fought their way through to the advancing units of the Army and Waffen-SS ...

Composition of the Garrison of the "Fortified Place" of Ternopol on March 23, 1944

Fortress Commandant with Staff (*Generalmajor* von Neindorff)
Two battalions of the 949th Grenadier Regiment (of the 359th Infantry Division)
Demba Fusilier Battalion
543rd Regional Defense Battalion
500th Proving Battalion
Mitscherling Battalion (3rd Battalion, 4th SS-Volunteer Regiment of the *Galizien* Division)
Kampfgruppe Grundmann (company strength)
The remnants of Third Battalion, 4th SS-Volunteer Regiment (*Galizien* in company strength)
Alert Company from elements of the 8th Panzer Division
Alert Company Vogel
4th Battalion, 359th Artillery Regiment with 3 batteries
A company of *Panzerjäger* with 6 guns
A battery of assault guns with 9 assault guns
Self-propelled artillery battery of the "LAH" with 6 guns
The remnants of 4th Battery, 384th Flak Battalion with 7 guns
Other smaller units.

Notes:
[1] Written by G. Fricke: *Fester Platz Tarnopol.*
[2] A fully-stocked supply dump was on hand.
[3] *Oberst* von Schönfeld, commander 949th Grenadier Regiment.
[4] Army Group A was designated Army Group South Ukraine.
[5] Only the Galicians of the 4th SS-Volunteer Regiment became disheartened and gave up.
[6] Commander of the 9th SS-Panzer Division *Hohenstaufen.*
[7] From this time on the Germans differentiated between "*Rückkämpfer*" (men who had made their own way back to the German lines) and "*Rückkehrer*" (men who were sent back by the Russians).

Crimea:
The Seventeenth Army

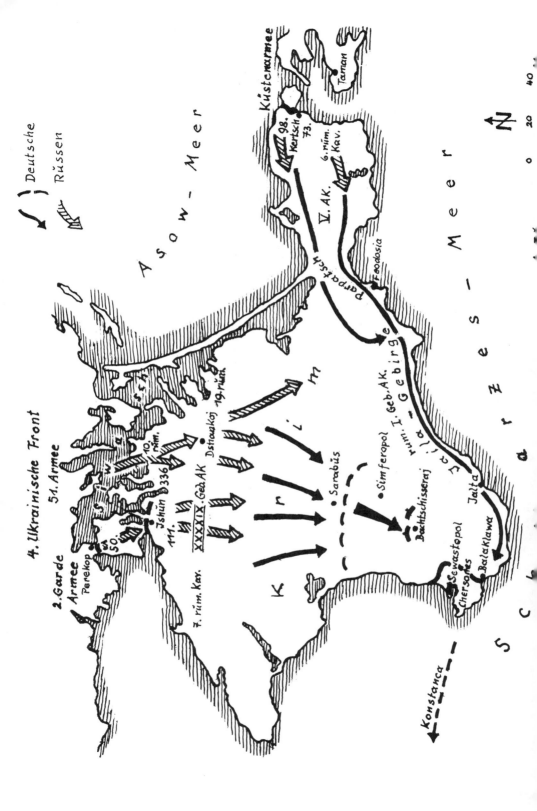

Deutsche
Rüssen

4. Ukrainische Front

2. Garde
Armee
51. Armee

Perekop

50.

111.

10. rüm.

Ishūn

336

Dstioukoj

XXXXIX. Geb. AK

7. rüm. Kav.

19. rüm.

W

Sch

Asow - Meer

K r i m

Sarabūs

Simferopol

Bachtschisseraj

Parpatsch

Feodosia

Küstenarmee

Kertsch

98.

73.

V. AK.

6. rüm. Kav.

Taman

rum. I. Geb. AK.

Ja i la - Gebirge

Jalta

Sewastopol
Chersones

Balaklawa

Konstanca

S c h w a r z e s - M e e r

N

0   20   40 k

Crimea: The Seventeenth Army

Tragedy on the Black Sea

The Crimea – virtually a large island, joined to the mainland in the north by the six- to eight-kilometer-wide Isthmus of Perekop and a rail line whose raised embankment crosses the Sivash. The Sivash, the "foul lake," is a shallow, island- and lagoon-rich body of water. To the south and west extends the Black Sea, and in the east the four- to fifteen-kilometer-wide Strait of Kerch separates the Sea of Azov from the Black Sea and at the same time the Crimea with its Kerch Peninsula from the opposite Taman Peninsula. The Crimea is largely flat, with wide, open plains. Only in the south do the plains rise to form the Jaila Mountains, part of which run along the southern coast. There were few rail lines and a couple of overland roads. In the southwest corner of the Crimea is the city, fortress and harbor of Sevastopol, with a small tongue of land, the Khersonyes Peninsula, with a number of bays, steep rock faces and narrow beach. It was here that the tragedy of the Seventeenth Army was to be played out.

Defense of the Crimea – Cut Off from the Entire Eastern Front

After months of heavy and costly fighting the Seventeenth Army was finally permitted to evacuate the Kuban bridgehead, and in an extremely well planned and executed operation crossed the Strait of Kerch from the Taman Peninsula. By October 9, 1943, the army had reached the Crimea with all of its soldiers, horses, heavy equipment and vehicles. If the troops had expected to be given time to rest and recover, they were soon disappointed. Eight divisions were immediately transported to the north, where they were thrown into further heavy fighting. The remaining German and Rumanian divisions stayed where they were for the time being. Hitler wanted to hold onto the Crimea for reasons of prestige. He was concerned about the negative political effects a loss of the peninsula would entail, especially where Turkey, Bulgaria and allied Rumania were concerned. However, political considerations and motivations only make sense when they correspond to a nation's military position and strength. Moreover, the argument that holding onto the Crimea would provide flanking protection for the southern end of the Eastern Front did not ring true, as this could have been better achieved by barricading the Perekop Peninsula. And the claim that was often repeated in such situations, that the Crimea would tie down significant enemy forces, was also invalid, because since 1943 the Red Army, with its great superiority in troops and materiel, had been in a position to launch offensives simultaneously in several sectors.

The Commander-in-Chief of the Seventeenth Army, *Generaloberst* Jaennecke, realized this and ordered plans drawn up and preparations made for a fast, staged evacuation of the Crimea along the Isthmus of Perekop toward the lower Dniepr River. It was his belief that holding on to the Crimea was of no military value whatsoever; on the other hand, his army could significantly strengthen the southern wing of the German eastern front.

For the reasons already outlined, however, Hitler refused to permit the Seventeenth Army to evacuate the Crimea over the Isthmus of Perekop. Then it was too late. On October 24, 1943, the Soviet Fourth Ukrainian Front under General Tolbukin broke through the front held by the German Sixth Army north of Melitopol. Soviet armored and mechanized units raced across the Noga Steppe toward the lower Dniepr. On October 30 the first Soviet tanks appeared at the northern end of the Isthmus of Perekop. The Seventeenth Army was cut off from the mainland and the southern wing of the German front, which finally stabilized beyond the lower course of the Dniepr, with bridgeheads near Kherson and Nikopol. On October 31 and November 1 Soviet armored forces advanced toward the Crimea from the north, making initial gains until they were halted by hastily-assembled German units. The Russians had crossed the Tartar Wall and advanced to the outskirts of Armyansk, and had begun to establish a large bridgehead on the islands and spits of land of the Sivash. Soviet pressure on the isthmus was maintained, but the German defences there firmed up after the arrival of the 50th Infantry Division. The 88mm batteries of the 9th Flak Division proved particularly effective, their accurate and devastating fire providing valuable support to the hard-pressed German infantry. An armored flak train also distinguished itself, destroying 24 enemy tanks in the early days of the battle for the Crimea.

While the army was mastering the situation on the northern front, a new crisis developed on the Kerch Peninsula. The Soviets had gone on the offensive there as well, sending forces across from the Taman Peninsula. Following successful landings in early November, they established a bridgehead near Kerch, which, try as they might, the Germans could not eliminate, leading to continued heavy fighting by the 98th Infantry Division holding the line there.

The Seventeenth Army was already cut off from the mainland and on its own, it was engaged in battle with enemy forces near Perekop and Kerch, and the army's commanders were convinced that an evacuation by sea was inevitable in the near future. In spite of this Hitler stuck to his decision: no matter what, the Crimea was to be defended with all means available. To back up his decision Hitler had two more German divisions[1] sent to the Crimea as reinforcements, though two divisions was completely inadequate.

The army carried out its orders and prepared to defend the peninsula. In the north was XXXXIX Mountain Army Corps, whose 50th Infantry Division was holding positions on the Isthmus of Perekop. Holding the areas opposite the Sivash and the Sea of Azov were the 336th Infantry Division and the Rumanian 10th and 19th Infantry Divisions. Far to the east on both sides of Kerch was V Army Corps, with the 98th Infantry Division, the recently arrived 73rd Infantry Division and the Rumanian 6th Cavalry Division. The Rumanian I Mountain Corps and two additional Rumanian cavalry divisions were holding the Russian partisan units in the Jaila Mountains in check, while guarding the lengthy coastline. Until it was sent into action in the Ishun Narrows in the north, the 111th Infantry Divisions, the other of the two divisions sent to the Crimea by Hitler, was the army reserve. This role was later assumed by the so-called *"Gebirgsjägerregiment Krim"* (Mountain Infantry Regiment Crimea).

This made a total of five weak German divisions and seven Rumanian divisions. Other than two assault gun brigades there were no mobile armored units. The defenders' heaviest firepower was provided by the proven heavy flak batteries of the 9th Flak Division, which performed in the dual role of anti-tank and anti-aircraft defence.

As well there were army and corps units, rear-echelon services, coastal batteries, naval units, Luftwaffe personnel, Russian volunteer troops and laborers, as well as a giant "Wehrmacht entourage" which had been assembled in the Crimea following its capture by the Wehrmacht in early summer 1942. The result was an imposing rations strength of 235,000 men[2], of which only a small percent were pure combat troops.

With the exception of Kerch, where bitter fighting continued around the enemy foothold, the winter months of 1943/44 passed relatively quietly. German naval and air superiority on and over the western Black Sea ensured a regular,

smooth and almost unhindered flow of supplies from the mainland to the Crimea.
The Seventeenth Army received all the supplies it needed. Nevertheless, the
Seventeenth Army and Army Group A continued to press for the evacuation of the
Crimea, which had long since ceased to be of any significance militarily. Discount-
ing the logical arguments of his Generals, Hitler insisted that the Crimea was to be
held, and confirmed this in Operations Order No. 7 of April 2, 1944.

The Russians knew that the Crimea, and if it stayed, the Seventeenth Army,
were theirs. They dropped leaflets urging the defenders to desert, mocking the
German position: The Crimea is our largest and most secure prisoner-of-war camp.
The Germans feed themselves, guard themselves and when they go on leave they
even return voluntarily. We are in no hurry to take the Crimea.

Then, however, the entire situation on the Eastern Front began to deteriorate.
From mid-March the Germans were forced to abandon their defenses on the Lower
Dniepr, and Soviet offensives along the entire southern front forced Army Group
A back beyond the Dnestr. On April 10, Odessa, the Seventeenth Army's most
important supply base and port, fell to the Russians. This meant that the army was
now totally isolated, 300 kilometers from the new German front, and that from now
on it would have to be supplied from the Rumanian port of Constanza, which meant
a much loner sea journey. There was till time, however, to evacuate the army by
sea with all of its men, horses and materiel. But Hitler stubbornly refused and
forbade any evacuation.

This was the prelude, and now the first act of the tragedy began. The Soviets
set out to "liquidate" the German army in the Crimea. General Tolbukin's Fourth
Ukrainian Front massed in the north, with the Second Guards Army (6 rifle
divisions) near Perekop and the Fifty-first Army (5 rifle divisions and 1 tank corps
with 500 tanks) in the Sivash. Near Kerch the Coastal Army under General
Yeremenko was ready to attack with 11 rifle divisions and 1 tank brigade with 100
tanks. Air support was to be provided by the Eighth and Fourth Air Armies with
a total strength of about 2,000 aircraft. In April Marshall Vasilevski's headquarters
took over coordination of the two fronts.

From mid-March the Soviet air force became more active, an indication that
the expected enemy offensive was not far off. The Soviet assault began on April
8, when vastly superior forces attacked the German northern front. At nine o'clock
in the morning, following an hour-long artillery barrage, the Second Guards Army
advanced against the German positions on the Isthmus of Perekop, supported by
aircraft of the Soviet Air Force. At first the 50th Infantry Division held fast, and,
with elements of the 111th Infantry Division, even launched counterattacks to
eliminate enemy penetrations. The 336th Division on the west side of the Sivash

also held firm. On April 10, however, the situation abruptly began to change. The 50th Division was unable to hold any longer and fell back toward the Ishun Narrows, which were occupied by the 111th Division, suffering heavy casualties in the process. In the Sivash area the Rumanian 10th Infantry Division, which had been hit by the full weight of the attacking Soviet 51st Army, fought with great determination throughout the 9th and 10th, launching several counterattacks which resulted in heavy casualties. On April 10, however, the Rumanian division's resistance suddenly collapsed. Unexpectedly – on account of the difficult nature of the terrain – Soviet rifle divisions and tank brigades emerged from the lakes and islands of the Sivash and drove into the deep flank of the German defences on the isthmus. Working by night over a period of months, employing German prisoners as laborers, the Russians had built raised roadways and foot bridges, the tops of which lay just below the surface of the water so as to remain undetected by German aerial reconnaissance. They used these, as well as barges and boats, to move their troops across the "foul lake." The German positions in the Ishun Narrows could no longer be held. With the German northern front smashed, the enemy had a free entrance to the Crimea. As there were no further forces or reserves available, and since the rear of XXXXIX Mountain Corps was also threatened, on April 10 the Seventeenth Army gave the order for a withdrawal toward Sevastopol. The German and Rumanian forces faced a difficult retreat over 160 kilometers of open terrain lacking significant natural obstacles. The result was a race with the pursuing Soviet tanks and motorized infantry.

A 240-Kilometer Withdrawal in Four Days

The hasty retreat by XXXXIX Mountain Corps began during the night of April 11/ 12. Early on the morning of April 12 Soviet forces occupied Ishun. Constantly on the move, mostly on foot, the long German and Rumanian columns strove southward, pursued relentlessly by the Soviets and all the while facing the threat of being overtaken and enveloped, especially on the left flank. Near the rail junction at Dhankoj the Mountain Infantry Regiment "Crimea," the army's last reserve, held out against numerically far superior forces until it was overwhelmed. Flak detachments, assault guns and the remaining elements of the Luftwaffe provided support and relief when the Soviets got too close or broke into the retiring units and generally delayed the pursuit. German fighters, Stukas and close-support aircraft flew 2,390 sorties. *General* Deichmann, commander of I *Fliegerkorps*, directed his units from the forward infantry positions. In one instance a *Gruppe* of

KG 27 carried out a low-level attack on Soviet armored units and put 50 tanks out of action. The flak detachments destroyed 58 enemy aircraft and 62 tanks.[3] All of this gave the withdrawing forces breathing room, but only temporarily.

Once again the German troops, and with them the Rumanian soldiers, were forced to march and fight simultaneously. Every officer and man knew what was at stake, hoping that if they could reach Sevastopol, ships would be waiting to take them off and that the Crimea was finally to be evacuated.

The retreat continued in a somewhat orderly fashion. It was a forced march for men and animals, with the Soviet tanks and mounted and motorized infantry close on their heels. There were no bivouacs or night quarters, just a few hours rest and then on the move again. The withdrawal covered 40 to 60 kilometers daily. Everything considered superfluous was thrown from the horse-drawn wagons to make room for the wounded and footsore. The motor vehicles were covered with clusters of soldiers, hanging on for dear life. Although there were prepared intermediate and blocking positions, they had not been manned by reserve forces and were therefore useless. As the columns raced onward, rearguards tried to brake the enemy's pursuit, fighting until they were outflanked or until the Soviets broke through. Some battle groups were temporarily surrounded, but managed to fight their way out and back to the main body. Across the flat, coverless plains echoed the hard roar of Russian tank cannon, the crack of 88mm anti-aircraft guns, the rumble of hastily positioned German batteries, the thud of Stuka bombs. Soviet close-support aircraft roared overhead. German assault guns drove to the most threatened positions and backed up the hard-pressed infantry. All of the resistance and countermeasures were unable to hold up the enemy for long, however, and on April 13 Soviet forces entered Simferopol, the capital of the Crimea and the former site of Seventeenth Army Headquarters. And who knows if XXXXIX Mountain Corps would have reached Sevastopol at all, if it had not been for the former commandant of the fortress, *Oberst* Beetz? He recognized the danger facing the approaching columns and established a blocking position in the Belbek Valley near Bakshissery with two battalions, six batteries and several assault guns. There Beetz inflicted a heavy defeat on a Soviet force advancing from Simferopol in an attempt to overtake the retreating German forces. The Soviets threw caution to the wind, advancing in a densely-packed column of tanks and vehicles. Suddenly, accurate fire began to smash into the column. Beetz won twelve precious hours, which allowed the mass of the German and Rumanian units to stream into the fortress and hurriedly prepare to defend its northern section. On the evening of April 14 the first enemy units appeared and tried to break into the fortress, but were repulsed.

XXXXIX Mountain Corps had just made it, although it had suffered heavy casualties. In only three days, fighting day and night under constant enemy pressure, it had covered 160 kilometers, bringing its heavy artillery with it.

The exhausted men breathed a sigh of relief, they had made it. They had reached Sevastopol, and here was the harbor from which they would sail across the Black Sea to freedom. Unbeknown to them, however, a new order from Hitler, issued on April 12 while the retreat was still under way, had arrived, striking the army command a crushing blow: although the Crimea had been lost, the fortress of Sevastopol was to be held indefinitely. That those in the Führer Headquarters imagined the battered units could do so was inconceivable.

First, however, the Seventeenth Army had another concern. XXXXIX Mountain Corps had arrived, but V Army Corps was still far to the east near Kerch. Until it arrived the eastern and southern zones of the fortress were guarded by units of the I Rumanian Mountain Corps.

The retreat by V Corps was to be far worse. On April 10 the corps received the code word "*Adler*, which meant it was to retreat to Sevastopol to link up with the remaining elements of the army. Like XXXXIX Mountain Corps, V Corps had to cover a tremendous distance in a few days – 240 kilometers – to reach the fortress before the Soviets, and it, too, had to travel mostly on foot. The start of the withdrawal by the fighting elements of the 73rd and 98th Infantry Divisions and the Rumanian 6th Cavalry Division was fixed for 1900 on April 10. That evening, however, the retreat began to develop into a fiasco. Again there was a foot race – and this time an especially dramatic one – between the foot and horse-drawn German units and the tanks and motorized units of the Soviet Coastal Army. The Soviets immediately gave pursuit and sacrificial actions by rearguard units were unable to halt them. On April 12 the retreating German and Rumanian forces reached the intermediate position at Parpatsch, having already suffered considerable losses. Nevertheless, the position was held until evening. As elements of the Soviet Fifty-first Army were now approaching from the north, the corps was forced to abandon its westward march and veer south to cross the Jaila Mountains along the coastal road. In order to speed up the withdrawal, about 10,000 men were picked up by small ships of the *Kriegsmarine* at Feodosia and other small coastal ports and delivered safely to Balaclava.

Between April 10 and 14 the lives and freedom of the stalwart former defenders of Kerch hung by a slender thread. The entire corps faced the possibility of death or capture. The withdrawal, which was ordered much too late, had deteriorated into a chaotic retreat. On April 17, between 1000 and 1100, the last elements of the corps, completely exhausted after their tremendous march, reached the fortress area south and east of Sevastopol. The corps had suffered destructive losses in men, horses, vehicles, weapons and equipment, including all of its heavy artillery.

The history of the 98th Infantry Division described the retreat:[4]

> "The division was still unaware of the disaster already brewing on the northern front. Irretrievable time was lost before the order came for the withdrawal from the Kerch Front. Not until April 10, Easter Monday, two days after the beginning at Perekop, did the division receive orders to begin its withdrawal at 1900.
>
> The first pulled back toward the west during the course of the afternoon: all the Rumanians, the flak units, the train units, the assault guns. The seriousness of the situation was evident at a briefing held at the division command post at noon. Not only had the enemy broken into the Crimea at Perekop, but across the Sivash as well, and was already advancing from Dshankoj toward Simferopol with many tanks. He was thus half again as close to Sevastopol as the defenders of the Kerch Front. Everything was now to become a race against a double enemy – the one from the north and the one which had broken out of his large bridgehead near Kerch – a race between tanks and men on foot. The withdrawal was to take place as follows: each regiment (if they could still be called such) was to release a battalion to the rearguard led by *Oberst* Schmidt. Those so designated were 1st Battalion, 282nd Grenadier Regiment under *Hauptmann* Fritz, 1st Battalion, 290th Grenadier Regiment under *Hauptmann* Mez and the 85th Replacement and Training Battalion under *Major* Krauss. They were to remain in the main line of resistance until 0300 and then withdraw.
>
> The regiments began to leave their positions at 1900 as planned. Regiments, battalions – how high were the combat strengths of these units? The 290th Grenadier Regiment, for example, numbered 200 fighting men. The 282nd Grenadier Regiment was in much the same shape, as was the battered Fusilier Battalion . . . Soon after 1900 the 13th and 14th Companies with their heavy weapons experienced the reality of the withdrawal. The companies had to haul their heavy anti-tank guns and infantry guns through the spring mud using the resources at hand. After hours of backbreaking, fruitless labor most of the guns had to be rendered unusable – on the first evening of the retreat! A short time after the withdrawal began the vehicles of the 198th Signals Battalion broke down and had to be blown up. On April 11 the 282nd Regiment occupied an intermediate position at the Tartar Wall. The enemy had recognized the withdrawal and began to follow up. At about 1500 heavy tanks with mounted infantry broke through the 73rd Division in the right sector and set about encircling the '282nd.' At the last minute, as if by some miracle, they escaped the tanks and managed to restore a semblance of

order. During the march to the Parpatsch position, which continued after dark, exhaustion proved the undoing of many. The 8th Company, which stopped to rest, was surrounded by tanks and scattered. The company commander and many others were killed by enemy fire and many went missing. *Gefreiter* Lemberger, one of the 'old warriors,' reported back alone the next morning, an *Offenrohr*[5] and one round of ammunition over his shoulder.

At first the '290th' seemed to get away from the position smoothly, but near Bagerovo elements ran into enemy tanks and were surrounded. All were taken prisoner. Also lost were the last two heavy anti-tank guns and the division's radio station.

Late in the morning of the first day of the withdrawal the commander of the 289th Regiment received a report that one of his battalions had been completely scattered by enemy air attacks, and that most of its men were dead or wounded. The enemy close-support aircraft, which had been in the air since first light, found a rich harvest among the former defenders of the Kerch Peninsula, who were virtually powerless against them. The few German fighters which did appear were unable to challenge the absolute Russian air superiority. It soon became obvious what had happened to the rearguard battalions. The enemy had not been fooled, and he had not failed to notice the nocturnal withdrawal. The numerous columns of smoke from burning quarters and camps, the large-scale demolitions and the explosions as rear-echelon Rumanian units blew up their ammunition had alerted the enemy the previous afternoon.

Enemy tanks from Kerch surrounded the 1st Battalion of the 282nd Regiment, which had stayed too long in the main line of resistance, and shot it to pieces. Few escaped. *Hauptmann* Fritz was severely wounded. He ordered the stretcher bearers to leave him and get themselves to safety. Fritz remained behind alone.

The 85th Training and Replacement battalion suffered the same fate. The few survivors, among them the battalion commander, were captured. The 198th Light Pionier Column met the same end. 1st Battalion, 290th Regiment also failed to get away. The battalion, which was to have occupied an intermediate position at the northern edge of the Bagerovo airfield at 0900, was attacked by Russian tanks and destroyed. Only a few men escaped.

By April 11 the entire rearguard regiment under *Oberst* Schmidt had ceased to exist. The *Oberst* had only a group of about 40 survivors with him.

Groups of 40 to 50 enemy tanks with numerous anti-tank guns and truck-mounted infantry were already rolling westward. Here and there the Russians still encountered determined resistance. On April 11 the

3rd Battalion of the Artillery Regiment was in position behind the Tartar Wall, ready to fire. The 105mm field howitzers destroyed several marauding enemy tanks with direct fire. The guns poured fire and destruction into the enemy formations until late afternoon, although there were losses among the guns and their crews as well. During an attempted change of position the limbers were destroyed by tank gunfire. The batteries used their last rounds to spike their guns. It was a bloody end after the battalion had sacrificed itself to prevent the certain destruction of the fighting elements of the 'division' and avert an enemy breakthrough. The remnants of the battalion, now a small 'battle group' under the battalion commander, *Major* Kern, were forced to withdraw that evening in the face of superior forces.

Like the A 1 intermediate position which had been planned by the army, a halt in the A 2 position was out of the question. Any baggage the troops still had with the had to be destroyed. All that was still allowed was 'flight baggage,' a rucksack.

By the evening of April 11 there was no longer a 289th Grenadier Regiment. A battle group assembled from survivors of the regiment, about equal to a battalion, was placed under the command of *Oberst* Schmidt. But before the unit could reach the Parpatsch position (A 3 position) – the narrowest part of the peninsula, which should have been defended from the beginning – disaster befell the battle group. Lacking any sort of defence against enemy armor, the unit was attacked by Russian tanks from in front and behind and was shot to pieces. The survivors were led off into captivity.

Exhausted and at the end of their strength, the survivors of the 290th Grenadier Regiment arrived in the Parpatsch position singly and in small groups. Here, together with elements of the 73rd Division, they were to defend against an enemy vastly superior on the ground and in the air. After three days of retreating and fighting the force was completely inadequate. The defenders of the Parpatsch position held off the pursuing enemy until 0600 on April 13. Twenty-five to thirty men of 1st Battalion, the 13th Company with one heavy infantry gun and three light infantry guns, and about thirty stragglers – this was now the strength of the 290th Grenadier Regiment.

Also in the Parpatsch position on the morning of April 12 was the 282nd Regiment. It consisted of a single battalion as well as the attached 'Battle Group' Kern and a battalion of conscripted rear echelon personnel, mostly from units not belonging to the division. By about noon, following heavy fighting, especially around Ssemissotka, all resistance by the rear echelon battalion collapsed. The entire battalion disintegrated and the survivors were taken prisoner. Russian motorized infantry drove into the gap, but direct fire from a battery of the 1st Battalion,

198th Artillery Regiment forced them to retire.

In the mean time more than 100 enemy tanks had assembled on the southern flank. In position there was the regiment's artillery, with the 1st, 2nd and 4th Heavy Battalions, whose fire had repeatedly forced the enemy back. Now, late in the afternoon, the main attack began. At 1700 heavy fire from a concentration of weapons began to fall on the regiment's positions. As the guns of 1st Battalion were already under enemy machine-gun fire, the battalion commander ordered the unit to spike its guns after expending its ammunition. The gun crews managed to escape in waiting trucks.

The 2nd Battalion was positioned around a quarry southeast of Ak-Monai. With its guns in the main line of resistance, the battalion knocked out 12 enemy tanks and smashed one infantry attack after another. Our infantry was numerically so weak that it was unable to provide adequate protection for the guns. The battalion watched as the strength of the exhausted defenders diminished. Obus Toge was lost. Late in the afternoon the batteries smashed a massed tank attack with infantry in front of their firing positions with direct fire. There was no longer any possibility of moving the guns to another position. The last rounds of ammunition were used to spike the guns. *Hauptmann* Gerhard and the remains of his battalion fell back, and were employed as infantry behind a blocking position in a valley.

Through the exemplary use of its light 105mm batteries, the 4th Heavy Battalion succeeded in getting its 150mm guns out of their firing positions with tractors as darkness was falling.

The remnants of three grenadier regiments began another night march, and in doing so escaped total destruction. From sun up to sun down April 12 had been a battle of life or death for the 98th Division, or rather what was left of it.

After these events and the experiences of the past days and nights since the beginning of the withdrawal, there was a growing feeling among the troops that they had been left in the lurch. They were not surprised by what the enemy threw at them, but the division was surprised by the lack of countermeasures against the enemy's superiority. No air force, no assault guns – nothing. But they listened to their orders. They made the tremendous foot marches and the gave of the last of their strength without a murmur. This attitude would later be broken down by desperation and bitterness when the supreme command broke its word and delivered the troops into the hands of the enemy.

It had become clear that the division was going to have to fight its way through the Jaila Mountains. Enemy armored forces were already in burning Simferopol and the division had only a few hours to reach the coastal road.

The division's medical services, themselves constantly on the move, performed outstanding feats in the indescribable confusion. Ambulances were frequently chased by strafing Soviet aircraft and the drivers were often barely able to save themselves and their cargoes of wounded. Many experienced low-level air attacks on the train station, watching helplessly as the waiting transport trains went up in flames.

Before dawn on April 13 *Oberst* Schmidt and a collection of surviving members of various units, in total about 120 men with 5 machine-guns, began to fall back toward Ssaly. With this small force he was to defend the northern entrance to the pass road through the Jaila Mountains. The remnants of the train units and other columns set out at about the same time. The last to leave were caught and captured by the Soviet armored spearhead, which appeared at about 0900.

A battle group led by *Oberst* Faulhaber, a battalion reinforced by stragglers from other units, stopped a further enemy advance in the hills due south of Zurich Valley. However, the unit was too weak to withstand the increasing pressure from the north and east for long. During the late morning this rearguard also withdrew from the Zurich Valley into the mountains, which seemed to offer the only hope of escape. Not a moment too soon! As the troops approached Ssaly, Soviet tanks which had advanced along the Stary-Crimea road and from the direction of Karabsubasar began to fire into the columns stalled at the entrance to the pass.

In Ssaly itself there was a terrible jumble of soldiers and vehicles of all kinds. Rumanians mixed with Germans and horse-drawn and motor vehicles became wedged together in a terrific traffic jam. Everyone was trying to get through the mountains to Sevastopol. It was a scene of defeat, but not of an orderly withdrawal.

The battle groups of *Oberst* Faulhaber and *Oberst* Schmidt were able to hold the enemy at arm's length from the pass entrance until 1130. This was the bitter end of the road for the 198th Artillery Regiment. It was impossible to evacuate the guns, which had been saved at such effort, by sea, and the six-horse teams could not negotiate the mountain road. With heavy hearts the gunners blew up the last 14 light and 6 heavy guns near Ssudak. The artillery vehicles were destroyed and the horses shot. The drivers watched with tears in their eyes. The men of the battalions were assembled in 'artillery companies' for use as infantry.

By evening the pressure from the advancing armored battalions of the Soviets was so great that the defensive battle in the barrier north of Ssaly had to be abandoned. In the meantime, all of the other surviving units were moving through the Jaila Mountains. By now the term 'battle group' had replaced the misleading designations 'battalion' and 'regiment.' Battle group could mean 10 men or 100.

The unending columns, mostly train units and surviving German and Rumanian units, streamed south in the direction of the fortress of Sevastopol. There was now no one who could restore order. The many small groups of infantry interspersed among the columns stopped, fought briefly and then hurried westward again. Late on the afternoon of April 13 the 'main body' of the 98th Division reached Ssudak and halted. The hours of waiting made the soldiers jumpy and uneasy. It became dark. Firing began. First it was only an anti-tank gun. Shell after shell landed in the village. It was the opening act of a partisan ambush of the columns as they prepared to move on. Hand grenades came flying down. Submachine-gun fire sprayed from windows and rooftops. There were muzzle flashes everywhere. Several trucks drove away, but became lost in the darkness and got stuck. The columns were close to panic. There was still a few of the 'old warriors' left, however, and they saved the situation by placing well-aimed bursts of fire on the muzzle flashes. Soon things had quieted down; the threat of panic had been averted. The columns resumed their march at about midnight. This dance was repeated several times before the sun rose again.

Once again *Oberst* Schmidt and 'Battle Group Mez,' which now consisted of about 40 men, guarded the flank of the retiring columns, establishing a screening position north of Uskut. The battle group remained there until 1100 the next morning, then followed as rearguard. The next afternoon, as he was establishing contact with the division command, *Oberst* Schmidt was wounded in an air attack.

The bright morning sun illuminated the depressing scene of long columns in flight. At the sides of the coastal road along which the army columns were moving lay burning vehicles and dead and dying horses. Soldiers stood to the sides, lightening their packs. Broken down vehicles were pushed down the slope to the sea. The march continued to Aluschka unhindered by the enemy. There the fleeing troops received an unexpected gift – a few hours of rest. There were still depressing signs of their plight, however: the horses, which could no longer be taken along, were led into a field and shot. Once again the drivers, their friends and providers, stood with tears in their eyes. It was a sad blow for those who had worked so hard to save their faithful animals, but there had not been many left to lose; virtually the division's entire complement of horses and vehicles had already been destroyed. By scraping together the remnants of diverse units, the 290th 'Grenadier Regiment' under *Major* Mez had grown to 250 men and 3 machine-guns, but no heavy weapons. Strong security forces were deployed to the north, and the columns spent the night of April 14/15 in Aluschka. For the soldiers it was the first proper night's sleep since the beginning of the retreat.

After entering Yalta the division's columns rested. There was ample food in the abandoned depots of an evacuated base. A few hours later the columns resumed their march toward Alupka. Partisan ambushes from the hills bordering the road resulted in halts and brief firefights, but at least the dreaded fighter-bombers were absent.

By now the rearguard, which was accompanied by the division commander in a radio vehicle, had discarded everything not absolutely necessary. All that remained in the trucks was ammunition. Everyone was armed to the teeth. If a truck developed mechanical trouble it was pushed over the cliffs into the sea. At a place where the forest extended close to the road the columns again came under fire. A few minutes later, after an immediate counterattack, the enemy disappeared. There were six new wounded in the trucks as they drove past great houses and palm trees. Behind them glittered the sea . . ."

Despite extreme pressure from the enemy, heavy fighting and terrible casualties, the withdrawals by the two army corps toward Sevastopol had succeeded at the last moment. German losses were 13,131 men killed, wounded or missing; the Rumanians lost 17,652 men.

The 73rd Infantry Division had lost 79% of its authorized strength. Only a handful of stragglers returned from the Rumanian 19th Infantry Division, which had been at the Sivash. The artillery lost 70% of its guns; three-quarters of the anti-tank guns had been lost.

This was the first act of the tragedy.

Sevastopol is No Longer a Fortress

An orderly evacuation from Sevastopol of the remains of the Seventeenth Army would still have been possible had it not been for Hitler's order to hold and defend the fortress. At least he had no objection to the evacuation of the quite superfluous "Wehrmacht entourage," which included members of the military and civilian administrations, the labor service, specialists, members of the Todt Organization, field railway engineers, the army postal service, women auxiliaries, Red Cross personnel, civilian officials and so on. Also to be evacuated were the now useless headquarters and rear-echelon services, so-called Eastern Legionnaires, whose reliability was doubtful, Russian POWs, Rumanian units and, of course, the wounded. More than 100,000 people were evacuated to the Rumanian mainland. Most were sent back in supply ships, which were empty on their return journey to Rumania anyway, but some went by air. Everyone belonging to a combat unit was forced to remain, however.

The sea convoys were still running relatively unhindered. Soviet aircraft made only sporadic attacks and were held in check by the Luftwaffe.

Sevastopol at that time was the scene of tremendous confusion. Commanders assembled their troops, headquarters tried to establish contact with their units, new units were created out of thin air, supplies and munitions were organized, sectors assigned and command posts set up. A steady flow of stragglers, men who had escaped the Russians, was arriving from all over the Crimea, in ones and twos, on foot or in overcrowded vehicles. Parking areas were filled with large numbers of useless and abandoned vehicles of every kind. An especially sad fate awaited the many horses.

The army command had succeeded in assembling the wreckage of both corps within the fortress area, reorganized all of the available troops and men from the train units, navy and air force and organized a stronger, united defense. The main line of resistance extended in a semi-circle around Sevastopol from south to north with a radius of 20 kilometers in the south and 10 kilometers in the north. Behind it was the city, the harbor and then – the sea.

Deployed on the northern front was XXXXIX Mountain Corps with the 50th and 336th Divisions, while on the eastern front (facing south) was V Corps with the 98th, 111th and 73rd Divisions, as well as newly-formed combat units from Rumanian divisions and other scratch battalions. As before, the heaviest firepower was provided by the 9th Flak Division, which had brought back more than 300 light and heavy guns. As the Rumanian units had little fighting value left they were evacuated, with the exception of the 1st Mountain Division and three battalions of the 2nd and 3rd Mountain Divisions. On Hitler's orders no more units were permitted to leave the Crimea. The order from the army command on April 16 read: There will not be one step back in the defense of the fortress of Sevastopol!

Viewed in the short term, this order was justifiable in permitting an orderly evacuation of the many personnel still on the peninsula. The fighting troops saw this, and even though conditions were extremely difficult they retained the necessary fighting spirit. Even after the deep disappointment caused by Hitler's renewed order to hold out, the soldiers still trusted their Commander-in-Chief, the man who had brought them out of the Kuban Bridgehead in an orderly manner. They were prepared to fight on until the order finally came to evacuate the Crimea and the ships arrived to take them away. Keeping the harbor and coast free for this purpose depended on their steadfastness.

Sevastopol was not the fortress it had been in early 1942, when it took German forces weeks of the heaviest fighting to capture it. The mighty fortress works had been shot up and blown apart, German-installed naval guns and coastal batteries faced seaward, the existing bunkers, forts and casemates had not been repaired and were serving as bullet-proof accommodations for headquarters, hospitals, assembly areas and so on. The field positions in the main line of resistance had been beefed up, with barbed wire in front, but there was no in-depth system of defenses with strongpoints or a second and third line. Because of the hard limestone the trenches could not be dug deep enough. The only well-built rear position was on the small Khersonyes Peninsula.

The poor state of the fortress was not the only disadvantage facing the defenders. During the retreat the Luftwaffe had lost all its airfields in the Crimea and was left with only two fields near Sevastopol and on the Khersonyes Peninsula, which would soon be under Soviet artillery fire.

Then, of course, there was the enemy, who knew the terrain and the fortress installations very well, and who was assembling his numerically-superior forces for the final battle. The Fourth Ukrainian Front now numbered 24 rifle divisions, 1 tank corps, 1 artillery division, 2 anti-aircraft divisions and other combat units. The Coastal Army had likewise been reinforced.

One of the defense orders was especially painful for the troops but was unavoidable. It was obvious that when the evacuation came they would be unable to take the vehicles and horses with them. The vehicles had already been assembled in preparation for destruction. The order of April 21 instructed that all horses were to be shot and thrown into the sea, as there was a shortage of fodder, but also to prevent them falling into the hands of the enemy. They stood patiently in long lines until their turn came, the four-legged comrades of the long war years. When the German drivers, handlers and blacksmiths hesitated, Russian volunteers took over the bloody job. The Rumanians were not satisfied with single shots, they drove the animals to the edge of the cliffs and sprayed them with machine-gun fire. Thousands of horse cadavers choked the waters around Sevastopol and Khersonyes – 26,000 in all. Thousands more were set free out of pity. These grazed freely in the valleys near the front until most of them met a painful end under heavy fire when the final battle began.

The second act of the tragedy was about to begin.

•

The Soviets gave the defenders no more time to fortify their positions and prepare for the defence of the fortress. The german forces had scarcely reached the fortress when the first battles with the hotly-pursuing Soviet advance battalions took place. The following days saw the fighting intensify along the entire forty-kilometer front.

Initially the Soviet efforts were limited to strong scouting raids and probing attacks supported by tanks, especially against the northern front and the 336th Division. On April 17 enemy air activity increased, and on the 18th Soviet artillery began firing into the city.

As of April 18 there were still 124,000 men in and around Sevastopol. The evacuation of non-combat units was continuing. Then Hitler intervened once more.

Instead of an order for the final evacuation of the entire army, which was becoming more imperative day by day, Hitler once again issued strict orders that the "fortress" of Sevastopol was to be held. Hitler even went so far as to send reinforcements, in total two replacement battalions with 1,300 men[6] – a number which was laughably inadequate. These unfortunate troops found themselves thrown into the midst of the impending defeat.

The initial difficult and costly positional fighting saw all enemy attacks repulsed; the northern front held firm. On April 27 the Soviets felt strong enough to launch their first major attack. Supported by large numbers of tanks and close-support aircraft, they struck in the southeast, attacking toward the Sapun Heights. The attack collapsed with heavy casualties. The Soviets had not yet completed their artillery buildup, however. Mercifully, the troops had not learned of Hitler's obstinate, completely incomprehensible order. However, it was clear to the Commander-in-Chief of the Seventeenth Army that Sevastopol could not be held much longer, and that a total evacuation was imperative if the army was not to be lost. The enemy was building up his forces rapidly, the situation was becoming ever more acute and it was only a question of time until the German front was overrun, which would mean the end. *Generaloberst* Jaennecke therefore decided on an unusual step. On April 28 he flew to Führer Headquarters to convince Hitler to authorize an immediate and total evacuation. In spite of his forcible presentation Hitler remained unmoved. Finally, his rage became so great that he relieved Jaennecke as Commander-in-Chief of the army and forbade him from returning to Sevastopol. *General* Allmendinger assumed command of the army.

By May 4 the Soviets had completed their great buildup for the decisive attack. They now had 470,000 men, about 600 tanks, more than 6,000 mortars, guns and "Stalin Organs" and a massive force of bombers and close-support aircraft. Facing this array on the German side was a total of 64,000 men in largely makeshift units comprising troops from every branch of the armed services. In early May the total available reserves were three battalions.

The men in the fortress still believed that everything would turn out well. But the Russians were already working their way toward the main German positions in nightly battles on the approaches to the fortress.

By May 5 the Soviets were ready.

•

A tremendous, several-hour bombardment from 300 heavy guns, 400 multiple rocket launchers and numerous heavy mortars opened the battle. At 0930 the rifle divisions of the Soviet Second Guards Army and the Fifty-first Army, supported by bombers and close support aircraft, attacked XXXXIX Mountain Corps in the north. The corps was now under the command of the one-armed, one-legged *General* Hartmann. A cloud of smoke and dust hung over the entire front. The main force of the assault by four Soviet divisions struck the 336th Infantry Division, which held fast. The 50th Division also helped prevent a Soviet breakthrough. Counterattacks sealed off or eliminated enemy penetrations. Although the Soviets made repeated charges against the German lines, all of their tank-supported attacks were repelled during three days of heavy fighting, with heavy casualties to both sides. However, as a result of the overall situation both German divisions were forced to fall back beginning on May 7.

Following their standard practice of staggered attacks, which kept the Germans in the dark as to their real intentions and caused them to commit their reserves prematurely, the Soviets did not launch their offensive against the eastern and southern fronts until the morning of May 7. Here they had packed 200 guns into each kilometer of front. This tremendous assembly of artillery opened the assault with a terrific bombardment. Then the infantry of the Coastal Army, accompanied by tanks and masses of close-support aircraft, operating in groups of up to 50 machines with fighter escort, stormed the positions of V Corps. In the south the attackers smashed a wide breach in the front held by the 50th Division and achieved major penetrations against the 111th Division. On May 8 the Sapun Heights were lost; located south of the city, they offered a commanding view of Sevastopol, the coast and the sea. By evening the two divisions had lost about 5,000 men. The army was forced to order the recapture of the commanding heights in order to prevent a collapse of the entire defense. Units withdrawn from the northern front, which from the 7th had been forced to pull back toward the city and the south bank of Severnaya Bay, threw back the enemy spearheads and firmed up the front held by the hard-pressed V Corps.

The hills and valleys around Sevastopol rang with the crash of bursting shells, the thunder of bombs, the rattle of machine-guns, the roar of gunfire and the thud of exploding hand grenades. The scene was typical of a major enemy offensive: the air was filled with smoke, dust and the flashes of impacting shells. Dirt-encrusted German infantrymen crouched in their battered positions as the earth-brown waves rushed toward them with their piercing shouts of "Urray!" Crying, moaning wounded staggered toward the rear and crawled or were dragged under some sort of cover. Messengers dashed across the shell-torn terrain. Command posts lay under falling bombs and artillery fire as a steady flow of bad news came in. Officers led counterattacks with a handful of men. Commanders scraped together the last reserves. In the headquarters the field phones rang steadily, radio messages poured in and messengers arrived from every quarter. The headquarters tried to direct, lead, help and support the fighting troops, but there was little they could do. The battle raged on into the night. The darkness was illuminated by Russian parachute flares and bombs whistled and howled before bursting.

The Maxim Gorki I fort was the site of one of the field hospitals in the Sevastopol area. Beneath its thick ceilings and behind its mighty walls long lines of wounded lay in the gloomy passages. Moaning – groaning – whimpering – requests for help. Doctors and first aid teams did everything in their power until they were ready to drop. The flow of wounded was continuous, with the injured men supporting each other or being dragged or carried in. A trench had been dug in the nearby steep slope so that the severely wounded could be taken down to the wharves for evacuation by ship. Others were evacuated by air. The crews of the Ju 52s performed magnificently. Arriving during the hours of darkness, they came in through Soviet searchlights, flak and fighters to land on the dark runway, which was marked for a brief period by illuminated flashlights. Many of the transports crashed while attempting to land or went up in flames before they could take off again. The ambulance drivers, who braved enemy fire to take the wounded to the unit dressing stations by day and then transported them to the airfield at night, witnessed some gruesome scenes. On several occasions transports were hit by Soviet bombs and set on fire, and the drivers were forced to look on helplessly as they listened to the screams of the wounded on board above the crackle of the fire.

Where are the Evacuation Orders and the Rescue Ships?

Still the defenders of Sevastopol continued to hold out. The commanders of the army, the corps headquarters, commanders of divisions and other units and every man was waiting for the order to clear out, for the evacuation and an escape from this inferno, for salvation.

And finally, finally – at 2300 on May 8, 1944, in distant Berchtesgaden, Hitler gave his consent for the final evacuation of Sevastopol and the embarkation of the rest of the Seventeenth Army. Once again the order came too late, much too late! By the early morning hours of May 9 the evacuation order was in the hands of the Army Commander in Chief. *General* Allmendinger immediately ordered a withdrawal to the final position, the Khersonyes position. The remains of five German divisions, as well as Rumanian units and thousands of stragglers, began a fighting withdrawal toward the small Khersonyes Peninsula. In some places, however, the fighting withdrawal was more like a flight. The troops in the north pulled back through the battered, rubble-filled fortress of Sevastopol, fighting their way through enemy forces which had landed on the shore of the bay west of the city. The last rearguards from the 50th Division began to fall back at about 1600 and moved in good order into the new defensive position. That evening *Oberst* Beetz, who had become division commander following the wounding of *General* Sixt, was killed. It had been Beetz who had provided such effective support to XXXXIX Mountain Corps near Sevastopol on April 16. In the east Soviet loudspeakers scoffed: "Yes, yes, you are already encircled, the best thing you can do is give up and become a prisoner!" *Oberst* Faulhaber of the 282nd Grenadier Regiment (98th Division) and two squads covered the withdrawal of the remaining elements of his regiment. He was wounded twice by machine-gun bullets and lost a leg. As so often before, the flak proved its worth, covering the withdrawal with the last of its guns and shooting up pursuing tanks and infantry. Frequent air attacks resulted in fresh casualties, and the dead and wounded were left where they fell.

The enemy pursued sharply in an attempt to break through and roll up the Khersonyes Peninsula before it was occupied by the Germans, but failed. The worst part of this hurried, and in some places panicky, withdrawal, was that the Luftwaffe, which had so far provided such effective help and support, was forced to leave Sevastopol. The last usable airfield on the Khersonyes Peninsula now lay under directed enemy artillery fire. Battered by bombs and shells, landings and takeoffs were no longer possible. Soviet air superiority was now absolute. From then on the fearless Ju 52 pilots were forced to make night landings on two hastily-converted sections of paved road, which had intentionally remained unused until now – so as not to betray their positions to the enemy – and continued to fly out the wounded.

Here is a brief summary of the Luftwaffe's accomplishments: in the period April 8-22 its bomber, close-support and fighter units flew a total of 3,796 sorties, shooting down 226 enemy aircraft and destroying another 23 on the ground as well as destroying 186 tanks and 633 vehicles. German losses were 31 machines.

On April 25 Luftwaffe strength on the peninsula was 46 machines. In the period May 4-14 a further 253 enemy aircraft were shot down against the loss of 5 German machines. A further 23 aircraft, which could not be recovered due to damage, were blown up when the airfields were evacuated.

From April 8 the Luftwaffe's transport units flew 21,457 soldiers out of the Crimea, 16,387 of them wounded.

From April 16 to May 12 the 9th Flak Division shot down a total of 207 Soviet aircraft and destroyed 127 tanks in surface actions, including 72 in the period May 8-12.

These figures show that the Luftwaffe had made great efforts, but what were these successes against the hundreds of Russian tanks and aircraft.

For the army command everything depended on two things: that the Khersonyes position, as the last defensive barrier hold out until the bulk of the remaining soldiers – just over 50,000 on May 8 – had embarked, and that the ships necessary for the evacuation arrive in time. The badly battered German units found themselves manning a front barely 10 kilometers wide, which extended across the completely flat, naked plateau of the Khersonyes Peninsula. In the short term, however, the position still offered advantages: it was relatively well-fortified, there were even adequate stocks of food and ammunition. The northern part was occupied by the remaining units of XXXXIX Mountain Corps, the southern part by V Corps. The Soviets immediately made a major effort to break through this last German defensive front, but their attacks on May 9 and 10 were beaten off everywhere. The troops knew that this was the final battle, and that they only had to hold on for another day or a few more hours, until the ships came for them.

The following description of the final phase of the Battle of Sevastopol is taken from a report by the Chief-of-Staff of the Seventeenth Army, *Generalmajor* Ritter von Xylander:[7]

"On May 5, at 0930, the enemy began his attack, which we were expecting as we had observed his preparations, committing an unheard-of mass of materiel which eclipsed anything experienced before. The Russians were confident that their forces were sufficient. I do not need to repeat what the army looked like at that time, but I might be allowed to mention that, in the end, all that the army received from the promised large-scale reinforcement program was two replacement battalions, as well as 15 heavy anti-tank guns, 10 howitzers, 4 heavy field howitzers, and several infantry guns and mortars, which all in all was not enough to cover a fraction of the ongoing losses.

The focus of the enemy attack was in the north against the B-Stellenburg sector – Belbeck Valley. The sector was bombarded for 48 hours by 400 guns and an equal number of multiple rocket launchers and mortars. This was followed by a charge by the entire Second Guards Army. We had only just regrouped and had handed over this entire sector to *Generalmajor* Hagemann (336th Infantry Division), who performed magnificently in holding against this attack.

There were battles of insane bitterness, deep penetrations and crises, and finally the entire B-Stellenberg position was lost. Losses among our troops climbed alarmingly and we finally withdrew all German units in the sector of the XXXXIX Mountain Corps from the front, replacing them at great risk with Rumanian and alert units, so as to have some reserves in hand. We took no reserves from V Corps, as it was obvious that the enemy would attack there as well. Instead we took them from the 98th Division's sector. The northern front was still holding on the morning of May 7, although weakened and with only two companies in reserve. As well as to Hagemann, this was due to *General* Konrad (XXXXIX Mountain Corps), who was forced to hand over his corps to *General* Hartmann that day. He received no recognition before he was sent into the wilderness. On the morning of May 7 the enemy attacked V Corps from the coast to the Sapun Heights. The Russians committed an even greater mass of materiel, and their air force was so active that our fighters were able to shoot down 90 enemy aircraft that day and the flak another 33. The defenders were simply killed in their positions, until at about noon the entire front was ripped open except for the 186th Infantry Regiment under Oak Leaves wearer *Major* Ziegler, which continued to hold in front of the windmill hill. Soon, however, the regiment was outflanked to the north. The remaining reserves (a total of 5 battalions, a figure which we were proud of in our situation) were quickly used up.

The situation in the late afternoon: On the coast Battery Hill lost and recovered, Karan taken from the enemy, then a gap to windmill hill-saddle road, where the 186th Grenadier Regiment was holding, groups of enemy tanks advancing through the gap, small battle groups from the remains of the 111th Division on the Sapun Heights. Enemy break-through along the 'serpentines' of the Yalta road as far as the road fork near Dumskij. In the rear not one company in reserve. A situation had arisen where the relative strengths of the opposing forces caused us to expect the worst. The army had to decide between standing idly by and watching the enemy breakthrough toward Sevastopol, which would undoubtedly take place the next day, or withdrawing the northern front to form new reserves. The first option would have meant the end of the rest of the army in one or two days, so *General* Allmendinger's[8] only choice was 'Wildcat' (codeword for the prepared evacuation of the northern sector). Since the order could not be issued until early evening, the withdrawal took place in two stages, the first night seeing a move back to the so-called harbor protection position. As usual with a well-planned operation, the withdrawal went smoothly. By morning two battle groups had been formed from the forces released by the withdrawal: one near Dumskij under *Oberst* Faulhaber (98th Division) with 4 battalions, and one near Nikolajevka Hill under *Oberstleutnant* Marienfeld (111th Division) with 2 battalions. Each battle group included several assault guns.

The enemy resumed his attack on the morning of May 8 following intensive artillery and air preparation. In the south the 73rd Division was forced back, but the front did not crack. Killed in the fighting were a regimental commander and the commander of the pionier battalion, as well as many other members of the division. The enemy broke through across the Sapun Heights, took Nikolajevka, the vineyards there and the 'English Cemetery.' Battle Groups Marienfeld and Faulhaber launched a counterattack. In the afternoon the former established contact with the 186th Grenadier Regiment at the saddle road, while the latter got to within 800 meters of the 'Serpentine.' In the meantime, the Soviets were thrown out of the wine estate through the efforts of *General* Hagemann. The 'English Cemetery' was the scene of heavy fighting, but it remained in enemy hands, as did part of the Nikolajevka position.

We still had no permission to evacuate and no ships. The army therefore decided to continue to hold on and, as a necessary precondition, to order the recapture of the Sapun Heights (from which the enemy had an excellent view of the entire peninsula). We had to bet everything on this card and were aware that if it failed all that would be left would be to withdraw the remains of the army to the last Khersonyes position. Elements of the 50th and 336th Divisions which arrived on the south shore of Severnaya Bay in the coming night were sent in the direction of the Sapun Heights.

At 0215 on May 9 the following order reached the army: 'The Führer has authorized the evacuation of the Crimea.' In carrying out this order the army decided to defend the windmill hill in the south, as well as the Nikolajevka position, and to win back the parts of the position already held by the enemy. In doing so the enemy was to be prevented from getting close to the embarkation points. The battle now was to win time, because as a result of the order not to evacuate German combat troops from the Crimea, on May 5 there were almost 70,000 soldiers in Sevastopol and evacuation by ship was expected to be slow at first.

A serious crisis developed on May 9. The 73rd Division was driven back and resistance collapsed in the southern sector. In the north, energetic commanders led all available forces in an attack on the Nikolajevka position, in particular *Oberst* Beetz (formerly fortress commandant, now commander of the 50th Division), who managed to reach the heavily-defended farms of Nikolajevka, and, further to the east, General Hagemann. The exhausted troops were unable to advance any further, however. From the east, enemy forces broke through the 98th Division, which had left a weak force to occupy the Inkerman position. In the afternoon the decision had to be made to withdraw toward the last Khersonyes position. Numerous groups of infantry, as well as batteries and flak artillery resisted to the end. The remains of the northern divisions (50th and 336th) had to fight their way through the enemy, elements of which had crossed Severnaya Bay. Losses were considerable; *General* Hagemann was wounded seriously and three regimental commanders were killed.

The city and harbor of Sevastopol were evacuated.

•

Meanwhile, in the Khersonyes position we had deployed XXXXIX Mountain Corps as ordered and were able to use the still relatively intact battalions of the Rumanian 1st Mountain Division as a security force, while V Corps withdrew its troops still fighting to the east. Those who came back were few and badly scattered; they were met outside the position and were assembled into battle groups as they arrived. The enemy followed up sharply and tried to break into the position that night. By employing all command personnel and officers we created a make-shift garrison and held the position. The Russians quickly moved in their artillery and were soon making full use of their superiority in materiel. We had brought 120 pieces of artillery and anti-aircraft guns back into the position. Enemy artillery and aircraft pounded the last airfield on the Khersonyes Peninsula. With the runway pitted by over 100 heavy bomb craters, the last 13 fighters took off for the Rumanian mainland just before darkness fell on May 9.[9]

With the arrival of the first naval landing craft it became possible to embark some of the unnecessary personnel, including the operations sections of the Seventeenth Army, of V Corps and the last Rumanian headquarters. The Commander-in-Chief and I remained with XXXXIX Mountain Corps, which was now in command, intending to leave with the last units to embark.

May 10 saw a series of enemy attacks repelled. Assembled in small battle groups, the men continued to fight well. Casualties in the open, rocky terrain grew atrociously, especially in the vicinity of the embarkation points, where the units preparing to board the ships and the wounded had been assembled.

Oberst Beetz, commander of the 50th Division, was killed in the position. XXXXIX Mountain Corps' artillery commander, *General* von

Gallwitz, was badly wounded and died the next day. Announcements by the navy indicated that sufficient ships would be available to embark the last remaining units during the night of May 11/12. Command of the ships on one hand, and of the troops at the assembly points on the other, was confused and complicated by conflicting orders. Despite the loss of much of the communications system, orders reached the troops everywhere during the night of May 11. At 2000 the enemy began to lay down destructive fire on the rear areas, especially on the piers. Some time later the fire was shifted onto the defensive positions and soon after the enemy attacked on a broad front. Once again the enemy attacks were beaten off everywhere, and on Battery Hill, where a penetration was made, the enemy was driven out again.

The heavy fire and enemy attacks continued throughout May 11. Our troops continued to hold fast. Ammunition was running dangerously low. The enemy had exhausted himself, however, and at 2300 the troops made a general withdrawal, followed at 2400 by the rearguards.

Covering positions were occupied around the embarkation points, in which the last companies held on under ceaseless Russian fire . . ."

Drama on the High Sea

The penultimate act of the tragedy began.
What all the officers and men on the small Khersonyes Peninsula did not know was the following:

When Hitler finally authorized the evacuation, the German Navy, supported by Rumanian military and commercial shipping, began a major, planned evacuation operation. *Großadmiral* Dönitz himself had intervened and issued the appropriate instructions. More than 190 German and Rumanian ships left at intervals in a number of convoys, the first sailing immediately. The 400-kilometer voyage from the main harbor of Constanza across the Black sea to the Crimea took one to two nights and one day.

The evacuation began well. About 15,000 personnel were picked up during the night of May 9/10, but after that things did not go so smoothly. In the early morning hours of May 10, at about 0200, the large transports *Totila* (2,773 BRT) and *Teja* (3,600 BRT) arrived in the waters off Khersonyes and halted two nautical miles offshore to avoid enemy artillery fire. As the ships refused to come any closer, embarkation was delayed from the beginning. As well, a storm at sea that day accompanied by high waves damaged a considerable number of the following ships. In spite of these difficulties the first units, which had already assembled at the piers carrying only their small arms, were delivered to the ships lying offshore by Siebel ferries and pionier boats in a calm and orderly fashion. The embarkation was further delayed, however, by the loading of a large number of wounded, and dragged on from 0400 until 0730, well into broad daylight.

The enemy, who had spotted the embarkation, did not sit idly by, and soon the ships came under heavy artillery fire and continuous air attack.

•

Death on the sea now joined death on land. There was no safety, even on board the large ships. *Totila* had taken about 4,000 men aboard when Soviet bombers and close-support aircraft approached. There were no German fighters left. The ship's anti-aircraft guns hammered away, firing tracer into the sky. At 0545 *Totila* was struck by three bombs and left dead in the water and on fire. On board all hell broke loose. Water streamed into the lower compartments, while topside everything was in flames. The ship was wracked by thunderous explosions. Those who were not drowned below decks or killed by bomb fragments, gunfire or the flames leapt into the water, which was covered by sheets of blazing oil. Clusters of men clung to life preservers and floating pieces of wreckage. Most of those who tried to swim clear went under. The *Totila* sank at about 0800. The mine-sweeper R 209, which rushed in to help, was only able to rescue a few hundred men.

More air attacks followed and exploding bombs threw up great fountains of water. The next vessel to be hit was the motor ship *Teja*. With about 4,800 to 5,000 soldiers on board, it had sailed off toward the southwest escorted by two mine-sweepers. The *Teja* was caught by Soviet aircraft. Heavily damaged by aerial bombs and torpedoes, it went down at about 1500, 23 nautical miles southwest of Khersonyes. Once again casualties were heavy. The mine-sweepers picked up about 400 survivors and arrived back in Constanza on May 11.

About 8,000 soldiers on the two transports had drowned in the waters of the Black Sea.

The small steamer *Helga* still had ammunition on board when it arrived and approached the coast. The crew spent half an hour throwing the now useless ammunition overboard. As soon as the ship had taken aboard as many soldiers as it could hold the *Helga* set sail. Soon afterward Soviet aircraft appeared. The ship took a direct hit amidships, the ship's boiler exploded and fire broke out. All of those uninjured jumped overboard. Three pionier landing craft crisscrossed the scene in an attempt to rescue survivors. Four times they returned to shore with survivors they had fished out of the water, some of them wounded. The Rumanian torpedo boat *Naluca* was also sunk.

Like thousands of others, *Unteroffizier* Werner of the staff of the 98th Infantry Division experienced an air attack on a smaller ship, a navy landing craft, which was forced back to the coast by enemy aircraft:

> "The vessel, its deck was teeming with men, shoved off. At once artillery shells began to land to the right and left and before and behind us. Scarcely had we escaped the enemy fire when enemy aircraft roared in and began to circle round us. They opened fire with cannon and machine-guns. I was lying next to an empty canister, when a burst of fire suddenly severed an arm and a leg from a naval officer next to me. The deck was covered with dead and wounded, and everywhere there were cries and wailing. A motor boat was riddled by gunfire. The surface of the water was dotted with floating pieces of wood and the heads of swimming men. A sailor roared: 'We're taking on water, we're going down! All baggage overboard!' At once knapsacks, rucksacks and pieces of equipment began to fly over the railing. Now even we land soldiers could notice the ship settling in the water. Some of those in the water were swimming alongside, but many had already drowned. We turned back toward land and reached the coast without further air attacks. Apparently the Russians did not want us to escape. We dragged the many dead and wounded ashore, where the medics began their work . . ."

Other fully-loaded ships managed to get through on May 10, bringing about 10,000 men to the Rumanian mainland. This was nothing from the point of view of the army, which wanted to be completely evacuated in the coming night. The navy certainly failed to do this, however, the heavy seas had forced many convoys to turn back, while others had been delayed. It was soon clear that the urgently-awaited new convoys could not arrive at Khersonyes until May 11 at the earliest. The decision had to be made to hold the Khersonyes position for another 24 hours. The soldiers at the front now received the depressing news that the promised embarkation had been delayed a full day. Once again they settled in to hold on and keep the enemy at bay. Their stubborn defense was to be poorly rewarded. It is estimated that 25,000 men were still crammed together on the peninsula. Only a small number of troops were evacuated during the night of May 10/11.

The shoreline, with its bays, embarkation points and gangways, lay under constant artillery fire and was subjected to waves of air attacks. The passageways in Maxim II fort were full of wounded. Crowded about the steep slopes, where two- to three-meter-wide ladders led down to the landing places, were countless stragglers about whom no one was any longer concerned. Gradually order broke down here and there. Everyone was possessed by the same thought, to get to the ships which still might save them at this late hour. The men knew nothing of the sinkings at sea, and thousands of eyes still scanned the sea for ships, but the sea was empty.

At dawn on May 11 a large convoy with ten to twelve ships appeared in the waters off Khersonyes at a distance of 25-30 kilometers. Getting the troops to the large ships was now even more difficult, because the Siebel ferries and most of the pionier landing boats were no longer available. They had either been lost the preceding day or had sailed away to the west with other ships. Navy landing craft and a pilot boat had to take over the job of ferrying the troops to the ships lying at sea.

The slaughter of the transport ships was about to resume.

Enemy air units carried out running attacks on the 3,152-ton Rumanian auxiliary ship *Romania*, which, fortunately, had only taken on a few troops. A survivor, *Oberzahlmeister* Feucht, described the sinking of the Rumanian ship: "Russian attack aircraft roared in. *Romania* increased speed. Despite the fire from its quadruple-flak the ship was hit. Wood and glass splintered and there moans from wounded men. Fresh wounded were added to those already lying below deck. Again the alarm bell sounded throughout the ship. The anti-aircraft guns fired. Aircraft roared round about us. Again bombs whistled into the water. Later, when the ship stopped to take on a newly-arrived shipment of men, it happened: the aircraft reappeared. There was a splitting and cracking and a rending crash, which shook the entire ship and extinguished the lights. A bomb had smashed into the engine room and had at once set the outpouring oil on fire. Everyone pressed toward the exits. Biting smoke and hot air made it difficult to breathe. The screams of the wounded mixed with the hiss of escaping steam and the rattle of exploding anti-aircraft ammunition. We plunged head first into the sea, anything to get away from the sinking ship. Then we swam for our lives . . ."

Battered by artillery fire and bombs, the *Romania* lay dead in the water, burning and smoking, for almost a day, before sinking in the early hours of May 12.

At about 0730 the Rumanian steamer *Danubius* was hit by a bomb and blew up.

The steamer *Geiserich* also sank after several bomb hits and a torpedo from a Soviet submarine.

A further Rumanian ship was lost, as well as a number of lighter vessels and tugs.

It was later determined that, on average, only a tenth of the troops on board the stricken vessels were saved by escorting *Kriegsmarine* ships.

Then followed the tragedy of the final act.

•

The withdrawal of the remaining divisions from the Khersonyes position was set for 2300 on May 11. The rearguards were to follow an hour later and cover the coming night's evacuation from Kruglaya, Omega, Kasatscha and Kamyschewaye Bays and the western coast. A report from the navy indicated that a large convoy was expected to arrive at about midnight. It was calculated that the newly-arrived shuttle craft would require two trips to take the approximately 10,000 men to the large ships. After completing this task they too would set sail with a full load of troops.

The Naval Commander Crimea, the man responsible for the evacuation, pinned great hopes on this night, as did all of the troops from the General down to the last man. The final evacuation and escape simply had to succeed.

At 2100 – as per an order received that afternoon from Army Group South Ukraine – the Commander-in-Chief of the Army and his staff left Khersonyes for the Rumanian mainland aboard a fast motor torpedo boat.

Exactly half an hour later the Sea Commander Crimea left under heavy artillery fire aboard the command vessel of the 1st Motor Torpedo Boat Flotilla. As radioed orders and instructions were no longer getting through to the incoming convoys, *Admiral* Schulz wanted to personally direct the expected ships as close to the landing sites as possible and organize the shuttle service to save valuable time.

In the meantime, increasing numbers of soldiers were streaming to the embarkation points, landing bridges and makeshift moles, waiting, worrying and hoping. When would they get away – where were the ships – why didn't they come?

The ships arrived offshore, but they did not come in to pick up the waiting troops. An especially tragic climax was approaching. Suddenly there was fog, spreading from land out to sea, becoming heavier and thicker and making orientation on the water more difficult. The landing sites were visible only from a short distance, especially since the beacon lights had been knocked out by enemy fire. It became all the more vital for *Admiral* Schulz to bring the convoy ships as close to the coast as possible.

But where had the fog come from? Fog was an unusual phenomenon at this time of year. As it was later to be discovered, Russian artillery had set alight a number of smoke generators which had been installed to protect the harbor installations in the event of a major air attack. The German forces had not destroyed the generators, planning to use them to cover their withdrawal, not suspecting that they were contributing to their own downfall. To be sure, the artificial fog prevented the ships at sea from suffering further losses, but it also rendered useless all the efforts of *Admiral* Schulz. He managed to find the steamer *Dacia*, which was guided toward the coast by a Siebel ferry and a navy landing craft, before contact was again lost. Schulz was unable to locate any of the other convoy ships. So it was that many ships, especially smaller vessels with poor means of navigation, crisscrossed and stumbled about off the coast in the fog and darkness and just barely or failed to find the planned landing sites. During the night there were about 60 ships off the Khersonyes Peninsula, only a few of which found their way to the coast and undertook to embark troops.

The embarkation points and the sea approaches lay under heavy artillery fire, which had begun on the evening of May 10 with a destructive barrage and continued the whole following day and throughout the night of May 11/12. Continuous bombing and strafing attacks, by night as well as day, supplemented the artillery fire, and a series of landing sites was smashed.

The groups of soldiers clustered around the bays and inlets and along the narrow beach on the west side of the peninsula saw all hope disappear. Most of those still remaining were the combat troops who had held out until the end. The rescue attempts went on, however, and several thousand more still managed to escape.

Quite by chance *General* Reinhardt, commander of the 98th Infantry Division, came upon five Siebel ferries and several smaller boats at a remote coastal position, where the commanders of the vessels had steered their craft up to the shore. Reinhardt alerted elements of his division and nearby units of the 111th Division and brought them to these ships. The General waited for stragglers in the last landing craft, where he was joined by the Chief-of-Staff of XXXXIX Mountain Army Corps. Finally at 0300, as dawn approached, the ship pushed off.

The Soviets also failed to notice the 50th Infantry Division's withdrawal to the pier and about 3,000 of its men were rescued. The same thing happened to the 336th Division, whose severely-wounded commanding officer had been flown out. Some of the 73rd Division's men got away in landing craft, the rest aboard a sub-chaser. Not a single ship found its way to the piers allocated to the 111th Division.

Since a massive attack by Soviet air units was expected in the morning, against which the convoy ships would be defenceless, the Naval Commander Crimea could not accept responsibility for a continuation of the evacuation. Therefore, at

0133 on May 12 he sent the following grave message to the senior Admiral Black Sea: Embarkation by day out of the question. Request that all convoys arriving Khersonyes after 0200 be turned back. A further message followed at 0205: Situation demands the breaking off of rescue operation. Embarkation to end at 0230 at the latest.

The last large convoy left the waters off Khersonyes and suffered losses on the return trip. The Rumanian ship *Tisza* was damaged by a bomb and had to be taken in tow by a mine-sweeper. The steamer *Durostor* was hit by several bombs and a torpedo from a Soviet submarine and sank. A severely-damaged submarine chaser had to be scuttled.

Navy landing craft remained on the scene beyond 0230, taking on further troops at various embarkation points. They were under orders from the naval commander to take aboard as many men as possible. These small ships, which had been designed to carry 250 men, took aboard as many as 750, and in some cases as many as 1,100, before sailing off toward the west. At 0330 the boats of the 1st Motor Torpedo Boat Flotilla under the command of *Admiral* Schulz sailed for Constanza, the last vessels to leave.

In spite of all the difficulties and shipping losses, the tireless and unselfish actions of the German and Rumanian navies resulted in the rescue of 25,697 troops and 6,011 wounded from Khersonyes and their transport to Constanza.

One other outstanding incident should be mentioned. During the night of May 9/10 fifty Ju 52 transport aircraft landed at the two makeshift airfields to pick up wounded. Badly overloaded, with as many as 30 severely-wounded men on board, they flew back. Quite miraculously, the lumbering transports returned without loss, having rescued more than 1,000 wounded.

The Final Hours on the Khersonyes Coast

The history of the 98th Infantry Division described the final days and hours on the peninsula:[10]

> "The number of combat troops who withdrew into the Khersonyes position, which extended in a semi-circle around this peninsula west of Sevastopol, from the formerly-held positions on May 9 was small. Squads were formed and sent into action. For those 'up front' the position was a great surprise. It was well-constructed with an extensive trench system and concrete living, ration and munitions bunkers, in which were stored an abundance of excellent rations. Ammunition, however, was in short supply. The horseshoe-shaped position, which

extended around the embarkation points on the deep bays of the north coast, was only two kilometers deep opposite the central Bay of Kamyschewaya.

Crammed into a very small area, the final act of the entire drama began for the many thousands of Crimean fighters. The stage on which it was to be played out, the western tip of the Khersonyes Peninsula, was in full view of the lost Sapun Heights and lay before the enemy like an exhibit.

On the evening of this black 'day of flight' the troops learned of Hitler's order that the Crimea was now to be evacuated. What three weeks ago would have been perceived as an act of reason, as proof of a sense of responsibility guided by a growing awareness, was now received with scorn and derision. For the first time there were open expressions of doubt, bitterness and anger. If the Crimea could be evacuated now, it could just as well have been evacuated a few weeks earlier, before thousands more had been stubbornly and irresponsibly sacrificed.

The night of May 10 was used to prepare the defences for the coming day. Above all order had to restored in the sectors, which were the scene of unimaginable confusion, for the 'battle groups.' As dawn broke the battalions and companies awaited the enemy without sufficient heavy weapons and low on ammunition: on the right the 289th Grenadier Regiment, left the 290th Grenadier Regiment.

Many of those in the final main line of resistance on the Crimea, among them signals men, rear-echelon soldiers, drivers, clerks and cooks, were not fighters like the trained and experienced infantrymen, but all of them had stood the test and exhibited a high level of courage, toughness and self-control. To the final day the remnants of the 98th Division fulfilled their duty with discipline, uninfluenced by the signs of collapse all about them. Thus were all of the attacks on May 10 beaten off with bloody losses to the enemy. Now everyone waited for the embarkation which must take place soon.

During the course of the day a new '*Führerbefehl*' was announced and was circulated among the troops. It stated that the entire German and Rumanian Black Sea Fleets were at sea and that Sevastopol was to be evacuated during the coming night. Air support was promised, and an entire *Geschwader* of long-range close-support aircraft was to intervene during the afternoon of May 10. Could this really be possible?

The long-range close-support aircraft did not come. There were none on the entire Eastern Front! And the ships! There were ships, but . . .

The losses among the soldiers waiting to be evacuated rose alarmingly, especially near the embarkation points. Many non-fighting elements and large numbers of wounded had assembled there. One after another, circling Russian aircraft peeled off to bomb and strafe the helpless men. After darkness fell on the evening of May 10 everyone waited for the order to fall back. It did not come. The ships promised by the navy were not there. The navy was unable to arrive in time. There was nothing else to do but delay the order to withdraw for twenty-four hours.

Twenty-four more hours of holding on! In this situation! With ammunition running out, and exposed to the powerful artillery and air force of the enemy!

The Russians attacked with the powerful support of heavy weapons and tanks. However, all their attempts to break through were repulsed by the men fighting for life and freedom. Losses were heavy everywhere, in the positions and at the embarkation points. At this time the last commander of the Crimea left the Khersonyes Peninsula and sailed to Constanza. he was obeying a 'Führer Order.'

At 2000, following a heavy bombardment, the enemy launched another attack on the main line of resistance and the embarkation points. This, too, was successfully repelled. Finally the eagerly awaited hour of the withdrawal for embarkation to freedom was near. Sufficient shipping space had been promised for the night of May 11/12. The withdrawal began at 2300, following a final salvo from the rocket launchers. After an eerie march to the sea, past burning vehicles, dead and injured horses, and burning ammunition dumps, the small groups of soldiers reached the piers from which they were to embark. The main body of troops, as well as the rearguard, was scarcely molested by the enemy. Now the ships could come.

The embarkation points assigned to the division were located 30 to 40 meters below the bluffs of the western coast. These fell away sharply at first, before becoming a rocky slope with large boulders and smaller stones. Near the coast the water was shallow, but ships with a low draught could come in quite close to shore.

Two hours of feverish waiting passed in complete inactivity. Nothing happened. In these two hours alone a large part of the waiting men could have embarked. But no ships came. Among those waiting was one of the last survivors of the 282nd Regiment, *Hauptmann* Vockentanz. He reported: 'At the loading place the land ended suddenly, as if cut by a knife. Twenty to thirty meters below roared the sea. Two- to three-meter-wide ladders had been placed against the rock wall for us to climb down. The night was lit bright as day by the 'Christmas trees' dropped by enemy aircraft. The men crowded in front of the piers. Equipment, weapons and packs lay in jumbled heaps. Then enemy bombs began to fall. Every security measure was disregarded, all restraint disappeared. The instinct of self-preservation eliminated any semblance of order. In the thunder of exploding bombs the desperate men jostled down the bluffs, hanging from ladders, climbing over one another and falling on the dead, the wounded and the boulders tossed up by the sea. More low-flying enemy aircraft approached the bluffs from the sea, however, and fired their guns into the clusters of men.'

Leutnant Klotz wrote: 'We're lying on a spit of land. Bombs fall into the sea. Nearby are some artillerymen and signals people who have been waiting for some time. Out to sea a ship catches fire. Soon it is a blazing torch. What could be happening out there? No ships come for us. We are lost, they are abandoning us. The sea is calm. Another half hour and darkness will be falling. And the sea is empty! Where are the promised ships, where are the German air units? Several men try to take to the sea on rafts, so as to escape the dreaded Soviet captivity. Every attempt is foiled by the barricade of enemy shells.'

It was certain that no ships were going to come to where the fighting elements of the 98th Infantry Division were waiting. There were other places where troops were still being taken off to vessels on the high sea, but that was not enough. It was later learned that the navy transport fleet in the waters around Sevastopol was strong enough; however, the naval commander's command and communications organization broke down under the heavy enemy fire. As a result, most of the embarkation points remained largely empty of boats and landing craft, and the assembled troops waited in vain.

Oberstleutnant Lau, the Division Ia, refused to get on board as the last fully-loaded boat was preparing to depart. All of the staff had not yet embarked. He led the remaining 50 men to another location, where an air traffic safety ship was preparing to depart. At his urging the ship took aboard fifteen of his men. *Oberstleutnant* Lau remained behind with the rest. He has been missing since then.

At the foot of the bluff the small group that was all that was left of the 198th Fusilier Battalion stood and waited. Then a navy landing craft approached the shore, guided by the division's liaison officer with the navy. *Hauptmann* Dr. Maull, the commander of the fusiliers, directed the loading. The only ones still not back were the last pickets. With the words: 'I wouldn't think of leaving my people in the lurch!' the *Hauptmann* disappeared into the darkness. After waiting a brief while the boat pushed off on orders from the flotilla commander. *Hauptmann* Dr. Maull has been missing since. And with him so many others . . .

The enemy aircraft returned as dawn began to push back the darkness. The Russian artillery came back to life. Salvoes from Stalin Organs rushed down, laying a barricade of fire across the surface of the water. Thirty, perhaps forty salvoes fell before it was completely light.

Then it daylight. The morning of May 12 had begun. Russian tanks rolled forward on a broad front and began to fire. The wounded wailed. Many men were as if lost in thought, many ran into the enemy fire. Then an officer said: 'There are no more ships coming! We've been written off, betrayed.' There was no longer any purpose. Any attempt to continue the battle was senseless, the continued slaughter of the trapped German troops could not be justified. The order was given to cease fighting and show white flags, which was generally obeyed . . ."

Walter Winkler described the final hours of the 50th Infantry Division:[11]

"On the evening of May 9 we heard that Hitler had finally given the order for the evacuation of the Crimea. It was clear to everyone that the order had been given much too late. The evacuation by sea would now have to take place under heavy enemy pressure while fighting was still going on. A Soviet attack in divisional strength on May 10 was beaten back all along the line with heavy losses. A replacement unit made up of soldiers who had recovered from their wounds arrived from Constanza and was sent into the front lines.

These events gave the troops new courage and confidence. Because of foul weather the embarkation, which had been scheduled to begin on the night of May 10/11, was put off. The German front held throughout the following day. As part of XXXXIX Mountain Corps the division withdrew from the Khersonyes position. The enemy did not notice this movement, as he was deceived as to our real intentions by two combat patrols sent against his own lines. Only a third of the garrison remained in the trenches of the Khersonyes position. The withdrawing units were directed by a traffic control officer to embarkation points on Kruglaya and Omega Bays, from where naval launches took them to the transport ships anchored off the coast. The first groups of combat troops were taken off without incident.

Some time before midnight *Major* Teschner, who was in command of the rearguard on the left wing of the Khersonyes position, received a report that wounded and train personnel at Omega Bay had already been waiting many hours for their ferries. His suggestion, to delay the abandoning of the Khersonyes position for twenty-four hours so as to create more favorable conditions for the embarkation, was rejected by division. He was told that more ships were still expected. At about midnight *Major* Teschner and his men began to withdraw, as the rearguards on the right wing were leaving their positions. Teschner's unit moved into a blocking position around the bays chosen for loading to cover the embarkation. The scene at the embarkation points was a miserable one. So far only a few ferries had arrived. They had only been able to take aboard a few hundred soldiers, while the beach teemed with

wounded and members of the trains and other units. It was no better with
the 336th Infantry Division on our right. Only with the 50th Division's
121st Infantry Regiment did the evacuation go as planned, although
even there many units were still waiting to be picked up. Another launch
appeared at about 0200. It was loaded calmly, although the word was
that this was the last boat. It was in fact the last.

Early on May 12, when no more ships appeared, *Major* Teschner
and the rearguard units under his command once again formed a semi-
circular line around the embarkation bays. He hoped that further
evacuation ships might yet arrive during the coming night. He also
attempted to include the units to his right in this blocking position and
thus extend it to the south. However, the neighboring units had only a
few fighting troops left and no heavy weapons. Late that morning the
Russians attacked following a heavy bombardment. The attackers were
beaten back, but to the south of the blocking position they drove through
to Omega Bay. The Rumanians there surrendered. Further south large
groups of prisoners could be seen forming.

Red Army troops now pressed in from the rear. The situation in
Teschner's blocking position was impossible. Therefore, at 1200 *Major*
Teschner ordered all fighting to cease. The sad fate of the German troops
which could not be evacuated began to unfold . . ."

A report from a member of 1st Battery, 86th Light Flak Battalion:

"A few days ago we could still say – near Sevastopol. Now it was
only Cape Khersonyes, the cape of a thousand curses. We didn't know
that this was the last day, but we suspected as much. Enemy artillery
hammered the small area left to us, the bombs fell without pause.

Along the bluffs sat thousands of soldiers whose units no longer
existed, stragglers, waiting to be evacuated. Every niche in the rock,
every bit of cover was alive. Every half hour the Russian close-support
aircraft came to claim more helpless victims. The doomed group still
held off the enemy, but it would all be over in the coming night.
Somewhere on the beach lay a single ferry – two pontoons, across them
a platform, on it a bridge and beneath the engine. It was waiting for
darkness, because by day the IL-2s and larger bombers were always
overhead. It had sailed the previous night, but no ship had come to take
off its living cargo, so it was forced to return. Most of the soldiers on the
ferry had been flak artillerymen. Their guns had been destroyed, their
ammunition exhausted, they should have been evacuated days ago
'according to plan.'

During May 11 the commander of 1st Battery, who had by chance
spotted the ferry, assembled his scattered people. The battalion had
disbanded three days earlier and had received orders to evacuate the

peninsula.

Embarkation began as dusk fell. Two foot bridges led to the ferry. The soldiers crossed with rapid steps. Many of them were from the flak artillery, but other branches were represented as well. They were dead tired, hungry, ragged, but once again they had hope in their eyes. The crush began when the ship was full. The *Hauptmann* stood on one footbridge, the adjutant on the other, with pistols drawn. The faces of the two officers betrayed no emotion whatsoever. If at least some of the men were to be saved they had to appear hard and pitiless. Overloading the ferry would mean death for all.

Slowly the ferry chugged to one of the official embarkation points and there took aboard several dozen wounded. While this was taking place the *Hauptmann* scoured the loading platforms on shore, picking up the rifles of those killed in the last air attack and giving them to the soldiers on the ferry who had none. 'A soldier should at least bring his weapon with him,' he said. He also tossed rifles to the many others lying around: 'You might need them yet.'

So the last ferry left Cape Khersonyes. It would not return. One pontoon was already leaking, and besides, the three submarine chasers we hoped to meet were the last ships. We could not reach Rumania on this ferry, so the three sailors which made up its crew would be going with us.

Suddenly, an enormous landing craft appeared from out of the darkness and took on the wounded. They had been looked after as well as possible by their comrades on the ferry. There was no medical assistance, but the *Hauptmann* gave instructions that 'in five minutes I don't want to see a wounded man without a schnapps in his stomach, as long as he can take it and has nothing to eat.' We had schnapps, there had been plenty of it in Fort Maxim Gorki II at the bluffs. The food situation was not so good, but there was always something left for the wounded in the knapsacks, even if it was only prunes, which many of the men had in their pockets. We never learned if the landing craft carrying the wounded reached Rumania. We, however, chugged on through the night. The three sailors peered tensely into the darkness. There – a brief flash, and again, and soon light signals were passing back and forth. A shadow came alongside: 'Climb aboard!' Then from over there: 'Stop, enough, the next boat is coming.' Another shadow, and again the hasty clambering over the railing. Then a third shadow. Finally everyone was off. The last to leave were the three sailors, who left their ferry to sink in the darkness.

The three submarine chasers were small boats with small crews. There was no room for anyone below deck. Side by side we crouched on the narrow deck. The sailors could scarcely move about their boat, but they endured this with good humor. Only in the event of an attack would it have been critical, because the crew could not have got to their weapons. The sailors broke out the last of their provisions, and on this fast, streamlined boat we finally felt as if we had been delivered. Only when we thought of the comrades who had been left behind was our joy mixed with bitterness.

We sailed for a night, a day and on into a second night. Then, finally, the contours of the coast and a harbor emerged. We were in Constanza. A brief 'Thank you, comrades!' and the shadow of the boat disappeared into the darkness of the unlighted harbor, almost as unreal as the whole rescue and voyage had been. Twelve hours after our departure the battle near Khersonyes had come to an end . . ."

It was the final act of the entire tragedy.

For more than half a year the Seventeenth Army had held the Crimea, following an insane order. Now the end was near for the remaining defenders. No more ships came to pick them up. When the morning of May 12 dawned the Black Sea was again empty and quiet and endlessly wide.

Since any further resistance had become senseless, at about 0800 the bulk of the remaining troops in the area of the northern embarkation points, including the commander of the 73rd Infantry Division, *Generalmajor* Böhme, surrendered.

Artillery fired on the barely 25-meter-wide beach between the bluffs and the sea at the embarkation points on the western coast, where several thousand men still cowered among the rocks and crevices and at the steep cliffs. Then Russian tanks attacked the last line of defence. Further resistance was useless. *General* Gruner, commander of the 111th Infantry Division, walked toward one of the tanks to surrender. The tank opened fire, killing the General. Then, as was so often the case with the Soviets, the officers and highly-decorated soldiers were led away from the others. This was followed by shots and screams. The remaining Russian auxiliaries who had served the Germans were lined up along the cliffs and shot.

Then, on this hot summer day, the last remnants of the Seventeenth Army, over 15,000 Germans and Rumanian troops, were assembled into long columns and marched past the whirring Soviet newsreel cameras into captivity. For most of them there would be no return.

Other groups of German troops refused to surrender and continued to hold out. German aerial reconnaissance revealed that elements were still holding out around the embarkation points at 1500, probably in the desperate hope that they would still be rescued. They held out until their ammunition was gone.

Others preferred to risk everything rather than be captured by the Soviets. They set out alone in small boats and on makeshift rafts, taking their chances on the open sea in hopes of being found and picked up. In fact, during the night of May 12/13 German motor torpedo boats scouring the sea found and picked up another 83 men. These were the last troops of the Seventeenth Army to be saved.

Altogether about 130,000 of the 230,000 men in the Crimea were picked up by German and Rumanian ships and taken to the Rumanian mainland in the evacuation initiated by the Seventeenth Army on April 12 and the officially sanctioned one which followed. In the same period the Luftwaffe evacuated a further 21,000 soldiers by air, most of them wounded. The losses reported by the Army High Command were approximately 57,500 killed and wounded (including prisoners). In addition there were at least a further 20,000 men whose fate remained completely unexplained, including a large number who drowned. Thus the Battle of the Crimea had cost about 78,000 German and Rumanian soldiers.

In addition to the human losses a tremendous amount of war materiel of all sorts was lost. Between May 1 and 10, 5,261 tons of munitions had been sent to the defenders. Most of this failed to reach the fighting positions or could not be used by the decimated units. Only 720 tons of ammunition was recovered.

Once again an entire army with two army corps had been lost, and Hitler alone bore the responsibility for its destruction.

Excerpts from Wehrmacht Communiques:

May 10:
. . . In the Sevastopol bridgehead German and Rumanian troops are engaged in further heavy fighting with the advancing enemy. In the course of our withdrawal the rubble of the city of Sevastopol has been abandoned. Yesterday close-support aircraft destroyed 30 Soviet tanks. 19 enemy aircraft were shot down air battles and by flak artillery . . .

May 11:
. . . Yesterday our troops, together with Rumanian mountain infantry battalions, halted bitter attacks by powerful enemy forces in the area west of Sevastopol. 20 Soviet tanks were destroyed . . .

May 12:
. . . Yesterday German-Rumanian units continued to offer stubborn resistance against superior enemy forces in our narrow bridgehead west of Sevastopol, destroying a large number of tanks . . .

May 13:
. . . Yesterday near Sevastopol our rearguards engaged in bitter fighting

with numerically far-superior enemy forces, and with exemplary bravery covered the evacuation of German-Rumanian units . . .

May 14:
. . . On May 13 the last German-Rumanian troops were transported to the
mainland . . .

In a unique operation units of the German and Rumanian navies and merchant
marine, as well as transport units of the Luftwaffe, evacuated the allied troops
deployed in the Crimea in the face of heavy enemy resistance.

Disposition of the Seventeenth Army

Headquarters Seventeenth Army:
Generaloberst Jaennecke (from April 30, 1944 *General der Infanterie*
Allmendinger).

Army:

Headquarters V Army Corps:
General der Infanterie Allmendinger (from May 5, 1944 *Generalleutnant* Böhme).
73rd Infantry Division: *Generalmajor* Böhme
98th Infantry Division: *General der Infanterie* Gareis, then *General* Reinhardt

Headquarters XXXXIX Mountain Army Corps:
General der Gebirgstruppen Konrad (from May 7, 1944 *General der Artillerie*
Hartmann)
50th Infantry Division: *Generalmajor* Sixt (from May 2, 1944 *Oberst* Beetz)
111th Infantry Division: *Generalmajor* Gruner
336th Infantry Division: *Generalmajor* Hagemann
Mountain Infantry Regiment "*Krim*"
Two assault gun brigades (191st and 297th)
Two army anti-aircraft battalions (275th and 279th).

Luftwaffe:
I Fliegerkorps: *Generalleutnant* Deichmann

Operations Staff Crimea of I Fliegerkorps: General Staff *Oberst* Bauer with aviation units of varying strength and composition (on April 1, 1944, for example, 126 operational Stukas, close-support aircraft, fighters and reconnaissance aircraft).

Flak artillery:
9th Flak Division: *Generalmajor* Pickert
(3 flak regiments).

Kriegsmarine:

Headquarters Naval Commander Crimea: *Konteradmiral* Schulz with harbor masters at Sevastopol, Feodosia and Yalta, harbor and supply service centers on the Crimean coast, and landing craft in transport, motor torpedo boat and coastal patrol units.

(According to *Großadmiral* Dönitz: eight motor torpedo boats, twelve minesweepers, three submarines, six naval artillery directors, 60 landing craft.

Rumanian Units:

Headquarters I Rumanian Mountain Corps:
1st, 2nd and 3rd Rumanian Mountain Divisions.
Headquarters Rumanian Cavalry Corps:
2nd, 6th and 9th Rumanian Cavalry Divisions
10th and 19th Rumanian Infantry Divisions.

Notes:
[1] The 73rd Infantry Division was sent to the Crimea by sea at the end of January 1944, the 111th Infantry Division in early March.
[2] State as of April 9, 1944.
[3] From April 8-14.
[4] Excerpt from: M. Gareis: *Kampf und Ende der 98. Infanteriedivision.*
[5] Anti-tank weapon similar to the American "bazooka."
[6] Arrived from May 1-12.
[7] Von Xylander wrote this report to his departed Commander-in-Chief, *Generaloberst* Jaennecke, on May 16, four days before the end of the Seventeenth Army near Sevastopol.
[8] New Army Commander-in-Chief.
[9] On orders of I. *Fliegerkorps.*
[10] From: M. Gareis: *Kampf und Ende der 98. Infanteriedivision.*
[11] Excerpt from W. Winkler: *Der Kampf um Sewastopol.*

IV

White Russia:
Army Group Center

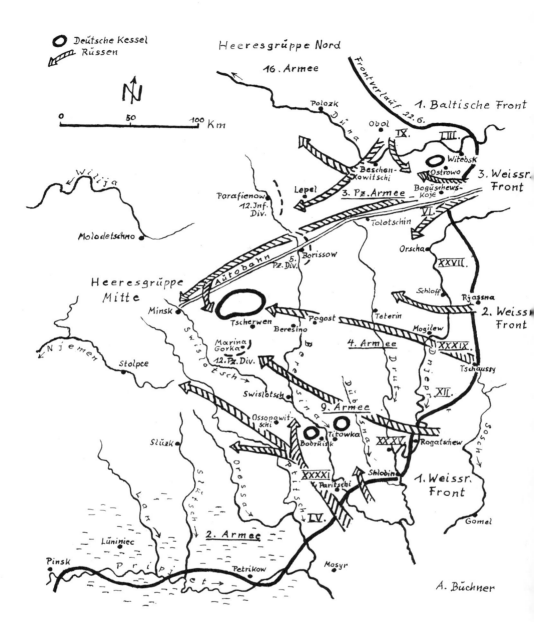

Deutsche Kessel
Rüssen

N

0   50   100 Km

Heeresgrüppe Nord

16. Armee

Frontverlauf 22.6.

1. Baltische Front

Polozk

Düna

Obol   IX.   LIII.

Witebsk

Beschen-
Kowitschi

Ostrowo

3. Weissr.
Front

Lepel

Boguschews-
Koje

Parafienow
12. Jnf.
Div.

3. Pz. Armee

VI.

Molodetschno

Tolotschin

Orscha

XXVII.

Wilija

Autobahn

5.
Pz. Div.

Borissow

Schloff

Rjassna

Heeresgrüppe
Mitte

Minsk

Tscherwen

Pogost

Teterin

2. Weissr.
Front

Beresino

Marina
Gorka

Mogilew

XXXIX.

12. Pz. Div.

4. Armee

Tschaussy

Swislotsch

Drut

XII.

Njemen

Stolpce

9. Armee

Dübssna

Swislotsch

Dnjepr

Ossopowit-
schi

Titowka

Sossch

Slusk

Bobruisk

XXXV

Rogatschew

Beresina

Shlobin

1. Weissr.
Front

Oressa

XXXXI

Paritschi

Ptitsch

Gomel

LV.

Sluzsch

2. Armee

Lan

Lüniniec

Pripjet

Petrikow

Mosyr

Pinsk

A. Büchner

White Russia: Army Group Center

The Worst Defeat Ever Suffered
by The German Army

White Russia – a land rich in history. It was here that the soldiers of Napoleon I marched across the land-bridge between the Duna and Dniepr Rivers toward Moscow, the metropolis of the Czarist empire, and during its retreat from Moscow the "Grand Army" perished while crossing the Beresina. Something similar was to take place 132 years later, only this time not in the depths of an icy winter, but during the hot summer of 1944. White Russia – hilly, with great, sometimes jungle-like, forests interspersed with marshes, fields and villages, small lakes and streams, marshy lowlands, traversed by the northward-flowing Duna and the southward-flowing Dniepr with its many tributaries, among them the Beresina. Among the country's large cities were Vitebsk and Orsha, Mogilev, Bobruisk and, of course, Minsk, the capital city of White Russia, from where the first Russian highway led through Smolensk to Moscow. In those summer days this entire country was to play an especially tragic role for hundreds of thousands of German soldiers.

The German Army Group Center –
An 1,100-Kilometer Front

The campaign against the Soviet Union had also passed through White Russia. Great battles raged there in the summer of 1941 until the noise of battle moved more and more toward the East. However, Army Group Center was unable to capture Moscow and the war returned, until following its retreat the army group was able to occupy a new, and this time, so it hoped, permanent front.[1] Six defensive battles were fought along the front in one year, but it held firm. From

Polotsk in the north, where it linked up with Army Group North, the front extended eastward in a great salient around Vitebsk, then between Orsha and Rogatchev in a large bridgehead east of the Dniepr, before running increasingly westward and then straight south from Pinsk to a point near Kovel, where it met Army Group North Ukraine. Thus Army Group Center – at that time the strongest German army group – under its Commander in Chief *Feldmarschall* Busch occupied an extended, semi-circular, eastward-facing salient approximately 1,100 kilometers in length and held by four armies.

The northern wing from Polotsk consisted of the Third Panzer Army[2] with IX, LII and VI Army Corps (nine divisions), in the center the Fourth Army with XXVII, XXXIX and XII Corps (nine divisions) and finally the Ninth Army with XXXV, XXXXI and LV Corps (ten divisions).

The southern wing along the Pripyat Marshes was formed by the Second Army with three army corps. There were thus about 500,000 German soldiers (without Second Army)[3], about 400,000 in the actual front area, certainly an imposing number. This figure meant little, however, because most of the infantry divisions, which would have to bear the brunt of the fighting, were far below strength and had only five to seven battalions instead of the usual ten. The entire infantry combat strength of the Third Panzer Army, for example, was only 21,500 men, while the Ninth Army had only 24,000 trench fighters in the main line of resistance. The entire divisional artillery of the three armies numbered only 1,260 light and heavy guns. In addition to these weakened divisions, whose job it was to hold the front (Third Panzer Army about 220 kilometers of front, Fourth Army 200 kilometers and Ninth Army 280 kilometers), the entire army group had only six infantry and security divisions and a single panzer division[4] in reserve, which it had moved into positions behind the individual armies. There was a further negative factor in addition to the projecting front, the weakened divisions and the lack of reserves, and that was the Luftwaffe. It was so tied down in the West and with the defence of the Reich that the commanding *Luftflotte* 6 had available only a very few flying units, including a mere 40 fighters. To compound the situation there was a shortage of fuel. The Luftwaffe was scarcely to appear during the coming heavy fighting.

The army group's commanders had another cause to worry. The entire rear zone in the area of forests and swamps between the Dniepr, Beresina and Pripyat Rivers was controlled by partisans[5] as on no other front. Repeated large-scale anti-partisan actions were carried out, but were unable to eliminate the nuisance of the partisan bands. Even in periods of relative quiet German forces could only travel the Mogilev-Beresina road in convoy, and movement by smaller units was quite impossible off this major road. The situation was similar in other sectors. The partisans mined roads, ambushed staff vehicles, killed motorcycle messengers, cut telephone lines, and so on.

The army group's overall situation was seen as only marginally stable and therefore as early as April the army group command proposed two plans to shorten the front, a move which would save forces and result in better defensive positions. One plan, the so-called "small solution," would have seen the Third Panzer Army abandon the salient around Vitebsk and the Fourth Army evacuate the bridgehead beyond the Dniepr, while the "big solution" would have seen all three armies pulled back behind the Beresina. Although the army group and the armies pushed for weeks for a withdrawal of the front to shorter lines, Hitler once again rejected any such move, even forbidding further work on positions in the rear and instead ordering the establishment of "fortified places," a concept "invented" by him. Vitebsk, Orsha, Mogilev and Bobruisk were so designated. The army group's Commander in Chief gave in and issued orders that the existing main line of resistance was to be defended no matter what.

Another factor made the coming disaster inevitable. Although previous experience tended to indicate that the Soviets would launch their new offensive against the eastward-projecting salient occupied by the army group, Hitler, and with him the entire High Command, assessed the situation quite differently. They expected an enemy offensive all right, but they calculated that it would be directed against Army Group North Ukraine[6] from the area south of Kovel. It was anticipated that in doing so the Soviets would undertake to cut off the salient held by Army Group Center from the rear and then drive in the general direction of the Baltic, causing Army Group North's front to collapse.

Thus the German High Command completely misinterpreted the situation and in its operational assessments credited the Soviets with greater capabilities than did they themselves. The plan devised by the Soviet high command (STAVKA) was not as complex as the one expected by the Germans. They intended to launch their offensive in several phases – first they would smash Army Group Center, then advance to the Baltic, cut off Army Group North and finally a resume their offensive toward the west through Poland as far as the Vistula. In early 1944 planning and preparation for the first phase of the operation, code-named "Bagration,"[7] were proceeding at full speed.

The Prelude – Partisans Open the Soviet Offensive

During the previous winter the Soviets had launched heavy attacks, especially near

Vitebsk, but the Third Panzer Army had stood fast. The Soviets had also failed to achieve the desired success in five "highway battles" on the Minsk-Smolensk highway in the area of the front held by the German Fourth Army. Now, following the end of the heavy winter fighting, quiet settled over the front, a deceptive quiet. The German troops were pleased – what soldier wouldn't be – their positions had been beefed up in every way possible, and they felt secure. Following the defensive successes of the winter the general mood was one of confidence. When relieved, the soldiers could rest in the rear areas and soldier's homes, swim in the rivers, there was leave, the supply service was functioning smoothly and the troops took the routine of positional warfare – the sentry duty, harassing fire and occasional enemy advances – in stride. What went on in the rear areas with the partisans interested few, there were security divisions to deal with that.

The quiet held, but with his unfailing instinct the front-line soldier sensed that something was up "over there." There was something in the air. Prisoners brought in by patrols reported attack forces assembling behind the Soviet front, while agents provided similar information. Surveys by observation battalions identified powerful new artillery units in several sectors. As early as June 7, Headquarters Ninth Army reported strong enemy forces massing opposite its front. The army group's reply: Out of the question! From June 10 the threatening signs of a giant Soviet buildup increased. German listening posts intercepted enemy orders, new armies appeared on the Soviet radio net, and aerial reconnaissance reported a considerable increase in rail traffic and lively column traffic on the roads. The Soviet buildup intensified day by day. Soviet artillery began ranging in on June 14, and continuous air attacks were directed at lines of communication in the rear of the German armies and against airfields. Repeated enemy advances in the period from the 17th to the 21st were obviously intended to probe the German front for weak spots, provide information and capture jumping-off positions for the offensive.

The units on the German side right up to the army level realized that a terrible threat was brewing. This was no diversionary buildup, no deception, especially since – quite contrary to the beliefs of the German high command – there were no similar indications on the front held by Army Group North Ukraine.

However the reports reaching the senior commanders were not taken seriously and were dismissed as unimportant, they simply did not want to admit that they might be true. The prevailing opinion was still that this was a diversionary or containing move and that the main blow would fall upon Army Group North Ukraine. As a result, when the Commander in Chief of Army Group Center tried to convince Hitler that everything was pointing toward an imminent, massive

Soviet offensive against his army group, the Führer refused to listen. Hitler talked him out of the idea, refused to send further forces and ordered that the present positions be held. Since the OKH was of the same opinion as Hitler, *Feldmarschall* Busch decided that an offensive against his army group was indeed out of the question. Thus convinced, he even left to go on leave in Germany – three days before the beginning of the enemy offensive.

By mid-June the Red Army was ready. Once again it possessed a tremendous superiority, with which it was about to fall upon the three German armies and their twenty-eight divisions on a 700- kilometer front. The Soviets had assembled four "Fronts": the First Baltic Front (Army General Bagramyan) with five armies[8], and the Third White Russian Front (Lieutenant General Chernyakhovsky) with six armies[9], under the overall command of Marshall Vasilevsky, and the Second White Russian Front (Lieutenant General Zakharov) with three armies[10] and the First White Russian Front (Army General Rokossovsky) with five armies[11] under the overall command of Marshall Zhukov. This made a total of nineteen armies with 138 divisions and 43 armored units, together with 2.5 million troops, 31,000 mortars, guns and rocket launchers, 5,200 tanks and assault guns and more than 5,200 aircraft in five air armies. Sheer weight of numbers ensured success, and the Soviets were certain of victory and confidently looking forward to the end of Army Group Center.

The Soviet High Command had deliberately chosen June 22, 1944, the third anniversary of the beginning of the German offensive against the Soviet Union, as the date for the attack. Now they would demonstrate that their offensive, timed to begin in several phases, and employing tremendous amounts of men and materiel, could run as precisely as clockwork with great speed.

During the night of June 21/22 the Soviet Air Force launched massive attacks on every large city in the combat zone. At the same time partisans began a campaign of sabotage against German railroads in the rear areas. 10,500 sections of track were blown, although 3,500 mines were removed from the roadbeds before they went off. As a result of these demolitions, the largest partisan operation to date, almost all German rail traffic was cut for twenty-four hours or more. In addition, communications cables along the highway, which ran to the army group, were destroyed at many locations.

Then the Russians began their great offensive, which in scale and power far exceeded any so far during World War Two. (In order to ensure the continuity of the multifarious events, the effects of the attack on each German army will be described separately).

Third Panzer Army – Situation Already Critical on the First Day of the Attack

The Soviet offensive began early on the morning of June 22. For several hours the positions of IX Army Corps on the army's left wing were pounded by artillery[12] and close-support aircraft in a devastating bombardment. The Soviets paid special attention to the German artillery positions and some batteries scarcely had a chance to fire. Then the Soviet rifle divisions attacked northwest of Vitebsk, supported by large numbers of tanks. East of Obol the 252nd Infantry Division took the brunt of the Soviet attack. Fighting desperately, it held out against the superior enemy forces throughout the day, but already there was a breach in the front eight kilometers wide. In subsequent night attacks the enemy pushed the corps' front back still further. After fresh massed attacks on the morning of the 23rd the Soviet assault waves broke through on a wide front south across the Polotsk-Vitebsk rail line while some of their forces veered southeast. Outflanked on two sides and in some cases already split up into battle groups, the units fought their way back through heavy rain. In spite of the ongoing difficult fighting against numerous enemy breakthroughs, which went on throughout the night of June 23/24, in the course of the next morning the corps succeeded in establishing a bridgehead position east of the Düna. Every available alert and construction unit was committed. The individual combat units, under constant attack from the Soviet Air Force, fought their way back, fending off repeated Soviet attacks. During the afternoon of the 24th the enemy broke through the hastily erected Düna position in numerous places and soon had tanks across the river near Beshenkovitchi. Still, in some places the defenders managed to repulse the marauding enemy forces, which were engaged in encircling every German unit they could. An endless column of train units and divisions which had been in positions around Vitebsk streamed back along the Beshenkovitchi-Lepel road, the only one still open, under almost constant attack from enemy fighter-bombers. Throughout the 25th the elements of *Korpsabteilung* B already surrounded in Beshenkovitchi held out in extremely heavy fighting. That evening they were ordered to fight their way back to the German lines, which they did.

During the course of the day the situation for all of IX Corps became increasingly more serious. The 24th and 290th Divisions, which late that morning had been sent by Army Group North to provide some relief, had been forced to withdraw back toward the north in the direction of Polotsk. The corps' two divisions, already badly battered, carried out counterattacks and established blocking positions in an attempt to ward off the continuous enemy pressure and withdraw further to the south and then west.

The situation on the army's right wing, in the southeast where VI Corps was engaged on the land bridge between the Düna and Dniepr Rivers, looked even more catastrophic. The situation there on the first day of the attack was more than critical. Southeast of Vitebsk the northern attack group of the Third White Russian Front (18 rifle divisions, 9 tank brigades) achieved deep penetrations in two places. The corps' shattered front was driven back eighteen kilometers. Here, too, the fighting raged on through the night of June 22/23 and continued on into the next day without pause. Employing far superior forces, supported by heavy fire from heavy infantry weapons, mortars, artillery and multiple rocket launchers, but primarily by tanks and close-support aircraft, the focal point of the enemy attack lay further south, where the Russians broke through to the south on both sides of the Vitebsk-Orsha road. A major part of the available army reserve, the 95th Division, had to be committed. The division launched desperate counterattacks and tried to seal off enemy penetrations. The army had been forced to send the remaining elements of the division to hard-pressed IX Corps.

The evening and night of the 23rd saw events begin to follow in rapid succession. The Soviets had broken through the rear positions everywhere and in the northern breakthrough area were continuing their advance toward the north-west, west and southwest. In the southern breakthrough area, too, (see Fourth Army) Soviet tanks were already rolling into the hinterland, and the gap to the neighboring XXVII Corps was already 20 kilometers wide. Nevertheless, those German units still able to resist did so, throwing themselves against the overpowering enemy. However, with its front again broken during the night of June 24/25, VI Corps was in no position to halt the Russians. Outflanked in the north in the area of the highway and in the south near Bagushevskoye, it was forced back. While LIII Corps around Vitebsk had so far been spared by the enemy, there was already a gap of 45 kilometers between the army's left and right wings (IX and VI Corps), which was expanded further on the 25th. VI Corps was completely overrun by the Fifth Guards Tank Army following behind the masses of Russian infantry. Its divisions were smashed and dispersed, and all the bravery and willingness of the troops to hold out could not change the outcome. In the following days individual battle groups tried to escape to the west or fight their way through to XXVII Corps in the south. Harried by tanks and pursued by cavalry, the remaining elements were again dispersed and surrounded in several small pockets, such as at Schilki, where they were wiped out. The commanding general was among those killed. As of June 25, VI Corps and the reserves sent to help it no longer existed.

The Fighting around Vitebsk –
And with The German High Command

The Russians had now enlarged their breakthroughs on both sides of Vitebsk to such an extent that they achieved freedom of movement with their motorized units in the rear and at the same time turned their inner wings toward Vitebsk, sending spearheads from the northeast and southwest. The threat facing the city and the salient occupied by LIII Corps was obvious. It was now that the battle for the corps began – not with the enemy, but rather with the German High Command.

Feldmarschall Busch, who had immediately cut short his leave and returned to his headquarters in Minsk following the beginning of the Soviet offensive, was forced to recognize the threat facing his army group. Nevertheless, the *Feldmarschall* vigorously rejected the immediate evacuation of the Vitebsk salient ordered by Third Panzer Army on the evening of June 23.

Nevertheless, those "far above" saw the situation as so alarming that early on the morning of the 24th *Generaloberst* Zeitzler, Chief of the Army General Staff, arrived in Minsk himself. *Feldmarschall* Busch brought him up to date on the situation and requested the withdrawal of LIII Corps himself. Zeitzler refused, and only authorized a withdrawal by the corps' three divisions as far as the positions on the outskirts of Vitebsk. He was not authorized to do any more. Then the Chief of the General Staff left again by plane.

In the meantime the enemy spearheads had reached the Ostrovno area. Vitebsk, the largest city in the region was – as had been predicted – surrounded.

Now the Commander-in-Chief of the Third Panzer Army pressed, not for an evacuation, but for a breakout while there was still time.

In the afternoon Zeitzler called *Generaloberst* Reinhard from the Obersalzberg near Berchtesgaden, where Hitler was staying at that time, to see whether the proposed evacuation of Vitebsk was absolutely necessary. In a few words Reinhard described the extremely dangerous situation. Orders for the breakout had to be given now. With every quarter hour the enemy ring around Vitebsk and LIII Corps was drawing ever tighter.

Then another call from Zeitzler: The Führer has decided that Vitebsk is to be held as a "fortified place." The three divisions are to allow themselves to be surrounded.

A short time later a message from the commandant of Vitebsk reached Third Panzer Army, advising that the roads to the west had been cut, the city was completely encircled and that LIII Corps was surrounded. Once again the army's Commander-in-Chief pressed *Feldmarschall* Busch to give up Vitebsk. At 1610 the army group commander informed him that Hitler was standing by his decision.

The battle for the survival of LIII Corps went on. After several radio messages, at 1312 the already surrounded corps reported: Situation fundamentally changed. Completely encircled as a result of continuous reinforcement of the enemy. 4th Luftwaffe Division no longer exists. 246th Infantry Division and 6th Luftwaffe Field Division in heavy fighting on several sides. Various enemy penetrations into city. Bitter street fighting there.

Once again Third Panzer Army urgently requested permission for LIII Corps to break out, and repeated the request several times. Finally, at 1830 that evening, the army received word that Hitler had authorized LIII Corps to fight its way through to the German lines. At the same time, however, he demanded that Vitebsk continue to be held as a "fortified place" by a single division (the 206th Infantry Division) and defended to the last man. Now the "command," or more accurately interference, effected by Hitler from thousands of kilometers away took on a terribly grotesque aspect. Namely, he demanded that a general staff officer parachute into the surrounded city to deliver his written orders. Not until *Generaloberst* Reinhard declared that only he could carry out such an order did Hitler relent.

At 1833 the corps reported: Overall situation makes necessary a breakthrough toward the southwest with all forces. Will commence on the 26th at 0500. At 1930 another radio message arrived, asking for delivery of supplies by air. These were sent during the night. Meanwhile, following the receipt of approval the corps prepared to break out, if the complete confusion which reigned in such situations could be called preparation.

The 26th of June, filled with fighting like the day before, began with the rising of the blood-red sun. LIII Corps began its breakout. At 0830 a German reconnaissance aircraft reported the leading elements of the corps about ten kilometers southwest of Vitebsk. At 1210 *Feldmarschall* Busch sent another radio message to the 206th Division, ordering that all elements still in Vitebsk were to fight and hold out to the last man. It was the last confirmed radio contact with the city. Aerial reconnaissance reported German troops at various locations in the Vitebsk area moving toward the west and southwest. Fighting between small groups of German troops and enemy forces was observed at several lake narrows. Another report came in that there were larger German concentrations in the villages and woods along the road ten to fifteen kilometers southwest of Vitebsk, and that the area was the scene of fighting and enemy air attacks.

The commander of the 206th Division, *Generalleutnant* Hitter, had no thought of defending Vitebsk to the last man. On the afternoon of the 26th he reached the decision to break out of the burning, smoking city. Hitter's troops set out that evening at 2200, taking the wounded along in several horse-drawn vehicles and a prime mover. The assault teams leading the way failed to break through. They were intercepted by Russian blocking units and surrounded. A final charge with fixed bayonets failed. In a small wood the survivors were either killed or captured.

Late on the morning of the same June 27 a radio message from LIII Corps advised that it had broken through several enemy positions in continuing its breakthrough thirteen kilometers southwest of Vitebsk. The troops were suffering heavily from enemy air attacks and ammunition was running low . . . It was the last radio message from the corps.

The desperate battle by the remnants of LIII Corps, individual battle groups and smaller units, ended in the villages and forests fifteen to twenty kilometers southwest of Vitebsk. A few small groups were able to save themselves. Following long, arduous journeys on foot the survivors reached the German lines, where they described the fate which had befallen the rest of the corps.

On June 29 Soviet radio announced the end of the German defenders of Vitebsk – 5,000 dead in the city, 20,000 men killed in the desperate defense of Vitebsk and in air attacks, and another 10,000 who obeyed a Soviet demand for surrender. Among the latter was the corps' Commanding General and with him a small group of 200 men, 180 of them badly wounded. The end came quickly for the rest of the Third Panzer Army. With the loss of two corps (VI and LIII Corps) the army was left with two completely open deep flanks and only the remains of the hard-pressed divisions of IX Corps and the reserves, which were scarcely worth mentioning, having been formed from all available alert units and train personnel and the Artillery Weapons School. The enemy continued to advance, overrunning the hastily-established blocking lines and positions in the rear even before the had been occupied by the makeshift units which were thrown together or the few reserve units arrived. *Feldmarschall* Busch issued orders forbidding a further retreat, but it was no use, the enemy was too strong. The 252nd Division now had to pay the price for the army group's refusal to authorize a timely withdrawal beyond the Ulla River. Already badly battered, the division reached the river to find all the bridges gone. The troops were forced to swim across. Many reached the west bank, but a large number drowned. Most of the division was now barefoot, the men having lost their boots crossing the river. Many of IX Corps' units had already been cut off, surrounded and wiped out. Others fought their way through toward the southwest in the direction of Lepel – which the Russians entered late on the morning of the 28th – and further to the Upper Beresina, where they were picked up by the approaching 112th Infantry Division.

There had long since ceased to be an army front. While on the completely open right flank of the army the enemy continued to advance toward Minsk, enemy forces on the equally open left flank veered toward the northwest. The Third Panzer Army was thus separated from the neighboring Sixteenth Army (Army Group North). An attempted counterattack by Sixteenth Army was smashed at the outset by the Soviet Air Force. From June 27 there was a great, gaping gap in the north, which was steadily enlarged and which could not be closed, and which finally led to the isolation of the entire Army Group North. After five days of heavy fighting and appalling casualties the Third Panzer Army had ceased to exist.

The events of those days were described by an *Obergefreiter* of the 505th Army Pionier Battalion:

>"Our battalion was assigned to the 246th Infantry Division and built a spar bridge over the Düna between Polotsk and Vitebsk. The bridge was planned for the supply of the Third Panzer Army. The spars were already standing and the bridge was provisionally passable. The thunder of guns had been heard in the distance from the direction of the front since June 22 and there were many Russian aircraft to be seen in the sky. This did not concern us greatly. Enemy attacks on both sides of Vitebsk were nothing new, this had happened often in the past. The number of enemy aircraft was unusual though.

>On June 23, before it got dark, the *Spieß*[13] ordered us to fall in. The company commander, *Oberleutnant* Krause, appeared and reported on the situation: During the night we were to dig in at the north end of the half-finished bridge over the Düna, on which we had been working, to guard against its possible seizure by the enemy.

>I managed to snatch two hours sleep, then we moved out. The battalion staff was ahead of us. The night was filled with the distant sound of fighting, and the horizon was lit by gunfire, bursting shells and fires.

>The three companies of our battalion reached the bridge unhindered. In front of the bridge hastily moved in infantry and Luftwaffe troops were already digging foxholes. We, too, dug in. Out of a sense of urgency the bridgehead was established before midnight. Meanwhile vehicle after vehicle rolled across the bridge heading south. As we crouched in our holes facing north orders came down that the bridgehead and the bridge were to be held until all of the units had passed through and reached safety.

>Some time later we pioneers were assembled once again. 'To the bridge!' The flow of trucks, guns and horse-drawn supply trains across

the bridge the day before and throughout the night had left it in a sad state, especially since it had not quite been completed before the Russian offensive began. It had also already suffered damage from enemy air attacks. Our job now was to shore up the bridge for the new stresses it was expected to have to bear.

The first Russian aircraft appeared with the dawn and soon the first bombs were falling. Then more aircraft came. The Russian Air Force appeared on a scale never before experienced during the war. Bombs hailed down on the bridge, but fortunately most of them landed in the water. Vehicles continued to rumble across the bridge. Enemy forces were already around the bridgehead and these now opened fire with artillery.

Vast numbers of troops with their equipment were backed up before the bridge waiting to cross. Officers shouted and brandished their pistols, each wanted his unit to be the first across. Our company and the other companies of the battalion worked under fire. I was assigned to be company messenger and had to take the company's requests for material to the south bank, where the command post was located.

I can't remember how many times I crossed the bridge under enemy fire, perhaps ten times over and back. Dead pioneers lay where they had been hit, an axe, a saw or a hammer still beside them. I sought cover behind them. Several times I lay there for half an hour or longer, unable to rise, while shell fragments splintered the beams and hits tore apart the superstructure. When the firing abated medics ran onto the bridge to the screaming wounded, and I ran to the command post or to the work detail.

Late in the morning the Russians attacked with tanks. They were beaten off and were unable to break into the bridgehead. But from then on the T-34s stayed within sight of the bridge and kept it under direct fire. On top of it all it was a clear day with its roasting summer heat.

Still a continuous flow of men and trucks and horses raced across the bridge. Whatever was hit by enemy fire was tipped over the side. That evening the bridgehead was still holding but the bridge itself had become impassable for motor and horse-drawn vehicles. Under the enemy fire the bridge was being swept away from the pioniers piece by piece. Dead men and horses floated among the beams and posts, while wounded clung to pieces of wood.

'Pioniers fall in!' came the order. There were not many left to assemble. Those still alive took their rifles and disappeared to the south bank of the Düna. Hand over hand we crossed the battered bridge, which was hanging into the water and under continuous enemy fire. Now and again someone fell into the water or was wounded.

After us came the troops who had been defending the bridgehead. The rearguards stayed behind, however, and were shot or captured.

Great quantities of war materiel, horses, vehicles and ammunition had to be left behind. We could see it lying and standing on the north bank of the river, mostly intact and fully useable by the enemy.

Beyond the south bank we ran across an open field, pursued by enemy close-support aircraft. The enemy stood all along the north bank firing at us. The wounded were tended to but were no longer taken along. Save yourself if you can was the new watchword. The Russians were said to have crossed the Düna somewhere else and were already ahead of us. My friend Feichtinger and I found a motorcycle and sidecar and drove off across the dry, open plain.

The first Russian soldiers appeared, there was only a·few of them. But the enemy had in fact crossed the river already. We drove several more kilometers and spotted more Russians, about two battalions or more, ahead of us and to the sides. Their tanks swarmed out of the evening horizon everywhere, including to the west of us.

There was an outburst of rifle fire and our machine was hit. We left the motorcycle where it was, having no time to destroy it, and ran off on foot. Like rabbits before the hunt we raced across the field as bullets chirped all around us. There were many other soldiers with us. The enemy fire so intensified that one could not hear the individual shots above the whistling, there was just a rising and falling buzzing and whirring. When it became too bad I threw myself to the ground. There were plenty of others on the ground, but many of them did not get up again.

When we were out of the heaviest rifle fire there followed mortar and artillery fire. Despite all the losses more and more followed. Everyone who could get away did so.

Then several air attacks. Squadron after squadron raced over the ground at low level, fighters and close-support aircraft. They attacked with fragmentation bombs and machine-guns. I lost sight of my friend Feichtinger. I didn't know where he was, and didn't see him fall.

We escaped the enemy fire in the twilight, and the damned aircraft, too, left us in peace. Everyone was feeling the effects of hunger and terrible thirst, and the many stuck and abandoned vehicles were scoured for food and drink.

We assembled in a wood. Orders passed among the cluster of troops to had got this far. Numbers of units were called out. In this way I made contact my the company, or at least what was left of it. There were barely ten men from the battalion's other two companies. The battalion staff no longer existed.

Our company commander was still there, though, as was the *Spieß*. I'm not exactly sure how many there were, perhaps thirty or forty men. I searched in vain for my friend Feichtinger.

A large number of troops had assembled in the dark wood, at least several thousand men. There were also some soldiers from the divisions which had broken out from Vitebsk, some of whom had reached safety over our bridge. There were also many vehicles there and several tanks and assault guns, but they were almost out of ammunition.

A General came with several officers and informed us that we were surrounded. The Russians had crossed the Düna northwest of us while we were still holding the bridge. They had also come from the southeast over the land bridge between the Düna and Dniepr. The word was that at dawn we would attack in order to force a breakout to the west. Every soldier was to fight as an infantryman, no matter which branch of the service he belonged to. The infantry attack would have to smash a breach in the enemy lines, then the tanks and assault guns would follow up to complete the breakthrough. Our chances were good, said the General. It was expected that we would meet only light security forces. Everything not needed for the breakthrough was to be destroyed.

Before midnight the Russians began to lay harassing fire from artillery and Stalin Organs on the wood. It was impossible to sleep. I sought cover behind tree trunks, but had to constantly change positions, listening for the howling of incoming shells before leaping behind the nearest thick tree or into a depression in the ground. Wounded screamed. They faced the worst fate of all. Anyone who could not walk had to be left behind.

The morning of July 26 came and we assembled for the assault. There was no artillery to prepare our attack, as the guns and ammunition had already been blown up. We were told that we were to break through the Russian line of security in a surprise attack. All we had left was light machine-guns and our small arms. I still had my rifle with about forty rounds, as well my steel helmet and light pack.

Silently the soldiers, among them members of the Luftwaffe and Luftwaffe field divisions, walked into the starting position at the forest edge. Behind them were the Russian volunteer auxiliaries, men and women. What faced them if we failed to get through would be worse than death.

No medics followed the assault groups, there was no longer any sense. The badly wounded could not be taken along. Those with minor wounds were helped by their nearest comrades, but the more seriously wounded had to be left behind. Many of the decimated units went to the attack without officers, there were none left. Our company commander, *Oberleutnant* Krause, was still with us, however.

As it became light we left the cover of the wood and worked our way forward, creeping and crawling. On a rise we could see the heaps of dirt belonging to a Russian position. Those at the front leapt to their feet and charged the position with loud shouts. Everywhere behind them figures in field gray, blue-gray and camouflage uniforms stood up.

Enemy fire began to whip toward us. Shouts of hurray mingled with the screams of the wounded. The heaps of earth were like a fire-spitting wall. The first assault wave fell, the second hesitated and went to ground. The surprise attack had failed.

We worked our way forward in stages under enemy fire. Nearly every man who stood up was hit. The Russians were firing into our attack with rifles, machine-guns, mortars, anti-tank guns and, soon, artillery. These were no weak pickets. The enemy had obviously been expecting our breakout and had fortified the area during the night. A shell fragment ripped up the company commander's back. Luckily I was able to drag him to a small, shallow ravine without being hit myself. A comrade tossed me a packet dressing. I dressed the chief's wound, as I had done to so many others before. When the fire had abated somewhat, two of us puled him behind a bush and from there back to the cover of the wood. The *Oberleutnant* had been badly wounded and did not recognize me. I don't know if he survived his wounds and captivity. I saw him for the last time in the wood. He was a good officer. We left him with the other seriously wounded.

A Major I did not know appeared and got us moving again. My friend and I went back to the forest's edge, ran from its cover and threw ourselves down in one of the ragged skirmishing lines, in which living and dead, wounded and unwounded lay side by side. A new attack was ordered. A young *Leutnant* tried to lead the way. 'Let's go men, only another fifty meters! Everyone follow me!' A number of men jumped up to follow him – and fell with him.

Individual soldiers repeatedly made attempts to work their way toward the hill. They were shot down or forced to take cover. Some tried to approach the enemy positions with hands raised, but they, too, were shot. Our assault guns did not leave the cover of the forest, probably because they had no ammunition.

Another charge, again murderous fire, more losses. We were forced to take cover again at once. No one made it to the top of the rise. All of those still alive pressed themselves into the ground and tried to find cover. Finally the enemy fire was so heavy that it drowned out the cries of the wounded. The Soviets were now firing on the slope with everything they had, even though there was no one left standing.

I lay among the dead, living and wounded under the blazing sun, not moving and almost without any sensory perception. I no longer felt my thirst or the heat. To stand up meant certain death. I lay there until afternoon, when the firing and bursting shells began to abate. The Russians probably realized that they were not going to be attacked again, because they had already eliminated most of us. Finally the firing stopped.

A little later I saw several soldiers to my right get up without being fired upon. Then I stood up, too feeble and shaky to still be afraid of surrendering.

I saw hundreds of dead comrades lying on the long slope. There were few complaints from the wounded, because most of them had been hit more than once, often a third or fourth time . . ."

The first days of the Soviet offensive had seen the army corps and all three armies and their corps rendered virtually helpless. There were no reserves and, worst of all, command was almost impossible. The effects of the lack of communication with the divisions, and even between these and their individual units, were disastrous. The heavy artillery fire and the ongoing air bombardment had destroyed the field telephone lines and much of the radio equipment. In the rear areas partisans destroyed the communication cables. With the constant battles of retreat new lines of communication could not be set up, and Russian transmitters interfered with long-range radio communications. Increased use was made of messengers, but these were usually forced to take circuitous routes, and most orders reached the units too late. Often the orders did not arrive at all, because the unit in question had changed positions or the driver had been killed or captured en route. Executive officers had the same experiences. On several occasions general staff officers or even generals were forced brave the threat of enemy fighters to deliver orders by Fieseler *Storch* aircraft. After June 24 the transmission of orders and the movement of messengers became even more difficult, and the strict command vital in this critical situation became extremely difficult and finally impossible. Practically every corps and division was fighting on its own. In the end unit commanders were left on their own and were forced to make decisions without the requisite knowledge of the enemy's and their own situation and events further afield. No one knew any more where their own troops were, how far the enemy had advanced, and so on.

Breakthroughs on Fourth Army's Left and Right

June 22 saw only scouting and reconnaissance attacks, which were repelled everywhere. A day later, however, the enemy offensive also hit Fourth Army, and by June 23 the Soviets were concentrating their efforts at two points. One was on the left wing, where the southern group of forces of the Third White Russian Front (25 rifle divisions, 11 tank brigades) attacked north of the highway against XXVII

Army Corps in the direction of Orsha, while the other was in the center against XXXIX Panzer Corps in the Chausy area, where the Second White Russian Front advanced in the direction of Mogilev with 16 rifle divisions and 2 tank brigades.

The attack began at 0530. It was unlike anything experienced before, even by the veteran Russian Front soldiers. Shells from countless guns of every caliber pounded the German positions. Meter after meter of ground was torn up, giant craters changed the landscape, everywhere there were shell holes and crater after crater. In this howling, crashing, roaring, exploding inferno individual shell bursts could not be distinguished. Obstacles were torn apart, bunkers and dugouts were flattened and buried, whole trenches were levelled, direct hits struck machine-gun and mortar positions. Artillery positions disappeared under gray-brown-black clouds of smoke, guns were tossed into the air, ammunition being kept at readiness exploded. Dead, bloody and dying men lay among the fountains of earth and muck which constantly sprang up. Those who survived cowered in their battered trenches and half-destroyed positions, scarcely aware of what was going on around them. Aircraft bearing the red star roared overhead, dropping sticks of bombs and leaving behind them walls of fire. Then the Soviet rifle divisions attacked. A few German troops stirred, automatically reaching for their weapons. A few guns began to fire, then the defensive fire intensified and grew heavier. Nevertheless, masses of earth-brown Red Army troops, escorted by waves of tanks, broke into the shattered German positions under the cover of smoke.

The surviving defenders fought bitterly and in some places repelled the enemy attacks. Penetrations against XXVII Corps north of Orsha and XXXIX Corps east of Mogilev were initially sealed off. However, the major Soviet penetration against VI Corps (see Third Panzer Army) on the land bridge between the Düna and Dniepr Rivers grew significantly. The enemy drove the 78th Assault Division of XXVII Corps, which was on the far left, back from the highway. That evening, in the face of the enemy's manifest superiority, the corps was forced to commit the only reserve still available to the army group, the 14th Division, in an effort to head off the enemy assault and at least prevent a breakthrough on the first day. The next day, however, when the Soviets sent in their massed tank brigades, the existing gap in the front to Third Panzer Army was quickly expanded to 100 kilometers. There were virtually no German combat units left in the gap. Russian armored and motorized units poured west virtually unhindered, advancing north of and along the highway. The elements of the corps already cut off were forced to fight their way back toward the rear positions.

In the center, east of Mogilev, two Soviet armies smashed the 337th Division of XXXIX Corps and achieved a deep penetration on the Rjassna-Mogilev road.

Once the first and second German trench lines had been stormed, the T-34s began to roll into the corps' rear areas. On the evening of the June 23 the Panzergrenadier Division *Feldherrnhalle*, which was being held in reserve there, was given the task of closing the gaps which had been torn in the defensive front, but was unable to do so.

A deadly threat which was to spell the end of the Fourth Army began to appear on the evening of the second day of the offensive on the army's left wing. The enemy breakthrough there was especially dangerous for the divisions far to the east on the other side of the Dniepr. A request by the army to immediately withdraw the divisions in the bridgehead back across the river was rejected by Hitler. As if to mock the troops there, Russian aircraft dropped leaflets over the front: We will get you the same way!

On the 25th the Soviets broke through the shortened, but still weak, lines of XXVII Corps in the area of Lake Orechi, forced the corps back from the highway and advanced across the PK road.[14] The Soviets thus gained a free hand west and north of Orsha, allowing them to move further west and south and thus threaten the entire left flank of the army. Bitter fighting raged day and night. In the area of penetration in the center the Soviets continued to attack in the direction of Shkloff and Mogilev in spite of all German countermeasures. When, on the third day, contact with the Ninth Army was broken north of Rogachev (XII Corps), leaving the army's right wing isolated, the entire salient east of the Dniepr was ripe for encirclement. *General* von Tippelskirch now decided on his own authority to evacuate the bridgehead, following Hitler's rejection of the idea on the morning of the 25th. However, this decision by the army's Commander-in-Chief came too late.

The main and secondary roads leading to the Dniepr, many of the latter little more than narrow tracks through marshy areas, were completely crammed with retreating combat trains and units of the various divisions. Enemy infantry and tanks broke into the retreat in several places, scattering units and overrunning rearguards. The leading Soviet elements reached the Dniepr at about the same time as the Germans. All high-level command in the combat zone had ceased. A radio message came from XII Corps: The troops are to fight their way through to the west – then the corps went silent, there were no more communications. While the retreating units were crossing the Dniepr during the night of June 25/26 and the following day, the Soviets were crossing the river between Orsha and Mogilev at the same time as XXXIX Corps. The last halfway intact division, the 25th Panzergrenadier Division, which had formed XXVII Corps' rearguard south of Orsha, fell back. By the 26th about half the army had reached the west bank of the

Cherkassy

*Battle in the pocket —
an artillery barrage.*

*German troops wait
for a new enemy
attack by the rail line
to Korsun — in the
foreground a light
machine-gun, behind
a heavy anti-tank
gun.*

*Column traffic in a
village near Steblev.
In the right
foreground the
pennant of a division
command post.*

Russian troops on the attack again — a large proportion of the soldiers are carrying submachine-guns. On the right is a Maxim heavy machine-gun.

Relief attack — initially the German panzer divisions bog down in the morass . . .

. . . the cold returns.

Supplies have run out — letters marked out in the snow with straw request an air drop of fuel.

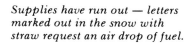

Preparing for the final advance toward Oktyabr.

Shenderovka, the "Hell's Gate," under enemy fire.

Men of the first breakout wave wait for the order to attack.

Behind, long columns march into their assembly areas.

Breakout to freedom.

Left behind in the pocket.

Some of the lucky ones who escaped.

Ternopol

The Russians advance toward Ternopol — a heavy gun behind an artillery tractor.

Passing one of the few German tanks, now disabled, Soviet infantry advance into the city.

Soldiers of the Red Army during a pause in the fighting. Their armament is typical — the soldier on the left has a submachine-gun, the one on the right an anti-tank rifle.

On foot, the panzergrenadiers fight their way toward Ternopol kilometer by kilometer . . .

Another relief attack — the Commander-in-Chief of Army Group North Ukraine, Feldmarschall Model (in background, left) accompanied the attack in the leading half-track.

. . . but in spite of their efforts the attack bogs down.

East of Chodaczow-Wielki a few figures appear out of the morning mist — they were the first fighters from Ternopol.

A wall of fire, smoke and dust —
the Soviet offensive against the
Isthmus of Perekop begins

Hasty retreat in the north and
east of the Crimea — a panje
wagon with wounded

Crimea

The final battle for
Sevastopol

Russian infantry fight
off a German
counterattack

One of the last German
defensive positions on
Severnaya Bay.

The small Khersonyes Peninsula with
the steep cliffs of its western coast and
the Black Sea.

Naval convoys still run
relatively unhindered to
the Rumanian
mainland.

Arrival of an overloaded
naval landing craft in
Constanza.

Minsk-Bobruisk

June 22 — German troops await the imminent Russian attack against the Third Panzer Army.

June 23 — Barrage fire on Fourth Army's sector of the front.

June 24 — Soviet breakthrough against the Ninth Army.

Heavy 75mm anti-tank gun in action.

Every village is the scene of bitter fighting.

Rearguard covers the retreat.

Trucks are blown up.

German troops from Bobruisk, picked up by the 12th Panzer Division.

For most there was no escape - long columns on the way to the prisoner reception camps.

The march through Moscow by German prisoners of war — leading the way a group of Generals . .

. . . followed by approximately 56,000 men.

"Rückkämpfer" — these lucky ones soon found their way to new German units.

Following behind the barrage were Soviet tanks and motorized infantry.

The German armored counterattack grinds to a halt under enemy fire.

Brody

Wounded panzergrenadiers take cover behind a tank.

The end in the pocket.

These two managed to get through . . .

. . . as did this group, seen on its way to the reception center.

Several "Rückkämpfer" report to General Lange.

Russian preparatory fire in the Jassy area.

Kishinev-Jassy

A Soviet anti-tank gun supports an attack by infantry.

Following enemy breakthroughs further resistance was mounted from the intermediate positions.

A shell bursts among a group of charging Soviet soldiers.

A Russian tank breaks into a contested village.

Tall pillars of smoke indicate the destruction of vehicles and equipment.

The bitter road into captivity.

Dniepr. The prepared positions there[15] could not be held on account of the hotly-pursuing enemy. In the morning hours of the 27th the Dniepr position was blown up.

On June 26, with the army group's position worsening by the hour (as well as that of the Third Panzer Army and the Ninth Army), *Feldmarschall* Busch flew to Führer Headquarters at Rastenburg, East Prussia, where he reported to Hitler. The latter approved a withdrawal in stages by the Fourth Army toward the Beresina, but insisted that the "fortified places" Orsha and Mogilev be held. There was no longer any question of the two cities being held – Orsha, the transportation center, fell into Russian hands that evening, before the Germans could organize a defense. The last transport trains carrying wounded and Wehrmacht materiel just managed to escape before the city was encircled. They did not get far, however. A few kilometers beyond the city twenty-five trains were caught by Soviet tanks and shot to pieces. The weak garrison of Mogilev (elements of the 31st Infantry Division) went down to defeat the next day.

And still the weight of the Russian attack increased. On the 27th enemy armored and motorized units drove west through the wide-open front north of XXVII Corps as far as just east of Borisov on the Upper Beresina. Near Tolotchin the Soviets veered southeast across the highway into Fourth Army's deep, open flank. The army now ordered an accelerated withdrawal to the Beresina.

Retreat to the Beresina –
The Russian Air Force Commands the Sky

That same day the battered divisions of XXVII Corps pressed themselves together into a sort of "wandering pocket" in the area south of Orsha, while near Mogilev XXXIX Corps sought to assemble what forces it had left, and the wreckage of XII Corps set itself in motion from the Rogatchev area. To the Beresina – that was clear. However, the general direction of the retreat was already being dictated by the enemy. In the north the Soviets had seized the highway and were pressing from that direction, while from the south (Ninth Army) they were advancing up both sides of the Lower Beresina and had already reached Osipovichi. Thus the retreat to the Beresina could only lead through Beresino and the major road bridge there on the Mogilev-Minsk road.

The distance to the Beresina was about 200 kilometers. And if there had been no defensive line on the west side of the Dniepr, then surely there would be one behind the Beresina – or so the Generals, officers and men believed, hoped and expected. The mass of troops moved out, with the remnants of the surviving divisions forming the core, followed and accompanied by army and corps units, train units, rear services and countless numbers of men separated from their units.

This was no longer a retirement, not an orderly withdrawal, rather a mass of men hysterically fighting their way back through an extended area of forests and swamps, crisscrossed by many rivers and streams whose crossings had already been destroyed, over mostly poor roads, in tremendous heat, without adequate provisions, and threatened from all sides. Soon assailed from the flanks and pursued from the rear, the decimated regiments and battle groups had to hold off well-armed partisan bands and regular troops of the Red Army, cover and protect the main column, and fight their way through Soviet blocking positions. Soviet tanks with mounted infantry were often faster, overtaking and positioning themselves in the path of the retreat, driving through individual march groups, scattering columns, seeking to cut off and trap them. Soviet close-support aircraft repeatedly strafed the defenceless foot and horse-drawn columns by day and bombed them by night. There were no German aircraft to be seen.

German-speaking Russians in uniforms taken from captured German officers appeared. These tried to assemble stragglers and send them in the wrong direction or divert the columns so as to weaken the already limited cohesion of the German forces, spread confusion and finally deliver them up to Soviet troops. On many occasions German troops threatened to shoot unfamiliar officers in German uniforms who tried to give them orders, suspecting them to be disguised Russians.

The retreat was marked by fire and smoke, seesaw battles for woods, stream beds and hills, vicious, costly battles on roads and paths and for villages and river crossings, roaring tank cannon, crackling rifle fire, the roar of low-flying aircraft, the rattle of aircraft machine-guns, the crump of exploding bombs, machine-gun and anti-tank fire from the forests. The brief summer nights were colored red by the many fires, and everywhere there were confused, panicky groups of men and vehicles.

On the 28th and 29th German forces had to capture crossing sites on the Drut River so that bridges could be built. On the evening of the following day the Osslik was reached, and as the bridges there had already been destroyed, it had to be forded. On to the Beresina, across the river to where German troops were supposed to be waiting . . .

The minuscule numbers of fresh troops arriving were far too little and too late. They were supposed to strike out toward the remains of the army and form solid pillars against the flood of the onrushing enemy – but this move succeeded for only a few days. When Russian tanks advanced on Borisov on June 27, they were slowed down and halted briefly by the 5th Panzer Division, which had just detrained there. The division, together with those forces that could be scraped together – including companies of the Pionier-Lehr Battalion, police units, and so on – was then sent to a bridgehead on the highway near Borisov to temporarily hold the area east of Minsk. For the army group, which was facing annihilation, this was of little significance. The 12th Panzer Division of the Ninth Army also arrived. Attacking from the area southeast of Minsk it achieved limited success (see Ninth Army).

One other event from the already threatened deep rear of the Fourth Army is worthy of note: At the end of June *General* Flörke[16], on orders from the army command, established a blocking position east of Minsk with the scraped-together remains of various units. The position was held until July 3. Flörke and his troops were unable to prevent the encirclement of the army, which was imminent, but they did allow Minsk and its hospitals to be evacuated. On July 1 and 2, 8,000 wounded left the city. Three hospital and forty-three evacuation trains carried about 12,000 rear echelon Wehrmacht personnel, including a large number of female auxiliaries, to the west. Then the Russians arrived. On July 3 they entered the undefended capital city of White Russia. Battle Group Flörke, which was still trying to escape south of Minsk, was caught by the enemy and dispersed, and most of the rearguards were killed.

Already caught between the enemy spearheads from north and south, the only direction left to the main body of the Fourth Army was toward Beresino. As of July 1 German troops were in fact holding a bridgehead east of the river.[17] The columns which had managed to fight their way back to the bridgehead streamed in from different directions, lining up one behind the other to cross the long bridge over the Beresina. Although a second span and a foot bridge for the infantry had been built, it took days for the accumulated mass to get across. And while the pursuing enemy came ever closer, and began to attack from the south, the Soviet Air Force mounted continuous strafing and bombing attacks on the stationary masses of troops and vehicles. From time to time the bridge was hit by bombs and rendered unusable until repaired by the pioneers. The scenes there were indescribable. Officers drove their troops, trying to get the decimated units across the bridge as quickly as possible, motor vehicles pushed forward recklessly, horse-drawn vehicles became inextricably entangled, drivers shouted, teams of horses bolted. There were burning trucks everywhere, as well as tanks and guns which had been blown up, bleeding and dying men and the bodies of horses. It was complete chaos and the overriding sentiment was: save yourself if you can!

The following description was provided by a survivor of the crossing at Beresino:[18]

"No one was safe from the Russian aircraft. We moved along the 'highway' toward the Beresina bridge. The close-support aircraft visited this 'highway' at brief intervals and pounded the columns which were bunched together.

We moved on another three kilometers to a point just short of the bridge near Beresino. There everything stopped. An incredible mass of every possible type of vehicle: horse-drawn and motorized, cannon, howitzers, supply train vehicles, assault guns, tanks, light and heavy anti-aircraft guns – column after column on the 'highway' in front of the bridge one behind the other, beside one another, left and right of the road up to 100 meters to the side. Everything was striving toward the bridge. Just get to the other side! But first we had to pass through this dangerous place. The later one crossed, the more dangerous the operation. To be over there! – Safe and sound! We imagined we would be safe there, in so far as one could speak of safety in war, especially in our desperate situation. We worked our way forward. 300 meters to the bridge! The bridge itself lay under constant fire from artillery and aircraft. We were forced to wait. There was no moving forward in this crush. The aircraft returned, about 20 of them. They strafed the lines of vehicles and dropped large numbers of small bombs, most with delayed action fuses. To our left dirt whirled high from the explosions. They had us square in their sights. There was no cover. The drivers had to stay with their horses on the road. The animals sensed what was happening. We lay flat beside the road, pressed close to the ground, which was quite flat. We tried to scratch into the earth with our fingers in an effort to find some cover. Bullets whistled! Bombs burst all around us! Fragments whirred and hissed. It was difficult to imagine not being hit. A minute there seemed like an eternity. All the while the Red Air Force remained overhead, showering us with bombs. Yes, one needed a foxhole . . ."

And another description:

"There were many assault guns, tanks light and heavy artillery and vehicles, out of fuel, blown up, burnt out, bombed. Close to the bridge, where the crush was greatest, scenes like none I had seen before were played out. Vehicles pressed toward the bridge from all directions, each one trying to be first across. This obstacle had to be passed as quickly as possible. How much longer would the bridge be standing? Seconds, moments, even longer? The next artillery salvo could bring it down for good. Drivers were given orders not to allow any strange vehicles into their columns, and they were told not to stop. About ten columns pressed toward the bridge side by side; however, only one could cross at a time. The vehicles on the 'highway' had intentions of being the first across. There was cursing and fighting. One horse-drawn wagon drove into another. Wheels broke. More wrecks were added to the vehicles already destroyed. The military police were powerless. Finally everyone ran for his own life. The bridge had to be crossed! . . ."

About 13 kilometers north of Beresino, near Zhukovets, the 110th Division had built its own bridge, over which crossed elements of XXVII Corps.

The main bridge near Beresino was blown at about 2000 on the evening of July 2, after the last rearguards had fought their way back from the bridgehead. Further stragglers and small groups of troops arrived the next day and were ferried across by pioneers.

Those who had made it across the river now experienced their next bitter disappointment. There was no defensive line there, no prepared positions occupied by German troops. Even the hopes that they would be beyond the grasp of the Soviets on the west side were dashed. As the last elements were crossing the river, to the north near Borisov the 5th Panzer Division was being forced back. On June 30 the Soviets had begun crossing the Upper Beresina at several places, and soon afterward their tanks were outside Minsk. Approaching from the south, where the 12th Panzer Division had also been forced to withdraw (see Ninth Army), by July 4 they had reached the vicinity of Tscherwen, blocking the corps' path to the west.

No Escape for the Remains of Three Corps

There was no escape. The end of the Fourth Army was fast approaching.

Without knowledge of the enemy's situation or that of the two other armies, without communications with its own army command and unaware that there was no longer any such thing as a German front, the remains of the army tried to continue their march. On July 4 the leading elements ran into powerful enemy forces in an area of difficult, hilly wooded and marshy terrain, about ten kilometers northwest of Tscherwen, still thirty kilometers southeast of Minsk. The Soviet forces barred the way to the west. The first attempts to break through, on July 4 and the following night, were unsuccessful, and the attackers suffered heavy casualties. The following columns soon ran into the rear of the stalled units. Soon the enemy appeared on all sides. A pocket quickly began to form in the Pekalin area in a triangle between the Minsk highway and Tscherwen (which the Russians had taken on July 1). Squeezed together inside the pocket, which was twelve kilometers wide and five kilometers deep, were the jumbled elements of eleven divisions, security units, army and corps units, trains, etc, including about four to five-thousand wounded. The situation very quickly became hopeless. The Russians poured heavy fire into the pocket. There were twenty to thirty enemy aircraft overhead at all times, and the forces in the pocket were under continuous air attack. Losses mounted. The last artillery rounds were used up in futile local attempts to break out. The infantry were also almost out of ammunition. In places the infantry had to leave their foxholes and attack with fixed bayonets in order to repel enemy attacks. The last hand grenades were used up. There was no more food, ammunition or fuel.

In this situation the Commanding Generals of XXVII and XII Corps (*General* Völckers and *General* Müller)[19] called all of the Generals in the pocket together for a conference. The result was a decision for an immediate breakout. The short time available was insufficient to restore order and assemble the various units forced together in the pocket. On July 5 *General* Völckers dissolved his corps and issued orders by radio for the units to break through on their own toward the west – general objective Baranovichi. But Baranovichi was 170 kilometers away.

During the night of July 5/6, beginning at 2300, the majority of the surrounded troops initiated the breakout toward the west, intending to bypass enemy-occupied Minsk to the south. The units encountered heavy defensive fire and soon split up into individual battle groups and other small groups. Overrun Soviet units in the path of the breakout soon regrouped and were reinforced by motorized troops. The Soviets then began to pursue the fleeing groups of German troops and encircle them.

Several divisions had launched a breakout attempt across the highway on July 6, intending to bypass Minsk to the north. The final breakout attempts ended on July 9. The German forces trying to escape suffered further heavy losses, especially at the hands of the Soviet Air Force. According to Soviet reports *General* Müller ordered all resistance to cease near Tschalin on the 8th, after the ability to resist of the units and stragglers with him had almost ended and there was no hope of reaching the distant German lines. All concerted German action ceased. Many groups of troops, large and small, nevertheless continued to try and make their way to the German lines through fields, forests, swamps and abandoned villages. Only a few men succeeded, however (see *"Rückkämpfer"*). Most were killed in hopeless battles, were murdered by partisans, starved to death in the forests or went into Soviet captivity. About 60,000 men, including 13 Generals, had been killed, captured or had gone missing forever . . .

The following are accounts of the army's individual divisions:

XXXIX Panzer Corps

Suspicions that an enemy offensive was imminent grew stronger from early May. Movements of guns and tanks, the construction of gun positions and the assembly of infantry forces had been detected along the corps' entire front. Poor observation conditions and the fact that the Soviets were maintaining absolute radio silence, contrary to earlier practice, prevented the formation of a clear picture of the enemy's intentions. Predictions as to the likely focal point and the date of the expected enemy attack changed constantly, until about the middle of the month when it became clear that the enemy was massing particularly strong forces on both sides of the road to Rjassna. The 337th Infantry Division which was deployed there was holding a sector of the front almost 40 kilometers wide. To permit a concentration of its forces, the 110th Infantry Division, which had been sent to the corps, was inserted on the 337th Division's left wing. Criticism grew of the senior command, which, instead of pulling Fourth Army back behind the Dniepr, inserted further forces into the salient, where they were in danger of being cut off at any time by an enemy breakthrough north and south of Fourth Army. None of the 30 assault guns promised each division had arrived.

On June 16 Russian artillery began laying down adjustment fire on the corps' entire sector, especially on both sides of Rjassna, where alone 120 enemy batteries had been detected. The Soviet offensive against Fourth Army followed on June 23.

Following heavy air attacks on many positions the previous night, at 0530 an artillery bombardment began which was so heavy that it completely obliterated the forward trenches, killing the troops manning them. This was followed by attacks against the corps' entire front by far-superior enemy forces. As expected, the main effort was directed against the sector held by the 337th Infantry Division on either side of the Rjassna-Mogilev road, where the Russians committed six to seven divisions with 100 tanks, supported by fire from 140 batteries, in a very small area. While the enemy managed only minor gains near Chausy and northeast of Gorki, at the point of main effort he was able to penetrate to a depth of six kilometers within a few hours. With the help of the only partially mobile and less than fully combat ready *Feldherrnhalle* Panzergrenadier Division, the Russian attack was held up temporarily at the Resta east of Suchary, without, however, being able to establish contact with the 110th Infantry Division, which had been forced to bend back its right wing north of the point of penetration. Russian attempts to roll up the 12th Infantry Division's front through attacks south from the area of penetration were prevented with some difficulty, but the 12th and 31st Infantry Divisions were forced to withdraw toward the northwest in heavy fighting.

On June 25 the enemy also broke through the Resta position. The entire corps now began to move toward the Dniepr between Mogilev and Kopys, while holding off the pursuing enemy. On the morning of the 26th it was still east of the river. The enemy was approaching Mogilev from the southeast and east. His air force completely controlled the air above the corps. By midday the Russians had crossed the Dniepr about twenty kilometers north of Mogilev, before turning north to attack the rear of the 110th Infantry Division and XXVII Corps still fighting on the east side of the river.

There was no longer any thought of holding the Dniepr Line. The divisions of the corps had already been smashed. Moreover, that which had generally been feared had happened – the enemy had broken through both neighboring armies and had set about closing the ring around the Fourth Army at the Beresina by launching rapid thrusts deep into the rear.

For the corps everything now depended on reaching the Beresina as quickly as possible. The corps' Commanding General, *General* Martinek, was under orders from the highest level to leave the 12th Infantry Division behind to defend Mogilev, which had been declared a 'fortified place.' Early on June 27 he ordered the 31st Infantry Division to withdraw toward the southwest along the rail line from Mogilev, and what was left of the 337th Infantry Division and the *Feldherrnhalle* Division to fall back toward the west on and north of the Mogilev-Belenitchi-Beresino road. The 110th Infantry Division, with which only radio contact existed, was to fight its way back to the Beresina with XXVII Corps. Until this time *General* Martinek had tried to lead his five divisions in spite of the loss of the communications network and uncertainty over the general situation. Now he was forced to leave them to their own fates.

At about 1700 on June 28 the *General* set out from Belenitchi in the direction of Beresino, where it was planned to set up a new corps command post west of the river. The road was jammed with fleeing columns, which were repeatedly bombed and strafed by low-flying Soviet aircraft. During one such attack *General* Martinek, who had taken cover a few meters from his vehicle, was killed when a bomb exploded nearby. A large fragment struck the general in the head, killing him instantly. Martinek was thus spared the pain of watching the final and total destruction of his corps.

Proof of the pitiless harshness of those days is provided by the fates of Martinek's two successors. Within twenty-four hours both *General* Pfeifer and the corps chief, General Staff *Oberst* Masius, had died soldier's deaths, which was unique in German military history."

The 110th Infantry Division
"When the Soviet offensive began the division found itself east and southeast of Gorki, defending a sector twenty-five kilometers wide. The main line of resistance

ran along the west bank of the Pronja. The unit was fully ready for action, morale and fighting spirit were good, all positions were well equipped.

June 22: At 0530, following an extremely heavy artillery bombardment, the Russians attacked on the division's left wing in the left sector of the 245th Grenadier Regiment. At the same time two containing attacks were made against the regiment's sectors in the center and on the right. In extremely heavy and confused fighting, which included several counterattacks, the enemy was beaten back with heavy losses. That evening the main line of resistance was firmly in our hands, and the enemy had failed to achieve his objective, the capture of the city of Gorki.

June 23: Continuing the offensive begun yesterday, after heavy artillery preparation the enemy once again advanced against the left wing of the 255th Grenadier Regiment. Despite the large number of guns employed by the enemy the division was able to fend off all attacks and in the evening was in possession of the main line of resistance.

June 24: In expanding his offensive the enemy launched heavy attacks against the entire sector of the neighboring division (337th Infantry Division) and achieved penetrations. In order to protect the division's right flank, the 321st Division Group[20], the 120th Replacement Battalion and an alert company formed from supply troops were sent into the Robotka-Kischisy area to screen to the south.

June 25: The Russians repeated their attacks against the sector to our right. Powerful armored forces (80 tanks) succeeded in breaking into the main defensive area. Immediate counterattacks by two reserve regiments stemmed off the penetration somewhat, but were unable to prevent the enemy from driving deeper into our lines with fresh reserves. Late in the evening the 110th Infantry Division was forced to pull back its lines on orders from corps due to the situation on the right. Despite heavy air attacks the withdrawal was carried out smoothly during the night.

June 26: The Russians began to pursue energetically. Thanks to their good motorization and extensive armored forces they were able more often than not to outflank and press the division, which was carrying out a staged fighting withdrawal. Especially heavy fighting broke out along the Orsha-Mogilev road. The road and the bridge sites near Schkloff were bombed continuously by enemy close-support aircraft. South of Shkloff the Russians succeeded in advancing up to the Dniepr, where they blocked the road with stout log barricades and mines. An attack from the south by assault guns under the command of *Generalleutnant* Schünemann of the 337th Infantry Division, which was supposed to open the road, stalled in front of this Soviet barricade. All the while the Russians were pouring in a continuous stream of troops, reaching the Dniepr and sending elements of their motorized units across before the German troops had reached the west bank of the river. The division commander recognized the dangerous situation. He shortened our bridgehead on the east bank of the Dniepr, took out the 254th Regiment and sent it across to the west bank by vehicle, with the assignment of establishing a southward-facing front and preventing an advance toward the north and northwest by the Soviets.

June 27: As the Russian crossing points lay outside the division's sector, the 254th Grenadier Regiment was able to reach the assigned area and occupy a defensive front there. In order to prevent further enemy forces from crossing the river, at dawn an attack was carried out against the bridgehead under the command of the regimental commander. The objective of the attack was to occupy the enemy bridgehead and prevent a further advance. The attack achieved the element of surprise and was completely successful. In the meantime all of the division's troops had been withdrawn to the west bank of the Dniepr. The 255th Grenadier Regiment secured to the east and north, the supply troops to the northwest around Schkloff. In the afternoon the 254th Regiment was suddenly attacked from the southwest in its right flank. The regiment was forced to bend back its right wing and establish a front to the southwest. This was done successfully. The Russians attacked the regiment's right flank all day with superior infantry and armored forces. Several penetrations were achieved, but all were cleared up by counterattacks. 1st Battalion, 252nd Grenadier Regiment, which was attached to the 254th Grenadier Regiment, was nearly wiped out. In an effort to reinforce the regiment a pionier battalion from another unit was placed under its command and the division's own 321st Division Group was inserted into the line beside it. That evening the division withdrew further to the west.

June 28-29: In the afternoon the main body of the division reached the Prut and crossed the bridges near Teterin. Late in the afternoon heavy enemy pressure developed from the southeast. The bridges were in poor condition. Columns of motor and horse-drawn vehicles backed up in front of the bridges. The enemy was drawing nearer. Toward evening the columns and the bridges near Teterin came under fire. During the night the division marched toward the west and southwest into the area of Shepelvitchi and south. There were ongoing battles with partisans and enemy motorized units, which had arrived in the division's rear. The division was still firmly in the hands of its commanding officer.

June 30: The first elements of the division reached the woods east of the Beresina near Zhukovets and halted there, as the division's 110th Pionier Battalion and the attached construction battalion had to erect a 16-ton and a 4-ton bridge over the river. There was constant enemy pressure from the east as well as tank fire from the north until we reached the Beresina. The bombardment and enemy air attacks lasted throughout the entire day. Elements of the battered divisions from the battles for Orsha and Mogilev had assembled in the woods east of Zhukovets. There were elements of the *Feldherrnhalle* Division, the 78th Assault Division, the 157th and 337th Infantry Divisions, as well as flak units, a tank (Tiger) unit and elements from Headquarters, XXVII and XXXIX Army Corps. Supply problems were great, there were not enough rations, the wounded could not be properly cared for due to a shortage of dressings and medicines, ammunition, especially for the artillery, was running short, as was fuel, so that all non-vital vehicles, which excluded tanks, self-propelled guns and motor vehicles for the wounded, had to be blown up.

July 1: The battered units assembled in the Zhukovets woods begin to move through. The main body of the 110th Division followed next to an unfamiliar division. In Borovino, 12 kilometers west of Zhukovets, an advance message center was set up by the commander of the 110th Signals Battalion, which intercepted all arriving elements of the division and attached units and, as per orders, directed them into the Borovino area. All other units not attached to the division continued on toward the west.

July 2: At about 1800 orders came that the entire train was to move on at once toward the west in the direction of the Minsk-Bobruisk 'highway.' The advance message center was disbanded and the division resumed its withdrawal toward the west.

July 3: According to a briefing by the Chief-of-Staff, XXXIX Panzer Corps, who was killed later that day, the division was supposed to break through on two march roads south of Minsk to the Ptitsch, where it would meet our forces. The southern march road lead through Dratshkovo-Kotjagi, while the northern one, which was also to be used by the 110th Infantry Division, ran from Wolma (30 km east of Minsk) to Kojaditsche. In the course of the late afternoon the division's advance battalion reached Wolma and established a bridgehead across the river of the same name. An order from XXVII Army Corps had instructed the division to hold the area for one day, so the day was used to further reduce the train and destroy superfluous vehicles.

July 4: Air drops of rations and fuel at 0500, but on a very limited scale. During the night of July 4/5 the division broke through toward the west. Its disposition was: advance battalion, 254th Grenadier Regiment, Division Headquarters, 255th Grenadier Regiment, 321st Division Group, artillery, anti-tank and further division units. The division reached the vicinity of Gatovo, 20 kilometers southeast of

Minsk.

July 5: Heavy air and tank attacks throughout the entire day. Following the successful breakthrough across the Bobruisk-Minsk road and the reaching of Gatovo, the advance battalion and the 254th Grenadier Regiment undertook an attack aimed at forcing the Soviets further toward the southwest. The attack was a success, but the Russians committed strong forces to a counterattack. A force of six tanks with 250-300 mounted infantry severed contact with the forward battalions and the regimental headquarters. Immediate counterattacks by the regimental reserve and remaining elements of the division headquarters were unsuccessful. There were attacks by waves of enemy aircraft, increasing in intensity by the hour. At times there were 30-40 close-support aircraft in the air. At the same time the Russians undertook an attack from the east from the direction of Gotwaskije against the wood 2.5 kilometers west of Gotwaskije.

All the elements of the 254th Grenadier Regiment, the advance battalion, two artillery battalions, train vehicles, vehicles carrying the wounded and the division headquarters had been squeezed into the wood. The other two regiments were still far behind. Intercepted radio messages revealed that it was impossible for them to fight their way through to the main body of the division. The wood west of Gotwaskije was systematically placed under fire by the Russians through artillery, air and tank attacks. Because of shortages of ammunition and fuel the division finally decided to destroy most of the vehicles and heavy weapons. One motorized column was kept for the wounded. As well, a column of horse-drawn vehicles was formed to carry wounded, which was to follow the division on the road.

July 6: During the evening the division, armed only with small arms, broke out to the west and early the next morning reached a wood 500 meters west of Kanjutschisy. The division planned to break through further to the west in smaller battle groups, taking the wounded with it. The artillery regiment and the anti-tank battalion, without guns like all the other units, now formed infantry-style battle groups. The only motor vehicle left to the division was a 5-watt radio station. The battle group of the 254th Grenadier Regiment and the division headquarters, with a total strength of about 400 men, remained in the wood the entire day.

July 7: During the night of July 6/7 the individual battle groups set out in a generally northwesterly direction and crossed the two 'highways' north and south of the Dzherzhinsk-Minsk rail line. In the early morning hours they reached a wood about 10 kilometers west of the rail line, where the units stopped to rest. The enemy must have spotted the battle groups during the night, however, because they surrounded the wood that morning and attacked from all sides. The battle groups initially took up positions at the edge of the wood, but when the artillery fire grew too heavy and losses began to climb, they broke out toward the west. In an unequal battle of pursuit the Russians drove the remains of the battle groups before them, attacking from all sides, until they had been completely scattered. The commander of the 254th Regiment was badly wounded and taken prisoner.

The little that is known of the fate of the individual battle groups following the complete destruction of the last somewhat intact units of the division comes from statements by soldiers who managed to fight their way back to the German lines. The majority may have fallen into Russian hands. The division commander, *Generalleutnant* von Kurowski, was last seen on July 12 together with 13 men, probably in the area of Lida. There are no clues to the fate of the division headquarters or unit commanders, other than *Oberleutnant* Reeder, commander of the 254th Regiment. Elements of the column transporting the wounded, namely 10 trucks and 15 panje wagons with about 400 wounded, were ambushed by Russian forces southeast of Minsk on July 6. According to reports by *"Rückkämpfer,"* all the wounded were shot. Days later about 150 men managed to reach the German lines.

Those elements of the division which had earlier escaped from the pocket assembled west of Grodno, including the complete 110th Workshop Company. Following a move to Chmielowo, near Stawiski in Poland, the survivors were counted. The assembled troops totalled 16 officers and officials and about 1,100 men. This included about 450 men who had been on leave or assigned to other units and had not participated in the retreat, as well as 350 stragglers from Personnel Replacement Battalion 110/4. Thus only about 300 of the division's men had escaped – from a total of about 12,000.

On its way to the 110th Division was Personnel Replacement Battalion 110/4 with about 1,400 men, which had entrained in Detmold on June 25. As the Stolpje-Minsk line had been blown, the battalion detrained in Stolpje, remaining there until June 25, when it was committed in the infantry role. Stolpje station fell into Russian hands and had to be recaptured, as a hospital train carrying severely wounded cases was stranded there. The attack was a success and the train moved three to four kilometers toward Minsk. Its subsequent fate is unknown. In the course of further fighting the replacement battalion was smashed and scattered . . ."

The 57th Infantry Division

Late May: "The division was deployed on the right wing of the Fourth Army with XII Army Corps on the Drut. In the division's rear lay an extended area of swamp and forest with strong partisan groups. Supply was possible only from the north, from Mogilev.

June 22: Beginning of the Russian summer offensive. Enemy attacks against XXXIX Panzer Corps on either side of the Rjassna-Mogilev road repelled. Still quiet in the division's sector.

June 23: A Russian reconnaissance advance against the division was beaten back and collapsed amid the barbed wire obstacles with heavy losses.

June 24: An enemy penetration on the division's right wing against XXXV Corps in the wooded area near Chomitschi. The 707th Personnel Replacement Division was sent to the threatened area. XII Army Corps was to remain in its present positions.

June 25: At about 0400 very heavy artillery fire on the sector of the division's right regiment and – extending far to the south – on the front of Ninth Army. A penetration on the right wing of the 164th Grenadier Regiment was cleared up. All available officers and men of the division command were set in march to the area of penetration. Late in the afternoon a medical company, the 'large' train and all other non-essential elements were evacuated to the west as a precaution. They returned unhindered.

June 26: A quiet day for the division.

June 27: At 1100 in the morning the acting Commanding General personally brought orders to evacuate the position when darkness fell, reach the area of the point of intersection of the Mogilev-Bobruisk road and the Drut and prevent a Russian advance from the south. All available elements of the division were sent ahead to the specified area to carry out the assignment. Two armored cars of the 18th Panzergrenadier Division were sent to the division and placed under its command. The Commanding General had already withdrawn the corps' other two divisions across the Dniepr on June 27 without waiting for orders 'from above.' An army pionier construction battalion was placed under the command of the 57th Infantry Division for the withdrawal through the swampy, partisan-infested forest region. Later, the division was to owe much of the credit for the success of its withdrawal to this battalion.

After issuing the necessary orders the division commander drove to the Drut crossing, familiarized himself with the terrain and deployed the elements of the division and attached units as they arrived.

The commander of a regiment of the 707th Security Division also turned up with one officer and nineteen men. He informed the division CO that this was all that was left of his regiment and went on to say that:

On the morning of June 25, while en route to the assigned area, the 20th Panzer Division's armored group had received orders to return to Bobruisk at once. The

707th Security Division was committed instead. Its assignment was to send one regiment toward the former border between the Fourth and Ninth Armies and another into the former sector of the 57th Infantry Division, throw back the enemy and retake the former front line. Late in the afternoon the division encountered weak retreating elements of the 134th Infantry Division about 30 kilometers west of the front line, which reported that the Russians had broken through on a broad front. A short time later the division was attacked by powerful Russian forces with tanks and completely scattered.

That same evening the 57th Infantry Division was able to withdraw without difficulty and during the night reached and occupied the assigned area.

On June 28 strong enemy forces attacked from the east and south without success. Early in the afternoon the acting Commanding General of the corps called the division commander and ordered him to break contact with the enemy, as the situation with the 18th Division made this necessary. In carrying out the order the heavy artillery battalion became completely bogged down in swampy terrain, was attacked by enemy tanks and had to destroy its guns.

In the days that followed, the division commander led the division in scouting missions, road building and battles with partisans as it continued its retreat, while the commander of the 217th Infantry Regiment provided exemplary leadership to the rearguard, which saw some heavy fighting against pursuing enemy forces. July 1 found the division continuing its withdrawal in the direction of the Beresina, after defeating an enemy tank attack the night before in which eight Russian tanks had been destroyed. When the division commander reported to the command post of XII Army Corps on the morning of July 2 he was told something like the following by the acting Commanding General: Two hours earlier the army commander had arrived in a Fieseler *Storch* and had handed over to him command of all units of the Fourth Army; however, there were few units left which were fit for combat. The Ninth Army had collapsed completely. That day the division reached the area twelve kilometers northwest of Beresino.

On July 3 the division resumed its march in a northwesterly direction, in an attempt to reach the highway near Borisov. That morning the spearhead of the division ran into strong enemy forces with tanks and assault guns on the north bank of the Uscha. The Fusilier Battalion and 1st Battalion, 217th Infantry Regiment went straight to the attack from the march and forced a crossing of the river, destroying several enemy tanks in the process. The two units had to be halted at about 1100, however, as orders had arrived from corps to break of the battle at once and continue the march toward the northwest, as Borisov had been given up in the face of heavy Russian attacks. When the division commander reported to XII

Army Corps, he found the Commanding General of XXVII Corps there and a large number of division commanders. Following lengthy discussions the rest of the Fourth Army was split into two groups for the resumption of the march on July 4. The right march group was placed under the command of XII Corps and the left under XXVII Corps.

On July 4 the division, as the only corps unit fit for combat, led the way as XXVII Corps resumed its trek toward the west. The scenes within the march groups were indescribable. Thousands of men from various units, railroad workers, members of the labor service, and so on, mostly unarmed, walked along with the division's units. The bridges which the division built over small streams were so blocked by these groups that our heavy weapons, guns and vehicles could not cross for hours. Late in the afternoon the forward battalion encountered the enemy. An attack was begun immediately, but could not be carried out as the heavy weapons had been left behind and the many weaponless soldiers from other divisions made command and the communication of orders impossible.

Under these conditions the division commander was forced to report to the Commanding General that an attack and a resumption of the march were impossible, especially since elements of the division had been committed against enemy forces approaching from the south. Afterward two further divisions were placed under the command of the 57th Infantry Division. However, only the two division commanders and their Ia Officers reported, as they had no units left.

The march to the west could not be resumed, and the march groups' rearguard was forced to engage the pursuing enemy in heavy fighting in order to prevent the march groups from being pressed together, suffering serious losses in the process.

On the morning of July 5 XXVII Corps held a lengthy conference of all division commanders. In the face of strenuous objections the Commanding General gave the order to stand and fight. During the drive back to their units the division commanders decided to act independently and break out toward the west that evening. At about 1930 a radio message from XII Corps was picked up, instructing that all the divisions were to be dissolved. All guns, heavy weapons, vehicles, munitions, and so on were to be destroyed, and small battle groups were to be formed, which were to try and break through in a southwesterly direction. General departure at 2230. As difficult as this decision was, there was no other solution. Orders were issued quickly. At 2220 our artillery fired for the last time. Amid the thunder of the guns our vehicles were blown up, and the last shells were used to destroy the guns themselves. At 2230 a mass of men, estimated at 40-50,000, rolled over the surrounding Russians, completely destroying them in their desperate rush.

Most elements of the 57th Infantry Division remained together during the march to the west. At dawn on July 6 they came upon the remains of the *Feldherrnhalle* Division, which had been part of the right march group. It had veered southwest between the enormous, water-filled craters of what had once been a German munitions depot. Strong enemy forces had dug in north of the Tscherwen-Minsk road, frustrating all attempts to cross the by day. Ceaseless air attacks unlike any experienced so far inflicted considerable losses. The two division commanders decided to cross the road in a southerly direction in two groups that evening, the 57th Infantry Division with all the foot troops was about 6 kilometers to the west, and the commander of *Feldherrnhalle* with the remaining vehicles, into which the wounded had been loaded, directly to the south.

The two groups moved out after darkness fell. The *Feldherrnhalle* group was unable to cross the road. It was scattered and suffered heavy casualties; most of its men were captured.

The 57th Division group, on the other hand, made it across. Once beyond the road the group, which was still 12-15,000 strong, broke up into small battle groups. Each tried to make its way as far to the southwest as it could as quickly as possible.

The march by the division commander's group, which had been the last to cross the road, lasted until the late morning of July 7. Two VW Schwimmwagen were still on hand, and these were used to carry wounded. The group determined that the north-south bridges over an open, eastward-facing bend in a river were manned by strong Russian forces and a rail bridge leading west was blocked by tanks. The group took cover in a large rye field, waiting for dark before resuming its march. Heavy fighting had taken place in the river bend, which lay about twelve to fifteen kilometers southeast of Minsk. It was agreed to meet at the western edge of the rye field when darkness fell and cross the river away from the road using the two *Schwimmwagen*. Exhausted, the men fell into a deep sleep, from which they were awakened at about 1700 by rifle fire. The Russians had surrounded the rye field and now began firing into it with mortars. One by one the small groups were rounded up. The division's remaining groups also got no further, and those troops who had not been killed in the most recent battles were captured south of Minsk on July 8 and 9.

Little is known of the other breakout groups: July 8: *Oberstleutnant* Rößler, commander of the 164th Grenadier Regiment, *Hauptmann* Müsse, commander of 1st Battalion, 164th Grenadier Regiment, and many of their men were killed in a further breakout attempt. Under the command of the regimental adjutant, *Hauptmann* Krefting, the rest of the regiment pushed on. *Oberst* Zunke, commander of the 217th Grenadier Regiment, went into captivity with the rest of his regiment, severely wounded.

July 9: *Hauptmann* Krefting, wounded, was captured southeast of Minsk with the remains of the 164th Grenadier Regiment.

Between the 5th and 16th of July the Denzlinger group (I./217 and attached units) was able to cross the Orsha-Minsk road east of Minsk and then turned northwest in the direction of Molodetschno. There the group was picked up as the result of an operation by fresh German forces. The 57th Infantry Division no longer existed. Until the evening of July 5, when the order to disband was given, every member unit of the division had been a willing, determined and capable unit in the hand of its commander . . ."

Panzergrenadier Division Feld*herrnhalle* (brief summary)
"Following costly battles with Army Group North, the division had been transferred from the Narva front into the Mogilev area to rest and recover. When, in the course of his major offensive, the enemy broke through north and south of the city, the division was deployed along the 'highway' leading to Chausy. Two days later, however, as Soviet troops had already advanced west past Mogilev on the right and left, the division was ordered back and given the job of holding open the road to Minsk. The division was unable to fulfil this task. Before reaching the Beresina near Beresino, the division suffered heavy losses to enemy air attack on a stretch of road blocked by numerous vehicles. The crossing of the Beresina led to further losses. The guns and heavy weapons had to be blown up, as there was no fuel left for the prime movers. The panzer regiment's Second Battalion was deployed to guard the river and suffered very heavy losses on June 29. Travelling in small vehicles and on foot, on July 5 the remains of the division reached the area southeast of Minsk. Completely surrounded by the enemy and hard-pressed by partisans, the regiments broke up into small groups which tried to fight their way to the west through the grain fields and forests. Most, however, failed to get through . . ."

The 78th Assault Division[21]
"On June 21 the assault grenadiers were lying in their trenches on both sides of the Smolensk-Minsk highway, waiting for what was to happen next. An enemy attack seemed imminent. Only limited enemy movements were observed that day.

The enemy air force opened the battle between 2155 and 0150 during the night of June 21/22. The bombardment, which was aimed primarily at the artillery, blanketed the main defensive area.

As the morning of June 22 dawned, an eerie stillness hung over the front. The enemy bombardment began at 0700 and the fire directed at the highway was especially heavy. At the same time the Soviet Air Force reappeared over the artillery positions and so plastered the batteries with bombs that some of them never had a chance to fire. The first attacks, which were made under cover of smoke, were reported only ten minutes later. The day ended without any great success for the enemy, but his attacks were viewed more or less as a feeling-out of the German front.

On June 23 the enemy went over to attempts to break through. During the night his air force made extremely heavy attacks on the main line of resistance and the rear areas. At 0100, under the cover of this hail of bombs, the enemy infantry moved into their jumping-off positions. Beginning at 0500, Soviet artillery pounded the entire main line of resistance, the command posts and in particular our artillery. All the while the Russian infantry moved closer to the main line of resistance, while tanks assembled close behind them. In spite of the furious enemy artillery fire the batteries of the 178th Artillery Regiment were able to open fire.

The attacks began at 0600. Waves of Soviet bombers and close-support aircraft dove on the main line of resistance and artillery positions. The front faltered in places. Counterattacks by 3rd Battalion, 122nd Infantry Regiment, which was attached to the 215th Assault Regiment, began. These were not always successful. Several strongpoints in the main line of resistance continued to hold out. Smoke laid by the enemy infantry reduced visibility.

An event occurred on the left wing, held by the attached 480th Grenadier Regiment, which at once illustrated the seriousness of the situation. The enemy had broken into the line there at about 0730, and soon afterward broke through.

Soviet battalions and regiments continued to attack all along the division's front. Penetrations were made against the 14th Assault Regiment, which could not be cleared up or sealed off by counterattacks, until an assault gun battery approached from the north and intervened. The situation with the 195th Assault Regiment was much the same.

The last reserves were brought forward. Alert companies were deployed. The assault pioneers arrived rapidly. The situation was serious as seldom before. The battalions nevertheless scraped together whatever people they could and counterattacked, one of which even managed to reach the first line of trenches.

The waves of Soviet tanks, about twenty per wave, were already advancing toward the west.

Late in the afternoon the division announced a new main line of resistance, which was to run along the second line of trenches – the artillery protection position. The position was occupied during the evening and night, but due to a shortage of forces was only weakly manned. The artillery moved its positions further to the rear. – The front held by the 78th Assault Division was seriously threatened by heavy pressure from the north (where the 480th Grenadier Regiment had been). Everything now depended on maintaining the integrity of the front and falling back in stages to establish a new, determined defence in the 'Tiger Position' north of Orsha.

The pressure from the enemy continued on June 24. There was still loose contact between individual units. However, between the right wing of the 215th Regiment and the left wing of the 14th Regiment, where the 178th Replacement and Training Battalion was, contact had temporarily been broken. Waves of Russian tanks poured through this gap into the rear of the new defensive line. This was the situation at about 1600 when the division was forced to order a withdrawal to the 'Tiger Position.' At the point of intersection between this position and the Pskov-Kiev road lay Lissuny. This was the Russians' next objective. Their tanks and infantry moved in from the northeast, but fortunately darkness fell before they could launch their first attack.

Throughout that evening and night the glow of burning villages on both flanks showed how far the enemy had advanced against the neighboring divisions.

By the evening of June 24 the deep flank of the Fourth Army was already seriously threatened. Further north the 78th Assault Division was still holding, and the withdrawal of the northern wing into the 'Tiger Position' had avoided the worst, but the situation was threatening nonetheless.

In the early morning hours of June 25 heavy fighting developed around the 'Tiger Position' and the Pskov-Kiev road. An enemy breakthrough was cleared up. A subsequent breakthrough against the neighboring division on the left was more serious, as it could not be sealed off. Enemy tanks were already hurrying along the Pskov-Kiev road, while others rolled across the road in view of the defenders and rumbled off to the west. The front on the division's left began to crumble. The situation on the division's left wing (480th Grenadier Regiment) would soon be impossible if the gap to Lake Kusmino was not closed.

At that critical moment the division ordered the two regiments in the north, the 215th and 480th, to fight their way back along the Pskov-Kiev road in the direction of Orsha, where they were to occupy a defensive line. The enemy ring around Orsha began to close.

The situation was becoming ever more confused. How could it go on? The men of the 78th knew only one thing – by pulling back they had frustrated the enemy's attempt to break through in their sector.

On June 26 Orsha was surrounded from three sides. The only way out left to the division was to the southeast. Orsha fell into Russian hands that evening, before the division's units were in the city. Hitler had decreed Orsha a 'fortified place' and the 78th Assault Division was to have formed its garrison.

The only way for the Fourth Army to reach the new German line of resistance, which it was hoped had been established further to the rear, was over the Mogilev-Beresina-Minsk road. The road became a guideline for the withdrawal, and north of it the 78th Assault Division was to fall back with XXVII Army Corps. The unit which began the retreat was no longer a division; it was only the remnants of what only a few days before had been such a steadfast formation. However, the men were still possessed by an iron will to break through and establish contact further to the rear. On June 27 the divisions of XXVII Corps assembled in Dubrovka, which lay about thirty kilometers south of Orsha. Heavy fighting had taken place the day before near Bryanzowo, where the division's few remaining assault guns had knocked out fifteen Russian tanks. During the course of the 27th the 78th, 25th and 260th Divisions arrived. Some elements of these units had had to fight their way through to the assembly area. This was the first indication of the 'wandering pocket' in which three divisions were to fight their way southwest in the direction of Minsk. That evening the division held a briefing. The CO described the situation and went on to explain that it was only a matter of hours before they were encircled and that the route they were following, over poor roads and its direction dictated by the enemy, offered no likelihood of the supply of ammunition, fuel or food. Taking along the many wounded was impossible or at best very difficult. In the interests of mobility the number of vehicles had to be kept to an absolute minimum, because the speed of the retreat was decisive for the fate of the entire force.

The time for frankness had come. Even the greatest optimist could not deny the desperate seriousness of the situation. Everything which might hinder movement had to be left behind. That the wounded had to suffer as a result of these measures was the most bitter part of all. All that mattered now was to get as many men as possible to the safety of the German lines, who knew how many kilometers to the west. The will to win through still existed – but it was opposed by the will to destroy of a far superior enemy drunk with victory.

The corps' retreat began on June 28. At about 0800 a Russian battalion broke through the German line of security in the direction of Dubrovka, causing a significant disruption in the withdrawal. Through the action of the division's heavy weapons and 6th Battery, 178th Artillery Regiment, the enemy was turned away. The line of security was pulled back at about noon and was set up in a circle around the site of a difficult river crossing. Due to the difficult crossing conditions the division ordered all vehicles left behind, as they were hampering its mobility. The

178th Artillery Regiment was ordered to destroy all horse-drawn guns, but this order was not followed in all cases.

The division started out again at 0400 on June 29. The advance guard soon ran into the enemy. Assault guns, Tiger tanks and escorting infantry attacked. The enemy was thrown back four to five kilometers and the withdrawal route was reopened. In this hard battle *Oberleutnant* Birk and his men captured three guns, six anti-tank guns, five heavy and twenty light machine-guns. Four-hundred dead Russians lay on the battlefield. The assault grenadiers were fighting for their lives and they made the Russians pay a high price. When the retreat resumed, with the advance guard now covering the rear, waves of enemy close-support aircraft appeared and attacked the columns with bombs and guns. Casualties were high.

When the division reached the Drut that evening the enemy the enemy was close behind. An energetic counterattack was launched to buy time to repair the destroyed crossings. The 25th Panzergrenadier Division crossed the river near Krugloye, while the 78th, 260th and *Feldherrnhalle* Divisions and the List Regiment of the 57th Division crossed further south near Teterin. The corps hoped to establish contact with the 110th Division, which was ahead of the rest, on June 30 and finally be through the enemy. Like so many other hopes in those days, this one too was unfounded. The 110th Division was not to be found. The enemy had already reached Borisov.

In the afternoon of June 30 the Russian broke through the march columns between the 260th and 78th Divisions about five kilometers west of the Drut. The division counterattacked and reopened the road. The sun burned down pitilessly. Close-support aircraft again attacked the march columns. That evening the division reached the Oslik, only to find the crossings there destroyed as well. Finally a ford was found, through which the division crossed the river. Heavy prime movers towed the lighter vehicles across. In Schnepelewitschi the division posted sentries and stopped to rest. A single village was now large enough to accommodate the remains of the division . . .

The adjutant of an assault regiment described the subsequent retreat: 'The Russians felt their way forward on the morning of July 1. Subsequently they attacked our thin lines from the east with strong support from heavy weapons. Heavy barrages and air attacks accompanied the attack. As corps rearguard, the division had the difficult task of defending its positions until about ten o'clock so as to give the whole march column a chance to get away through a forest west of the rest area. The forest was difficult to negotiate, with badly rutted roads and the way frequently blocked by burning ammunition trucks. The division carried out its assignment in bitter defensive fighting. The lines shortened as the rearguard slowly withdrew toward the forest. The division mobilized every available vehicle to rescue the remaining troops in contact with the enemy. The move was a success.

After a forced march we reached a strip of woods before the Beresina near Zhukovets, in spite of repeated Russian attacks and encircling attempts and heavy air attacks. Late that evening the troops stopped there to rest while the way to the crossing site was scouted. The narrow forest road was so jammed with vehicles and men that one often waited for hours, before moving ahead a few meters and then waiting again. Most of the assault guns, Tiger tanks and self-propelled guns had long since been blown up due to lack of fuel.

By the late afternoon of July 2 the bulk of the division was across the river. The units were directed to designated rest and assembly areas by the division headquarters staff, which had stopped next to the bridge. For the first time we were able to assess what was left of the regiment. Scarcely 100 men remained from those who had manned the trenches of the first day of the battle. It was likely that there were stragglers elsewhere, but the bulk of our people had been lost. By intercepting and commandeering men separated from their units we were able to form two weak companies. The strength of the regimental headquarters was now equivalent to a company headquarters in normal times. Excess officers were used to form mounted rations search teams in an effort to at least supply the troops with the most important items. In the meantime the enemy had reached Tscherwen and was now astride the main route of retreat for the remains of the Fourth Army near Pogost.

Early on July 3 the withdrawal was resumed, direction still southwest. Hopes were now that the pressure from the enemy would not be as great after crossing the Beresina. But at about 1100 the Russians were back. They launched a strong attack with fresh forces from the south in an attempt to seal off the line of retreat and finally smash us once and for all. In possession of the Mogilev-Minsk highway, which was in good condition, it was easy for the enemy to bring in new forces and throw them into the battle. The area where the enemy planned to complete the encirclement was west of the Beresina, north of Tscherwen.

In an effort to foil this plan a blocking unit was formed from almost every element of the corps. Its assignment was to defend a line of resistance about three kilometers south of the line of retreat until 1600 on July 4 and hold open the road until the arrival of the leading elements of the 267th Infantry Division, which was following behind the 78th Assault Division. Combat strength of the blocking unit was about 700 men, armed mostly with rifles. Ammunition for the few remaining machine-guns was very limited. As well there were two self-propelled 20mm guns. That was all.

The first Russian attack at 1230 was repulsed. The second followed at 1500 and was likewise beaten back. At about 1700 the Russians sent over two captured

German soldiers with a demand for unconditional surrender. The division refused. The makeshift front collapsed under the weight of the enemy attack which followed at about 2000. The troops streamed back, but were halted after one kilometer and put into a second line. The width of the thinly-manned line was about 800 meters. Ammunition was scarce, the fighting strength of the troops low. Only a limited amount of ammunition could be gleaned from the elements passing behind us. Losses were heavy. Nevertheless, no one thought of surrendering voluntarily. There were no deserters. Everyone still hoped for a way out of the pocket which was forming. During the early morning hours of July 4 the line had to be withdrawn again due to a shortage of forces. The new line ran along a village and was very favorable for defence. Between us and the enemy was a 400-meter-wide band of swamp. 500 meters to the rear was the road which we were protecting.

At about 1130 Russian infantry attacked on a broad front with heavy fire support. The focus of his attack was the village. We had already been outflanked on the right. The last reserves were sent in. House-to-house fighting raged in the village. Then the enemy took the village, the Russians were only 300 meters from the road. Our men fought their way back. Finally they settled down again and halted the Russians. The units regrouped hastily and launched a counterattack. The remaining elements of the 17th Grenadier Regiment appeared at this decisive moment and joined the attack. The enemy faltered and the village was retaken. The village was held until the leading elements of the 267th Division arrived. The two self-propelled guns of the 178th Anti-tank Battalion played a decisive part in the success of the counterattack. At about 2100 the regimental elements of the 78th Assault Division with the blocking force, which had been relieved, rejoined the division.

The division held a situation briefing. The remnants of about twelve German divisions and several army and corps units were now pressed together in a pocket about 12 to 13 kilometers in diameter. Powerful enemy forces blocked the road leading west. Repeated breakthrough attempts had failed with heavy losses. The few combat-ready troops from the various units manned the thin defensive lines at the edge of the pocket. The majority of the wounded, as well as the horses and vehicles, were in camouflaged positions in the center of the pocket. As well there were the corps and division headquarters. Deep depression reigned there on account of the hopelessness of the situation. The general fighting strength of the troops had been diminished by shortages of food, physical overexertion and lack of rest. The repeated breakouts from one pocket to another had made a deep impression on the morale of the troops. The anxious question being asked was, what happens now? A rumor spread that the combat units had been unable to reopen the road in spite of their great bravery. Under these circumstances the retreat could only be continued by leaving behind all the vehicles and dividing the units into small battle groups.

Appropriate orders were issued, and at 2300 on the night of July 5/6 the surrounded forces launched a surprise breakout in regiment-size groups. The objective was the German front which had been reestablished in the Baranovichi area. But as the remains of the divisions prepared for battle, they were unaware that the Russians had already been in Minsk for three days, in Slutsk for five days and were already in battle with the remains of the Ninth Army[22] thirty kilometers east of Baranovichi.

On the evening of June 5 a field kitchen turned up and issued hot rations to a regiment of the 78th Assault Division for the first and last time.

The final preparations for the breakout were made with determined desperation. Everything not absolutely necessary was left behind. The sick and wounded were assembled in the center of the pocket. They were to be surrendered to the Russians.

The troops formed up for the assault at 2300. Individual units began to sing the *Deutschlandlied*.[23] The survivors will never forget that night. Burning villages, howitzer and rifle fire, dull explosions mixing with the thunderous hurrays and singing of the attacking units. Enemy forces which tried to resist were overrun and thrown back. The breakout succeeded . . .

By dawn of July 6 the enemy encircling positions had been left behind. However, the scattered Russian units quickly regrouped. Enemy motorized forces arrived. The larger breakout groups were soon caught and surrounded again. The only chance was to break up into very small groups. There was uncertainty as to the enemy situation. Finding a way through an area heavily occupied by the enemy was left to the resourcefulness of individuals. The retreat had gone from pocket to pocket and had covered 200 kilometers.

The bulk of the 78th Assault Division, like all the other divisions, was listed as missing. the division commander, *Generalleutnant* Traut, was also posted missing . . ."

The Assault on the Ninth Army

The Soviet offensive against this army followed a similar pattern to those against the Third Panzer and Fourth Armies, but it was not until June 24 that they extended their attack further south to involve the Ninth Army. Probing and preparatory attacks on the 23rd had been beaten off. Then, however, it was the same as at Vitebsk, Orsha and Mogilev, only this time the destructive fire began at night, at 0230, and was concentrated on the army's left wing in XXXV Corps' sector near Rogatchev. For three-quarters of an hour shells of every caliber rained down on trenches, strongpoints, artillery positions and command posts. Scarcely a square meter of ground was left untouched. The grenadiers in their battered positions dared not raise their heads and the gun crews could not run to their guns. Field telephone lines were blasted and most of the radio equipment was knocked out – no more communications. Then the enemy fire abruptly shifted to the rear. At first light formations of close-support aircraft dove on the still-smoking forward positions. Then the enemy came – two tightly-massed armies of the First White Russian Corps attacked.

The remaining German infantry crouched behind their guns could scarcely believe their eyes. They had felt themselves relatively secure with the natural obstacles of the Drut River and nearby swampy terrain between them and the enemy. But now masses of Russian infantry came storming across the stream on numerous footbridges and Soviet tanks, which had crossed the Drut over under-water bridges, were rolling through the swamp over log roads.

Close-quarters fighting with the shouting Red Army troops broke out. The first enemy assault was repulsed, but the second broke into the German positions. Those who were still able fought back with determination. An example of this determination was provided by 3rd Battalion, 446th Grenadier Regiment (134th Division), which destroyed thirty Soviet tanks by midday. The other units also accounted for a large number of enemy tanks. There were successes here and there, but they were too little in the face of the enemy's overwhelming numerical superiority. The Russians made their first penetrations against the 134th and 296th Divisions, precisely at the boundary between the Fourth and Ninth Armies. Strong enemy forces began to take hold of the wooded area west of the Drut. Against this dangerous penetration east of Bobruisk the army command committed the only panzer division it had in reserve (20th Panzer Division). The panzers attacked that evening and achieved some success.

However the area east of Bobruisk was not the only focal point of the Soviet offensive. A second lay south of Bobruisk, near Paritschi, where a second group of forces with two armies had attacked XXXXI Corps on June 24 following a heavy bombardment lasting from 0450 to 0530 and had achieved a major penetration against the 36th Division. As the situation here seemed to be worsening, orders were issued for the 20th Panzer Division to launch a counterattack to the south. The division was turned 180 degrees and had to drive more than 100 kilometers over poor roads into XXXXI Corps' area during the night of June 24/25. The division had not had sufficient time to have much effect with XXXV Corps, and now it was too late to help XXXXI Corps. When dawn broke on the morning of the 25th the breakthrough near Paritschi was already forty kilometers wide, and the 20th Panzer Division was unable to prevent it, even though it destroyed sixty Soviet tanks. On June 26 the Russians reached the rail line south of Bobruisk. More forces followed and motorized units advanced west and northwest on a broad front. On the 27th Soviet spearheads were as far as Osipovichi. East of the Beresina XXXXI Corps and its battered divisions were forced to conduct a fighting withdrawal toward the north toward the Beresina bridges leading to Bobruisk.

In the north the Russians had forced a breakthrough against XXXV Corps on the 25th and then continued their attack toward the northwest and west with undiminished strength. Already they were threatening the roads leading to Bobruisk from the east. An attempt by the 707th Security Division to close the gap to Fourth Army failed. The Soviets broke through the corps several more times on the afternoon of the following day, and major German elements streamed back in the direction of Bobruisk. The enemy had already cut the major Mogilev-Bobruisk road, sent a strong force of tanks to Titovka from the northeast and blocked the bridge over the Beresina there.

The army once again requested permission for XXXV Corps to withdraw toward the north, while there still might be time for some units to escape. The army group's answer (based on an order from Hitler): Permission to withdraw is absolutely out of the question. The enemy was too strong, however, and events now began to develop like an avalanche.

XXXV Army Corps Encircled

On the east side of the Beresina, XXXXI Corps, which was withdrawing from south to north, sent the 20th Panzer Division ahead to seize the bridges leading to Bobruisk. The division was unable, however, to reach the bridges against the powerful enemy forces around Titovka. Only the railroad bridge about three kilometers to the south was still open. A tremendous traffic jam developed there as troops and train units pressed toward the bridge, under constant air attack. The raised approach to the bridge and the bridge itself were filled with burning vehicles and dead men and horses. Nevertheless, most of the foot elements were able to get across to the west side of the Beresina and into the city.

This was no longer possible for the mass of XXXV Corps. Withdrawing from the east, its path to the river crossing had already been blocked near Titovka. An enemy spearhead from the north grew stronger on the 26th and began to surround the corps. The increasingly surrounded, attacked and pressured corps defended itself on all sides, while other columns and elements of various divisions streaming in from the east strove to escape across the remaining rail bridge to Bobruisk, under heavy air attack the whole time. The area east of Titovka held by units of XXXV and XXXXI Corps was reduced considerably and the confusion in the forming pocket was great. The corps command was unable to restore order to and lead the partially-smashed, scattered units. There was no other course of action but to break out through the enemy ring toward the northwest, as there appeared to be no way west across the Beresina. Appropriate orders were issued at 1700 on the 29th, and the first still-cohesive units and battle groups set out against initially weak opposition. Luck was with the surrounded German units at the outset.

The same terrible scenes were played out over and over again. Because of the swampy terrain on both sides of the road on the east bank of the Beresina there was no possibility of seeking cover to the right or left. The units and trains of about six divisions, corps units and so on, assembled, waited, marched, then halted again. All the while they were subjected to hours of air attacks against which there was no cover or defence. The situation worsened as wrecked vehicles added to the congestion on the road. Losses were extremely heavy.

During the night of 27/28 June the Russians reported a major attack by 500 aircraft lasting an hour and a half on the German forces still in the pocket.

East of the Beresina the otherwise black night was lit by gunfire, tracing ammunition, bursting shells, exploding bombs and burning villages. When day came the Soviets moved in tanks and strong infantry forces, broke up the columns and largely smashed them on the 28th and 29th. The fate of one battle group, which included the corps' Commanding General, was typical. It was formed early on the 28th from remnants of the 296th Division. The group succeeded in crossing the Mogilev-Bobruisk highway that morning without interference. It spent the day in the area between the highway and the road which branched off to Podretschje. That evening, as it moved out across the road toward the north, the battle group came under fire from a battery of 122mm artillery. Most of the group were pinned down by the artillery fire. No trace was ever found of *Generalleutnant* von Lützow.

The remains of the units attempting to break out now assembled into small groups and tried to escape to the northwest. During the next few days most were captured or wiped out. A few small groups reached the Beresina north of Bobruisk. These tried to swim the river, believing that they would be free from the Russians on the other side. In some places, however, the Russians were already waiting on the west bank. Only a few individuals managed to make their way back to German units.

The entire XXXV Corps had been wiped out within five days. But there was still Bobruisk and XXXXI Corps.

By the 26th the Russians were already three kilometers southwest of the city, and the next day it was enveloped from the south, west and north. The Soviets had been able to completely surround the city so quickly because an undefended road bridge fifteen kilometers north of the city had fallen into their hands. Only a small bridgehead around the rail bridge remained in German hands on the east bank. For the mass of the cut-off XXXV Corps it was of little significance.

Another order from the army group on the 27th: 'Fortified place' Bobruisk is to be held with one division no matter what. It was the same as before at Vitebsk, Orsha and Mogilev: there was no 'fortified place' – no appropriate fortifications, no stockpiles of supplies, no powerful, cohesive garrison – nothing but a massive aggregation of men. Named fortress commandant, *General* Hamann, who was later hanged by the Russians, had nothing with which to conduct an effective defence.

The ruinous game of existence or non-existence was played out again. On the 27th the Commander-in-Chief of the Ninth Army again requested a breakout to the west by all the surrounded units. *Feldmarschall* Busch again refused and gave orders for Bobruisk to be defended to the last round.

The first powerful attacks from the south and west failed in the face of defensive fire from the 383rd Division, the 20th Panzer Division[24], assault guns and security units. During the day and the coming night thousands of soldiers, mostly stragglers from the east and from the army's rear area to the west of the city, streamed into Bobruisk, most of them without weapons, however. The night of June 27/28 was quiet. Heavy attacks began early in the morning from the south, west and northwest and lasted throughout the day. Russian infantry gradually reduced the outer positions and pressed toward the city limits. At 0825 *Generalleutnant* Hoffmeister, the "commander" of XXXXI Corps, who had moved with his staff to Bobruisk, radioed to Ninth Army: 383rd Infantry Division is engaged in fighting for Bobruisk. In the city are the commanders of the 36th and 45th Infantry Divisions and the 707th Security Division. Commander of the 134th Division has shot himself. Since dark on the previous day elements of every division have been streaming into Bobruisk in disorder, some without weapons and after destroying their heavy weapons. Flow across the rail bridge continues. No radio contact with XXXV Corps, which ordered all guns blown up. Request complete freedom of action.

Breakout from Bobruisk – Only 15,000 Escape

Finally, at 1250, word arrived from the army group: On rders of the Führer the 'fortified place' Bobruisk is to be abandoned, surrounded units are to break out toward the north along the Beresina. As so often before the order had come one or two days too late.

By this time, those in "high places" had already written off the men of the Ninth Army. This is reflected in an extract from Army Group Center's war diary from June 28:

> This morning's reports of the catastrophe involving the main body of the Ninth Army surrounded in the area around Bobruisk leave no doubt that the unit has no more fighting value, even if the intended breakout battles could be successfully carried out.

An entry in the war diary of the Ninth Army the same day read:

> The enemy ring around Bobruisk has closed. For practical purposes the army has ceased to exist as a fighting unit.

In the overcrowded city, in which there were an estimated 70,000 men, hell began to open up. Ammunition and food were running low, there was no water. A supply drop was made, but most of the canisters landed among the Russians. The wounded from the individual dressing stations were taken into the unprepared casemates of the citadel, a relatively safe location, which eventually held 5,000 wounded. They remained there with first aid personnel, as it was impossible to evacuate them. While most of the attacks were being repulsed and individual penetrations were being cleared up by counterattacks, the Soviets began to lay down an increasing weight of fire on the entire city area with artillery and rocket launchers, including numbers of phosphorous shells. Waves of Soviet aircraft dropped their bomb loads on the city. Groups of houses caught fire, supply dumps burned. In the meantime the Russians used a surviving telephone line to demand that the commandant surrender. In great haste the defenders tried to organize a breakout, which was to take place in three waves. The breakout was ordered to begin at 2300 and was to be made on the west side of the Beresina in a general northerly direction.

As the masses of men and machines were trying to achieve some sort of order, an almost impossible undertaking, the enemy artillery fire intensified. Whole areas of the city were in flames, black swaths of smoke stood out against the blood-red night sky, thick smoke filled the streets, roof frameworks collapsed in showers of sparks and walls crashed to the ground. Over a city sinking into an orgy of rubble and ash roared the Russian bombers. A stream of men fled into the northern quarter of the city, from where the breakout was to take place. Column after column gathered on the broad arterial road until it was completely filled. Among those waiting to break out were large numbers of men separated from their units, Wehrmacht personnel and lines of Russian civilians trying to flee the Red Army. Those wounded who could still walk joined the columns. Rumors spread in the terrible confusion and in some places there were outbreaks of panic. With great difficulty the first wave, with its combat units and spearhead, an armored group from the 20th Panzer Division, which still had several tanks and twelve armored personnel carriers, assembled for the breakout. Supporting this force were several self-propelled guns and ten assault guns.

By about midnight enemy fire and the sea of flames were reaching for the central and northern areas of the city. Then something stirring happened – all at once singing was heard in the burning, bomb and shell-shattered city of Bobruisk. Several began, hundreds joined in, and soon thousands of German soldiers were singing the song "*O Deutschland hoch in Ehren.*" It was a prelude to the breakout.

Tensely the troops waited for the breakout to begin. At about 2330 the advance units of the first wave began to move. The enemy had not yet noticed anything. After four kilometers, however, came the first Russian blocking position. Rifle fire cracked from the German ranks. With wild determination they overran an anti-tank position. After further enemy resistance had been overcome other march groups, often clustered into small groups, followed along the bank of the Beresina. Then it began to get light in the east and soon the Russian close-support aircraft were there, roaring over the columns at low altitude, firing their cannon and machine-guns into the columns. The columns split up and sought cover. The march went on – but not much longer. T-34 tanks appeared ahead and the few remaining tanks and assault guns took up the uneven battle. Soon they lay shot-up and burning at the side of the road. Nevertheless, the first wave fought on and advanced thirty-five kilometers toward the northwest, even though partisans in German uniforms tried to sow confusion among the columns and battle groups. On June 30, however, the escaping Germans were completely scattered by a strong Russian force coming from the east across the Beresina. The Commanding General of XXXXI Corps and the commanders of the 36th and 45th Divisions were captured. The remaining small groups of German soldiers continued toward the northwest. Most of them succeeded by various means in reaching the Swisslotsch area, where they were picked up by the 12th Panzer Division, which was advancing toward them from the area of Marina Gorka.

On the west bank of the Beresina the situation was no different than on the east bank. For unknown reasons the second wave did not leave Bobruisk until around midday of the 29th and was surrounded after five kilometers. Few escaped.

The last wave, which included elements of the 383rd Division, whose task it was to hold off the pursuing enemy, as well as many wounded and survivors from the second wave, was supposed to follow on the evening of June 29. Its breakout got nowhere, as the Russians had meanwhile completely blocked any escape to the north and west. Only a few small groups and individuals managed to get through.

The wounded suffered a particularly tragic fate. By June 26 many wounded were waiting to be transported out of Bobruisk, but there was no way to get them out of the city to safety by rail or road. Many of the ambulatory wounded left the hospitals and joined the breakout waves, others hobbled on crutches or even crawled in order to avoid capture and the certain fate of German wounded who fell into Russian hands.[25] About 5,000 wounded, mostly serious cases, remained behind in Bobruisk, as did many stragglers and the city commandant.

Frantic and scattered, the remains of XXXV and XXXXI Corps stumbled about for days between the Drut, Beresina and Swisslotsch. Only about 15,000 men[26] had reached the lines of the 12th Panzer Division by July 3, when it was forced to withdraw again south of Minsk. Those who had escaped were loaded aboard trains in Marina Gorka and transported to the west. Further losses were suffered in the overloaded rail cars through partisan demolitions and air attacks.

The number of German soldiers killed in the fighting, drowned in the rivers or who had succumbed in the dense forests and swampy lowlands is unknown. The Soviets claim a figure of 73,000 dead and wounded in the pocket east and west of the Beresina.

There was still the right wing of the army, LV Army Corps. The corps and its two divisions were cut off during the Soviet breakthrough near Paritschi, as was XXXXI Corps' 129th Division. The army group placed these units under the command of the Second Army, which was not attacked. The three divisions were the only ones of the entire army group to escape – but under what circumstances.

The 129th Division was forced to find its way through the difficult, partisan-controlled Pripyat Marshes. Beginning June 24, and for fourteen days, the division fought its way through swamps, moors, rivers and forests, marching great distances under the hot sun with little to eat, often over log roads and bridges built by the pioneers. On July 6 the division came upon a railroad with an empty train. The troops climbed aboard and the train headed off toward Pinsk in the west. The division was saved. The 102nd and 292nd Divisions withdrew through Ptitsch, Oressa, Slutsch and Lan. On July 5 the two divisions and the corps headquarters arrived in the area north of Luniniece.

The fate suffered by the Ninth Army has been described in many division histories:

The 45th Infantry Division[27]

"XXXV Corps directed whatever troops and combat units could be withdrawn from the units not attacked or still holding into the Rogatchev area, where the enemy had achieved a major penetration against the 134th Infantry Division. All that was left in the 45th Division's sector was the 135th Infantry Regiment, the 45th Fusilier Battalion and several artillery, pionier and anti-tank units. Everything else was hastily sent to the northeast to the Ninth Army's existing flash point.

The 134th Division's situation was desperate when the two battalions of our 133rd Infantry Regiment arrived. An overall view of the situation had been almost totally lost as a result of the tremendous enemy pressure. Employing masses of tanks, artillery and, in particular, close-support aircraft, the Russians had torn up the German lines, destroyed communications and surrounded many units in several small pockets. The newly arrived units struggled to occupy favorable positions, but were soon overrun, outflanked or forced to fall back by the irresistibly advancing enemy in spite of attempts to stand their ground. All the commanders could do was assemble their badly weakened forces for limited counterattacks and conduct a fighting withdrawal to new sectors where they might perhaps be able to halt the enemy. The extreme severity of the fighting was illustrated by the heavy casualties on both sides.

Despite all efforts the 133rd Regiment's battle group was completely encircled northeast of Bobruisk on June 27. Even though the discipline of the men and their officers had not weakened for a moment, here and there the first signs of despair were beginning to show in this almost hopeless situation, evidenced by the first suicides. No wonder: involved in heavy fighting day and night without interruption or perhaps only a short breather, almost no rations, bled white and completely exhausted, the men were reaching the end of their endurance. And still the Russians continued to drive into the fluid lines within the pocket, squeezing the surrounded troops into an ever smaller area. Once again the men assembled for a last, desperate breakout attempt. Patrols discovered a 'weak' spot in the Soviet lines, and it was there that the attack was to be made. The remaining troops in the pocket assembled during the evening. Their orders: break through in a northerly direction in two assault groups without regard to losses, leaving behind all vehicles and unnecessary equipment!

As part of one march group the regiment was able to move forward to within a few meters of the Russian lines unnoticed under the cover of darkness. When the enemy opened fire the battle group broke into the position with shouts of hurray. The regimental commander, *Oberst* von Horn, was wounded twice in the thigh and was captured. The men stormed irresistibly onward and groups of them broke through the enemy's deep zone in difficult close-quarters night fighting, finally reaching open terrain. The breakthrough was a complete success. The remaining men, scarcely 300 of them, assembled on the morning of June 28 and set out in hopes of reaching our lines. There were frequent firefights with partisans and Russian troops. Without food, and almost without ammunition, exhausted and worn out, they reached the Beresina. While the officers were developing a plan to cross the river, strong enemy forces once again surrounded the small battle group. Escape was impossible, further resistance futile. Bursts of Russian machine-gun fire decided their fate: it was captivity. Individual groups which had become separated during the breakout from the pocket also approached the Beresina and some – in the most dramatic circumstances – even managed to reach the far bank. This was the end of the 133rd Regiment.

The battle group under *Oberst* Kammerer, which had been formed from the newly-formed elements of the 130th Infantry Regiment and various other units, suffered a similar fate. It, too, was deployed north of our division's sector. Unfortunately no details have surfaced, although *Oberst* Kammerer is said to have been killed.

The division's sector between Paritschi and Plesovitchi was initially spared by the Russians in the first days of their offensive. Not until Sunday, June 25, did the abrupt beginning of an unusually heavy artillery bombardment announce the onset of the enemy attack. Enemy tank units, which had crossed the swampy terrain in front of our positions over log roads, achieved the first penetrations. Immediate counterattacks threw the enemy back. It was the last successful day of fighting for the 45th Infantry Division on the Eastern Front. Nevertheless, that same evening orders were given to abandon the position, as the enemy had already advanced to the north and west in the neighboring sectors. At midnight the two battalions of the 135th Regiment and the 45th Fusilier Battalion occupied strongpoints further to the rear. By morning, however, this position proved untenable as the enemy had moved in considerable armored forces during the night. Several companies were able to counterattack and hold, but the others were simply overrun by the crushing weight of the enemy. In a few hours the first Russian tanks appeared behind our positions. During the subsequent withdrawal the lack of any sort of communication between the elements of the division caused great difficulties, and orders and reports from the senior commanders rarely got through. There were confirmed reports on June 27 that enemy armored spearheads advancing from the direction of

Rogatchev and Mogilev had reached the Beresina bridges near Bobruisk and further west had cut the Bobruisk-Minsk road. That evening the division was still struggling to pass on a corps order, which instructed the divisions still east of the Beresina to break through toward the north at dawn on June 28 and attempt to make contact with the Fourth Army, which ostensibly was still holding a bridgehead there. It was maintained that there were only weak enemy forces in that direction. The order specified the area around Babino, north of the Rogatchev-Bobruisk highway, as the general assembly area.

The division's units largely succeeded in evacuating their positions during the coming night unnoticed by the enemy. The batteries of the 98th Artillery Regiment, which no longer had guns or ammunition, joined the various battle groups and fought as infantry. The 'highway' itself offered a chaotic scene. It was completely jammed with motorized and horse-drawn vehicles of every type, forming confused, and in some places burning and exploding, snarls. Worst of all, the Russian bombers and close-support aircraft attacked the packed columns without pause on a scale not before experienced. The foot troops fought their way forward past dead and wounded men and horses, shot-up vehicles and abandoned guns and equipment of every kind. Scarcely had they reached the designated area when an executive officer brought amended orders for the division: the breakout was not to be made toward the north, but toward Bobruisk! The remaining elements of the division were now to establish a defensive position in and around Bobruisk. The city itself had been declared a 'fortified place' on orders of the Führer, which was to be held at all costs, even if the enemy advanced past it on the left and right.

The nearer they came to the saving Bobruisk bridges, the closer the troops pressed together. The Russians had by now already destroyed the bridge built by the pioneers, and their tanks were firing into the city. In spite of this, many tried to swim the river, but only a few succeeded. Most were swept away by the current or sank in the swampy terrain along the riverbank. Other battle groups, which had not received the revised orders or had given up on a crossing of the Beresina at this location as hopeless, continued to withdraw toward the north. There too, however, there was no success. Groups which reached positions where they thought they had some breathing room soon found themselves surrounded again or faced by masses of Russian troops. The remaining elements of the division were soon surrounded in several small pockets. With their ammunition running low it was obvious that the end was near. East and northeast of Bobruisk one group after another went into captivity.

A few groups were lucky and escaped death or capture. Moving mostly by night, a group of about 240 men from the 133rd Regiment under the command of *Oberfeldwebel* Kiraly made its way back to Minsk, and from there to Dünaburg and German-held territory. Several other groups also withdrew in the direction of Minsk, but were forced to veer southwestward when threatened by Soviet armored spearheads thrusting toward the city.

An unpleasant fate awaiting the masses of captured German troops. The many wounded were put aboard primitive panje wagons, in which they travelled for days. Many died before the survivors were assembled in overcrowded Russian field hospitals. There was much suffering there and little medicine, even though the Russian female doctors did what they could. Although completely exhausted from the terrible days of the past weeks, the remaining soldiers were forced to assemble in columns of several hundred men each and were marched to a large assembly camp at Shlobin, receiving nothing to eat for three days. Once there the prisoners received their first food: thin soup once a day. Those who could tolerate it ate a paste made from common grass. In this way they were able to sustain themselves and avoided death by hunger and deprivation in the initial days of their captivity . . ."[28]

The 6th Infantry Division (condensed)[29]

"Apart from enemy artillery fire, it was quiet in front of the division at the beginning. Not until the Russian spearheads were close to Bobruisk was the division attacked.

On June 23, following a heavy artillery bombardment and unusually heavy air attacks, the Soviets broke through the thin lines to the north and southwest of the division. The gaps could not be closed. The 6th Fusilier Battalion had to be deployed to the north to protect the flank, and on the evening of the 24th the 58th Grenadier Regiment had to be pulled out of its sector and sent to help the 296th Infantry Division. When the 58th Regimental Headquarters arrived at the command post of the 296th Division in Koschary early the next morning, it received orders to occupy a rear position on the west bank of the Dobriza where it was to receive the withdrawing elements of the 296th Division. When the companies arrived they found that the Russians had already occupied the position. The enemy was thrown out and by midday the specified line was in the hands of the regiment. It was unable, however, to link up on the left with the 134th Division. The regiment with which it was to have made contact had been wiped out. As ordered, at about 2300 the 58th Grenadier Regiment evacuated the position, unhindered by the enemy. The regiment pulled back toward a new sector beyond the Dobyssna, under constant attack from enemy aircraft, arriving at first light. Once again, however, it was unable to establish contact with the 134th Division. Several enemy attacks during the day were repelled. In the afternoon the Commanding General of XXXV Corps came to the regiment, just as enemy tanks were spotted driving west. *General* Freiherr von Lützow expressed the opinion that what was at stake here was not just a local penetration against the 296th Division, but whether or not the Russian advance from the south toward Bobruisk on the west bank of the Beresina could still be stopped. If not, the entire corps would be surrounded.

On June 26 the regiment once again evacuated its position. The next morning it occupied a new line behind the Olsa. There 3rd Battalion encountered superior enemy forces, was unable to drive them back and was forced to withdraw. Further north Russian infantry units were marching westward en masse. A thrust by Soviet tanks against the rear of the regiment was beaten back by three assault guns attached to the regiment. At 1500 the regimental adjutant received the following orders at the 296th Division's command post in Krasnaya Dubrova: 'XXXV Corps is surrounded east of the Beresina. The corps will fight its way out toward the northwest to Bazewitschi on the Olsa, which is being held by units of the Fourth Army. Attack is to begin at 2300. Attacking on the left will be the 58th Grenadier Regiment, on the right a regiment of the 134th Division. All heavy weapons, vehicles, etc, are to be destroyed, the horses are to be shot. The men are to retain only their small arms! The army order on which this corps order is based reads: 'XXXV Corps will link up with XXXXI Panzer Corps in Bobruisk. Should this prove impossible, it is to break out toward the northwest and reach Bazewitschi.'

Behind the 58th Regiment the Rogatchev-Bobruisk road was already under constant fire from enemy forces south of Chernev and from tanks from the Krupitschi-Barak area. In the face of the threat of encirclement the regiment's commander ordered the battalions to pull back through Leititschi toward the edge of a forest. As the road had already been blocked by enemy fire, the troops had to swim the stream near Leititschi. Flanking fire from the north and south inflicted heavy losses. Near Dolgoroskoye the regiment went into defensive positions. As darkness fell, all around the scene was one of chaos. The series of detonations from demolitions, bombs and bursting shells was uninterrupted. Soldiers stumbled about everywhere, searching for their units. Once again the regiment failed to establish contact with the 134th Division. Nevertheless, at 2300 the regiment set out in the direction laid down in the orders. North of Welitschki it crossed the Mogilev-Bobruisk road unnoticed. Then the regiment found itself in a swampy area. The night was pitch black, and the need to skirt numerous obstacles made

orientation by compass extremely difficult. Early on the morning of
June 28 the regiment ran into Russian pickets at the edge of the forest
south of Morchowitschi. The pickets were brushed aside and the
regiment continued in the direction of Bazewitschi, which was still
believed to be in German hands, but which had already been occupied
by the Russians. West of Ljubenitschi the spearhead suddenly came
under heavy fire. The enemy had barricaded the edge of the forest to
prevent a further advance to the north. The regiment attacked and one
enemy position after another was taken in close-quarters fighting. The
enemy superiority was too great, however, and a further advance was
impossible. To make matters worse, contact between battalions and
companies had been lost during the attack in the forest. As a result the
58th Grenadier Regiment practically ceased to exist as a unit. Those not
killed, captured or wounded tried to escape in small groups.

The main body of the 6th Division (less the detached 58th Regiment) left its former positions during the night of June 25/26 as ordered,
in order to establish a new front beyond the Dobyssna River. The next
morning heavy fighting raged near the command post of the 37th
Grenadier Regiment. The regiment's CO, *Oberst* Boje, was shot in the
head and killed during an attempt to recapture a village west of
Kabanovka. His place was taken by *Major* von Ribbeck. He was killed
the next day. The 37th Regiment suffered heavy casualties. Several days
earlier the division's pionier battalion had built a 24-ton bridge across
the Dobyssna. In the evening *Oberfeldwebel* Möller blew the large
bridge on the Shlobin-Bobruisk road at the very last minute, even though
Russian tanks were on the approaches and the bridge itself.

With complete chaos in its rear, the division continued to battle
against increasing enemy forces from the northeast, east and south.
There was no longer any contact with 'above.' Finally, on June 26 came
a puzzling radio message: '6th Infantry Division is to blow up and
destroy all materiel, and rifles in hand fight its way through the enemy
in a northerly direction to the right wing of the Fourth Army near
Bazewitschi on the Olsa.' Early on June 27 the main body of the division
was engaged in heavy fighting beyond the Ola along the Shlobin-
Bobruisk road. As ordered everything was destroyed, including the still
intact and well-supplied artillery. A final briefing was held in Kumy,
about 20 kilometers west of Bobruisk, and the commanders were told of
the plan and assigned their objectives. As evening fell the division set
out on in an exemplary, serious manner on what was to be, in spite of the
confident conduct and mood of its men, its last march.

The 18th Grenadier Regiment, with a pionier company, an assault
gun and an anti-tank platoon, formed the rearguard. The division
stormed across the Rogatchev-Bobruisk road, storming enemy-held

villages which lay in its path. Men whose identities remain unknown gave their best. A *Wachtmeister* from the 6th Artillery Regiment shot the crew of a Russian anti-tank gun, which was barring the road, with his rifle, then was killed himself. His conduct was typical of many.

The division's route led in a generally northerly direction in a fold in the terrain. From the few areas of high ground it was possible to see the entire division, now strung out in a long line, its numbers steadily shrinking. The line of men became ever smaller. Once the Russians realized the division's intentions they sent their motorized units onto the hills to the left and right, where they set up anti-tank guns and machine-guns. From there they fired into the division and made repeated attempts to bar its way. The wounded had been taken along under the leadership of the division's medical officer, *Oberstabsarzt* Dr. Lorenz. It was not his fault that the horse-drawn wagons sank in the swamps. Dr. Lorenz shot himself after being wounded in the pelvis, *Oberstabsarzt* Dr. Schulz likewise after being shot in the stomach.

The so far cohesive breakthrough came to a halt at the Mogilev-Bobruisk road, where the enemy had hurriedly moved motorized and tank units into position. Following repeated, but unsuccessful, attacks, the concerted actions gave way to individual efforts. Losses were extremely heavy, many men were killed attempting to escape encirclement, while many others were wounded and taken prisoner. *Oberst* Höke, commander of the 18th Regiment, and *Hauptmann* Geisel, commander of the pionier battalion, were taken to a house, both badly wounded. Soon afterward the house was hit by a shell.

The spearhead of the remaining elements, which included the division commander, managed to cross the road and by the evening of June 28 was approaching the village which was the division's objective. As the units were quite mixed up, there was a hasty regrouping. However, before a clear picture of the strength and position of the enemy could be obtained and preparations made for an advance toward Bazewitschi, scattered firing from all sides developed into heavy fighting in the falling darkness. It was obvious that Soviet forces had been waiting or had rapidly been moved in. The fighting, which lasted into the morning of the next day, resulted in the complete destruction of the division. No further details exit.

The division commander, *General* Heyne, with his Ic, *Oberleutnant* Ahrens, and a *Gefreiter* reached the west bank of the Olsa, and there they were taken prisoner.

Several small groups of forces, including elements of the 18th Grenadier Regiment, succeeded in crossing the railway bridge to Bobruisk. One group fought a hopeless battle there for a short time, while another took part in the breakout from Bobruisk. The men who got through were assembled by the commander of the 6th Artillery Regiment and sent back to Warsaw. Two trucks were sufficient. In addition, a very few members of the division managed to escape through Russian-occupied territory. In a journey lasting weeks they managed to reach their own lines, which had meanwhile been pulled back hundreds of kilometers . . ."

The 35th Infantry Division

"After all attacks had been repulsed on June 23, at 0400 on the morning of the 24th the enemy launched a major attack following an hour-long bombardment on the division's sector, and soon achieved deep penetrations and breakthroughs. The next day the main body of the division was forced to withdraw toward the west, as radio communications had been interrupted and it had lost all contact. On the 26th the division was surrounded by far superior enemy forces near Osemlja (about 40 kilometers south of Bobruisk). After destroying all of its vehicles, heavy weapons, equipment and documents the division, with only its small arms, broke through the Russian encircling ring with loud shouts of hurray. It then withdrew to the Ptitsch, pausing briefly before setting out again. During the further course of the retreat the division fought its way through the Pripyat Marshes toward the southwest, constantly pursued by enemy tanks and its flanks threatened. Thanks to its great march performance a north-south thrust by the Soviets failed to cut off major elements of the division as they left the swampy terrain . . ."

The 36th Infantry Division (268th Artillery Regiment)

"On June 26 the Soviet offensive began in the division's sector. It mattered little that the division was able to hold its positions for three days with strong support from the 268th Artillery Regiment, the entire front of Army Group Center collapsed. This collapse also saw the end of the 268th Artillery Regiment. The guns and materiel were blown up at the Beresina opposite Bobruisk and rendered unusable. About 2,000 officers and artillerymen were taken prisoner. Of these only a few ever saw their homeland again, most dying in the prison camps of the Soviet Union. About 700 men were killed or posted missing. A few were able to make their way to their own lines . . ."

After only ten days this battle, probably the largest single one in history, was over. By June 28 the German Army Group Center was no more. The three armies which had been attacked possessed no cohesive and combat capable units worthy of mention, and a section of the German front almost 350 kilometers wide (in a straight line) had been completely destroyed.

Hitler and the OKH must have realized that the total collapse had been caused by their faulty planning and complete underestimation of the Soviets.

Once again Hitler needed a scapegoat. It was none other than the Commander-in-Chief of the army group, *Feldmarschall* Busch, the very man who had followed Hitler's rigid defensive concept and had forbidden timely withdrawals, and thus likewise carried a great deal of the blame. Busch was relieved of his post on the evening of June 28 and replaced by *Feldmarschall* Model, who was also in command of Army Group North Ukraine. But Model could not change what was taking place or save the army group; all he could do was try and slow down the enemy advance with the few new divisions he was sent. A new German defensive front was finally established 400 kilometers further to the west.

To understand how such a catastrophe could take place, here and elsewhere, one must look once again at the disparities between the two sides.

On the one hand were the numerically weak German infantry divisions, depending on horses for transport and thus possessing limited mobility, in linear formation in an unfavorable front, without any great depth of defense, with a handful of reserves, including a single panzer division, and without any support from a missing air force.

On the other hand were the Soviets, with their tremendous superiority in troops, guns, tanks and aircraft which permitted a style of attack which the German soldiers, in spite of their determination and will to hold out, could not withstand. Battered by masses of men and materiel, entire sectors of the German front were smashed and destroyed. Additional forces immediately poured through the holes and gaps in the front, expanding them into ever larger breakthroughs. Powerful armored and motorized forces streamed west, northwest and southwest without regard to their open flanks, driving into German units trying to fall back and cutting all communications, before turning back to complete the encirclements. In the areas near the front the shattered and isolated divisions and corps were squeezed together by continued pincer attacks until surrounded. The inflexible orders to hold on and the panic and disorder in the trains and rear-echelon units caused by the enemy threat made an orderly, mobile conduct of the battle impossible. The few unmanned blocking and security positions in the rear were also soon overrun.

The many partisans in the German rear vigorously supported the regular Red Army. They interrupted overland traffic, attacked whole units and columns from ambush positions, on occasion intervened openly in the fighting and generally made the German retreat significantly more difficult.

The Soviet Air Force, which completely ruled the skies, played a special role. Appearing in numbers never before seen, its bombers and close-support aircraft flew almost without interruption. They blasted mine fields and barbed-wire obstacles, bombed defensive positions and artillery, destroyed bridges and crossings with precision attacks and harried the retreating columns without mercy, sowing chaos and confusion.

The Long Way Back to the German Front

Countless German soldiers had been killed, wounded or had gone missing for good. Those who had managed to survive were assembled by the Red Army and forced to march to the great assembly camps, suffering from hunger and thirst.

Still, there were thousands who had slipped through the enemy forces all around them and sought to make their way west to where the German lines must be. Their watchword was: Life and freedom!

Those who tried to make their way through in groups large and small may have numbered ten- to fifteen-thousand. They set out from Vitebsk, from Bobruisk and from the large pocket southeast of Minsk. Their numbers dwindled rapidly, however, and in the following days and weeks the majority were wiped out. Many were not equal to the increased hardships and fell behind from exhaustion, many were surrounded again and most were killed by Russian search parties or partisans. An order by the Soviet dictator Stalin, decreeing that all fleeing German soldiers were guerillas who had to be liquidated, contributed to this state of affairs.

The survivors, the later "*Rückkämpfer*," sought to make their way through the once again Soviet-occupied territory of White Russia to Poland or Lithuania, always heading west and northwest. Those who could not go any further, could not endure or were wounded were left behind and died alone and abandoned.

The Soviets did everything in their power to catch the scattered and fleeing German soldiers. They sent mounted Cossacks to pursue them, set up blocking positions and intensified their aerial reconnaissance. U-2 biplanes, the notorious "sewing machines" or "highway crows," which were normally employed on night nuisance raids, flew search patterns by day and occasionally dropped leaflets produced by the "National Committee for a Free Germany." These urged German soldiers to report at once to the nearest Russian command and made the usual promises about good rations, fair treatment and an early return home. Sometimes these obsolete, but still useful, machines switched off their motors and broadcast German military marches from loudspeakers. This was followed by a message to the soldiers with a brief description of the military situation and a final exhortation: Your situation is hopeless – give up!

The German troops paid little attention to these promises, they knew differently from experience and had seen and experienced too much to trust the Russians. The most determined and fearless among them, those who wished to avoid Soviet captivity at any price, wandered on through the enemy rear in ever smaller groups and finally in pairs or even alone. Most hid during the day and travelled only by night, some still carrying their weapons, some unarmed. They occasionally ran into comrades, exchanged experiences and stories, travelled together for a time and then separated again to improve their chances of getting through. They avoided roads and footpaths, making their way instead through almost impenetrable forests and undergrowth, wading large swampy areas, sneaking through cornfields and thickets by night, lying in wait next to Russian advance and supply roads throughout the day waiting for a chance to cross unnoticed, swimming rivers, slipping past villages and working their way around Russian outposts.

Without maps or compasses they found their way using the sun, moon, stars and signs of nature. They were always hungry and often licked the dew from the grass in the morning to quench their thirst. These desperate, hunted men lived off whatever they could find along the way: green berries from the forest, ripening grain from the rye fields and half-rotten potatoes left over from the previous year. They ate wild plants and stole chickens, sheep and calves from secluded houses at the fringes of villages. Sometimes they received milk, eggs and bread from sympathetic villagers. They drank unboiled water from brooks, moors and pools – but they did not despair or give up hope. Things were somewhat better in Polish or Lithuanian territory, but the inhabitants were too frightened of the Russians to offer much help.

The most difficult part of the long journey, with its almost unimaginable hardships and deprivation, was passing through the Russian lines to the German front. A large percentage of the fugitive German soldiers failed to negotiate this last obstacle and died with their goal in sight.

Those who did finally succeed in reaching their own lines, bearded, completely dishevelled, often dressed partly in civilian clothes and scarcely recognizable as German soldiers, were received with comradeship, but also with a certain degree of caution and mistrust.

The "*Rückkämpfer*" were questioned and interrogated thoroughly and were required to provide accurate information, because there could be those among them who had been released by the Russians after being appropriately influenced and schooled to act as agents, spies or saboteurs.

Once it had been determined that they were legitimate, the survivors were sent to Schloßberg in East Prussia, where they were all assembled. Often little more than human skeletons, covered with sores and completely exhausted, they received the best possible care. There were representatives from many divisions and many ranks. The most senior was a *Major*, a wearer of the Knight's Cross, who had made his way back alone, walking barefoot at the end. The higher ranking officers had failed to get through, mainly on account of their age. Only a very few, virtually indestructible men, travelling alone or in twos or threes or small groups, survived the weeks of hardship and made their way through hundreds of kilometers of enemy territory to reach the German lines. All in all, no more than 900 men escaped from the various pockets in which the units of the army group had ended up. Several of them reported:

> "There was only a small group of us prepared to continue on. The next morning we camped in a large wood near a major road. We were tired, hungry and battered. What was more, almost all of our ammunition was gone. We were completely at an end.
>
> Then our *Oberleutnant* called us together: 'People, there's no more purpose! For us the war is over. We're far behind the Russian lines. The best thing for us to do is to split up and each man find his way home the best he can. I thank you for your willingness and wish you all well . . .!'"

And another:

> "From the approximately 250-man-strong group to which I belonged, there were finally only two others left. They, too, were captured, and I alone got through . . ."
>
> One of the many tragic fates was that of a larger group under the command of the commander of the 267th Division, *General* Drescher. Its flight was halted by the Njemen River, as too many of the men were non-swimmers. After attempts to build rafts from the willows growing along the river failed, they fashioned a chain from their belts. It must have been a fairly strong one, as the river at this location was 110-120 meters wide. Once the chain was completed, several swimmers crossed to the west side of the river with one end. Too many non-swimmers tried to cross at one time, however, and the end of the belt slipped from the hands of the men on the west bank. There was no time for another attempt, as dawn was breaking and the German troops were soon coming under fire from Russian sentries. The Soviets deployed motorized troops to attack the group, and in the ensuing combat *General* Drescher and his staff met their end.

The Story of One Man Who Got Back

"On June 25 our battalion (12th Reconnaissance Battalion)[30] was sent in the direction of Cherovski, as massed enemy forces were attempting to break through there. I received orders from the CO to take over the train and follow as quickly as possible. At about 2300 we set out in the direction of Mogilev. As ordered, I camped in a small wood near the Rostan station. We had no idea that the Russians had meanwhile rolled up the main line of resistance, and that our battalion had been forced to move into a hastily-established bridgehead near Chausy. Eventually, however, we too received this disquieting news. There was no hiding the fact that the situation was becoming 'ticklish.' Soon afterward I received an order by motorcycle messenger to lead the train to Mogilev, which had been declared a 'fortress.' With mixed feelings I set out as instructed, and soon we encountered a tremendous mixup. Vehicles of every type streamed toward us, only our battalion train was heading in the direction of the enemy. Then the report came that Russian tanks had broken into Mogilev.

It was now clear to me that we would never reach Mogilev. With a heavy heart I ordered the train to turn around and sent *Oberwachtmeister* Sch. off on my motorcycle to redirect everything in the direction of Minsk. I remained on the main road with the munitions truck, as I wanted to get the ammunition through to the hard-pressed battalion at any cost. Unfortunately, by this time there was no 12th Reconnaissance Battalion. It had been overrun by the enemy and almost completely wiped out. But I did not know this.

Trucks, cars, motorcycles and every other type of vehicle roared past us as fast as they could, occasionally colliding with one another. Anything that stopped was immediately pushed off into the ditch. The panic grew when, all of a sudden, the first T-34 rattled in from one side and opened fire into the tangled stream of men, horses and vehicles. Soviet IL-2 close-support aircraft flew over the highway, their fragmentation bombs and cannon adding to the bloody chaos. Here and there vehicles were already burning. We had to shove the vehicles in front of and behind us into the ditch in order to get moving. The wounded moaned and screamed. We were still taking them with us. As their numbers grew and the vehicles became fewer, the equipment, then the ammunition, and finally the rations, were thrown overboard. Nevertheless, there was scarcely enough room for all the wounded. The soldiers in this stream of defeat swore and sometimes prayed aloud, and above it all could be heard the howling of bombs and the roaring of tank cannon. More and more vehicles halted, burning and smoking, and our munitions truck was also blown up. Increasing numbers of wounded had to be left behind, and more and more wounded men lay on the highway, which had become a mass grave.

I realized that there was only one chance: get away from the road. The enemy had already overtaken us on the left and right. Quite automatically, march groups formed. Men from all branches of the service formed up around an officer or NCO and set out cross-country toward the still-fighting German front, whose dull rumble could be heard in the distance to the west. Soon the hundreds and thousands of troops, who like my group were moving across the terrain, realized that they were far behind the Russian lines.

I had a total of 13 men with me. We made good progress and hoped to soon reach our main line of resistance. We travelled only by night and slept during the day. One noon we tried to prepare some hot food from the rations we had left in the cover of a thicket at the edge of a swamp. But the smoke gave away our position. Suddenly someone screamed: 'They're coming!' and there was firing from all sides. While the others ran away, I feigned death and the Russians paid no further attention to me. The area through which I was moving seemed to have been created by God in his anger. Swamps, dense thickets, reeds, pools, great flat marshes and lazy channels alternated with each other. Soon I noticed that I was not alone. By day the landscape lay under the bright sunshine as if dead and abandoned. By night, however, there were whispers from the woods, and in the swamp there were splashes from the hurried footsteps of German soldiers, all heading west. Soon I, too, had company. Here and there mounted Cossacks appeared on their nimble horses, accompanied by hundreds on foot. Partisans were also hunting down the fleeing. The area frequently echoed with the rattle of submachine-gun fire and the detonations of hand grenades.

Like us, many hundreds and thousands struggled on. Between Minsk and Baranovichi we assembled into a group of about 80 men.

The Russians had set up a small anti-tank barricade at the railway embankment to prevent larger German units from crossing. A young *Hauptmann* described the situation to us, and then we attacked. Our uniforms were torn and we were starved. Many had no boots. Nevertheless, the Russians ran away as we charged, shouting loudly. We ripped the breechblocks from the five guns and threw them into a nearby brackish pool. Of course, we had no explosives.

This action must have challenged the enemy, because now he committed stronger forces. The next morning, after many groups had already crossed the railway embankment, he attacked. Many of us were killed or wounded. I myself was hit in the upper thigh by a shell fragment and could go no further. According to my pocket calendar it was July 4.

I had no idea where the others were. All that were visible were a few wounded, lying on the ground like me. They called desperately for help.

The day before I had used my packet bandage on a comrade, and I now tried to stem the flow of blood as best I could using my dirty handkerchief. Then I tried to stand up. At once several bursts of fire whistled past. On all fours I tried to reach a nearby thicket. My wounds burned like fire, but I made it all the same. I had scarcely crawled under cover, when the first Russians came slowly across the clearing, rifles at the ready. The wounded began to cry again. I watched as the Russians approached carefully and then killed them one after another with their rifle butts. I didn't make a sound, and so they didn't find me.

Sometime in the evening I dragged myself away. The next morning I found myself facing of a small stream, in which Russian women were doing their wash. When they saw me they screamed – I was dirty, dishevelled and encrusted with blood. But one woman immediately called to me: 'Russki!' and gestured to a nearby village. Exhausted, I sank to the ground, I was past caring. The Russian women cleaned my wounds, bandaged them and placed green medicinal herbs on them. Two of the women slipped away. I was suspicious and was about to leave, but the others calmed me. They repeated the only German word they knew, over and over: 'Good, good!' In fact the two women did come back. They brought a loaf of bread, a couple of eggs and a Russian canteen with warm milk. Then they showed me which way I should go and warned me with gestures to avoid roads and villages. Having recovered my strength somewhat, I set out again. By midday I had developed a high fever, and there were times when I thought I couldn't go on.

My boots had chafed my feet so badly that they had long since been covered with blisters, and both legs were so swollen that I couldn't pull my boots back on. I therefore had to cut the shanks and tie them loosely together. My wounds seemed to be healing, and they itched terribly. But my fever had dropped. Over the next few days I fed myself on berries, green potatoes and even tried to eat strips of tree bark.

One morning I found myself in a proper jungle. Huge trees lay crosswise and the undergrowth was so dense that I could scarcely get through it. Suddenly, through the bushes, I saw several figures running toward me. I called out: 'Germanski!' Eight German soldiers with rifles and submachine-guns approached slowly. We greeted each other joyously. We exchanged stories of our experiences and there was even a medic among them, who still had dressings with him. He examined my wounds and said: 'It's perhaps lucky for you that the wounds are crawling with maggots. They probably saved your life by eating the pus. But now it's time.' Then he set to work with his pocket knife, which he had heated over a small fire. I went along with this small group of comrades. Hunger repeatedly drove us to leave the relative safety of the swamps and forests to approach local villages in search of food. Often we stole what we could, sometimes we begged for food at isolated farms. Actually, we were helped quite often.

After some time we came upon a large camp of German soldiers. Here, in the middle of the wilderness, were assembled almost 400 men with 30 horse-drawn wagons under the command of two officers. I was speechless, having no idea how they could possibly have gotten here. The joy at once again being among numbers of my comrades was so great that I, too, forgot caution. We stayed two days. There was relatively ample rations there. On the evening of the second day a patrol returned with the news that the enemy had spotted the camp and was preparing to attack. It was decided to break out at 2100, but at about 2000 the enemy began to fire on the camp with mortars and anti-tank guns. The horses raced away with the driverless wagons. The wounded screamed and fell from the vehicles. Together with a Luftwaffe *Stabsgefreiter* who had befriended me, I found myself on a wagon with a wounded *Oberleutnant*. We drove like the devil and got through the Russian blocking line. Unfortunately we had to drive through a village. Naturally there were Russian soldiers and partisans in it, and a wild chase began. But once again we got through and turned off into a large wood. At 0400 we stopped to rest. Soon afterward I noticed several civilians enter the wood, probably trying to determine our whereabouts and numbers. There were 16 of us, including 6 wounded. We suggested to the *Oberleutnant* that we disappear at once, but he suggested that there was no danger and that we should rest a while longer to regain our strength. At about 0700 we were ambushed by about 50 partisans. Fortunately, most of us got away, as did I and the Stabsgefreiter. The *Oberleutnant* and the horses were led away, the other wounded were killed with bayonets.

Days later we met a group of about 120 men, who immediately joined us, including an *Hauptfeldwebel* from the 89th Infantry Regiment and an *Oberfeldwebel* from the panzer troops. We deliberated. The *Oberfeldwebel* wanted to take the road to Lida, I was against it. But the others were for the road on account of the difficult terrain and the expected hardships, and so we marched off in groups toward the road. The *Oberfeldwebel* led the first group and set quite a pace.

I suggested that he should be more cautious and at least skirt the villages, but he failed to heed the warning.

There was not a sound to be heard as we reached the first village. But in the farmyards I saw Russian trucks, their crews evidently sleeping. We had just about reached the village when the first challenge came: '*Stoy!*' At the same instant all hell broke loose. We scattered to the left and right and my faithful *Stabsgefreiter* stayed right with me.

When we assembled outside the village the *Oberleutnant* and 3 men were missing. Our small band was now down to 14 men. We hurriedly left the road and struck out once again through the forest and swamp.

At 0300 on August 13 we reached the Memel about 50 kilometers south of Kovno. We crossed the river unhindered by night in a boat we'd found. For another five days, moving mostly by night, we worked our way across country. At the end of the day on August 18 we were lying in some thick bushes. Suddenly, my good chum the *Stabsgefreiter* stood up. 'Listen!' he whispered. Through the quiet of the late summer day the thunder of guns rumbled in the distance. At last we were close to the front. The most difficult part of our journey was about to begin.

Carefully we slipped through the enemy rear in the darkness and approached the Russian main line of resistance. The sky was filled with bright flashes, the night roared with thunder-like crashes. I had to explain to my friends that we had no chance of getting through the front in a group, and we spit up into twos and threes.

Only the *Stabsgefreiter* went with me. Three days and nights we lay just behind the Russian front. On the first day we crawled into a wheat field. The shells from the German artillery were bursting uncomfortably close. During the night we moved on. We heard Russian soldiers talking, saw their shadows, and often they were so close that we thought they must see us.

The following night we tried again and once more had to retreat, as we were fired on twice as we moved forward. Once again we lay in the wheat field, chewing on the ripe heads of grain in an effort to combat the gnawing hunger. The third night we decided to break through no matter what. We set out at 2200. Dark clouds raced over us, here and there a machine-gun rattled, tracers flitted through the night sky, rifle shots cracked. As we crawled along we determined that we had reached an enemy position. It consisted merely of a trench, which was weakly manned. Since the Russians were constantly on the attack, they had no need of strong defenses. Two sentries slowly made their rounds while another slept. As soon as the pair of Russians were some distance away we jumped noiselessly over the trench and crawled on cautiously. Nothing stirred. The enemy position was already behind us. Relieved, I rested on one knee. At the same instant a parachute flare hissed into the sky, fired by a nervous Russian or German sentry. A wild firefight suddenly began, and we were in the middle in no-man's-land. We prayed not to be hit now.

In the flash of a bursting shell I saw a shell hole just ahead and immediately slid my left foot inside. At the same instant I was blinded by the harsh flash of an explosion, and my ears rang. I tried to stand up but fell down. It was then that I realized that I must have stepped on a

German pressure mine, which had blown off my left leg below the knee. My comrade was there at once and helped me bind the leg with our belts. He said something, but I didn't understand, as the explosion had burst both my eardrums. My right hand was bleeding heavily and a fragment must have struck me just above my left eye. Surprisingly, I felt no pain. So in spite of the loss of blood, supported by my loyal comrade, I crawled onward.

Finally the *Stabsgefreiter* left me. I lay alone, not wanting to die. I began to feel pain, which gradually worsened. But then my comrade, who had reached the German lines, returned with several of our medics and dragged me into the German positions. It was the night of August 31. I had lost my left leg and was bleeding from my head and right hand. But we had done it – after ten weeks of a hellish journey. I never learned what happened to my other companions . . ."

There was also the case of the Diercks[31] group. *Unteroffizier* Diercks was a member of the 36th Army Artillery Battalion, which had been assigned to the 383rd Infantry Division:

"At first Diercks was alone. Then he was joined by *Unteroffizier* Brixius with four men. As stragglers, they moved to the Beresina the first night. For days they were stuck in the swamps. They were hungry and could hear the rattle of Russian columns moving west on the highway. Diercks had a map and Brixius a compass. Using these they planned their march. – At first the blueberries were still green, but as the days passed they became riper and riper. The men measured the passage of time by the color of the berries.

Diercks and his group exchanged fire with Russian patrols and search parties. They met other groups of Germans, including the crew of a shot-down He 111. They travelled together for a while before separating. They swam the Ptitsch, while the lone non-swimmer paddled across the river on a tree trunk. Then they crossed the highway from Minsk to Brest-Litovsk. Along the way they requisitioned bread from the farmhouses and occasionally a canteen of milk. It was more difficult to obtain a handful of salt or a box of matches. Later they encountered a larger group of forty men, which was led by an *Oberst*. The two groups soon parted, however, and went their own ways.

A platoon from the 52nd Nebelwerfer Regiment encountered Dierck's group and joined it. The *Leutnant* placed himself under the command of the *Unteroffizier*. The man led here, not the rank. They lay in a rain-soaked forest, studied the map and decided to head for East Prussia.

The small group crossed the Memel. They had become as wily and experienced as trappers or woodsmen. The soldier Jakobs, for example, stole a sheep from a stall noiselessly and quickly. The sheep's legs were bound and it was carried off. In a wood the sheep was butchered and roasted. The usual fare, however, was beetroot and rye grain.

Weeks passed. The uniforms were torn, bodies emaciated, faces bearded. The swamps now lay far behind, also Novo Gorodok. They passed through the Njemen River region in a sparsely-settled area of Lithuania. They marched on, now in the seventh week of their trek.

Where were the new German lines? They came upon fresh signs of battle. But the war was still ahead of them, and they could not catch up with it. They did, however, encounter the enemy. *Gefreiter* Hummel and *Stabsgefreiter* Rall were killed in one firefight. They were left behind severely wounded and dying. And then, finally, they heard the front: the thunder of cannon and machine-gun fire.

Before them was a Russian mortar position. They tried to sneak past but were spotted and fired on. Everyone was hit, but fortunately not in the legs. They tried to escape into a rye field. Nerves were strained to breaking. The men lay between a Russian observation post and the Russian main line of resistance. On the hills all around were Russian batteries. They had stumbled into an enemy artillery position.

The night was cool. Diercks and Bauer had crawled close together for mutual warmth. *Feldwebel* Seitz groaned in pain, he had a high fever. The hours passed endlessly. They dared not stand as there were Russians all around. They picked heads of grain and ate the kernels. There was no going back.

Fate forced them to take the last step. A Soviet sentry discovered them. Diercks knocked him down. Forwards! The Russians laid down barrage fire with their mortars. That meant that there were no occupied Russian trenches ahead. But there was a trench – empty. They leapt across and then they were in no-man's-land. Finally they heard German words.

The Diercks group reached the German front fourteen kilometers east of Suwalki on August 14. The men had covered 450 kilometers in a straight line, about 650 with all the detours. In a forward regimental command post of the 170th Infantry Division *Unteroffizier* Diercks reported: 'Five German soldiers from the Bobruisk pocket reporting back to the German Wehrmacht after 49 days! . . ."

The soldier on the run the longest was *Unteroffizier* A. Anzhofer of the 246th Infantry Division. He reached the German lines in the vicinity of Schaulen (Lithuania) with two other soldiers on September 2, sixty-nine days after beginning his trek. The trio had covered approximately 600-800 kilometers (400 kilometers in a straight line). Ten men had been left behind along the way.

By the time the Russian offensive began to peter out, even the expectations of the Soviet High Command had been exceeded. Within a month, the Red Army, with its tremendous superiority, had advanced into the Kuvno-Brest Litovsk area. A week later the Russians were on the Vistula and at the Reich's East Prussian frontier. In addition, further spearheads had reached the Baltic in the north and had cut off all of Army Group North, which from then on was isolated in the Courland. The bulk of Army Group Center lay behind the onrushing Russian troops. All of the Third Panzer Army, the Fourth Army and a large part of the Ninth Army[32] had been lost.

In a battle lasting barely fourteen days the Germans had lost:
– 7 of 9 army corps (VI, XII, XXVII, XXXV, XXXIX, XXXXI and LIII Corps)

– 28 of 34 divisions (6th, 12th, 14th, 31st, 36th, 45th, 57th, 78th Assault, 95th, 110th, 134th, 197th, 206th, 246th, 256th, 260th, 267th, 296th, 299th, 383rd, Korpsabteilung D, 707th Security Division, 18th and 25th Panzergrenadier Divisions, *Feldherrnhalle* Panzergrenadier Division, 20th Panzer Division, 4th and 6th Luftwaffe Field Divisions
   – numerous army and corps units

The remnants which managed to escape were of little military value.
Many divisions had been so completely destroyed that scarcely a man returned, and in some cases not until after years in Russian captivity. For example, the OKH center in Rudolfstadt, Thuringia, declared the entire East Prussian 206th Infantry Division, which numbered about 12,000 men, killed or missing. The official date for every member of the division, from General to the last soldier, was July 18, 1944, location: Vitebsk.

German losses have been placed at about 350,000 men, including 150,000 captured by the Soviets. Further losses, including those shot on the way to the assembly camps, deaths during transport to Russia in overcrowded rail cars and from starvation and disease in the prisoner of war camps are estimated at 75,000 – giving a total of 275,000 dead German soldiers. The exact numbers will never be known.

The Soviets issued the following figures for the period June 23 to July 27: 380,000 German soldiers killed and 158,000 captured, including four commanding generals and thirteen division commanders, a total of twenty-two generals.

In addition to these tremendous losses in personnel, Army Group Center lost virtually all of its war materiel. Its total collapse was the worst catastrophe in the history of the German Army, and the greatest in German military history.

The victor not only dealt with the vanquished in a cruel and inhuman manner, but also degraded them. This, too, must be told. After vegetating for five days in the large assembly camp at Shlobin, all the prisoners were loaded aboard trains and taken to Moscow, where 57,600 prisoners of war were packed like sardines into the Hippodrome – for a special purpose. A great victory parade on the occasion of the smashing of the German Army Group Center took place in Moscow on July 17. The pitiless finale took place the next day. On the morning of that July 17, 57,600 German prisoners, in blocks twenty men wide, led by a group of Generals and escorted by Red Army troops with fixed bayonets and mounted Cossacks with slung submachine-guns, were marched down the wide Leningrad Road and Gorki Street toward Red Square in the city's center. The population of Moscow lined the streets to watch this spectacle. Many of the onlookers hurled abuse and insults at the defenseless prisoners, threatened and spat at them. A few of the older women, who had lost sons or husbands themselves, wept. In the end the long columns of emaciated, half-starved and ragged German troops, who in spite of everything had not lost their composure, were not led across Red Square, but were turned away just short of it and directed to various train stations. There they were loaded aboard trains and sent to prison camps in the vastness of the Soviet Union. Only a very few would ever see their homeland again, and then only after many years of captivity.

Extracts from Wehrmacht Communiques:

June 23:
. . . In the central sector the Soviets have begun their anticipated offensive. The attacks, launched on a broad front with powerful tank and air support, have been repulsed, and local penetrations cleared by immediate counterattacks. Bitter fighting is still under way on both sides of Vitebsk . . .

June 24:
. . . The Soviet offensive in the central sector has grown in weight and has been expanded to other sectors. Powerful tank and infantry forces have broken into our forward positions on either side of Vitebsk. The defensive battle continues with increasing intensity . . .

June 25:
. . . In the east our divisions are engaged in heavy fighting all along the

central sector of the front against the Soviet offensive being conducted
with powerful infantry, tank and air forces. The enemy has succeeded in
expanding his penetrations, especially in the Vitebsk area . . .

June 26:
. . . The defensive battles in the central sector are continuing with
undiminished ferocity. Our forces are putting up a determined defense
against the superior enemy forces attacking in the Bobruisk area . . .

June 27:
. . . In the central sector of the Eastern Front our brave divisions are
engaged in heavy defensive fighting against the massed forces of the
Soviets in the Bobruisk, Mogilev and Orsha sectors. A fighting withdrawal to new positions is under way west and southwest of Vitebsk . .
.

June 28:
. . . Heavy fighting continues in the central sector of the Eastern Front
in the Bobruisk and Mogilev areas. Following the evacuation of Orsha
and Vitebsk the heavy fighting has shifted into the area east of the middle
and upper Beresina . . .

June 29:
. . . The Soviets have gained ground in several places in the central sector
of the Eastern Front in the course of bitter defensive battles. The
garrisons of Bobruisk and Mogilev are putting up fierce resistance
against the enemy's superior forces. Heavy fighting against the advancing Soviets continues east of the middle and upper Beresina and south
of Polotsk . . .

June 30:
. . . Bitter fighting continues in the center of the Eastern Front. Enemy
spearheads have been halted in several places between Slutsk and
Bobruisk. Heavy fighting has broken out with advancing enemy forces
near Borisov and southwest of Polotsk. Close-support units have intervened repeatedly in the ground battle, scattering enemy infantry and
vehicle columns . . .

July 1:
. . . Our troops are still engaged in heavy defensive fighting in the central
sector of the Eastern Front. Street fighting is in progress in the city of
Slutsk. Heavy, tank-supported, Soviet attacks are also taking place in the
Osipovichi area and near Borisov. The enemy attacks have been halted
in heavy fighting on the upper course of the Beresina as well as west and

southwest of Slutsk . . .

July 2:

. . . In the central sector of the Eastern front our brave divisions continue to offer determined resistance to the superior forces of the attacking Soviets. In the Slutsk area the bolsheviks have gained ground after extremely heavy fighting. The city has been abandoned. Near Osipovichi our troops are holding their positions against all enemy attacks. The battle groups from the Bobruisk area have fought their way through to our main forces. Heavy fighting is under way against the continuously-attacking Soviets on the middle Beresina. The enemy pressure continues in the area west of Polotsk . . .

July 3:

. . . In the central sector of the Eastern Front west of Slutsk powerful attacks by the bolsheviks have been repulsed in heavy fighting. In the Osipovichi area and on the middle Beresina our divisions are withdrawing into the area around Minsk in heavy fighting with pursuing enemy forces. Bitter fighting is under way for the city of Polotsk . . .

July 4:

. . . On the central Eastern front the intensity of the fighting has increased further. West of Slutsk enemy attacks are alternating with our counterattacks . . . Bolshevik tank forces have entered Minsk and are advancing westward. Southeast of the city our units are putting up bitter resistance to the Soviets attacking from all sides and are fighting their way back toward the west. Enemy spearheads have been driven back by a counterattack near Molodetschno . . .

July 5:

. . . In the central sector heavy fighting continues for the land between the marshes in the Baranovichi and Molodetschno area . . . Our units are continuing to fight their way through south of Minsk . . .

July 6:

. . . In the central sector bitter fighting continues in the area of Baranovichi and Molodetschno . . .

Disposition of Army Group Center

(From North to South)

Army Group Headquarters (*Generalfeldmarschall* Busch)

Army Group Reserve:
14th Motorized Infantry Division (*Generalleutnant* Flörke) captured
Third Panzer Army (*Generaloberst* Reinhardt)

IX Army Corps (*General der Artillerie* Wuthmann)
252nd Infantry Division (*Generalleutnant* Melzer)
Korpsabteilung D (*Generalleutnant* Pamberg)

LIII Army Corps (*General der Infanterie* Gollwitzer) captured
246th Infantry Division (*Generalmajor* Müller-Bülow) captured
4th Luftwaffe Field Division (*Generalleutnant* Pistorius) killed
6th Luftwaffe Field Division (*Generalleutnant* Peschel) killed
206th Infantry Division (*Generalleutnant* Hitter) captured

VI Army Corps (*General der Infanterie* Dr. Pfeiffer) killed
197th Infantry Division (*Generalmajor* Hahne) missing
299th Infantry Division (*Generalmajor* von Junck) missing
256th Infantry Division (*Generalleutnant* Wüstenhagen) killed

Army Reserve:
95th Infantry Division (*Generalmajor* Michaelis) captured
201st Security Division (*Generalleutnant* Wüstenhagen) killed

Fourth Army (*General der Infanterie* von Tippelskirch)
XXVII Army Corps (*General der Infanterie* Völckers) captured
78th Assault Division (*Generalleutnant* Traut) missing
25th Panzergrenadier Division (*Generalleutnant* Schürmann)
260th Infantry Division (*Generalmajor* Klammt) killed

XXXIX Panzer Corps (*General der Artillerie* Martinek) killed
110th Infantry Division (*Generalleutnant* von Kurowski) captured
337th Infantry Division (*Generalleutnant* Schünemann) killed
12th Motorized Infantry Division (*Generalleutnant* Bammler) captured
31st Infantry Division (*Generalleutnant* Ochsner) captured

Army Reserve:

Feldherrnhalle Panzergrenadier Division (*Generalmajor* von Steinkeller) killed
286th Security Division (*Generalmajor* Oschmann)

XII Army Corps (*Generalleutnant* Müller, Vinzenz) captured
18th Panzergrenadier Division (*Generalleutnant* Zutavern) killed
267th Infantry Division (*Generalleutnant* Drescher) killed
57th Infantry Division (*Generalmajor* Trowitz) captured

Ninth Army (*General der Infanterie* Jordan, later General der Panzertruppe von Vormann)

XXXV Army Corps (*Generalleutnant* Freiherr von Lützow) missing
134th Infantry Division (*Generalleutnant* Phillip) suicide
296th Infantry Division (*Generalleutnant* Kullmer)
6th Infantry Division (*Generalleutnant* Heyne) captured
383rd Infantry Division (*Generalmajor* Gihr) captured
45th Infantry Division (*Generalmajor* Engel) captured

XXXXI Panzer Corps (*Generalleutnant* Hofmeister) captured
36th Infantry Division (*Generalmajor* Conrady) captured
35th Infantry Division (*Generalleutnant* Richert)
129th Infantry Division (*Generalleutnant* von Larisch)

LV Army Corps (*General der Infanterie* Herrlein)
292nd Infantry Division (*Generalleutnant* John)
102nd Infantry Division (*Generalleutnant* von Bercken)

Army Reserve:
20th Panzer Division (*General der Panzertruppe* Kessel)
707th Security Division (*Generalmajor* Gittner)
Battle Commander Bobruisk (*Generalmajor* Hamann) hanged by the Soviets

Second Army (*Generaloberst* Weiss)
with XXIII, XX and VIII Army Corps)

Notes:
[1] On June 3, 1944, *Feldmarschall* Busch had said to the assembled division commanders in Minsk: "The Führer has ordered me to hold the army group's positions for as long as seven years."

[2] The Third Panzer Army had only infantry divisions under its command.

[3] Since the Second Army was not attacked in the time frame in question, it will not be mentioned further.

[4] 20th Panzer Division with the 21st Panzer Regiment, numbering 100 Panzer IVs.

[5] According to Soviet sources there were 240,000 partisans in the entire area occupied by Army Group Center, although this figure is probably too high.

[6] The OKH therefore transferred all available panzer divisions and replacement units from Germany into the area behind this army group's front.

[7] The name of a Russian General from the 1812 war against Napoleon I.

[8] 29 divisions, 8 tank brigades

[9] 43 divisions, 20 tank brigades

[10] 16 divisions, 2 tank brigades

[11] 50 divisions, 13 tank brigades

[12] In the Vitebsk area there were 380 guns per kilometer of front.

[13] *Hauptfeldwebel* (American equivalent: Top Sergeant)

[14] Pskov-Kiev highway

[15] Positions guarding the Dniepr.

[16] Commander of the 14th Motorized Infantry Division, the remnants of which had been taken over by the 110th Infantry Division.

[17] Units of the 31st and 267th Infantry Divisions.

[18] Excerpt from: R. Hinze: *Der Zusammenbruch der Heeresgruppe Mitte im Osten 1944.*

[19] The Commanding General of XXXIX Panzer Corps, *General* Martinek, had already been killed.

[20] Approximately regiment strength

[21] Excerpt from: L. Merker: *Das Buch der 78. Sturmdivision.*

[22] LV Army Corps

[23] The German National Anthem

[24] By June 28 the division had destroyed 213 Russian tanks.

[25] See R. Hinze: *Der Zusammenbruch der Heeresgruppe Mitte im Osten 1944.*

[26] When the individual units and wounded evacuated earlier were added the total was more than 20,000.

[27] Excerpt from: R. Geschöpf: *Mein Weg mit der 45. Infanteriedivision.*

[28] Other members of the Ninth Army who escaped from Soviet captivity said that they had been forced to march on foot from the site where they were captured to Shlobin, without any food, through hot, damp forests. Those who could not keep up and fell by the wayside were shot by their Russian guards. In Shlobin they were crammed into trains, eighty per boxcar, for transport to Moscow. When the cars were unloaded many of the men were already dead. It was there that the prisoners received their first hot food. A short time later they set out for the march through Moscow.

[29] Excerpt from: H. Großmann: *Geschichte der rheinisch-westfälischen 6. Infanteriedivision 1939-45.*

[30] 12th Infantry Division

[31] Abbreviated extract from: P. Carell: *Verbrannte Erde.*

[32] The attack against Second Army in the Pripyat region, which had not been affected by the Soviet offensive, began on July 14. In the initial onslaught the Soviets succeeded in separating the army from Army Group North Ukraine and drove it back across the Bug.

V

Brody:
XIII Army Corps

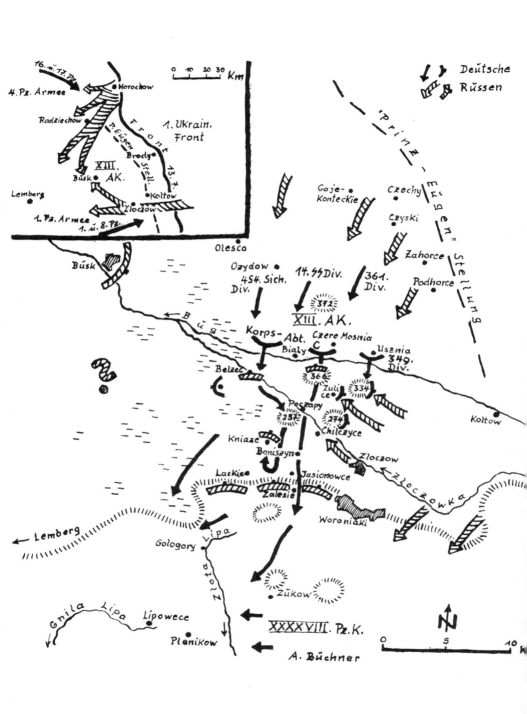

Deutsche
Rüssen

16. u. 17. Pz.
4. Pz. Armee
Horochow
Radziechow
Front
1. Ukrain.
Front
0 10 20 30 Km
PRINZ-EUGEN"Stellung
Lemberg
Brody
Busk
XIII. AK.
Koltow
Zloczow
1. Pz. Armee
1. u. 8. Pz.
"PRINZ-EUGEN"Stellung
Olesco
Gaje-
Konteckie
Czechy
Czyski
Zahorce
Podhorce
Busk
Ozydow
454. Sich.
Div.
14. SS Div.
361.
Div.
372
XIII. AK.
B
Bug
Korps-
Abt.
Czere Mosnia
Bialy
C
Usznia
349.
Div.
Belzec
366
Zuli
ce
334
Koltow
Poczapy
257
274
Chilczyce
Kniaze
Boniszyn
Zloczow
Zloczowka
Lackie
Jasionowce
Lemberg
Zalesie
Woroniaki
Gologory
Lipa
Zukow
Gnila Lipa
Lipowece
N
XXXXVIII. Pz. K.
Planikow
A. Büchner
0 5 10

Brody: XIII Army Corps

An End in the Pocket

During the Austro-Hungarian monarchy the land was known as East Galicia. Following the First World War it became part of Poland, before being occupied by the Russians early in the Second World War. It was a tranquil, out of the way region, with the watershed between the Northern Bug with its tributaries and the beginning Southern Bug, Strypa and the likewise southward-flowing Dnestr. The region featured wooded hills, valleys and forests, interspersed with villages large and small, among which was the small city of Brody. Brody was one-hundred kilometers from Lemberg (Lvov), the former capital of Galicia, and not far from Ternopol, which had been in Soviet hands for some time. Otherwise there was not much to say about Brody, other than it was located thirty-five kilometers southwest of the village of Zloczow, where the large overland road from Lemberg crossed the former Polish-Russian frontier and split in two to head off in the directions of Rowno and Ternopol. Now, in wartime, the road had become of special significance.

The war had passed through this land in 1941, when it was the scene of heavy fighting, which soon passed, however. Now, in 1944, the war was coming back. This time it was the Russians whose new offensive was pushing into Poland.

A New Soviet Offensive on Both Sides of Brody

Positioned in this militarily and strategically important area since its withdrawal from the Rowno area in mid-March was *General* Hauffe's XIII Army Corps. The corps, with its four divisions[1] deployed just east of Brody, already had "pocket experience." It had been surrounded around Brody from the end of March until mid-April, when the heavy losses inflicted by a stubborn German defence and a

counterattack by panzer units had forced the Russians to abandon the encirclement. From then until high summer the corps had spent a relatively quiet period
in its positions.

It was the calm before the great storm.

The Soviets, who were still in the process of completely destroying Army
Group Center and continuing their westward advance, were already preparing
their next offensive, the "sixth blow" as they called this part of their operations plan
for 1944. The attack was to be directed against Army Group North Ukraine, since
June 28 under the command of *Generaloberst* Harpe. The army group's situation
had deteriorated significantly since the total collapse of Army Group Center, and
most of its reserves had been taken away. The Russians, on the other hand, had been
massing forces for a new blow through Lemberg and Przemysl in the direction of
the San River since June 24 with their now customary overwhelming superiority.
Their initial objective was to capture the major road to Lemberg , necessary for a
rapid advance, and isolate XIII Corps, which was barring the way, especially at the
road fork near Zloczow. Once again they employed a double-sided envelopment
with great skill, striking precisely at the border between the Fourth and First Panzer
Armies so as to spit these two armies apart and encircle XIII Corps. On the corps'
left was XXXXVI Panzer Corps (Fourth Panzer Army), while on its right was
XXXXVIII Panzer Corps (First Panzer Army), both of which had infantry
divisions manning their fronts.

The Soviet offensive was to be carried out by the First Ukrainian Front, now
under the command of Marshall Konev. He assembled two groups of forces on
either side of Brody for the attack. The northern group consisted of two armies with
sixteen rifle divisions, two cavalry corps and twenty-nine tank brigades, as well as
five tank and mechanized corps. the southern group consisted of four armies with
twenty-nine rifle divisions and twenty-four tank brigades, as well as five tank and
mechanized corps. As well he had the usual overwhelming air forces in a
supporting role.

This time the Red Army's preparations were not concealed. Army Group
North Ukraine began noting increasing signs of an impending offensive in early
July. Appropriate directives were issued, and XIII Corps was placed on a
precautionary alert on July 6. This meant an immediate cancellation of all leave,
the movement of all combat troops to the front from rear areas and increased patrol
activity. Sentries were doubled, observation posts were manned around the clock,
while in the bunkers the men slept in shifts and never took off their uniforms,
helmets and weapons were kept nearby at all times. Increased supplies of
munitions were sent to the front, the artillery stockpiled ammunition, field
telephone lines were checked regularly and radio units stood by to receive

incoming messages every half hour. The field kitchens issued extra dry rations in the event that enemy fire made regular deliveries difficult, the aid stations prepared to accept a larger number of wounded, while the headquarters staffs were awake around the clock, ready to go to work.

The troops were calm and composed. Their positions were well-built, they were battle tested and had successfully defended against Soviet attacks before. Why should it be any different this time – when the Russians came again they would get a bloody nose.

But like the German front everywhere, there was only one infantry division next to the other, and behind them a second, but unmanned, rear position (the "Prinz Eugen Position") and nothing more. The Fourth Panzer Army had two panzer divisions in reserve (16th and 17th), as did the First Panzer Army (1st and 8th). At this point these units might have been better described as armored battle groups (*Panzerkampfgruppen*) than panzer divisions. With the exception of the 8th Panzer Division, these were the same ones which had seen heavy fighting at Cherkassy and Ternopol. But panzer divisions, especially ones which were nowhere near their authorized strengths, were no replacement for a defensive zone thirty, or even better, fifty kilometers in depth. The thin infantry lines would be all too quickly overrun and pierced. What was more, the defensive forces available were much too weak for the lengths of front they had to defend.

On July 13 every member of XIII Corps was listening to an ominous sound, from the Commanding General down to the last grenadier. At 0345 in the morning it had began to rumble and growl in the north, and soon afterward in the south as well. Only ahead of the corps' front did it remain quiet, and the men gave it little thought – the main thing was that nothing was happening there. But the corps command had already been informed what was taking place – the expected Soviet offensive had begun following a tremendous bombardment of the German lines which had lasted until 0930. Never before had the defenders seen such a concentration of materiel, especially of artillery, tanks and aircraft, followed by masses of infantry. It was not long before the forward infantry divisions broke. The enemy achieved deep penetrations near Horochow to the north of Brody and near Koltov to the south, which were soon expanded into breakthroughs. By the second day of the attack XIII Corps had been isolated from its two neighboring corps. Local counterattacks against the enemy spearheads failed to achieve anything.

Once Again – Panzer Divisions in a Futile Counterattack

The panzer divisions being held in reserve had been placed on alert on July 13, but it was not until two days later that they were thrown into the battle to close the front which had been torn open in two places. The 16th and 17th Panzer Divisions advanced in the north, while in the south the battle group comprising the 1st and 8th Panzer Divisions set itself in motion. Even before the German counterattack could get properly under way, Soviet armored spearheads were driving from Horochow through Radziechov in the direction of the Bug, and near Koltov were advancing toward Zloczow.

Panzergrenadiers mount up – weapons ready to fire – hatches shut – panzers forward! With roaring engines and rattling tracks the tanks, command and radio vehicles, armored personnel carriers and motor vehicles moved out. The armored forces encountered serious difficulties and suffered their first losses before the counterattack even got under way. The dreaded Soviet close-support aircraft, including Mosquito fighter-bombers delivered from Great Britain, roared in at low altitude. In swarms of twenty to thirty aircraft they dove on the advancing German armored battle groups, dropping bombs, strafing and firing rockets. The tanks zigzagged desperately but soon the first was shrouded in oily black smoke. Vehicles burst into flames and men leapt from disabled armored personnel carriers. The few self-propelled 20mm flak assigned to the battle groups, their crews unprotected above and with only light armor protection to the sides, fired wildly. Scarcely had they engaged one aircraft when the next roared toward them. A few German fighters appeared and tried to intervene, but they were too few.

The 8th Panzer Division's counterattack, which was led by the 10th Panzer Regiment's 1st Battalion, which had only one full-strength panzer company, the 4th, and the 301st Panzer Battalion, ran into superior enemy forces. The attack was halted and had to be broken off after suffering heavy losses. The way was now open to Zloczow for the Soviets. Elements of the 8th Panzer Division were forced into the area of XIII Corps. The 1st Panzer Division, which further south and east of Koltow had at first been able to contain the enemy penetration and set up blocking positions, was soon forced to withdraw toward the "Prinz Eugen Position." In places the attacking Russian forces had advanced so far that they reached the position before the German panzergrenadiers. In the afternoon the armored groups of both panzer divisions were deployed southeast of Zloczow for a counterattack toward the north, aimed at reestablishing contact with XIII Corps.[2] The attack got under way too late and after initial success was halted by several anti-tank fronts – the Russians spearhead heading toward Zloczow was too strong. The Germans had been unable to close the gap in the front or link up with XIII Corps. By this July 15 the Soviets had achieved decisive breakthroughs in both areas of penetration.

Like the 1st and 8th Panzer Divisions in the south, in the north the 16th and 17th Panzer Divisions had been unable to advance and their counterattack soon ground to a halt. The four depleted panzer divisions were unable to restore the situation in the face of the overwhelming tank, artillery and air forces of the enemy. In the next few days events began to concentrate in the south in an ever more dramatic fashion. There was no longer any possibility of a concentrated counterattack. In bitter fighting the 1st Panzer Division tried to prevent a complete enemy breakthrough, or at least slow it down. The Russians, who were pressing forward strongly in the area of penetration, attacked sharply throughout the night of July 15/16 and the next day, and every man of the division was pressed into action. The division's tanks and tank-destroyers threw themselves against the waves of Soviet T-34 and JS-2 tanks, while the panzergrenadiers, fighting on foot, sought to halt the masses of enemy infantry. Hours of massed artillery fire and attacks by heavy bombers delivered from America played havoc with the division's supply lines, and the fighting troops could only be supplied by night under extremely difficult conditions. The situation was no different for the 8th Panzer Division, which had also suffered heavy losses. It was pushed back toward the west and was given the job of securing the Zloczow-Lemberg road. In spite of bitter resistance the enemy occupied Zloczow on the 16th and during the afternoon of the 17th Soviet tanks of the southern group reached the Bug near Busk. The next day they linked up with cavalry units of the northern group. After six days of desperate fighting and futile counterattacks XIII Corps had been surrounded in the area north of Zloczow.

The Breakout is Delayed – in Spite of Past Experience

The corps command saw the situation as serious but not threatening. The clearly audible sounds of battle and the Russian breakthroughs in the north and south were certainly not good, however the corps had been surrounded before and had been freed. Why should it be any different this time, especially since it was known that four German panzer divisions were already engaged in a counterattack. But this time it would be different, very different . . .

The corps, together with the 349th Infantry Division which had been split off by the enemy, had so far only had to withstand minor frontal attacks. On July 16, following the loss of Zloczow on the right flank, orders came to withdraw to the prepared "Prinz Eugen" position. In spite of the rainy weather which set in on July 17 and the resulting poor road conditions, the withdrawal was carried out according to plan. A pionier battalion was assigned to secure to the west in the direction of Busk. The 349th Division and *Korpsabteilung* C were to march south during the night of July 17/18 and establish contact with the 8th Panzer Division – which was assumed to be advancing northward – in the area northeast of Zloczow. The attack failed, there was no link-up and the shattered right flank, where Koltov was still holding out, remained open. The expected relief forces (16th and 17th Panzer Divisions) also failed to arrive on the corps' deep left (northern) flank; instead it was earth-brown waves of Russian infantry and T-34 tanks which appeared. As a result the "Prinz Eugen" position had to be abandoned and the corps' left wing, the 454th Security Division and the 14th SS-Division *Galizien*, had to be bent back to form a front facing north.

Orders from the army for a breakout arrived on July 18. Once again, as in so many similar instances, the most senior German commanders delayed the decision until it was too late. The corps commander, *General* Hauffe, had also waited too long without acting. As the enemy was exerting heavy pressure from the east and north, and a difficult area of forests and marshes lay to the west, the only possible direction for a breakout was to the south. The appropriate warning orders were issued that afternoon. The corps command still believed that it could carry out a carefully planned breakthrough and establish contact with XXXXVIII Panzer Corps in an attack lasting a total of three days.

On the morning of the 19th at the corps command post in a small wood the Chief of Staff issued the precise orders for the breakout to the assembled Division Ia's:[3]

As the most effective remaining division, *Korpsabteilung* C was to form the spearhead. Its instructions were to advance across the Bug on either side of Bialy Kamien at dawn on the 20th, and after crossing the Zloczowka further to the south was to take possession of the area between Skwarzawa and Chilcyzce, deploying strong security forces to the south. A battalion of the 361st Division and the 249th Assault Gun Brigade were to be placed under its command for the attack. After the enemy took the former linchpin of Koltow, the 349th Division was instructed to set out simultaneously from the Usznia area with strong forces and take Hill 334, as well as the following hills, in order to guard the eastern flank of *Korpsabteilung* C.

Rear echelon units and the wounded were to follow as the attack progressed. The 14th SS-Division *Galizien*, the 361st Division and the 454th Security Division were to secure the rear of the two attacking divisions and await orders to fall back. – Not until the breakthrough had succeeded were the artillery, trains, supply services and wounded to be evacuated, then the three remaining divisions.

The corps command was still confident and hoped that a large part of the vehicles, guns and heavy equipment could be brought out of the pocket. All was expected to go well, as long as *Korpsabteilung* C and the 349th Division, with the support of the approaching panzer divisions, held the breakout area.

The attack was slated to begin at 0330 in the morning on July 20.

The Chief-of-Staff then described the situation: there were only Russian security forces south of the Zloczow-Lemberg highway to a depth of five kilometers, XXXXVIII Panzer Corps was still holding a solid front and a successful drive toward the corps by the 1st and 8th Panzer Divisions was under way – all three statements were in error and all were to have serious consequences.

The corps command had no idea what was really going on to the south.

The Relief Attempt Fails

The events on the deep flanks and in the rear of XIII Corps had already assumed extremely disquieting proportions. In the north the German relief attack had failed decisively, and the defenders were struggling to delay a further advance by the main Soviet force in the direction of Lemberg.

In the south the situation near Zloczow had likewise worsened considerably. On July 16 and 17, after the main body of the 8th Panzer Division had been forced to withdraw further to the west, the 1st Panzer Division remained engaged in heavy fighting in the area of the enemy breakthrough, the panzergrenadiers suffering extremely heavy losses. On the evening of the 17th the division was forced to order a further withdrawal toward Kabarowce, southeast of Zloczow. For the next two days the panzergrenadiers fought bitterly for possession of the village in the pouring rain. The enemy poured heavy fire into the German positions, while the numerically superior Russian infantry, supported by tanks, exerted pressure on the defenders. Not until the night of July 19/20 was the rubble of Kabarowce abandoned to the enemy, and on the 20th the division's forces pulled back in the direction of Pomorcany.

Meanwhile, on the evening of the 19th the remaining effective elements of the 8th Panzer Division had been withdrawn from their previous sector in preparation for a relief attack together with an armored battle group from the 1st Panzer Division. The attack, which was to take place the following day, was to be concentrated in a narrow area west of Zalesie. Its objective was the relief of the surrounded XIII Corps. However the counterattack failed to break through and was repulsed by the Russians with heavy losses. Strong Russian anti-tank positions and low-level air attacks, in spite of the rainy weather, foiled every attempt to advance into the wooded hill country south of the highway. The Russians proved to be stronger everywhere and the German battle groups soon found themselves in serious trouble.

The 28th Panzergrenadier Regiment's 2nd Battalion, part of the 8th Panzer Division, was surrounded by Soviet tanks. The 200 remaining panzergrenadiers held out for five days behind enemy lines before successfully breaking out. By then the battalion numbered 60 men. Three *Leutnante* and 140 men were left behind, most of them dead. Virtually alone, the 10th Panzer Regiment's 10th Company under *Oberleutnant* Pressberger fought on with its last remaining tanks on a broad stage against far superior enemy forces. The German tanks fought on until they ran out of ammunition or were destroyed. Only two *Feldwebel* and four men got back to their own lines; all the others remained behind dead or wounded, including the company commander, *Oberleutnant* Pressberger.

It was like at Cherkassy and Ternopol – the German armored relief attack got close to the pocket, but in spite of the efforts and readiness to attack of the German troops, was unable to break through. And once again the surrounded troops were certain that the German tanks were close and that relief was only a short distance away. In this case this is all the more incomprehensible, as the commanders of XIII Corps were in constant contact with Headquarters First Panzer Army by telephone. It is not know what forces were at work that allowed the formation of such an inaccurate picture of the situation.

Headlong Rush to Defeat

The area held by XIII Corps shrunk steadily. Following the loss of Koltow on July 19, about 65,000 men with their weapons and vehicles streamed into the hilly, wooded terrain between Czechy-Olesco-Podhorce and Bialy Kamien, an area no more than nine kilometers wide by eight kilometers deep. Inside the pocket all was confusion: columns stalled and blocked the muddy roads, halting or delaying all movement. Artillery units struggled to reach new firing positions. Units became mixed up with other formations as they strove to reach their new assembly areas. Traffic was chaotic. There was a great snarl of motorized and horse-drawn vehicles, and the assembly points were overcrowded. Inexcusably, huge numbers of train vehicles set out toward the south in broad daylight so as not to lose contact with the breakout forces, and in doing so revealed to the enemy the planned direction of the breakout.

Then came July 20. It was 0500, and thus completely light, by the time *Korpsabteilung* C, which had been delayed in reaching its assembly area, began the attack, one and a half hours late. On the right the 183rd Division Group made good initial progress. It quickly overcame light resistance and at 0725, after crossing the Bug, reached the edge of the enemy-occupied village of Belsec. In the center, the 217th Division Group ran into unexpectedly heavy resistance before Hill 366, where a number of Russian self-propelled anti-tank guns halted the advance temporarily. The Russians also committed tanks. Following a determined assault five of the self-propelled guns were captured intact, and three were immediately put to use by crews whose own anti-tank guns had been knocked out. At about 0900, however, the remaining enemy units were still defending bitterly, barring the way.

In the meantime the 183rd Division Group had already advanced through Belsec toward the southeast before encountering heavy resistance from the direction of Poczapy. On the other hand, it was not until noon that the armored group of *Korpsabteilung* C[4], which was supposed to be spearheading the attack, but which had been held up by strong Russian anti-tank defenses near Hill 336, reached the bridge across the Zloczowka near Poczapy. By then it had knocked out about twenty Russian tanks and anti-tank guns. By 1500, following fierce house-to-house fighting, the village had been cleared of the enemy and was securely in German hands.

The situation in the early hours of the afternoon did not look too bad, as the attack's initial objectives had been reached. The 183rd Division Group had occupied Hill 257 and the armored group had reached Poczapy, while the 217th Division Group was further back near Zulice. On the left, the 349th Division (with the attached 339th Division Group) had taken Hill 334 at dawn and had fought its way further toward the south. On the right, in the area of Skwarzawa, was the 361st Fusilier Battalion, which was screening the advance to the west. The breakout attack was thus going according to plan – at least initially. Still, all appeared to be going well . . .

The 183rd Division Group was now instructed to advance toward Kniaze. The 217th Division Group received orders to capture Chilczyce and establish a strong defensive position facing east, as the 349th Division was still lagging behind somewhat on the left.

The 217th Division Group, which had set out at about 1300 with part of the armored group from the Poczapy area, was able to occupy and hold Chilczyce and Hill 274 after a three-hour battle with determined enemy forces. At that point it may have been barely eight to ten kilometers across the Zloczow-Lemberg road to the south to the battle groups of the 1st and 8th Panzer Divisions.

Those eight to ten kilometers now meant life or death for thousands of German soldiers.

But now the situation began to change for the worse hour by hour. Continuous and increasingly heavy Soviet air attacks began in the afternoon. Bomber and close-support units blanketed the breakout units, following units, columns, battery positions and command posts with a virtually uninterrupted rain of bombs, and strafed every visible target on the ground. It was then that the German forces suffered their first major losses of men and materiel, especially among the following train units. A soldier later reported that Red aircraft were almost always overhead. Not a single German aircraft was to be seen.

On the ground, too, the enemy's forces were growing stronger. In the face of increasingly heavy resistance and difficulties with the terrain, the 183rd Division Group was unable to capture Kniaze. On the left the 349th Division made little further progress and was forced toward the center. Since afternoon Soviet troops had been attacking from the east and southeast. Hill 334 changed hands several times before being lost for good that evening. The German units near Zulice and Hill 274 also found themselves embroiled in heavy fighting. The breakout attack had come to a halt.

In addition to the threat to the whole breakthrough from the east, there now came steadily increasing pressure from the north against the divisions covering the rear. There was only one hope – get all the units out of the pocket as quickly as possible. The corps headquarters still believed that it could carry out the breakthrough and breakout according to plan, however. On the evening of the 20th it issued orders that the attack was to be continued at night in spite of the exhaustion of the troops. Objectives now were the Lackie area for *Korpsabteilung* C and Zloczow for the 349th Division. The corps' orders indicated that the 8th Panzer Division had already reached Woroniaki and would advance through Zloczow that night, and that the 1st Panzer Division was going to advance against Zalesie on the coming morning – which simply did not correspond to the facts.

The attack divisions were to resume the attack at 0100, but command of the units was becoming ever more difficult. All radio communications were out, and establishing contact with the units through executive officers and messengers was a wearisome and difficult process. There was little chance of mounting an orderly, concentrated attack, especially by night, and many battle groups and units were already trying to break out on their own.

•

July 21 dawned grey and cloudy.

The 183rd Division Group got no further. During the previous night's fighting for Kniaze it had been thrown back toward Hill 257.

As day broke the terrible Russian air attacks began again.

At about 0400 elements of the 217th Division Group, reinforced by numerous stragglers from other units, went to the attack. Unnoticed by the enemy it passed close by Jasionowce and reached the nearby commanding hills, but found no German tanks there. The group, which now included the remnants of the 249th Assault Gun Brigade (without vehicles), decided to push on toward the south on its own. That afternoon, after intermittent fighting, it came upon the rearguards of the 1st Panzer Division in the Zukow area. These were thus the first elements of the corps to break out. Other mixed units also got through.

In the early hours of the morning a battle group of the 1st Panzer Division under *Oberst* Neumeister had set out on one last attempt to relieve the forces trapped inside the pocket. It managed to create an opening into the pocket about ten kilometers west of Zalesie, through which about 3,000 soldiers of various divisions and 400 men of the 14th SS-Division *Galizien* managed to escape. That same day the battle group received orders to turn away to the west and capture Lipowece, as the Russians, who were advancing relentlessly from the northwest, had crossed the Zlota Lipa in the early afternoon. As the battle group's subsequent movements ran parallel to those of the troops escaping from the pocket, the panzer crews were forced to witness frightful scenes as they passed by. Hundreds, even thousands, of wounded, sick and completely exhausted men struggled toward the rear over muddy roads in the pouring rain. The roads were soon completely blocked, and individual columns stood in the same place for hours at a time.

In the days that followed, the 1st Panzer Division was withdrawn further to the south. The 8th Panzer Division, too, was forced to withdraw toward the west, where it became involved in further heavy fighting. XIII Corps was left on its own.

On the 21st, following the failure of the breakout attacks, the troops and rear echelon units within the pocket found themselves being squeezed into an ever smaller area. Heavy fighting developed against the enemy forces pressing toward the pocket.

The headquarters of the 217th Division Group, with its pionier platoon and some stragglers, fought bitterly against the flanking threat from the left around Chilczyze and held the village until evening. There was also heavy fighting for Poczapy. Two pionier platoons were holding out there, and the enemy finally resorted to heavy bombing attacks in an effort to break their resistance. Zulice was also defended stubbornly. The 183rd Division Group made a renewed effort to break through near Kniaze. Elements in battalion strength smashed a short-lived breach in the enemy ring and made contact with the 8th Panzer Division near Gologory.

The 454th Security Division had to be withdrawn from the northern front to cover the right flank in the Belsec-Skwarzawa area. Enemy pressure against the pocket's northern and eastern fronts had become so great, that by the evening of the 27th a breakout on a wide front for the bulk of the corps had become imperative – it was do or die. Once again the attempt was to be made without any idea of the true situation and under the continued false assumption that the corps would be met just south of the Zloczow-Lemberg road by the two divisions of XXXXVIII Panzer Corps, which were in fact withdrawing. The strength of the enemy forces in the south was to be demonstrated with disastrous clarity.

Once again orders were issued, if they got through at all, for a night attack, to be carried out on the night of July 21/22. With these orders any semblance of command in the pocket ceased to exist. The mood in the corps headquarters was a depressed one, there was doubt right from the start that the attack would succeed. There was terrible confusion in the pocket and the first signs of disintegration began to appear. Everything was caught up in the maelstrom of impending defeat. From this point on scarcely any details are known concerning individual units.

At about 0100, the remaining elements of *Korpsabteilung* C (339th Division Group) and a regiment of the 349th Division, which had found its way there, assembled into three groups at the railway embankment south of Boniszyn under the command of the two division commanders for the final attack. They set out at 0300, while it was still dark. So far the enemy forces in the south had done little of note. Now, however, they at once opened up with a withering fire from well-established hill positions between Woroniaki and Lackie. Tanks, anti-tank guns, anti-aircraft guns, mortars and heavy machine-guns tried to halt the attackers. In spite of a total lack of support from their heavy weapons and artillery, the officers and grenadiers stormed forward under the command of the two generals. With a thunderous shout of hurray! they stormed the enemy hill positions like a tidal wave, broke through with heavy losses and advanced as far as the highway. Several Russian tanks were destroyed in close-quarters fighting. Even the intensified artillery bombardment which began with the dawn was unable to halt the assault. At about 0500 the wooded hills near Jasionowce were taken, and the village, as well as Zalesie, were captured. This was followed by a breakthrough by the left assault group with about 5,000 men, which was able to fight its way through to the southwest.

The End for 30,000 German Troops

From July 22 there was no longer a XIII Army Corps. The assault groups on the right and in the center, which included the commanding general and his headquarters staff, had failed to break through. Once at least one assault group had succeeded in breaking out, there was no stopping for the following, compressed mass of the corps; each man wanted to get through and out of the pocket.

Pursued by the enemy in the north, under attack from ever stronger enemy forces in the east, and the way west barred by swamps and Russians, the only way to freedom was south across the highway, the major Zloczow-Lemberg road. It was a frightful, deadly path. The Russians had quickly sealed the gaps in their encircling ring, and now, in the light of day, the mostly open terrain lay under heavy, well observed and directed fire. Without order and organization, lacking coordination and contact with one another, wave after wave of German soldiers stormed forward. In dense ranks and columns, some led by officers, others on their own, thousands and thousands tried to break through in a desperate charge. Trains, wounded, supply units, elements of divisions which had previously been covering the rear, all fled together in disorder. Horse-drawn vehicles rumbled along, and motor vehicles swerved through the masses of men. In the midst of it all were spurting columns of flame, bursting shells, the howling of "Stalin Organs" and the cracking and rattling of light weapons. More and more of the fleeing troops were caught by the enemy fire, fell and were left behind, dead or wounded. There were scenes of horror everywhere – dead horses, shattered wagons, burning trucks and cars, the last few self-propelled guns and assault guns, now shot-up hulks. Those who fell were left behind – the only goal was to get through. The soldiers formed into groups and ran recklessly across the rail line south of Kniaze and the open meadows and broke into the Russian positions in places, resulting in wild hand-to-hand fighting. However, this massed charge up the open slope against the strongly-manned positions at the edge of the forest near Woroniaki, Zalesie and Lackie resulted in a tremendous increase in casualties. In addition to the fire from the Russian blocking positions, artillery fire poured into the breakout area from the east and west, and finally from the north. Added to this were attacks by Soviet aircraft. In this hellish fire from fours sides and from the air, the attacks, which lasted three and a half hours, were repulsed with appalling losses and many battle groups were completely wiped out. The German commanders suffered the same fate as their men. Corps General Hauffe was killed, the corps Chief-of-Staff died leading a battalion, the commander of the 454th Security Division sustained a serious head wound, the commander of the 361st Division was wounded and then captured, and the commanders of the 183rd and 217th Division Groups were listed as missing.

Only a very few succeeded in braving the enemy fire to reach the woods southeast of Lackie. There the small groups from the various divisions assembled, some still with their wounded. Completely exhausted and spent, it was several days before they made contact with the last units of the withdrawing XXXXVIII Panzer Corps. The accounts of the survivors can scarcely describe what took place during those terrible days.

Major Plähn of Battle Group Krüger (attached to the 349th Infantry Division) reported:[5]

> July 18, 1944:
> The battle group held Koltov against all enemy attacks at the cost of heavy losses. The artillery battalion fired most of its ammunition, saving only enough to spike its guns. Division described the situation as confused. Roads and paths had become poor due to the rainy weather which began on July 17.

> July 19:
> About midday the Russians launched a strong attack against Hill 374 and Koltov. Artillery and Stalin Organs bombarded the hill and our positions for twenty minutes in advance, and strong air units attacked Koltov. The enemy succeeded in taking the hill and the village. The panzergrenadiers withdrew to the northwest . . . Steady rain completely transformed the roads into mud. We were informed that our battle group was surrounded.

> July 20:
> The breakout attack toward the south began at dawn. The leading attack wave made good progress. 2nd Battalion, 8th Panzergrenadier Regiment advanced past Hill 334 toward Zulice, took the village, and pushed on toward the south, taking the wood between Poczapy and Chilczyze.

> July 21:
> In the afternoon the commander of the 349th Infantry Division received word from corps that he had complete freedom of action as of 2100. *Generalleutnant* Lasch immediately held a conference of unit commanders. Finally orders were given to break through the encircling ring . . . All elements were to break through to the south on foot . . . *Leutnant* Messerschmidt was to try and recover the wounded in an armored tractor . . .

After dark the remains of the division marched noiselessly toward the south in long columns . . .

July 22:

The enemy recognized our intentions . . . Defensive fire began abruptly as we reached the Zloczow-Krasne rail line. The breakthrough by night failed. As day arrived the enemy defense stiffened, Stalin Organs laid down barrage fire. The division disintegrated. Led by their officers some groups charged the Russian hill positions with loud shouts. Following a vicious battle lasting about an hour some elements penetrated the enemy positions and broke through to the south . . .

Over the next two days the remains of Battle Group Krüger arrived at the command post of the 8th Panzer Division south of Wisniowczyk . . ."

Following his return from Soviet captivity, catholic chaplain Bader of the 454th Security Division wrote of July 22:[6]

"I met my division's Ia Section that morning in Kniaze. To my dismay and horror, I watched as the Ib Section came under Russian fire and, paralyzed with fear, roared southwest straight into a swamp. In the afternoon I once again met *General* Hauffe at the northern exit from Kniaze. I asked what we were to do with the hundreds of men who had no idea what was happening. He answered: 'Their superiority is too great, there's no sense in going on. We can't continue to allow the men to be slaughtered uselessly. Perhaps we'll wait until night. The situation is hopeless!'

He walked away with *Oberst* von Hammerstein (Chief-of-Staff) and another companion; silently we took our leave. There was no longer any command authority in the pocket. The Stalin Organs hammered without pause into the troops now squeezed together in a small area. The Russian air squadrons bombarded the vehicle concentrations ceaselessly from low altitude . . . Positioned around the pocket, the Russian guns and mortars poured fire onto the plethora of targets. One German battery after another was stormed by the enemy, one company after another finished off – everywhere were burning vehicles, exploding fuel tanks and the moaning of wounded and dying men. Over the pocket the sun was completely blotted out by smoke and dust. The earth quivered and trembled. In the midst of this hell many men held out to the bitter end, others were paralyzed with fright and no longer capable of making decisions, many took their own lives.

The Russians had prepared this end for the corps, because it had repeatedly held up their advance for half a year. When the blood-red sun went down on that July 22, 1944, XIII Corps had been 'liquidated': about 25,000 to 30,000 German soldiers lay dead on the battlefield. A few thousand were still running for their lives. Over the rest sank the long night and deep silence of Russian captivity . . ."

There is little that can be added to these few sentences about the horror in the pocket. Those who had not fought their way out ended up being killed or captured in the ever-smaller pocket. Under ceaseless bombardment, it ended in terror, panic and chaos. Several larger, mixed groups did manage to slip through the Russian front west of Jasionowce on the night of July 22/23. Other elements held out throughout the 23rd in the forest west of Boniszyn and were later able to escape in small groups.

The fate of the many stragglers and *"Rückkämpfer,"* some of whom managed to endure terrible hardships and deprivation to cross the 300 to 400 kilometers to the new German lines in the Hungarian Carpathians by mid-August, was terrible.

The German XIII Corps was no more. The great highway to Lemberg (Lvov) was open to the enemy. Following its breakthroughs against Army Group North Ukraine, the Soviet First Ukrainian Front continued its expanding offensive against southern Poland. The Polish city of Lemberg fell to the Red Army on July 27, almost exactly three years after it had been taken by the Germans. The next day Przemysl was lost.

Exact figures for XIII Corps' losses were never known on the German side. Altogether, 12,000 men may have escaped from the pocket. The Russians spoke of more than 30,000 killed and 17,000 captured German soldiers – numbers which may come close to the truth.[7] In addition to these terrible human losses, the corps' entire complement of horses and all its materiel were lost.

The panzer divisions committed had also suffered heavily. The casualties sustained by the 8th Panzer Division were typical: in three weeks of heavy fighting during the month of July the division lost 2,361 men killed, wounded or missing. Materiel losses were 8 tanks, 77 armored personnel carriers and armored cars and 24 guns.

Few of the Germans taken prisoner at Brody ever returned. Among those who did were Generals Nedtwig and Lindemann, following ten years in Soviet prison camps.

Excerpts from Wehrmacht Communiques:

July 15:
. . . In the southern sector of the Eastern Front the Soviets have launched

their expected attack in the Ternopol and Luck areas. They were repulsed yesterday with the loss of many tanks, individual penetrations were sealed off . . .

July 16:
. . . In the Ternopol and Luck battle zones our divisions beat off Bolshevik attacks with heavy tank support. Penetrations were eliminated or reduced by counterattacks with the destruction of many tanks . . .

July 17:
. . . In the southern sector of the Eastern Front the defensive battle east of the Upper Bug has grown in intensity. Soviet armored forces attacking from the Ternopol and Luck areas were stopped in heavy fighting.125 enemy tanks have been destroyed here in the past two days of fighting . . .

July 18:
. . . On the southern Eastern Front the Soviets are continuing to attack east of the Upper Bug with powerful forces. Counterattacks by our divisions have smashed all attempts by the enemy to break through . . .

July 19:
. . . In the southern sector the fury of the enemy's attack has increased, especially east of the Upper Bug. Heavy fighting is raging there with enemy forces attacking in the direction of Lvov. 431 Soviet tanks have been destroyed in this sector since July 14 . . .

July 20:
. . . On the Eastern Front our divisions are engaged in heavy defensive fighting in the area east of Lvov. Attempts by the enemy to break through in the direction of the city itself have been halted . . .

July 21:
. . . In the East the fighting in the Lvov area and on the Upper Bug continues with undiminished intensity. Once again our divisions are putting up fierce resistance against the Soviets and have inflicted heavy losses on them . . .

July 22:
. . . In the East counterattacks by our troops east of Lvov have closed several gaps in the front. The Soviets have gained further ground northwest of the city . . .

July 23:
... In the East the defensive battle rages on great bitterness. In the Lvov
area enemy spearheads have reached the eastern edge of the city ...

Disposition of XIII Army Corps

Commanding General and Staff (*General der Infanterie* Hauffe)

Corps Units
Rear-echelon Services
454th Security Division (*Generalmajor* Nedtwig)
361st Infantry Division (*Generalmajor* Lindemann)
Korpsabteilung C[8] (*Generalmajor* Lange) with the 183rd, 217th and 339th Division Groups, each approximately of regimental strength
14th SS-Volunteer Division *Galizien* (*SS-Brigadeführer* Freitag)
349th Infantry Division (*Generalleutnant* Lasch)

Battle Group of the 8th Panzer Division, attached to the 349th Infantry Division,
consisting of Headquarters 8th Panzergrenadier Regiment; 2nd Battalion, 80th
Panzergrenadier Regiment; a mixed pionier company and the 249th Assault Gun
Brigade.

Notes:
[1] 454th Security Division, *Korpsabteilung* C, 14th SS-Volunteer Division *Galizien*, 361st Infantry Division
and the attached 349th Infantry Division.
[2] See disposition of XIII Corps.
[3] The 1st General Staff Officer of a division.
[4] Five captured Soviet T-34s with German crews.
[5] Excerpt from: W. Haupt: *Die 8. Panzerdivision im 2. Weltkrieg.*
[6] Excerpt from: W. Lange: *Korpsabteilung C.*
[7] See W. Lange: *Korpsabteilung C* and report by Chaplain Bader.
[8] For description of a *Korpsabteilung*, see chapter "Cherkassy."

VI

Rumania:
Army Group South Ukraine

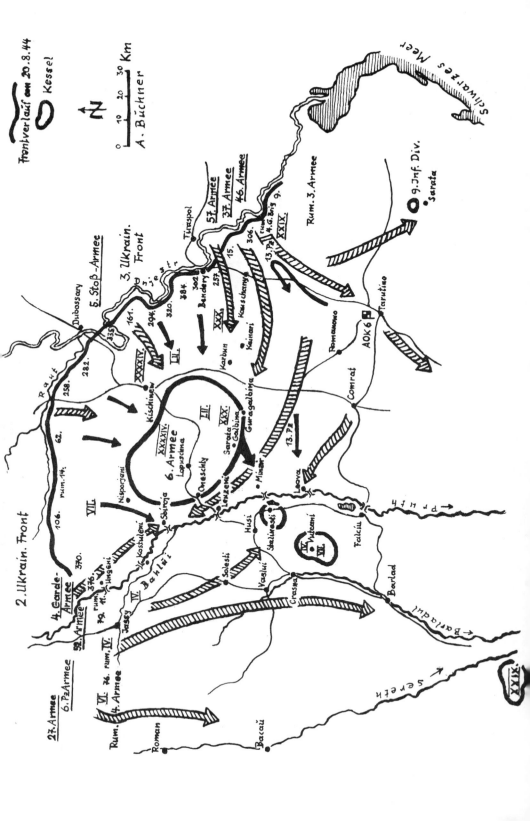

Frontverlauf am 20.8.44

Kessel

0   10   20   30 Km

N

A. Büchner

Schwarzes Meer

9.Inf.Div.
Sarata

57.Armee
37.Armee   46.Armee

XXIX

4.G.Brig 9.

306.

13.Pz

Rum.3.Armee

15.

302.

257.

Karburn

Kauschany

Kaintari

Tiraspol

5.Stoß-Armee

3.Ukrain. Front

Dnjestr

161.

294.

320.

384.

Bandery

XXXIV.

III.

XX.

Dubossary

335.

258.

282.

Rauf

Romanowo

AOK 6

Tarutino

Comrat

13.Pz

XXXIV.

6.Armee

Kischinew

II.

III.

Sarata
Gajbina

Gwasgalbina

Lopuschna

62.

106.

rum.14.

Nisporgeni

VII.

Skuleni

Leuzeni

Onreschty

Minari

Leova

2.Ukrain. Front

27.Armee

6.Pz.Armee

4.Garde-
Armee

52.Armee

376.

370.

rum. 11.
IV. Jungeni

rum.
V.

Kostuleni

Jassy

Bahlui

Husi

Vaslui

Soleschi

Stalineschi

Vutcani

IV.
VII.

Falciu

Barlad

Barladul

Sereth

XXX

Prut

rum. IV.

VI. zu. rum. IV.
4. Armee

Rum.

Roman

Bacau

Crasna

Rumania: Army Group South Ukraine

Catastrophe between the Dnestr and Prut

Bessarabia, in northern Rumania on the lower Dnestr River, is a quiet, isolated area with gently-sloping hills, broad meadows, forests and streams, with fields and farms, mulberry plantations and acacia groves, small villages with straw-roofed houses – an agrarian land with its provincial capital of Kishinev. Winding its way through the peaceful countryside, in some places with quite steep banks, was the mighty, slow-moving Dnestr River. Further to the west, amid forested hills, was the broad valley of the Prut River. Flowing through marshy areas and flooded terrain between lines of hills with steep slopes, the river and its many tributaries sought its way to the south.

This was the area where over 270,000 German soldiers were to meet their fate.

Until 1944 Bessarabia had been largely overlooked by the war. The German-Rumanian attack on the Soviet Union crossed the Dnestr, which was then the frontier, in a matter of a few days, ebbed far to the east and quiet returned to the land.

However, this tranquillity gradually began to change in early 1944. The first military vehicles and units began arriving from southern Russia. Their officers and soldiers referred to them as "advance parties." Then more came, long lines of motor vehicles of all types, horse-drawn train vehicles, and finally tired and worn-out German and Rumanian soldiers, arriving in endless columns. As the columns began to thin out, one could hear the approaching thunder of guns and see smoke rising from burning villages. The last rearguards arrived, and then came the Russians, who had now reached the Dnestr River in this southern part of the Eastern Front.

A Thin German-Rumanian Front on the Dnestr

Following major battles and months of retreat, the German and Rumanian troops withdrawing from Russia halted at the Dnestr and began occupying fixed positions once again. Here the enemy was to be halted and his advance stopped. Initially it seemed as if this might be possible.

The German troops breathed a sigh of relief – finally they would be once again manning a solid front behind the protection of a mighty river. Everywhere, in the rear, in the villages and larger cities, began the usual routine of soldiers settling in for an extended period of defense. The headquarters staffs of armies, corps and divisions sought out quarters, rear-echelon and train units moved into their billets, and supply dumps, munitions depots, supply offices and hospitals were set up. Members of the signals units laid down field telephone lines, motorcycle messengers went about their business and the artillery occupied firing positions. Further forward the heavy weapons – the mortars, infantry guns and anti-tank guns – were emplaced, and at the front the regiments, battalions and companies took over their defensive sectors.

There was a feverish period of digging in, building dugouts and bunkers and other installations. The forward trenches, with barbed wire obstacles and mine belts in front, with earth bunkers and communications trenches leading to the rear, formed the main line of resistance. Behind this a well-camouflaged system of positions was laid down. Based on previous experience, it consisted of further trenches, obstacles, strongpoints, command posts and, in places, anti-tank ditches. Following weeks of work there was a deep main defensive area, although the majority of the positions were still unmanned. This period was not entirely quiet; there were engagements of long and short duration. These operations included efforts by the Germans and Rumanians to hold onto a bridgehead on the far side of the Dnestr near Dubossary, while the Soviets attacked and won a large bridgehead near Tiraspol. In general, however, things remained quiet and the entire Dnestr line became a sector where nothing special was happening. The cities of Kishinev and Jassy became major communications centers in which the troops could relax and find some diversion from the routine of life in fixed positions.

This situation was to last into August 1944, when the land lay under the hot summer sun.

At that time the German-Rumanian defenses on the northern frontier of Rumania under the command of Army Group South Ukraine were aligned as follows:

On the right, along the lower course of the Dnestr to the Black Sea, was the Rumanian Third Army with three army corps. There were five Rumanian divisions, one Rumanian brigade, the German 9th Infantry Division and a German assault gun brigade. Next to it in a broad salient, which initially followed the Dnestr before veering sharply westward to the Raut River, was the "second" German Sixth Army[1] with four army corps, a total of fourteen German divisions, one Rumanian division and three assault gun brigades. Further west was the Rumanian Fourth Army and, finally, to the northwest the German Eighth Army, with a total of five Rumanian and three German corps with fifteen Rumanian and six German divisions as well as four German assault gun brigades.

In reserve the Army Group had:
One field training division, one panzergrenadier division and one panzer division, as well as a Rumanian armored division and several Rumanian infantry divisions and brigades (see Army Group disposition).

Altogether this was twenty-four German divisions and twenty-five Rumanian divisions or brigades with a total strength of about 650,000 men, including 340,000 German troops.

This seemingly impressive mass of troops might have sufficed for the long-term defense of the entire southern front if the Russians mounted no major offensive operations. Right from the beginning, however, there was the usual linear defense, too few reserves and not enough tanks and assault guns. In addition, two facts were deceptive: at this point in the war the German units no longer possessed strengths equivalent to their designations. It is true that the German infantry divisions there were almost up to strength[2] and, as far as one could say in wartime, were well rested. Their actual strengths were about 12-14,000 men with about 6,000 horses. But these were not the capable units of the early war years, confident and filled with belief in the "Führer." Nagging doubts about the outcome of the war were widespread. The news from all of the remaining fronts in the East and West was bad, and the homeland lay under a rain of Allied bombs. Too many experienced officers and soldiers had already fallen, and only about fifteen to twenty percent of the experienced Eastern Front troops had survived the last retreat to the Dnestr. The units had been stocked with young, insufficiently trained replacements or older men from non-combat units, including many who had never seen actual combat. Another factor was the limited mobility of the units. In most cases horse-drawn *panje* wagons had to take the place of combat vehicles, trucks and tractors. Anti-tank guns and other anti-armor weapons were in short supply, signals equipment was scarce and in some places there was a shortage of artillery ammunition.

The second major negative point was the Rumanian divisions. Their condition was even worse. As before, they were poorly trained and armed, and their morale had suffered badly from the constant German setbacks since early 1943. The Rumanians were war weary. Although the Rumanian head of state, Marshall Antonescu, remained firmly committed to the pact with Germany, secret efforts against Germany had been under way in the senior military command for some time, and some senior Rumanian officers were inclined toward treason and a coup d'état. The new Commander-in-Chief of Army Group South Ukraine, *Generaloberst* Frießner[3], quickly assessed the true situation and one of his first measures after assuming command was a proposal to the senior German commanders that the withdrawal of the front toward the Carpathians and behind the Danube was a military necessity. Naturally he met with a sharp rejection from Hitler, who still – in spite of past experience – wanted to hear nothing of withdrawals of the front. He justified this position by stressing the need to retain the loyalty of his Rumanian allies and the vitally important Rumanian oil fields. Once again, however, it was to be demonstrated that political and economic motivations make sense only when the necessary military force is available to back them up. The military forces were inadequate, Germany's Rumanian allies were preparing to change sides and the army group was about to be delivered up for destruction.

The Soviets had no thoughts of remaining on the defensive in the long term. What was even worse, was that the German side had no idea of a possible change of sides by the Rumanians and they badly underestimated the Soviets and their intentions, failing to realize what they were really up to. An increase in activity and a significant increase in traffic behind the lines was noted, but this was misinterpreted by most senior German staffs. They even believed that the Soviet command would withdraw forces from the southern front in order to bolster their huge and successful offensive against Army Group Center. Until early August there seemed to be no cause for concern. In general the enemy was quiet all along the front apart from local operations, the usual artillery activity and occasional air attacks. Appearances were deceptive, however, and the result was a misinterpretation of the situation by the German High Command, just as had happened in the case of Army Group Center.

Not until the troops movements opposite the western sector of the front persisted and expanded, did the German High Command become suspicious. Nevertheless, as late as August 16 the army group still believed that these were merely preparations for a larger local attack.

On August 16, for example, the Sixth Army in its projecting salient in the central sector on the Dnestr reported:

"Nothing special. Quiet everywhere!"

It was a fact in any case – and this was soon to result in general consternation – that the full extent of the massing of enemy forces for a new major offensive in the southern part of the Eastern Front had not been recognized in time. Even the usually very dependable "Foreign Armies East" Department in the OKH had erred this time over the timing and strength of the enemy offensive and had even gone on record as considering such an eventuality as very unlikely. The Soviets had once again cleverly disguised their tremendous buildup of troops and materiel and thus fooled the German High Command.

There was one other thing which the Germans at first failed to recognize and then paid too little attention to. Something was up with the Rumanians. There was nothing tangible or provable, but it seemed as if Germany's ally was up to something underhanded. There was even talk among the population of Jassy of an imminent revolution. It would not be long before the true state of affairs was revealed. Not only would the mass of the Rumanian troops fail to offer any resistance worthy of mention, but some units would openly rebel. As already stated, Soviets ambitions in the south went much further than the reaching of the Dnestr, the old Russian-Rumanian frontier. Quietly and secretly they assembled fresh attack forces, achieving a tremendous concentration of power – the Soviets now had seemingly limitless supplies of men and materiel in every sector of the Eastern Front.

The Soviet forces were under the overall command of Marshal Timoshenko. North of Jassy there was the Second Ukrainian Front (Army General Malinovsky) with six rifle armies, one tank army of two corps, an independent tank, mechanized and cavalry corps and the Fifth Air Army. In the large Soviet bridgehead at Tiraspol was assembled the Third Ukrainian Front (Army General Tolbuchin) with four rifle armies, two independent mechanized corps and the Seventeenth Air Army.

This made a total of ninety-four rifle divisions, six tank and mechanized corps, one cavalry corps and numerous independent units, all told 930,000 men with 16,000 pieces of artillery, rocket launchers and mortars of every caliber, 1,400 tanks and self-propelled guns and 1,760 aircraft.

Facing them at the focal point of the attack were only six German corps (four of these from Sixth Army) and two Rumanian corps with eighteen German and seventeen Rumanian divisions, as well as four brigades, two German armored divisions and five assault gun brigades, all in all about 270,000 German and 200,000 Rumanian troops with only 160 tanks (more than half of which were with the Rumanian armored division) and 283 assault guns and self-propelled howitzers. The Luftwaffe had only 232 aircraft in the area. Once again Russian superiority in artillery, tanks and aircraft was truly crushing.

It looked like a recipe for a repetition of the events at Stalingrad at the end of 1942, and it seemed that the lessons of that disaster had not been learned by the German command. Once again the German Sixth Army was involved – albeit the reformed one, created after Stalingrad – once again there were Rumanian divisions to its right and left, and once again it had no reserves. It was not only the enemy's tremendous superiority in forces which was to lead to this unsuspected and to this day misunderstood catastrophe. As at Stalingrad the Soviets sent the bulk of their infantry and tanks against the wings of Sixth Army, precisely at the boundaries with the two neighboring Rumanian corps west of the Raut River near Jassy and from their bridgehead at Tiraspol. An additional advantage of this tactic was that they avoided having to cross the formidable obstacle of the Dnestr under fire.

Once again the true nature of the approaching danger was not recognized by the German side. A recent assessment of the enemy position by Army Group South Ukraine forecast an imminent Soviet offensive near Jassy, but only a secondary attack near Tiraspol.

The command of the Sixth Army was no longer as comfortable with the situation as before. On August 19 it reported:

"The possibility exists that something is brewing on our right flank ."

It was already far too late for decisive countermeasures, because the same day brought the first early signs of the coming storm: that morning, following a heavy bombardment, the Soviets attacked the Rumanian Fourth Army on the right wing and the Sixth Army on the left wing.

The first attacks were reconnaissance attacks and probes in company and battalion strength, which were intended to feel out the German-Rumanian front for "soft" spots. In the afternoon the positions of the Rumanian VI Corps in the west were struck by an artillery bombardment lasting forty-five minutes. The subsequent attack broke into the Rumanian positions and took the commanding heights.

This was only the prelude, however. A somewhat eerie quiet hung over the rest of the front.

•

On the eve of August 19 German sentries reported something unusual: light signals and parachute illumination flares were seen from the Russian side, which were answered in places by the Rumanians. No one on the German side could make any sense of these signals, which might perhaps be coincidence, and they were assigned no great significance. The signals were of significance, however, and this was soon to be demonstrated in the worst fashion.

The "Black" 20th of August

The next day, August 20, was a Sunday.

The sun rose in the East like a blood-red ball. The early morning sky was cloudless and promised a hot summer day. It was precisely 0500.

Suddenly, there was a roar in the west as thousands of light and heavy guns, "Stalin Organs" and mortars abruptly opened fire.[4] It was the beginning of an enemy preparatory bombardment which swelled to a massed bombardment on a scale never before experienced. For an hour-and-a-half shells, mortar rounds and rockets poured down on the Rumanian IV and VI Corps and the German 76th Division to a depth of eight kilometers. The sun disappeared behind an impenetrable wall of smoke and dust thrown up from the dry earth. The hail of fire obliterated obstacles, covered trenches and positions, pounded bunkers and dugouts, destroyed guns and heavy weapons, severed lines of communication and killed or wounded many men. The Soviet Air Force sent whole squadrons to bomb the German and Rumanian rear areas.

At 0630 the foremost Soviet rifle divisions went to the attack. The Russian infantry and their supporting tanks advanced on a front of thirty kilometers behind the barrage, supported by large numbers of close-support aircraft.

This was not just a major attack, it was the beginning of a major offensive!

As the surviving German and Rumanian troops crawled from their half-destroyed bunkers and dugouts, dazed and terrified, they saw the leading Red Army troops emerge from the wall of smoke and dust and charge their positions, shouting and firing.

The Rumanian defense – where any was offered – collapsed quickly. Elements of both Rumanian corps, probably in secret agreement with the attacking enemy, abandoned their positions with scarcely any fighting, while the remaining units were quickly broken. Only the German 76th Infantry Division, attached to the Rumanian VI Corps, offered any resistance in what was already a virtually hopeless situation.

Individual machine-guns fired here and there, German troops threw hand grenades at the attackers, and groups of grenadiers gathered around a company commander or platoon leader and fired to all sides. Nevertheless, the defense collapsed under the Soviet assault, defense sectors were overrun, nests of resistance outflanked and taken from the rear, strongpoints were surrounded and later destroyed.

In spite of determined resistance in places and isolated counterattacks, the Russians also broke through the 76th Division's sector. Losses were heavy. Only a few of those at the front came back. The others? – killed – wounded – missing – captured . . .

A report reached the division commander of the "76th" from the division observation post: "The Russians are through!" The enemy was already rolling toward the Jassy road. Soviet tanks and trucks carrying infantry rolled through the Rumanian positions virtually unopposed. And, seemingly unmolested by Russian troops, the Rumanians pulled back on both sides of the 76th Division, apparently in disarray. A hesitant counterattack by a reserve division of the Rumanian IV Corps had scarcely got under way when the Rumanians pulled back again.

By about 1000 the Rumanian main line of resistance had been completely broken, its divisions withdrawing with scarcely any fighting. At about the same time Russian armored spearheads and motorized infantry appeared at the western edge of Jassy, and by midday enemy units were crossing the Bahlui River under the cover of a tremendous artillery barrage.

The incoming reports shocked the headquarters of Army Group South Ukraine, located far from the scene of events. The Commander-in-Chief ordered an immediate counterattack by all available reserves to restore the former main line of resistance. However, *Generaloberst* Frießner understood the situation completely: the enemy was already too strong and had penetrated deeply, the Rumanians had given up and the German reserves were much too weak in the face of the enemy's superiority.

Nevertheless, the 10th Panzergrenadier Division and the 258th Infantry Division, which had been hurriedly withdrawn from the Dnestr Front, its combat elements moved in by truck, threw themselves determinedly into the battle. As the Rumanian reserve divisions were already showing signs of disintegration, there was no joint counterattack, and the individual German advances were unsuccessful. The lone Rumanian armored division, "Greater Rumania" (equipped with German tanks), which went into action in the afternoon, met with initial success before it, too, was halted. Since it had proved impossible to throw back the far superior enemy forces or seal off their deep penetrations, the 10th Panzergrenadier and 258th Infantry Divisions struggled to at least screen to the west the large gap which had been torn in the front. The remaining elements of the 76th Division, which had been abandoned by the Rumanian divisions on its left and right, had no choice but to withdraw as well. The artillery hastily changed positions, and those units still on hand were able to pull back to the hills near Letcani, northwest of Jassy. All that arrived from the units which had been manning the front-line positions were scattered squads and small groups, bringing only the weapons they could carry.

As a result of the failure of the Rumanians to stand and fight, the Russian penetration quickly gained further ground. By evening the enemy had penetrated to the center of Jassy, which was the scene of heavy fighting.

Events in the east in the Soviet Tiraspol bridgehead went much the same as in the west before Jassy on this "Black" August 20.

The Russians were so certain of victory beforehand that they even sent some of their radio messages in clear text. One such message, intercepted at about 0300, read:

> "Marshall Timoshenko expects every soldier of the Red Army to do his duty!"

And another at 0345:

> "In fifteen minutes it will be night again!"

In fact, it would become dark as night again, in spite of the arrival of morning.

At 0400 – an hour earlier than at Jassy – there began a preparatory bombardment of fifty minutes duration. Here too the main Russian attack was preceded by smaller attacks whose aim was to capture important terrain features or make initial penetrations. These attacks were beaten off almost everywhere, and the men in the front lines and in the headquarters of the German XXX Corps in the rear breathed a sigh of relief, believing they had withstood everything the Russians had to throw at them.

It was 0700. Precisely on the hour hundreds of Russian guns opened fire. Numerous heavy batteries of 122mm and 172mm guns blasted away, "Stalin Organs" unleashed howling salvoes of thirty-six rockets each, whole mortar regiments opened fire and a huge number of the notorious *"Ratschbum"* all-purpose guns joined in – ever more, ever stronger, until finally there was just one tremendous flashing, rumbling, crashing and roaring.

The countryside, which until now had been largely at peace under the hot summer sun, was soon transformed into a torn-up battlefield. This was no local attack, this was the beginning of a major Soviet offensive, unsuspected and unexpected.

The tremendous bombardment lasted ninety minutes, until 0930. As the last shells burst, the massed Soviet infantry stormed forward, escorted by large numbers of Stalin heavy tanks and aircraft. With loud victorious shouts dense waves of enemy infantry broke into the positions of the German XXX Corps. In spite of their well-constructed positions, the defenders had already suffered heavy losses from the inferno of the Soviet bombardment and the bombing attacks.

The enemy quickly penetrated deeper into the defensive zone of the 15th Infantry Division, whose losses in soldiers and weapons already stood at about twenty percent, even though the troops who had survived the bombardment defended as best they could. Individual strongpoints stood their ground desperately, and in the burning villages every house was contested. When the ammunition ran out there was bitter hand-to-hand fighting. Counterattacks were carried out and the artillery laid down direct fire, destroying eighteen enemy tanks by evening. All in vain. The onrushing, overwhelming enemy took trenches and nests of resistance, penetrating deeper and pouring forward through the gaps and holes in the defense. With great effort the remaining troops from the fixed positions and the still intact division reserve established a makeshift line and finally a semi-circular defensive front around Kauschany, which held initially.

Even harder hit was the neighboring 306th Infantry Division, whose strength had been reduced by a third by the preparatory bombardment. The surviving troops manning the trenches were mostly eliminated in bitter close-quarters fighting, and the division's front collapsed. By 1000 the first enemy tanks were driving around the division command post. Fleeing grenadiers arrived from the front, many of them dazed and disoriented, some carrying their personal weapons, others with none at all. The division now committed its slender reserves. Blocking positions were manned, retreating infantry, stragglers and train personnel were intercepted and put into the line. Other than a few machine-guns and mortars, which were low on ammunition, all the defenders had to hold off the Russian assault groups, with their tanks and motorized infantry, was rifles. Only the heavily-fortified *"Leontina"* strongpoint was able to hold out until night, when it, too, succumbed. The Russians later reported 1,200 dead and 250 captured German soldiers as well as 37 captured guns in this one sector alone.

The communications net had largely been destroyed and the situation of the two divisions of XXX Corps was confused and unclear. In contrast there was no lack of clarity concerning the situation of the Rumanian Third Army's XXIX Corps on the right. The corps consisted of two Rumanian divisions and the German 9th Infantry Division.

It was the same as at Jassy: a large numbers of Rumanian troops left their trenches during the Russian bombardment and disappeared to the rear, others abandoned their positions when the attack began, threw down their guns and ran away, leaving great quantities of weapons and materiel behind. Only a very few put up any kind of resistance. It even seemed very likely that, as a result of secret negotiations between Russian and Rumanian officers the night before, some Rumanian units, in particular the 4th Mountain Infantry Brigade, had abandoned parts of their defensive sectors and had intentionally allowed the enemy to infiltrate their positions.

The entire sector of the Rumanian XXIX Corps had been broken without noteworthy resistance and brought to collapse, while the 9th Division, abandoned by its Rumanian neighbors, was forced to fight a bitter battle to all sides and was gradually forced back toward the south. At Tiraspol, too, the failure of the Rumanians had resulted in a large gap in the front. Located precisely on the right wing of the Sixth Army, it expanded and grew steadily.

All was not yet lost, however. The German command apparatus was still functioning, and late in the morning the first countermeasures were taken.

The Sixth Army's mobile reserve, the 13th Panzer Division, was alerted. But what was the status of this panzer division which was to carry out a counterattack on its own? Following earlier detachments to other units the division had available one panzer battalion with thirty-five tanks, two panzergrenadier battalions and elements of the pioneer battalion. And these weak forces were to throw back the Soviets and recapture the lost positions? From the beginning the counterattack was a questionable operation against such an overpowering enemy with his hundreds of tanks.

Nevertheless, the tanks and panzergrenadiers set out, advanced slowly in spite of strong resistance and by late afternoon even reached the high ground south of the Dnestr. Then, however, the division could go no further. The counterattack bogged down with heavy losses, without having closed the gap in the front. That was now out of the question.

On the afternoon of that first day of the offensive, as the remnants of the shattered German divisions struggled to master the situation in rear blocking positions and lines of security, and the weak 13th Panzer Division was forced back still further by the enemy, the roads leading to the rear were already jammed with fleeing Rumanian troops with and without weapons, on foot, on horseback, in motorized and horse-drawn vehicles. Suddenly the Commander-in-Chief of the Rumanian Army, Marshall Antonescu, arrived. Having learned of the conduct of his troops, he had come in person to try and halt them and bring them back to the front. Several senior officers were reduced in rank by his entourage and immediately relieved of their posts. As one German liaison officer reported, Marshall Antonescu employed draconian measures in an attempt to drive his soldiers forward – in vain. The Marshall had no idea that he would be deposed in three days and imprisoned.

It was a terrible duplicity of events. The "second" Sixth Army, like the first at Stalingrad, had been almost completely broken through on both wings and its deep flanks were increasingly threatened.

The army headquarters far to the rear in Tarutino was as yet unaware of the terrible danger. Late that evening, because of the limited numbers of reports arriving and the shortage of aerial reconnaissance, the army staff knew only that the right wing was under heavy pressure. The army commanders were unaware of the most important development, namely that the Soviets had gone to the offensive at Jassy simultaneously.

The commanders of Army Group South Ukraine were already well aware how the beginning battle would end. The Rumanian divisions had all but collapsed and had disappeared from the front. Nothing could be expected of them. There were scarcely any reserves available. The enemy had achieved deep breakthroughs, two giant gaps loomed to the left and right of the Sixth Army and there were no means available to plug them up or seal them off.

If there had at least been adequate numbers of air units, bomber and Stuka units, the enemy spearheads, the tank and motorized columns, could have been stopped. But the Luftwaffe was not there and could not help, because there were no aircraft for the hard-pressed Sixth Army. The few German machines which did appear were simply swept from the skies by the masses of Soviet aircraft. The two Soviet Air Armies flew more than 2,000 sorties on August 20, the Luftwaffe 230. The next day the Luftwaffe appeared only rarely or not at all.

Even though the battle had gone badly from the very beginning, the German commanders could not make the decision to withdraw the Sixth Army to the Prut. Furthermore, approval had not been received from Führer Headquarters. In the opinion of the army group's Chief-of-Staff the enemy penetrations would have to be "ironed out" before there could be any question of an orderly withdrawal.

He obviously had no concept of the true situation at the front.

One other thing must be mentioned which is scarcely believable: while the right wing of the Sixth Army had already been torn up, while the left wing near Jassy was "on fire" and enemy breakthroughs on both sides of the army were almost complete, the main body of the army – the divisions on the Dnestr and Raut Rivers – had no idea of what was in store for them or of the disaster which was approaching. The central front was still largely quiet, there had been no attacks there. Those troops not in the front-line positions went about their normal duties. For example, on August 20 and 21 the 257th Infantry Division held a division sports day, taking advantage of the fine weather. The suntanned soldiers heard a rumbling in the distance like a heavy summer thunderstorm, but no one suspected what it meant and few gave it any thought. None knew that their comrades in the other divisions were already engaged in a heavy, costly battle, and that soon they would be too.

On the morning of August 21 the Soviets resumed their attack, in order to expand the breakthroughs achieved the previous day and drive into the German rear with their tank and motorized units. The Germans, on the other hand, were forced to bend back their shattered wings further, and their open flanks were increasingly threatened.

Near Jassy a joint German-Rumanian counterattack was supposed to halt the Russians. The effort was in vain, even though the attacking 10th Panzergrenadier Division, with about twenty tanks and a panzergrenadier regiment, achieved initial success in the course of the morning. Then, however, the division ran into a powerful enemy spearhead with 100 to 150 tanks, suffered heavy losses and was forced back. The single Rumanian armored division played no part in the attack; it had simply pulled back and was not seen again.

The main burden of the increasingly heavy fighting was borne by the infantry, which were steadily pushed back. As the area of penetration could not be sealed off, it was now vital to extend the front to the south in order to prevent an enemy thrust into the deep left flank of the Sixth Army.

So the remains of the 76th Division fought their way back in a southeasterly direction and late that morning reached the area south of Jassy. But before the division was able to extend the front of the 10th Panzergrenadier Division, which had likewise fallen back, a mighty Russian spearhead, with about 300 tanks and mounted infantry, broke through to the south. What was left of the division was torn apart. Those elements which survived and managed to reach safety in the west fought on with other divisions. The 76th Infantry Division had virtually ceased to exist on the second day of fighting, the first German division to be destroyed.

In the western area of penetration the front now crumbled away piece by piece, like a landslide. Because of the worsening situation the 79th Infantry Division now left its positions and pulled back. Jassy was abandoned at about midday. In order to retain some semblance of cohesion it was necessary that evening to withdraw the 376th Division, which had not yet been attacked, from its defensive sector. The German IV Corps (*General* Mieth) struggled to master the situation by establishing new defensive lines. A new line on the Bahlui held, and all attacks against it were repulsed.

On the second day of his major offensive the enemy expanded his breakthrough near Jassy to an area 65 kilometers deep and 25 kilometers wide and by late morning had gone over to a rapid pursuit deep into Rumanian territory with tank and motorized units.

Things looked even worse in the Tiraspol battle zone. Reports from the observation posts in the grey dawn offered a depressing picture: in the distance long, dense columns of Russians were marching and driving south and southwest completely unmolested. There was no longer any question of a counterattack. The panzer battalion of the 13th Panzer Division had been reduced to about twenty tanks and was forced to attack here and there in an effort to help the hard-pressed infantry at least for a little while. Heavy defensive battles raged all day on the army's already largely open flank under the hot sun. Caught in the maelstrom of the enemy breakthrough, XXX Corps resisted the constant pressure from the masses of enemy tanks and infantry with the last of its strength. The 306th and 15th Infantry Divisions, which had been hardest hit, were pushed back steadily, but nevertheless sought to halt the enemy and in some places succeeded. Makeshift battle groups under the command of veteran officers formed breakwaters in the flood of onrushing Soviets. From midday there was no radio contact with the army, there had been no field telephone communication since the day before. Messengers failed to get through, there were no orders. The corps' Commanding General, *General* Postel, went forward himself to intervene and try and hold his divisions' wavering front. When two battalions faltered he drove forward under enemy fire and stayed with them until the soldiers had regained their composure and were standing fast.

The General threw his last reserve, the 153rd Field Training Division, into the battle, sending the men in by truck in an effort to establish a blocking position in the sector abandoned by the Rumanians – in vain. In a tank battle southeast of Kauschany which lasted until evening, the 13th Panzer Division and elements of XXX Corps destroyed ninety-two enemy tanks. It was a fine accomplishment, but what were ninety-two tanks to the Soviets, with their masses of armor.

When XXX Corps drew up the day's balance late in the evening, the situation looked dismal. In spite of their heroic efforts in defense the troops had been driven further back, there were new penetrations and various towns had been lost.

The 15th Division had been badly battered. The commander of the 306th Infantry Division had been killed in an air attack. His division was smashed. The 13th Panzer Division had no tanks left. The roads to the rear teemed with Rumanians fleeing to the south in panic, as well as a few German train units.

The worst thing was that the enemy was advancing further south and southwest in spite of all resistance. The danger for the entire Sixth Army on its open right flank, which could no longer be protected, became greater by the hour.

By the evening of August 21 the Russians had broken through to a depth of fifty kilometers in the Tiraspol area and were already fifteen kilometers from Tarutino, site of the headquarters of the Sixth Army.

The army command was now aware of the seriousness of the situation. It also knew that all available and committed reserves had already largely been destroyed. There was nothing left with which to halt the enemy. *Generaloberst* Frießner, the army group's Commander-in-Chief, was forced to realize that the two break-through areas to the left and right of the Sixth Army had become so deep and large by the second day of the enemy offensive, that the enemy and his masses of forces had won complete operational freedom of action. In the west, in the Jassy area, the Rumanian Fourth Army and the Rumanian corps attached to the Eighth Army had collapsed, were no longer fighting, were disintegrating and had virtually ceased to exist. The Eighth Army had ceased to play any role, as it was left with only its left wing with three German divisions and it was being forced to withdraw these to the southwest in the direction of the Carpathian Mountains.

General Mieth's IV Corps, now completely cut off from the Eighth Army, was placed under the command of Sixth Army as a result of the latest developments, but it, too, was of little significance. The corps, separated from Sixth Army by the enemy and the Prut, was out of contact and had to conduct its own battle on the west side of the river.

Advancing irresistibly, the Russians drove on deep into Rumanian territory, their spearheads fanning out. The two pincers now turned toward one another to begin the encirclement of the Sixth Army. Nevertheless, the commands of the army and army group hesitated to issue the most important and urgent order: Immediate withdrawal of the army to the west to the Prut!

Everyone was waiting for approval from Führer Headquarters.

Nothing Left but to Fall Back to the Prut – With The Enemy All Around

Heavy fighting lasted through the night. The next morning, August 22, finally brought a decision. Headquarters Sixth Army used its radio net to issue orders, specifying immediate relay to the units, for an accelerated withdrawal behind the Prut. Withdrawal to begin at 1930!

This was the army's last order, but it was already much too late for its implementation. By the time the order reached the corps and divisions during late morning it had long been overtaken by events. The Soviets were meeting virtually no resistance in their breakthrough areas. They were already marching south toward Barlad and Galatz unhindered, at the same time sending powerful forces to the southeast and southwest.

Now the Sixth Army was not only being threatened in its deep flanks, but had already been enveloped and there were clear indications that it was about to be encircled. Every hour was vital if the Prut was to be reached. Which would reach the Prut, where the Germans hoped to establish a new front, first – the Soviet tank and motorized columns or the unwieldy, mostly horse-drawn German infantry divisions?

This day was just as bitter and bloody as the one before. Far in the rear the Commander-in-Chief and his staff were forced to abandon their headquarters in Tarutino, as enemy tanks were approaching. The army headquarters initially moved to Comrat, but in the evening the enemy arrived there too, and the headquarters staff just managed to withdraw into the area southeast of Barlad. As a result the commanders of the Sixth Army were out of touch with their units for all the coming events.

In the west IV Corps was already engaged in heavy fighting south of Jassy, struggling to keep the Prut crossings near Kostuleni and Sbiroja open for the main body of the Sixth Army. However, in spite of continuous delaying battles by the already decimated divisions, by evening the villages of Kostuleni and Ungeni and the bridges there had fallen into Russian hands.

In the east the badly battered XXX Corps was forced to withdraw further, resulting in a very serious threat to the army's wide open right flank.

With desperate determination the decimated German units threw themselves at the onrushing enemy again and again. Hastily assembled battle groups fought to all sides. The remains of regiments, battalions and companies fought off enemy attacks all day but were forced back. They sought new lines somewhere among the hills and woods, defended villages and were forced back again before digging in once more at the next favorable location. Enemy tanks – artillery fire – strafing attacks – dead and wounded. Everywhere the sound of battle, black-gray smoke and dust, burning villages . . . Dead-tired soldiers, who had been in action for three days without rest, staggered back, taking their wounded with them.

A jumble of infantry, anti-tank crews, artillerymen, train soldiers and pioniers swirled into the night, which was filled with signal flares of every color and the red glow of burning villages.

The nearest division of XXX Corps, or what was left of it, the 306th Infantry Division, together with alert units, airfield personnel and an assault gun brigade, was still fighting off enemy attacks in a forward blocking position near Romanowo. When the defenders were outflanked they decided to break out to the west, led by the assault guns. The assault guns were running low on fuel and a longer rest stop was called in a large valley. Then, in the afternoon, disaster struck. A concentric Russian attack completely smashed the remaining units. There was no possibility of assembling the survivors. The 306th Division had ceased to exist.

In the meantime the badly battered 13th Panzer Division, which had lost all of its tanks, was engaged in a forced march through the enemy to the Prut, where it was to occupy two small bridgeheads for the expected arrival of elements of the Sixth Army. While at the end of the third day of fighting powerful enemy tank and motorized forces were driving the two spearheads further southeast and southwest and an encirclement of the Sixth Army was becoming more obvious, the German divisions in the salient on the Dnestr continued to remain oblivious to the true seriousness of the situation. They had received orders from the corps responsible to pull back and were preparing to abandon their well-fortified positions which had not been attacked so far.

•

Dawn came on the 23rd of August.

On the fourth day of the Soviet offensive the situation for the German troops between Jassy and Tiraspol was worsening by the hour.

In the west IV Corps and the remains of its three divisions (376th, 11th and 79th Rumanian) were defending south of Jassy. Initially the corps succeeded in repulsing all attacks, but then was forced to withdraw in a southerly direction. The corps was alone on a large stage. There was no contact with the main body of Sixth Army to the east and it therefore received no reports or orders. So *General* Mieth, the corps' Commanding General, held firm to his last assignment, to hold the Prut crossings near Sbiroja and Scoposeni for the army divisions expected from the east, in preparation for the occupation of a new position on the west bank of the Prut. It became clear that his corps had already been outflanked when the 10th Panzergrenadier Division, which was to have secured another bridge near Husi, ran into enemy tanks there. There was more bad news: the headquarters staff of VII Corps, which reached the Prut ahead of his divisions, was surprised by Russian tanks near the Leuzeni bridge in the afternoon and scattered. The enemy had also taken possession of this bridge. Only further south were bridges secured. The 13th Panzer Division was holding two bridgeheads near Leova and Falciu. Train and rear-echelon units from various divisions of the Sixth Army were already arriving there and were being sent across the river.

The main body of the Sixth Army now faced an extremely difficult withdrawal. It would have to be carried out under constant enemy pressure and in the face of increasing signs of encirclement. Four German army corps had to reach the Prut as quickly as possible.

VII Corps had the shortest distance to cover. Throughout the 23rd of August the three divisions of the corps carried out a rapid fighting withdrawal toward the Prut bridges near Sbiroja and Leuzeni, sixty kilometers away.

The men of the 370th Division marched in the sweltering heat, their tongues hanging out, so to speak, their feet hurting and sweat running down their faces. They had been marching for almost twenty hours, all through the previous night, the morning and into the afternoon with only brief rest stops. "To the Prut" was the watchword among the grenadier regiments, the artillery, the pioniers and anti-tank crews, the signals battalion, the medical companies, trains and other units.

And they made it!

During the coming night and the 24th of August the 370th Division crossed the river over the bridges near Sbiroja and Scoposeni and linked up with IV Corps, which from then on was referred to as "Battle Group Mieth." The other two divisions of VII Corps failed to reach the Prut. The Russians, who had broken through the rear Trajan position, were waiting for them. An attack by the two divisions to force their way through failed in the face of heavy resistance. The Rumanian 14th Infantry Division, the only one left in the army's zone, disintegrated and fled. The 106th Division was caught by Russian tanks and mechanized infantry from the north and south. A frightful battle ensued and within forty-eight hours the division had been almost completely destroyed. The 106th Division had ceased to exist like the 76th and 306th Divisions before it. Some minor elements of the division managed to reach temporary safety on the west bank of the Prut.

During the previous night XXXXIV Corps had begun an orderly withdrawal from the large salient on the Raut and Dnestr Rivers. The divisions marched out of their positions, which had not so far been attacked, and the enemy did not pursue until later. However, since the Russians had already broken into LII Corps' withdrawal from the east and were launching ever stronger attacks against the remains of XXX Corps from the south, a great mixup soon developed. The withdrawal by the three corps soon disintegrated into a disorderly retreat. The following radio message from Headquarters Sixth Army reached Army Group South Ukraine on the 23rd: "Withdrawal proceeding according to plan . . .", however the reality was much different.

The corps and divisions crossed on the few major roads, which by now were completely jammed. Columns ran into each other, units became inextricably entangled. Soon all order in the retreating masses of troops collapsed. By the early morning of the 23rd Kishinev was completely clogged, the major road to Husi totally blocked. The side roads, too, were filled with dense columns, often three and four abreast. They stopped, started again and stopped. Progress was slow and laborious. Tremendous traffic jams developed at crossroads as the columns became tangled. There were great knots of horse-drawn train vehicles, motor vehicles, supply wagons, field kitchens, heavy trucks carrying supplies, cars and *panje* wagons. Drivers cursed, officers shouted, military police tried to sort out the tangle of vehicles. In many places there was virtually no movement. There were already dozens of derelict vehicles at the roadsides with broken wheels or axles, unharnessed horses and motor vehicles abandoned for lack of fuel.

Rear area supply dumps and munitions dumps which could not be evacuated were already being set on fire and blown up. Those elements of XXX and LII Corps still able to fight tried to make a stand to buy some time, but they were soon forced to fall back.

The enemy pressure from the east, southeast and south was becoming increasingly heavy, and the penetrations and breakthroughs from three sides grew ever greater. For example, in the evening the Commanding General of LII Corps found himself forced to engage Soviet motorized forces with the help of assault guns, and during the night of August 23/24 XXXXIV Corps had to abandon Kishinev, after the enemy had crossed the Dnestr and was pressing from the north.

For Army Group South Ukraine there was no longer any doubt: The Soviets were driving deep into Rumania and were trying to complete the encirclement of the Sixth Army. On the evening of the 23rd Sixth Army was left with only a narrow corridor to the Prut near Husi. During the coming night the hard-pressed and pursued masses of German troops struggled to reach the river. Disastrous events were taking place elsewhere, however, of which most of the German soldiers would only learn much later.

Revolution in Rumania! Marshall Antonescu, who was well disposed toward Germany, had been imprisoned and the young Rumanian monarch had taken control of the nation. Rumanians were laying down their arms, but this was of little significance to developments at the front.

The catastrophe of the Sixth Army had begun and continued to develop at breakneck speed.

August 24 came.

•

The Soviets made fresh breakthroughs through the thin German defensive lines and rearguards. While the increasingly disorderly retreat by the masses of troops and vehicles ground its way to the west and southwest, small units, battle groups and rearguards sought to fight off attacks from all sides, weather the storm and fight their way through, until they were overwhelmed by the enemy advance. The Commanding Generals of LII and XXXXIV Corps arrived at the command post of XXX Corps, where the increasingly critical situation was discussed. The two Generals had seen plenty along the way, and their cars had made the trip along the plugged roads only with great difficulty. The three Generals, now without any leadership from Sixth Army, from which nothing more was heard, discussed possible joint measures aimed at averting impending doom and the threatening fate of complete encirclement. Depressed and disappointed, the three corps Generals took their leave. Inside they already knew that joint action with their unwieldy foot troops, gigantic trains of horse-drawn and motor vehicles and lack of communications would be all but impossible, to say nothing of the overpowering tank and motorized units of the Soviet forces closing in from all sides.

That afternoon near Husi developments began to follow in rapid succession.

For days trains and supply units from the various divisions had been rolling in an uninterrupted stream through the city, which lay in a deep valley a few kilometers west of the Prut. All of those who passed through Husi thought they had seen the worst. "Thank God that the Prut is behind us" was a common theme among the drivers and train soldiers passing through Husi in the early afternoon. Then, suddenly, the roar of tank cannon, and twenty or more Soviet tanks appeared from the west. They drove into the city, firing as they came, and charged into the German train columns, causing terrible chaos. Teams of horses were shot, vehicles smashed, trucks were set on fire. Everywhere there were dead and wounded. Those who survived ran away blindly. A few elements survived to reach the village of Falciu later that afternoon, where they reported the terrible news of the Russian surprise attack on Husi.

This ambush was not the worst however. Much more serious was that at about noon an entire Soviet tank corps of the Second Ukrainian Front had captured the important city of Husi from the west. The Soviets had immediately sent a spearhead ahead as far as the crossing over the Prut near Stalinesti, where they met tanks and motorized infantry of the Third Ukrainian Front advancing from the east.

The last gap near Husi had been sealed, the enemy ring around the Sixth Army had been closed for good. The word spread from unit to unit and from man to man: We're surrounded! We're in the pocket!

Those German units still capable of resistance continued to fight on against the Russian forces appearing everywhere. Thrown-together units formed new fronts and defended to all sides. The artillery's remaining guns drove into the open to engage the masses of Soviet infantry, while the anti-tank guns engaged the T-34s until they were out of ammunition. In spite of this the German units were outflanked, cut off, encircled, scattered, wiped out, destroyed.

During the course of the day LII Corps was pushed further back, its front was broken and outflanked several times, its units were being squeezed closer together.

XXX Corps, which earlier had been forced to bear the main weight of the Soviet offensive in the east, was worst off. After first clearing it of Russian forces, the remains of the corps' divisions, squeezed together and badly mixed up, held their ground in the Carbuna area, seventeen kilometers east of Guragalbina.

Great numbers of troops and vehicles from all arms were drawn into the large village, which extended toward the valley, from all sides as if by magnetism. This was where the gate to freedom was supposed to be, but Carbuna was fast becoming a witch's cauldron. The enemy was in hot pursuit from the east, was advancing from the south and had barred the way to the west. Russian fighters and close-support aircraft attacked with guns and bombs. An initial breakout attempt by elements of the corps early in the afternoon failed. Soviet bombers and close-support aircraft attacked the front of the attack wave, inflicting heavy losses. The commander of the 257th Division was among those killed. The orderly withdrawal was becoming a debacle. Motorized and foot columns flooded back in panic: The enemy is all around! Everyone pushed, hurried and drove southwest, where the only hope of escape now lay.

The roads were frequently blocked by destroyed or abandoned vehicles, and the forest tracks were jammed with train vehicles and littered with every type of equipment imaginable. Exhausted and worn out from the constant fighting, the heat and the strain of marching, dense rows of soldiers trudged along beside the roads. The wounded were in a pitiful condition, as treatment was all but impossible. The less seriously wounded made their way as best they could, on crutches or supported by comrades. The more serious cases were taken along in requisitioned farm wagons; many were unconscious, some near death.

Everyone wanted to get away as quickly as possible, just as long they did not fall into the hands of the enemy.

The area west of Guragalbina was to be captured after dark. That evening a major storm with heavy rain struck the area, which made the already poor dirt roads through the extended forest region all but impassable. Most of the vehicles and much of the horse-drawn artillery had to be abandoned. As darkness fell, loud explosions could be heard as the guns were blown up and the vehicles set on fire. All around could be seen muzzle flashes, showing that the enemy was drawing nearer and nearer.

That same evening Army Group South Ukraine came to the conclusion that the encircling ring around the Sixth Army had become so solid and thick that any escape from the pocket by substantial forces was unlikely.

Outside the pocket, Headquarters Sixth Army was receiving scarcely any radio reports from the corps. The only hope was that the bulk of the army might still fight its way to the crossing over the Prut near Husi, where "Korpsgruppe Mieth" was holding out on the west bank.

In the meantime, during the night increasing numbers of troops tried to make their way from the Carbuna forest region to the Guragalbina area, which had become the major assembly area for all surviving units. From here the trapped German forces intended to break out to the west via the shortest route, cross the Prut and reassemble on the west bank where there was still a German front – or so they believed.

During the night of August 24/25 *General* Postel, the Commanding General of XXX Corps, who had assumed command of the breakout attempt, reported by radio:

> "Are surrounded, beginning the breakthrough to the Prut in a southwesterly direction."

This was the last report from the Sixth Army, now surrounded in the Lapuschna-Oneschty-Guragalbina area. The distant army command did not hear from it again.

Sixth Army Encircled – Futile Breakout Attempts

General Postel now intended to break through between Guragalbina and Sarate-Galbina toward Husi in three columns.

There was bitter fighting in the entire encirclement area throughout the 25th of August and there were already increasing signs of disintegration. As dawn was breaking the commander of the 294th Division left Guragalbina, where the last conference of Generals had taken place. All around he saw the hordes of men, horses and vehicles which had gathered there, saw soldiers from every unit, saw exhausted, worn-out men lying about, heard shouts, cries, complaining and swearing. He noticed that train vehicles had been set on fire, documents were being burned, and that here and there weapons had been destroyed and items of equipment discarded. He also saw officers trying to restore order, saw shattered trucks, horses running loose, abandoned and disabled guns, train vehicles with their contents strewn about, shot-up vehicles and many dead and wounded from the latest air attacks. Clouds of smoke drifted over the partly-destroyed village.

As the swirling mass thinned out he came upon assembled groups of soldiers readying their small arms. They were the battle groups which were to force the breakthrough. The men in the valley meadow numbered about 1,000 men – 1,000 men from his entire division, which eight days ago was almost 14,000 men strong. Now there were no big guns, no heavy weapons, no vehicles and no field kitchens. As the soldiers gathered around him, soldier stood beside officer, grenadier beside artilleryman, anti-tank gunner beside pionier. Some of the men were already wounded. Haggard, dirty, hopeless faces looked at him silently and imploringly.

There was little more to say. A few words of thanks, then the final order: "Get ready! We're breaking out in an hour! Move out!" As the battle groups moved into position, *Generalmajor* von Eichstedt picked up a rifle and inserted a clip of ammunition.

Everywhere units were moving across the terrain, troops of soldiers who assembled, separated, mixed with others and left again. Several assault guns moved up, and two or three batteries drove into position. It did not look like a united, determined breakout.

Then they set out, led by the men of the "294th." They advanced through a valley, across a small stream bed and up a shallow slope. Scarcely had they reached the crest when Soviet machine-guns and anti-tank guns opened up. The General shouted "hurray!" and began to run. To the left and right his men stormed forward. The enemy fire intensified, especially from the right, smashing into the charging mass of men. In spite of losses the breakout appeared to be succeeding. Then tanks appeared on the flank. Flames spurted from their guns, shells burst and machine-gun fire raked the ranks of German troops, who had nothing more than small arms with which to respond. The numbers of dead and wounded grew, and several men ran back the way they had come. More and more followed until all of the survivors were running to the rear.

There was no breakout, no getting through. Here as in other places the renewed German attempts to break out collapsed in the face of concentrated enemy fire. Killed in the failed attempt from the Guragalbina area were the commanders of the 294th and 384th Infantry Divisions and many of their men.

The commander of the 302nd Division and the Commanding General of XXX Corps, who had personally tried to instil order into the breakout columns that morning, were wounded.

Minor elements of the three divisions managed to escape – temporarily.

While four Soviet armies in the north, east and south had received orders to destroy the surrounded German Sixth Army, a further army and a tank corps were in position with orders to prevent a German breakthrough to the west to the Prut.

The Soviets, who were squeezing the unwieldy mass of the German army ever tighter, now drove into the pocket from all sides and began to split it up.

On the German side, on the other hand, there was no unified action on account of the complicated nature of the terrain, the complete mix-up of units and formations, a lack of signals equipment, uncertain command and other reasons. There was no longer any overall command in the pocket. The remains of corps and divisions acted more or less independently, each seeking to break through on its own. The combat elements no longer stayed back to hold off the pursuing enemy, but rather were used to spearhead various breakout and breakthrough operations. Masses of vehicles, shattered units, stragglers, wounded and those simply trying to flee streamed together behind the fighting units, making the job of moving and fighting much more difficult.

In the end every soldier was motivated by only one thought: Get out of the pocket!

Still functioning were the doctors, medics and the personnel of the main dressing stations and field hospitals. They did their quiet, selfless duty as long as they could and helped as many as they could.

The medical teams recovered and cared for the wounded under the most difficult conditions. The less seriously wounded were provided with first aid and sent on their way in groups led by medics. The serious cases were loaded aboard available vehicles. The doctors and medical personnel stayed with those who could not be moved until the Russians came. Nothing more was heard of them.

There was no longer any planned withdrawal like on the 22nd of August, no orderly retreat like on the 23rd, no streaming back like on the 24th – this was a desperate battle to escape at any cost.

The catastrophe had come, the end of the Sixth Army was in sight. Pursued and harried from all sides by the tank units, motorized units and rifle divisions of the Soviet Third Ukrainian Front, the disorganized and disintegrating units of three German army corps sought to find a way through the enemy.

Squeezed together into several large march groups, often two or three columns abreast, the mass of surrounded troops moved in a generally westerly direction. It was like the past few days – the roads and lanes jammed with troops and vehicles, all driving forward in desperate haste – only with the difference that now the Russians were showing up everywhere. Enemy artillery fired into the columns, Soviet infantry swarmed from the woods and hills, Soviet tanks drove up on the left and right of the road and fired into the fleeing masses, which were under constant attack from the Soviet Air Force.

Every kilometer was bought at the cost of great sacrifice and heavy losses. In the lead were the battle groups, fighting their way through Russian barricades. Officers of every grade tried to maintain order and hold the columns together. The few remaining assault guns threw themselves at the enemy forces trying to split up the columns and drove them back, while the available artillery and anti-tank guns went into position at the roadsides and held off the Russian tanks with direct fire. To the Prut! To the river crossings! That's where the German troops are!

More detailed descriptions of the events of these days are provided in the histories of the units involved:

15th Infantry Division (XXX Corps):[5]

"There had been signs of an impending Russian offensive in the area of the Tiraspol bridgehead for some time. Movements and deliveries of troops were observed, and the sound of woodcutting (bridge-building) was heard. The troops also had indications that the Rumanians were about to desert. On August 17 the Russian artillery fire grew heavier. On the 18th the artillery fire was again heavy and several reconnaissance probes were beaten off. On the 19th there were more and stronger reconnaissance attacks and intense air activity by the Russians.

In spite of the indications observed and reported by the troops, the army group reckoned on a major Russian attack near Jassy in the area of the Eighth Army the next day, but only a secondary attack south of Tiraspol. The Russians had largely succeeded in concealing their preparations for a major attack south of Tiraspol. The morning of August 20 found the 15th Infantry Division ready and determined, but with a much superior enemy in front of it, with inadequate reserves behind it, with uncertain allies beside it and tied down by orders to hold the position. On August 20 the division's positions were bombarded from 0400 to 0450. Preliminary attacks followed along the entire front. As was their practice in the attack, the Russians wanted to determine whether the German main line of resistance was manned or if there had been a withdrawal to a rear position. The first attacks were repulsed everywhere. Most in the division thought that the matter was ended.

Russian radio messages were intercepted in clear text: 'All batteries ready to fire!' and 'It's about to start again!'

From 0700 to 0935 there followed a bombardment more powerful than any experienced so far, as well as air attacks. The division's forward command post on a hill west of Carnateni also lay under heavy Russian artillery fire. The view from there was terrifying. The entire Dnestr valley and the right divisional sector were shrouded in a single cloud of smoke. The sun, which had been shining from a clear, blue summer sky, had been obscured. The enemy barrage was followed by a massed infantry attack in an extremely small area by approximately two Russian rifle divisions with tank support. As a result of the barrage fire the 81st

Grenadier Regiment already had losses of over fifty percent in troops and equipment. Most of the remaining troops in the positions were overwhelmed in bitter close-quarters fighting. Only twenty-eight men from 1st Battalion, 81st Regiment reached the rear as stragglers, where they were picked up. The command post of the 81st Regiment was completely destroyed in hand-to-hand fighting. In other places strongpoints and nests of resistance continued to hold out, and there was still fighting at several points in the forward trenches. The first stragglers appeared in the vicinity of the division command post soon after the end of the preparatory fire. The enemy pushed through the gaps into the main defensive area very quickly, and Russian tanks were already driving past the division command post toward the rear. Remnants of the position garrison and a reserve battalion sent in by the army made a stand near Carnateni. The village was lost, but with the help of stragglers and the division reserve a semi-circular line of security was established and held around Kauschany.

By late morning the division command had learned of a successful Russian breakthrough against the neighboring 306th Infantry Division and on the right wing of their own division.

Many tanks with mounted infantry and troop-carrying trucks were already driving southwest, followed by dense columns of rifle divisions. During the afternoon the army sent the 13th Panzer Division to counter-attack, but it was unable to stem the enemy flood.

The 88th Grenadier Regiment (part of the 106th Grenadier Regiment was with the army reserve) had also seen heavy fighting. The main line of resistance was lost in several places. The division reserve, 1st Battalion, 106th Grenadier Regiment, was

committed to a counterattack; the battalion commander was killed leading his unit. In the evening all elements of the 88th Grenadier Regiment were withdrawn to a prepared position just east of Ursoaia.

The artillery had also suffered heavy losses in the first day of fighting. Most of the batteries were in battle providing direct fire. By the end of the first day it was obvious to the division that the Russian breakthrough had succeeded completely. The 81st Grenadier Regiment and significant elements of the 306th Division had been smashed. As the Rumanian units were no longer fighting, the right flank was completely open. It now appeared that the most urgent task was to establish a new front near Kauschany and secure the right flank along the enemy breakthrough position.

The division was unaware that the Russians had broken through the Eighth Army between the Prut and Seret the same day.

Daybreak on August 21 provided the observation posts on the hills northwest of the Botna with a depressing picture. Dense columns of

Russian troops were marching southwest. The defensive front around Kauschany withstood repeated attacks this day. The 88th Grenadier Regiment and the 15th Fusilier Battalion were placed under the command of the 257th Division for the day, so that the 15th Division commanded only the southern front on the Botna. All of the fighting troops there were combined into a battle group commanded by *Major* Nomanni.

In the evening the battle group was pulled back to the north bank of the Botna. Intervention by the 13th Panzer Division once again proved unsuccessful. The panzer division and the remains of the 306th Division were thrown back.

During the night of August 21/22 the division was withdrawn about ten kilometers further to the west. In the new line it would resist the hard-pressing enemy throughout the 22nd.

In the meantime, the Russian spearheads from Tiraspol were driving southwest toward Galatz and west toward Leova on the Prut, while leading elements of the Russian breakthrough near Jassy reached the area west of Husi between the Prut and Seret Rivers. The encirclement of the Sixth Army was at hand.

That day the retreat was ordered – too late. 'Withdraw at 1930, rearguards 2400.'

As ordered, the division began to withdraw during the night of August 22/23. Following a march of about twenty-five kilometers it reached the Emental-Kainari area. During the night there was scattered fighting, and throughout the 23rd the division fought off Russian attacks. The withdrawal was resumed in the evening. Before all elements had crossed the Botna near Emental, the enemy entered the village. The rearguard was scattered and many vehicles were lost.

By morning the Carbuna area had been reached. There was already a great deal of confusion there among the units of XXX Corps and the neighboring corps. Signals equipment was either absent or unserviceable. The officers of the division headquarters and senior unit commanders sought through personal intervention to restore order and to provide the units with clear march objectives and assignments.

Hanging over the retreat now was the signal: 'Enemy all around.' The Russians were in hot pursuit from the east, from the south their attacks were driving into the flanks of the march columns, in the west their fast units were already on the move on this side of the Prut, and from the air their close-support aircraft attacked the troops with guns and bombs.

The supply units under the command of the Ib had withdrawn in good time and were the only ones to escape the debacle as cohesive units. Nevertheless, there were no serious supply problems. The withdrawal route was littered with abandoned train vehicles, from which the troops could obtain food. On the other hand men and horses suffered from a shortage of water in the summer heat; the few village wells were not equal to the great demands of the masses of men and horses.

On August 24 the division fought in the Carbuna area and during the coming night was supposed to capture the area west of Guragalbina. As evening came it began to rain heavily. The poor roads, which led through a forested area west of Carbuna, became impassable for heavy vehicles. The 15th Artillery Regiment bogged down, and all attempts to free the guns failed. In view of the proximity of the pursuing enemy all the remaining guns – twenty to twenty-five light and three heavy howitzers – had to be blown up, after the preceding vehicles of the 257th Division had become blocked on the only still-dry road.

The first signs of disintegration began to appear on the 25th. Pursued by the enemy from all sides, the now completely entangled elements of several army corps sought to fight their way through the enemy, whose tanks and aircraft were firing pitilessly into the columns.

In the morning our Commanding General of XXX Corps had tried to intervene and instill order into the divisions. All control had been lost, however; the withdrawal had become flight. Every soldier knew that the pocket had been closed, and that survival meant reaching the Prut to the west. Every man called upon his last reserves of strength and followed orders. There was a brief outbreak of panic, a direct effect of the Russian tanks and aircraft. It was particularly unfortunate that the wounded could no longer be taken along.

That evening the main body of the division, entangled with other units, sought to break through to the Prut from the area of Guragalbina. The troops advanced until the morning of the 26th. Several Russian blocking positions were stormed and overrun. During the course of the day, however, the Russians launched tank attacks from all sides. Large elements of the division were destroyed that day. Other groups got as far as a marshy island in the Prut . . ."

The 62nd Infantry Division (XXXXIV Army Corps):[6]
"The division was deployed north of Kishinev on the Raut River. A well-fortified defensive system with five positions one behind the other had been set up. The division was up to strength in personnel and materiel, and the fighting spirit of the men was good. Then we received the completely surprising reports of the Russian attack and break-through near Jassy. The situation on the Raut-Dnestr front was thus untenable. But the withdrawal began much too late. The troops did not begin falling back until August 22. In the meantime Russian spearheads had already broken through to the south and had barred all the crossings

over the Prut. The troops of the Sixth Army knew nothing of this. Even in the event of an early evacuation of Bessarabia within a short time, the two bridges at Husi and Leova would have been insufficient to ensure a smooth crossing. Only on the first day did the withdrawal go as planned. On the 24th the fighting elements of the division, some of which had been sent ahead in vehicles, became involved with Russian forces which had advanced northwest from Tiraspol. At the same time Soviet forces were also approaching from the north. The few roads and lanes, which led through largely difficult terrain, were very soon jammed with vehicles of every type. The result was a kilometers-long line of vehicles, into which smashed the Russian attack from the north. One of the division's vehicle columns was overtaken and destroyed by the Russians on the first day. I found myself with the commander of the division supply troops. We stayed close to the Division Ib, so as to be able to immediately pass on his orders for the withdrawal to the units. During the march Soviet bombers appeared repeatedly, attacking the retreat roads with bombs and guns. There were no German combat aircraft to be seen, only a twin-fuselage reconnaissance aircraft.[7] Following an exhausting march with only brief rest stops and under continuous air attack, on August 25 we reached the small village of Stolniceni. There we found the Ib staff, elements of the Ia staff and many vehicles. Meanwhile the Russians were approaching from the north and northeast. The village lay in a valley. Stolniceni was abandoned when enemy tanks and motorized infantry approached over a rise. The last stand was made about two kilometers to the south by the division commander, *Generalmajor* Tronnier (died in Russian captivity), with about 350 men. The only heavy weapons were two 75mm anti-tank guns and four 120mm mortars. These weapons fired in every direction, as the enemy now began an attack from every quarter.

Another breakout was undertaken at 1700, which resulted in running battles with enemy units. Very many of the men were killed, the rest were captured. Earlier, south of Kishinev on the road to Husi, the sole regiment left behind by the division to cover the withdrawal had become involved in heavy fighting with Soviet tank spearheads advancing from the direction of Tiraspol. This led to further destruction of our units, as the result was the formation of a series of small pockets and the barring of the way to the west. A large number of enemy tanks were destroyed by *Panzerfäust* anti-tank weapons in close-quarters fighting. However, for us the battle ended on August 25 and the fate of our division was sealed.

The Rumanian 14th Infantry Division, which was deployed to our right, fought just as bravely in those days as the German divisions. Like all of the units in Bessarabia, it was all but destroyed, and those not killed went into Russian captivity. The same could not be said of the other Rumanian divisions, for example the 3rd, 5th and 7th Divisions, which it seems were led by traitors interested in the fall of Marshall Antonescu . . ."

The 10th Panzergrenadier Division (Army Group Reserve):[8]
"On the afternoon of August 20 the division, which until then had been in reserve, drove forward to the front. On the way we passed Rumanians streaming toward the rear. Other than the German troops there was only a single Rumanian unit moving forward: a heavy motorized artillery battalion.

Our regiment's assembly area[9] was a village left of the road, the regimental headquarters were located in a farm. The regiment was sent into action the same afternoon. 2nd Battalion was torn to pieces immediately, no one came back. Those not killed fell into enemy hands. 3rd Battalion was badly battered. Its commander came back with a wounded arm. He had to go forward again at once, his arm in a sling, to lead a counterattack. 1st Battalion was almost destroyed. Two company commanders, who had fought like lions, fell into the hands of the Russians. The battalion commander, two Lieutenants and a medic managed to reach the regimental command post. That 3rd Battalion escaped the worst in this action was thanks to the division's assault gun battalion. The latter lost two assault guns rescuing the battalion from the enemy.

This was the regiment's and the division's first action near Cotriceni (south of Jassy). In order to close the gaps in the front left by the Rumanians, the attack had to be made on too wide a front and was thus numerically hopelessly inferior to the Russians who were especially strong here – the focal point of their offensive.

On the morning of the second day of fighting the commander of an infantry division which had been destroyed at the front arrived at our regimental command post with an *Oberst* and two other officers. Other than the rear-echelon train units, they were all of the division which had escaped encirclement by the Russians. The four officers had sought out the nearest command post, so as to pass on 'to above' the news of the destruction of their division and inform them of the general situation.

In the afternoon the division marched east toward the Prut. Along the way it picked up stragglers from various infantry divisions. The three regimental commanders met at a station on the Jassy-Galatz line and exchanged bad news. East of the rail line the division moved forward in order to establish a makeshift front line.

The next day I had to undertake several dangerous liaison missions by motorcycle. The makeshift German 'front' was much too weak.

Russian tanks appeared, and soon afterward a Russian battalion attacked. Our force had to be shuffled back and forth to hold the main line of resistance. Fifteen Russian tanks tried in vain to cut off the elements of the division east of the rail line. Several of the tanks were destroyed.

Our withdrawal began on the evening of this August 22nd. The regiment once again occupied night quarters in Poeni Forest, from where it had set out two days before to take part in the fighting near Jassy.

The withdrawal continued on the 23rd, Husi lay behind us. The situation for the division had become extremely critical, the enemy encirclement was almost complete. The remaining units of the division had to break through, and were forced to use the west road. With their more heavily-armed and motorized units they had to leave the less-dangerous east road to the infantry divisions. As the Russians had attacked here from the north and west, there seemed to be less of a threat in the east.

The following day began with a costly attempt by the assault guns to break through Russian armor dug in on a hill in front of a village. Following this the assault guns, which were acting as the division's armored advance detachment, sought to fight a way through along another road in the valley. When this, too, failed, the division's spearhead began moving along a road over a mountain. The newly-created 4th Battery, which had been formed from the almost destroyed 3rd (Heavy) Artillery Battalion, tried to support the breakthrough with artillery fire. In doing so the battery suffered badly from enemy counterfire and the battery chief was severely wounded.

There now began a tremendous driving back and forth, forward and backward, up and down. Finally, a gap in the encirclement was found through which the division drove. The retreat passed by Crasna . . ."

The firm belief in the Prut crossings and a new German front on the west side of the river were to prove a frightful mistake for the elements of the Sixth Army breaking out of the Russian encirclement.

There were no more bridges over the Prut in German hands. West of the river Soviet troops of the Second Ukrainian Front had already advanced beyond Barlad.

"Korpsgruppe Mieth" had already lost the bridges near Sbiroja and Scoposeni, and the crossing near Leuzeni was also in enemy hands. On the evening of August 24 the 13th Panzer Division had been forced to give up the bridgeheads it was holding near Leova and Falciu. When strong Russian tank forces approached the rear of the exhausted division the bridges had to be destroyed. The last bridge, the one near Stalinesti, southeast of Husi, was to have been taken by an advance detachment of the 282nd Division[10], which had been hurriedly sent ahead. The surprise attack failed, however, as the bridge had been blown by the enemy some time earlier. While the German divisions were breaking out, suffering grievous losses in their attempts to fight their way through the enemy, there were already no more fixed crossings over the Prut. But that was not all.

The German troops, pressured everywhere by the enemy, shot at, pursued and repeatedly cut off, fighting their way forward with great difficulty and heavy losses, still had a firm belief in a German front west of the Prut where they would be taken in and could find safety from the enemy. In this, too, they were to be bitterly disappointed. There was no longer any question of a German front.

Even as the surrounded main body of the Sixth Army was facing complete destruction and elements of the army were breaking out toward the Prut, there were still German troops on the west bank of the Prut. They belonged to "Korpsgruppe Mieth," which had carried out a slow withdrawal of over 100 kilometers south from the Jassy area pursued by enemy forces from the north and threatened from the west. After picking up elements of VII Corps which had escaped across the Prut near Sbiroja and Scoposeni, Mieth assembled about four German divisions[11] in the Husi area, although the troops were exhausted and units were totally mixed together. Just as the doomed Sixth Army had no idea where the "Korpsgruppe" was, Mieth was unaware of the situation of the army and the elements breaking out toward the Prut, as there was no communications between them.

There was yet a possibility that the "Korpsgruppe," which was still engaged in heavy fighting against enemy forces pursuing from the north and west, might still stand a reasonable chance of fighting its way through to the west in the direction of the Carpathians and linking up there with the army group (remains of Eighth Army). But *General* Mieth took a fateful decision, which was to cost his life and the lives of hundreds of his troops. Completely unaware of the overall situation, he decided to hold a Prut crossing for the Sixth Army, which was still expected from the east, hoping at the same time to link up with it.

Mieth decided to retake Husi on August 25 in order to capture the crossing near Stalinesti.[12] However, the attack, spearheaded by the 370th Infantry Division, was halted beyond the northern edge of the city. Only the 666th Grenadier Regiment, barely a battalion strong, managed to enter the town, but was encircled there and completely wiped out. The attack was repeated the next morning and once again failed. In the face of the powerful enemy forces, Husi and the crossing near Stalinesti could not be taken.

"Korpsgruppe Mieth" was now also at the end of its strength and found itself increasingly threatened with encirclement.

The catastrophe of the Sixth Army was approaching its climax.

On the evening and night of the 25th all of the German forces which had been able to fight their way to the western and southwestern edges of the pocket – especially in the Guragalbina area – prepared for a final determined attempt to break out.

The better armed units assumed the lead and made initial progress under enemy fire. Several Russian blocking positions were stormed and overrun. When enemy resistance stiffened, hastily formed assault groups with assault guns were hurriedly sent forward to force the decisive breakthrough. Streaming behind the combat troops were thousands of men and vehicles.

On the morning of August 26 the Soviets used everything at their disposal to prevent a German breakthrough southeast of Minzir. However, the desperate Germans were able to punch a hole in the Russian lines, through which poured a stream of fleeing troops. The Russians poured fire into the narrow corridor from tanks, anti-tank guns, rocket launchers and artillery.

The German troops ran through fountains of dirt from bursting shells, vehicles loaded to beyond capacity rumbled through the flashing, rumbling thunderstorm of enemy fire. The last guns rattled along behind the trucks through the shellbursts. Death reaped a great harvest from among the masses of fleeing men, who had only one thought: on to the Prut – to freedom – to where their comrades were waiting . . .

An Island in the Prut Becomes a Trap

Finally, on the hills near Minzir, rifle pits, German uniforms, steel helmets, grenadiers in defensive positions. But the disappointment of those who had fought their way through was limitless. This was not a new front line, rather only a small bridgehead on the east bank of the Prut, which forward elements of the 282nd Division had occupied to take in the remnants of the Sixth Army streaming in from all directions.

Eventually there were ten to fifteen-thousand men assembled there. The final count may have been slightly more than twenty-thousand – no more. About twenty-thousand German soldiers had made their way to the Prut. Twenty-thousand from the 170,000 of the Sixth Army.

Within the giant encircling ring the end was fast approaching. Split into three smaller pockets, into which the enemy fired from all sides, outflanked, overrun and squeezed together, everything ended in confused fighting, chaos and defeat.

The noise of battle gradually died out. On August 28 – other sources say

August 30 – the final battles in the pocket between Kishinev-Oneschty-Guragalbina came to an end.

No further details are known.

An eternal silence began to settle over XXX, XXXXIV and LII Army Corps with their more than eleven divisions. There are no authenticated accounts of their final days. About 150,000 German soldiers died somewhere in the forests, valleys and villages, were captured, posted missing, presumed dead . . .

There were still more than 20,000, however, the remains of several corps and divisions, who believed they had reached a new German front at the Prut bridgehead. These survivors now crowded along the river within the protection of the bridgehead. The first disappointment was followed almost immediately by the second – the bridges over the Prut had already been blown, there were no other crossings for some distance and there were no bridging materials available. The way was blocked by the roughly thirty-meter-wide river, badly swollen by the recent rains.

All hell was ready to break loose at the Prut. Thousands of tired, worn-out, desperate men, including many wounded, gradually gathered along the east bank. The last guns, heavy weapons and vehicles were blown up or pushed into the Prut. The enemy was already firing into the bridgehead. Many men threw themselves into the water in an attempt to escape the enemy fire. Many drowned. Undaunted, on the 26th the pioneers began a ferry service across the river with the few available inflatable boats and whatever else was available, taking large numbers of men to the west bank. Shells burst near the boats as they plied the river, sending up fountains of water. Russian artillery and mortars fired on the numerous crossing sites, preventing the construction of a makeshift bridge and inflicting heavy losses.

For all of those who had been taken across the Prut and were about to breathe a sigh of relief, there followed a third bitter disappointment. To the general horror of all concerned it was discovered that they had not reached the west bank of the river at all. They were on an island, about five to six kilometers wide and about two square kilometers in area. The low-lying island, located between two arms of the Prut, was extremely marshy and was divided by two lakes. The first squads found a raised footpath through the marshes and waterways which lead to a footbridge to the west bank of the Prut near Stalinesti. It was then that they received the greatest and most depressing disappointment: it was not their comrades waiting for them over there as they had hoped, rather it was the Russians. The enemy had already barricaded the west bank!

Where was "Korpsgruppe Mieth," which was supposed to be somewhere west of the Prut? It was there, and not far away. Barely twenty kilometers separated the

"Korpsgruppe" from the rest of the Sixth Army. But the two groups could not find their way to each other and were incapable of joint action, because each was unaware of the other's presence. And besides – between them as well as in and around Husi were three Soviet divisions and elements of a tank corps, ready to encircle the "Korpsgruppe."

Throughout the night of August 27 and the following day the crossing from the east bank to the Prut island continued. There was heavy fighting on the heights east of the river as the bridgehead's defenders tried to prevent a rapid enemy drive to the Prut. Russian attacks from the east were repulsed. Once again German troops stood firm in a hopeless situation, not allowing the enemy to break through to the river. Russian officers appeared, escorted by Red Army soldiers with white flags. They were negotiators sent to arrange a German surrender. They were sent back unheard. On the evening of the 27th, at 2200, the bridgehead was evacuated. The last German defenders crossed the eastern arm of the Prut.

In the meantime, thousands of German troops had crowded together on the island in the Prut, among them the Commanding Generals of XXX, LII and XXXXIV Corps. After a week of uninterrupted fighting and constant retreat in the terrible heat, pursued by tanks and motorized infantry and under constant attack from the air, the troops were totally exhausted and dead tired. The hungry, thirsty soldiers and their officers and Generals now tried to dig in and camouflage themselves as best they could among the rushes, bushes and thickets.

The shattered remains of corps and divisions had long since ceased to be regiments, battalions and companies. They were not even makeshift battle groups as they had been yesterday and the day before. They were now little more than a mass of men who had escaped the pocket, many already lacking weapons, the others with only their small arms. Otherwise they had only what was on their backs – and the faintest spark of hope that they might yet escape their fate.

The Generals sat together in a small wood and deliberated. Soon they had devised another breakout plan. Exhausted officers

tried to get the men to their feet to form new battle groups.

The breakthrough to the west bank planned for the night of August 27/28 did not come off, however, because the troops earmarked to smash a breach through the enemy stumbled into a swamp in the darkness. The breakthrough across the western arm of the Prut was put off until the following night. It was never to take place . . .

Oberleutnant Baron of the 444th Corps Signal Battalion lived through those hours:[13]

"August 26: – Aided by the deep ravines (balkas) in the soft soil, we succeeded in establishing a defensive ring with several hundred officers, NCOs and men in the area of the villages of Voinescu and Razesi on the east bank of the Prut. I ran from strongpoint to strongpoint to see that all was in order and encourage the troops.

We had one notable experience: From the east came a German Kfz 2 with driver and – standing upright – a very tall and blond *Major*, who called to us: 'What more do you want, haven't you had enough?' And then he drove off again.[14]

Weaker Russian attacks were repelled. The Russians then committed tanks, three of which were destroyed with *Panzerfästen*. Afterward the enemy infantry and tanks left us alone until evening. The enemy artillery continued to make things difficult for us, however, pouring shells on the Prut valley and its eastern slope where we had dug ourselves in. Behind our line of security were thousands of stragglers, some in the balkas, but others below in the woods of the Prut valley. They all appeared to be leaderless, and as I learned later, many were also unarmed. When a group of shells landed nearby everyone jumped up and ran to another hiding place. In doing so they showed the Russians, who were certainly watching closely, where to place their next salvo. Accordingly, losses were high.

As darkness began to fall order began to break down at the front as well. Everyone raced for the Prut so as to get to the other side as quickly as possible. *Major* Söller and I also hurried down the slope toward the river with a small group which had stayed with us. There all was confusion. Russian shells exploded among the uneasy groups. There was a mood of panic. Wounded lay on the ground, and there were dozens of ambulances, all filled with badly wounded. When the noise died down one could hear the cries for help from men drowning in the Prut. Many, including some non-swimmers, tried to reach the west bank. Several tried to cross on the backs of their emaciated horses, others with parts of panje wagons. They too drowned. At this place there were no inflatable boats, nor was there a footbridge to be seen.

I lost contact with *Major* Söller and was seized by panic. I soon regained my composure, however, and set off down the river. The masses of troops and bursting Russian shells soon lay far behind me. To the south the sky was red with the glow of burning villages. I began to look for a suitable crossing, then heard calls on the other side. I recognized one voice – it was *Major* Söller. I answered, and he urged me to swim over. I took off my uniform and rolled all my things together. I placed the bundle on my back and climbed into the water, but the weight of my clothes and weapon forced me under. I gave up, informed *Major* Söller and wished him well. I never heard from him again. I was now desperate. I walked on southward, turned around and stumbled over something. It was a fuel canister. I stripped off once again, packed up everything I had, climbed onto the canister and swam off. In the darkness I failed to notice that my pistol, submachine-gun and boots had slipped from my bundle . . .

After reaching the other side and getting dressed, I set out through a stand of trees. Some time later I came upon a group of German soldiers, who informed me that a large group had assembled further to the north. From there on I repeatedly came upon large and small groups, lying exhausted in the grass or beneath trees. Scattered about were thousands of men, mostly stragglers, many only partly clothed and fifty to sixty percent unarmed like me. I reported to *General* Müller[15], although there were supposedly other high-ranking officers present.

In the meantime it had become light, it was August 27th. To my dismay, I now saw that the Prut valley was not yet behind us and that we still had about 1,500 meters of swamp before us. We were on an extended island in the marshy valley. As the hills on the far side were already occupied by the enemy, I could not imagine how we were going to get out of here.

We were lying close together when a tremendous bombardment began. Shells impacted in our midst and all around, fragments buzzed through the air. I dug a shallow pit with my fingers in the forest earth. I don't know how long the firing lasted.

The barrage had cost us dearly, we had many dead and wounded, who were a cause of special concern. I organized a collection of all available packet dressings, outer clothing and boots, and handed these over to the few remaining medical personnel and those who had lost some of their clothing. Most of the doctors and medics had remained with the wounded on the east bank of the Prut.

It was later announced that a conference of officers was to take place . . ."

The Soviets now set about to destroy these remnants of the Sixth Army. Mortar and artillery fire rained down on the mass of men holding out on the island. The Russian fire intensified as "Stalin Organs" joined in the barrage. Red aircraft attacked with bombs. The soldiers lay in the muck and swamp, unable to defend themselves. Losses climbed from hour to hour, and it was almost impossible to hold on in this witch's cauldron. At about 1600 in the afternoon the enemy began powerful attacks from the west. The desperate men could persevere no longer. Self-preservation drove them from their holes and hiding places. Here and there a few men got up, then small groups, which were soon joined by more men, running and stumbling forward among the bursting shells. Nothing could stop them now, the wild charge went on.

Without preparation, without orders, without any kind of order or organization, more and more soldiers, NCOs and officers got to their feet. They inspired others to do the same, and the forward movement expanded until most of the men in the Prut valley were on their feet and running. Loud shouts of hurray drowned out the enemy fire as about ten to twelve-thousand German soldiers, led by officers and Generals, surged forward like a tremendous wave, ignoring their hunger, thirst and exhaustion and the hail of enemy fire.

For these men, driven by hope and fear, scarcely half of whom were armed, there was no stopping now. They splashed through the swamps and mud under constant mortar fire, waded streams and crossed a 300 to 500 meter wide marshy lake, at times up to their chests in water, their rifles, submachine-guns, light machine-guns and *Panzerfaust* anti-tank weapons raised above their heads. Many sank in treacherous swamp holes, others drowned, many were killed or wounded and left behind.

However, in spite of the heavy enemy fire, the wave reached the steep western bank of the Prut, where the enemy positions near Stalinesti were taken in wild hand-to-hand fighting. The completely surprised and confused Russians disappeared in all directions. The heights on the west bank of the Prut were also stormed and all resistance overcome in close-quarters fighting. Finally the German troops reached the large forested area south of Husi, about three kilometers west of the Prut.

The remaining German forces assembled into small groups before setting out to make their way west through what was now enemy-occupied territory to a new German front somewhere in the Carpathians.

However, the Soviets recovered quickly from this surprise assault. On the morning of the 29th they surrounded the forest. The sound of heavy fighting was heard, which then gradually died away . . .

Scarcely any of the 20,000 men who had managed to fight their way to the Prut and finally to the Husi area under unspeakable hardships escaped.

Far away from these terrible events a single German division was facing destruction.

At the beginning of the Soviet offensive the 9th Infantry Division was at far eastern end of the front with XIX Army Corps, which was under the command of the Third Army. It was the lone German division there. The 9th Division occupied well-fortified positions right on the Dnestr, with Rumanian units to its left and right. The men of the division did not hear the sound of the battle which had begun, and they knew nothing of the Russian breakthrough from the Tiraspol bridgehead far to the west. When, on August 21, its neighbor on the left, the Rumanian 21st Infantry Division, was smashed and the corps headquarters pulled back to the west before the advancing enemy, the 9th Infantry Division suddenly found itself alone in the midst of a disintegrating Rumanian front. It did not receive instructions to pull back until August 22; these were the last orders issued by the corps. The only way left to the division was south. Fighting off the enemy as it fell back, by the evening of the 23rd it reached the village of Gnadenfeld and the next day got as far as the Sarata area. Caught from all sides, the division tried several times to break out of the encirclement. During the bitter fighting the division was almost completely destroyed. The survivors, including the division headquarters, laid down their weapons as the only sensible thing to do and marched into captivity.

These few sentences are all that is known of the 9th Infantry Division and its approximately 13,000 soldiers.

"Korpsgruppe Mieth" Surrounded in Vutcani

The horror was not yet over.

Back to "Korpsgruppe Mieth" – As the soldiers on the Prut island knew nothing of the "Korpsgruppe" not far away, so too the latter knew nothing of the desperate situation in the swamps and water.

General Mieth therefore stuck to his plan, still unaware of the true situation, to capture a crossing for the divisions still expected from the east. As the powerful enemy bulwark of Husi could not be taken, the *General* hoped to establish a bridgehead further south near Leova. On the night of August 26/27 the "Korpsgruppe" went to the attack to the south, west of Husi. There was heavy fighting in places with Soviet forces already near Leova, and during the course of the coming day the various units assembled in the wooded, hilly terrain about fifteen kilometers south of Husi, where they occupied an assembly area. Where were the expected combat units of the Sixth Army? Nothing had been seen or heard of them. A few troops from the 282nd Division had arrived in the villages occupied on the 27th, but that was all. Hopes of a link-up with units of the army expected from the east were dashed. The "Korpsgruppe" was forced to face the facts that it was by itself and would have to fight on alone. What was worse, they had stayed too long and now faced encirclement. The Russians were moving in from the north and had already occupied the villages just west of the assembly area. The "Korpsgruppe" would have to fight its way out to the west.

The staff of the "Korpsgruppe" were under no illusions. The divisions were even more mixed together, the fighting strength of the troops had dropped considerably. They had just completed eight days of difficult fighting in defense and on the retreat. Casualties were already high, losses of guns and heavy weapons great and there were only a few radio stations still intact. The was only one hope left. They would destroy all vehicles without fuel and all weapons for which there was no more ammunition and drive southwest through the village of Vutcani toward the Barladul River and then try to reach the Seret, where there would surely be a new German front.

A planned night attack on Vutcani had to be postponed as the troops were too exhausted. Not until dawn on the 28th did the attack begin, spearheaded by the 79th and 370th Divisions. Other formations, trains, etc, were to follow; the 258th and 376th Divisions were to cover the rear from a front facing north.

Vutcani was taken in spite of extremely heavy Russian artillery fire and almost ceaseless mortar fire, now from the south as well. Mobile advance detachments were to immediately take the Barladul bridges and hold them until the following main body of the "Korpsgruppe" crossed the river during the coming night. Four assault guns, all that were still available, rolled off carrying mounted infantry, but were halted in front of an extended anti-tank front. Reinforcements were sent in. The enemy was driven back and the attackers advanced to within one or two kilometers of the river. Events were coming to an especially tragic climax – because it was on the afternoon of the same day, the 28th of August, that the soldiers on the Prut island tried to escape into the forest south of Husi. The two groups were only twenty-five kilometers apart, and could have acted together – but they remained unaware of each other's presence.

In Vutcani, too, the end was approaching. The following elements arrived in the burning midday heat of the cloudless summer day. Located in a deep river valley, the large, extended village drew the battle-weary men like a magnet. Everything came together there and soon the large village was overflowing with men and vehicles. The troops dropped where they stood from exhaustion and were asleep in an instant. The enemy pursued sharply from the north, and the 370th Division, which was providing the rearguard, suffered heavy casualties. *Major* Rehm of the 79th Infantry Division[16] wrote of the events in Vutcani:

"However, the ominous events which took place in the afternoon and evening of August 28th placed in doubt the success of a breakthrough across the Barladul planned for the coming night by the troops which had streamed into Vutcani. First, a powerful attack from the north without tank support struck the right flank of the 79th Division, which was strung out in defensive positions. The elements deployed there were unable to hold out and were forced to abandon the small village of Babosi north of Vutcani. At the same time Soviet close-support aircraft began a series of attacks on Vutcani, with waves of aircraft attacking until evening. The bombing and strafing inflicted terrible losses in the overcrowded village. Several 20mm flak fired the last of their ammunition, without any visible success. Late in the afternoon Russian infantry began an attack against the southern section of Vutcani. There, too, the exhausted soldiers were unable to halt the attack, allowing Russian riflemen to occupy gardens and houses. Finally, an energetic counterattack by a handful of soldiers under the leadership of the Ia of the 79th Division, General Staff *Oberstleutnant* Labrenz, succeeded in driving the enemy out of the village again.

As dusk was falling *Oberst* Ringenberg, who had taken over responsibility for guarding Vutcani in the rear, or east of the village, reported to the 79th Division by telephone that the elements of various divisions under his command were under heavy attack. He urgently requested reinforcements. There were no available troops to be sent, however.

In addition to all of this bad news, the 1st General Staff Officer of IV Corps, General Staff *Major* Bucher, suddenly appeared at the command post of the 79th Division and reported that the entire corps headquarters staff had been scattered by a Russian ambush. The corps Chief-of-Staff had been killed and nothing is known of the fate of the Commanding General.[17]

Following the hopeful events of the first half of the day (when they had been able to reach Vutcani), the events after midday were nothing less than depressing. It was clear to the divisions being squeezed ever closer together in and around Vutcani from the north, east and south, some under attack and artillery fire, that the enemy knew their exact position. The ongoing air attacks were the first, very painful indication of this fact. The objective of the attacks was to decimate and demoralize the mass of troops trapped there. Both succeeded all too well. The attacks by the Russians in the late afternoon and evening against the southern section of Vutcani and the security forces east of the town were obviously intended to reveal the strength and ability to resist of the German units. It was therefore to be expected with certainty that the Russians would take all necessary measures during the coming night to ensure that reinforcements were on hand on August 29 to completely smash the now surrounded German divisions in Vutcani Valley.

On the basis of this assessment the commander of the 79th Division, *Generalleutnant* Weinknecht, decided to break out to the west from the witch's cauldron at Vutcani as soon as darkness fell. The attack was to be made on a broad front, and if successful, they would cross the Barladul during the night of August 28/29.

The plan ran into considerable difficulties. As a result of the events of the afternoon and evening in Vutcani the units had become inextricably entangled. Exhausted and dead tired, with no hope of escape, most of the troops lay sleeping in gardens and even on the roads and lanes. It took more than two hours to assemble about twenty officers at the command post of the 79th Division in Vutcani. The division commander made it very clear to them that they would face certain destruction if they were still in Vutcani at dawn the next morning. The enemy would certainly use the night to surround the village from all sides. The assembled officers were ordered to gather all available troops around them, regardless of rank or unit, to set out as the first attack wave from Vutcani at 2200. Experience indicated that the remaining soldiers would follow. The vehicles with the wounded were to follow the first wave. The advance detachment further to the west (the last four assault guns of the 825th Assault Gun Brigade, with infantry and pioneers) was ordered to advance from Idriciu-Rediu while it was still dark and seize and hold the road bridge over the Barladul east of Chitcani. After the mass of troops had crossed the river, smaller march groups were to be formed, which would attempt to break through to the west on their own.

There was no other choice. A final attempt had to be undertaken. The sooner the breakout began, the greater would be its chances of success.

The commander of the 79th Division briefed the commander of the 370th Division on the plan in a farm house in the sleeping, eerily quiet village of Vutcani. While the briefing was in progress *General* Mieth arrived alone and unannounced. He was informed of the situation, the decision which had been taken and the orders which had been given. In the meantime, an officer arrived and reported that it was impossible to get the sleeping soldiers into their departure positions and that a postponement of the attack was necessary.

On the basis of this report the breakout attack had to be delayed until 2400. Once again the attack failed to come off for the same reason. In order to avoid what appeared to be certain catastrophe in Vutcani the two division commanders and their staff officers personally shook the sleeping soldiers awake and led them to the west end of the village. So much time was lost that it was already light by the time the first wave set out. Some of the troops managed to get out of Vutcani, then streamed west in disorderly groups.

The last chance of forcing a breakout and breakthrough in the only fashion likely to succeed had been squandered. The German forces had been unable to evacuate Vutcani during the night of August 28/29 and thus missed their opportunity to advance to the Barladul under cover of darkness. Events between Vutcani and the Barladul crossings disintegrated into individual actions by isolated groups during the course of the 29th. Command at the division level was no longer possible.

The first moves from Vutcani at dawn were effectively frustrated by the enemy. A group of soldiers of all ranks from various units which had gathered around the commander of the 79th Division became involved in a close-quarters battle with Russian forces attacking from the south, and managed to drive them back. It soon became known that *General* Mieth had died of a heart attack that morning during fighting in the eastern section of Vutcani.

Under the command of capable officers, other groups in the first wave managed to get out of the overcrowded village in spite of heavy artillery and mortar fire from the south, southeast and southwest. The majority of the German troops did not succeed in making even this first step, however, as the Russians soon pushed into Vutcani from the east. Tanks and anti-tank guns created chaos among the masses of men and vehicles stuck in the village.

The leading ranks of soldiers, on the other hand, hurrying toward the Barladul, made one last great effort and broke through the first Russian blocking units they met just east of the river. Even the stronger enemy forces deployed in front of the bridge near Chitcani were overrun. By noon of the 29th a disorganized mass of German soldiers, most armed with only a rifle or submachine-gun, crossed the Barladul over this bridge. There were only a few vehicles with them. They all strived toward the hills and villages west of the river. That evening the last remnants of the "Korpsgruppe" were located in the area around Chitcani.

The enemy forces which had been taken by surprise by the ferocity of the German advance soon recovered, and by midday had halted the flow across the bridge near Chitcani. From a hill south of Idriciu a large concentration of German troops was observed to be stalled in front of the bridge. The unfortunate group was shot up by Soviet artillery and aircraft.

In these circumstances it seemed hopeless to try and get across the bridge. The group under the command of the CO of the 79th Division therefore set off in a southwesterly direction, without any notion as to how it was to cross the Barladul. The group consisted of about thirty soldiers, half of them wounded but able to walk. Also with the group were several officers and the radio station of the tactical group, as well as an assault gun which had been repaired in Vutcani. This sole remaining intact radio station sent the last situation reports 'blind' to the army group and the Eighth Army, as there had been no contact with these headquarters since August 23.

On the way the small group was showered with heavy mortar fire, which made a further advance seem senseless. The group planned to wait in a wood until nightfall before continuing west in smaller sections. The radio equipment, cars and the assault gun were set on fire. Before darkness fell, however, this group also met the unavoidable fate of Soviet captivity . . ."

In the days which followed, those elements which had reached the west side of the river tried to reach the Seret in small groups, most on foot with only a few vehicles left. It was hoped that they would find a new German line there. But here, too, all hopes were in vain – there was no new line. At this point everything disintegrated and each man tried to escape to the Carpathians, about 100 kilometers away.

Oberleutnant Kollmer of the 376th Infantry Division noted (excerpt):

> August 29:
> "After being repeated, the attack across the Barladul succeeded. Ordered to the west, to the Seret, direction Bacau.
>
> August 30:
> There are no more units, everything is mixed up. The division commander, *Generalleutnant* Schwarz, is still with us. German troops are supposed to be waiting on the Seret.
>
> August 31:
> On toward the Seret. The men are worn out physically. *General* Schwarz rouses their spirits. At about noon most of the troops to have got this far cross over an unoccupied bridge near Rogoaza on the Seret. Nothing to be seen of German troops.
>
> September 1:
> Reconnaissance reveals stronger enemy forces to the west. A decision is therefore made to head southwest to the Rumanian-Hungarian border. *General* Schwarz is completely exhausted. Also still with us are *Oberst* Heinz, *Oberstleutnant* Schirmer (Ia of the 370th Division) and *Oberstleutnant* Stein of the 370th Artillery Regiment.
>
> September 2:
> To the southwest the Trotosul Valley is also blocked by enemy troops. The order is given to break through in small groups . . ."

The Soviets gave the following brief description of the destruction of "Korpsgruppe Mieth":

> The German units located between Husi and Vutcani were surrounded. On August 29 the remnants of the shattered divisions, with a

total strength of about 20,000 men, succeeded in breaking out of the encirclement. Extremely tough fighting in the forests continued until August 30 as larger groups of Germans tried to break through to the west in the direction of the Seret to the Carpathians. During mopping-up actions on the 2nd and 3rd of September about 3,000 Germans were killed and a total of 35,000 captured. All remaining elements were smashed on the following day.

XXIX Corps Also Fails to Escape

The debacle was not yet over.

Already the entire Sixth Army had been destroyed, the nearly five divisions of "Korpsgruppe Mieth" had been smashed and the 9th Infantry Division had gone down . . .

There was still XXIX Corps, initially under the command of the Rumanian Third Army, now at the disposal of Army Group South Ukraine. All that was left of the corps was its headquarters; it had no troops left. The German 9th Infantry Division had been lost near Sarata, and the two Rumanian divisions of the mixed corps were no longer present. On the 26th of August the corps headquarters, which was withdrawing from the Barlad area, received orders to organize a defense on the Seret in the line Galatz-Foscani and establish a new front. For this purpose the 13th Panzer Division, the 10th Panzergrenadier Division, the remains of the 153rd Field Training Division and the recently-arrived *Panzerverband* Braun were placed under its command. All of this sounded good, but . . . The 13th Panzer Division, which had been in action since the first day, numbered only panzergrenadiers in regimental strength, four to six guns and a few anti-tank guns. The division had not a single tracked armored vehicle. The 10th Panzergrenadier Division was in much the same shape and the 153rd Field Training Division was even worse off. Only *Panzerverband* Braun, which had been sent by the army group, with elements of the 20th Panzer Division, twenty-one assault guns and the assault battalion of the Eighth Army, could be considered to have much combat potential – once again it was too little and much too late.

As the corps withdrew south toward the lower course of the Seret it was forced to fight a running battle against pursuing Russian forces. The 10th Panzergrenadier Division and the 13th Panzer Division found themselves facing encirclement. By the afternoon of August 26 the Russians had reached the area east of Foscani; the next evening, as the corps began to prepare its defenses on the Seret east of Galatz, Soviet armored spearheads were drawing nearer, having already reached Buzau in the corps' deep left flank. In spite of destroying a large number of enemy tanks, the 15th Flak Division's 12th Flak Regiment, positioned along the major Foscani-Buzau road with other elements, was unable to halt the rapid Soviet advance. In order to avoid being outflanked and encircled, the corps withdrew south from the Seret positions it had just occupied, with the motorized elements leading the way. Then, on the afternoon of the 28th, a report reached the corps command post in Cilibia that the Russians had taken Buzau. Afterward the corps' Commanding General decided to force a breakthrough to the west, south of Buzau.

Following an exhausting march during the night of August 28/29, and after the assault guns driving point had repeatedly encountered and driven away enemy forces, the motorized elements of the 13th Panzer Division, the 153rd Field Training Division and *Panzerverband* Braun reached the Cheraseni area, fifteen kilometers south of Buzau. The 10th Panzergrenadier Division had initially stayed behind in Cilibia to cover the rear. The horse-drawn and foot elements of the corps arrived later in the morning.

Hidden in a small wood east of the major road from Buzau to Bucharest, over which a steady stream of Soviet columns of all types was heading south completely unmolested, on the morning of August 29 four German Generals sat down for a discussion with the Corps General, *Freiherr* von Bechtoldsheim. How were they to proceed? Following the deliberations *General* von Bechtoldsheim gave permission for all the mobile elements of his corps to make their way under their commanders to the south toward the Danube and still friendly Bulgaria. All of the foot elements, on the other hand, were to set out that evening in an attempt to break out to the west. During the coming night an infantry attack led by *General* von Bechtoldsheim and supported by assault guns broke through the enemy southwest of Buzau. There were encounters with Russian infantry in corn fields, vineyards and forests. The troops ran into difficult terrain, where most were killed, wounded or captured. After pushing on through the Carpathians, on the morning of the 31st a group of about 100 stragglers led by General von Bechtoldsheim reached the road to the Buzau Pass. This small group with the Commanding General was one of the few from the entire corps to escape.

The motorized and armored elements also failed to get through. *General* Braun's group, which still had more than twenty assault guns and a lone Panther tank, met its end on the 30th at the Buzau-Mitzil rail line, which the Soviets had barricaded. Braun's forces tried to break through the blocking position and were scattered.

Setting out during the forenoon of the 29th, the 13th Panzer Division and the 153rd Field Training Division, which still had a number of guns, in total a mixed group of four to five-thousand men, reached the village of Calasari on the Danube. There the Rumanians barred the bridge and demanded that the Germans surrender for internment, which was the same as being taken prisoner. Since his troops did not appear capable of an attack on heavily-occupied Calarasi, and wishing to avoid further casualties, *General* Bayer declared to the assembled officers that he was unwilling to accept the responsibility for such an attack. As there was no other way out it was decided to lay down their weapons and surrender the next morning. The *General* left it to each officer and man to follow him or to try and get through on his own. He released the troops from his command. Such steps had already been taken by many generals and division commanders.

In the afternoon of the 30th the motorized group of the 10th Panzer Division came to a large wood west of Calasari, about fifteen kilometers north of the Danube. There all the remaining guns, vehicles, heavy weapons and radios were rendered unusable. That evening the troops assembled all of the available tires, inner tubes, canisters, gasoline cans, etc, as makeshift floats in preparation for crossing the river.

During the forenoon of the 31st about 100 men, including the division commander, crossed to the Bulgarian side of the river in spite of a heavy storm and gunfire from two Rumanian monitors anchored upstream. They were interned by the Bulgarians, and as soon as Bulgaria declared war on Germany were handed over to the Soviets.

The individual march groups had long since broken up. The men had been instructed to try and make their way to Bulgaria in groups of three to four men, as the way to the Carpathians was blocked. Only a few succeeded, and they too eventually ended up in Russian captivity.

Thus XXIX Army Corps, the last, had been completely smashed.

•

On August 31 victorious Soviet troops entered the Rumanian capital of Bucharest.

A battle group under *General* Winkler, hastily formed on orders of the army group and consisting of remaining army elements, primarily the 12th Flak Regiment, held open the northwest section of Buzau and the following day the Buzau Pass[18], before fighting a delaying action in the Buzau Valley. It was thanks to the efforts of this battle group that numerous train and rear-echelon units belonging to the army group, army and corps, which had been on the retreat to Buzau since the 25th, as well as many stragglers reached the Hungarian part of the Carpathians. With great difficulty the Germans succeeded in establishing a thin line of security in the Transylvania region using troops rushed to the area. Soon this line, too, came under pressure and was forced to fall back.

•

A few words about the Rumanians.

On August 23 a well-planned coup took place in Rumania. The former head of state Antonescu was imprisoned, and the same day the young King Michael went on the radio to announce a cease-fire with the Soviet Union and issued orders to all Rumanian troops to cease hostilities against the Russian armed forces. The serious consequences to Rumania's former German allies caused by the betrayal, the collapse of the entire German Army rear area in Rumania, which in places resulted in fighting between German and Rumanian troops, will not be gone into here. They had little to do with events at the distant German-Rumanian front, which was already collapsing, and had scarcely any effect there.

A few Rumanian units had carried out open betrayal shortly before the beginning of the Soviet offensive, such as the 5th Cavalry Division.[19] Others, like the 4th Mountain Infantry Brigade, immediately threw down their weapons and left the front. Other Rumanian units began to retreat without offering much resistance. Some senior Rumanian officers and commanders recognized the coming revolt and released their troops to go home, saying that the war was over. Other Rumanian units, such as the 1st Cavalry Division and the 11th Infantry Division, fought well, and their were cases where Rumanian troops abandoned by their officers fought on bravely with German units.

It was not the betrayal by the Rumanians which had led to the collapse of the German-Rumanian front. The German command should have learned from the events at Stalingrad in November 1942, where the Soviets broke through Rumanian units before encircling the first Sixth Army. Now they had repeated the process against the second Sixth Army. On account of their mentality, training, armament and command, the Rumanian soldiers were not equal to a major Soviet offensive. The German High Command should have known this.

The Soviets dealt with their new allies (Rumania declared war on Germany soon after the revolt) in a less than friendly fashion. Between August 23 and 31 the Red Army took more than 130,000 Rumanian troops prisoner during hostilities. The disintegrating Rumanian armies and corps were disarmed and about one-and-a-half-million Rumanian soldiers were sent to the Soviet Union, where they were employed as forced laborers. A new Rumanian First Army was formed from communist cadres and new recruits and was "allowed" to fight at the side of the Russians.

"Rückkämpfer" Fight Their Way Through

But back to the German troops. Here too there were those who wished to avoid capture at any cost and who sought to make their way across the many kilometers to a new German front. The area between the Prut and the Carpathians had long since been in enemy hands. Pursued and harried by the enemy, travelling on foot, these fugitives sought to make contact with friendly forces, enduring unspeakable hardships and deprivation. Their hopes were largely frustrated, however. The German front did not remain stationary in the wooded mountains, rather it got further away day by day. There may have been as many as 18,000-20,000 men who set out to reach the safety of the Carpathians. Many lost their way in the forests and were captured or died alone in the wilderness. Many more were shot or killed by Rumanian or Russian troops, while others succumbed to wounds or illness.

Only a very few managed to get through, and an even smaller number reached the German lines in Transylvania, Hungary. Others lost their way and wandered after the withdrawing German front for weeks. In the end, the reception staffs of the Sixth Army reported a total of only 350 returnees, the Eighth Army about 1,200.

Among the few were *Major* Schwammberger, *Oberleutnant* Steinmeyer and an *Obergefreiter* of the 161st Division, who reached German units in the Transylvania area on September 23.

There was also a ragged and scarcely recognizable member of the tactical staff of the 79th Division, the only member of his division to return.

There was *Oberleutnant* Baron of the 444th Corps Signals Battalion, who reached the German front near Neumark (Hungary) with five men of the 258th Division on October 3. The Commanding General of LII Corps, *General* Buschenhagen, and eight men managed to travel on foot from the forests west of Bucau to the Carpathians. They were betrayed by a Rumanian on September 13 and were handed over to the Russians.

There was *Hauptmann* Platz of the 258th Division, who, together with ten men, reached the German lines in the Hungarian frontier area on September 7 just before they were withdrawn.

There was a twenty-one-year-old *Gefreiter* of the 376th Division, who reached a unit of the 4th Mountain Infantry Division near Czikzereda on September 8 following a ten day journey. He took part in further fighting with the unit and was taken prisoner by the Russians six days later.

The following are reports from some of those who made their way back:

Oberleutnant Baron (444th Corps Signals Battalion):

"August 28 – were assembled in a wood south of Husi. There I reported to *General* Buschenhagen. I found him sitting on the forest floor. With him was *Oberstleutnant* Wollmann, his senior signals officer, and *Obergefreiter* Stein, his orderly. The General spoke with praise of the men because of their courageous conduct during the charge through the Prut marshes. He was very confident and firmly believed that we would succeed in fighting our way through to the new German front.

Following a brief rest we moved out in a westerly direction. As darkness fell we camped for the night after posting sentries. I and the few men still with me stayed very close to our General. In a brief conversation he informed us of his intentions.

During the following days and nights we marched on in a southwesterly direction. There was frequent contact with the enemy. We had practically nothing more to eat, except for one or two men who had some chocolate left. We quieted our hunger as best we could by gnawing on uncooked ears of corn from the fields. As a result of the lack of nourishment our physical endurance sank rapidly. Twice we captured some bread and once even some wine. Unfortunately, it was so little that it couldn't have satisfied even one of us. Throughout these days of marching through dense forests with no roads or paths the General remained an example of calm and confidence.

During the course of the 28th and 29th we were joined by *Major* Brückner, *Major* Dittfeld and *Hauptmann* Wissig. It was *General* Buschenhagen's intention to march in a southwesterly direction. He believed that we would reach the first German forces in the Barlad area. This hope was soon abandoned, however. The word now was that the new German main line of resistance had been established at the Seret, and the General suspected that we would find the Trotus-Seret line occupied by German troops. Unfortunately this assumption was also false, as it later turned out. Statements by civilians sounded less encouraging and were full of contradictions. One said the front was located at the Carpathian passes, while another maintained that the Russians were already in Budapest. At this point we decided to veer west and cross the Trotus west of Onesti. From there the General proposed to march up the Slanic Valley and then climb the high Carpathians. No one thought of giving up our flight. If necessary we were ready to march to Budapest. During the marching and fighting in the forested area southwest of Husi it had been my duty as executive officer to man the point (fortunately I still possessed a march compass), fight off Russian attacks, carry out counterattacks, lead patrols, etc. I had a great deal of luck in all these endeavours.

The captured food was divided equally. Together, the red wine and the German bread taken from the Russians revived our strength greatly, but unfortunately we obtained only a little food. Luckily the nights were still quite warm, and during the day it was still hot. Since we dared not leave the forest, we also suffered from thirst as well as hunger. It began to rain after we reached the Seret.

On August 28 our battle group still consisted of at least 2,000 men, but in the days that followed this number dwindled more and more. We suffered losses in dead, wounded and captured. Many remained behind out of weakness or a lack of energy. But many, mostly whole groups, lost contact with the main group during the night marches through the dense forest and as a result of combat with the pursuing Russians. As a result, four days later our numbers had dropped to about 500 men.

On September 1 we reached the end of the great forests near Albesti. From here on the way led largely over open terrain. Moving out of the forest and marching across the open fields would have been impossible for our still strong battle group. The General therefore decided to split up into small units of about thirty men. I remained with the General's group.

We moved out of the forest during the night of September 1/2 under heavy fire. We had to run for our lives for about two hours, before we managed to shake off our pursuers. The same night we crossed the Barlad Valley. In the days which followed we passed through the area between the Barlad and Seret. By day we hid in small woods, and marched by night. Russian columns frequently passed close by our hiding places, but we were not discovered. The march demanded the last of us. Every night we had to climb uphill and down seven to eight times, straight through almost endless corn fields, always avoiding roads and settlements. Only three times during these days did we sneak into Rumanian villages to steal food. There wasn't much left, the Russians had been very thorough. Nevertheless, we gladly accepted any supplement to our regular diet of young corn. Occasionally we managed to obtain some milk, but more often it was just some cheese, and very rarely a few eggs and some bread or grapes. *General* Buschenhagen ate the same as the rest of us.

Since we got no night rest our endurance decreased in spite of the now readily available, if primitive, supply of food. Especially tiring was the climbing up and downhill. The worst, however, was clambering through the deep ravines, which the rain had transformed into quagmires. We had to increase the frequency of rest stops. At each halt everyone fell at once to the ground and went to sleep.

We reached the Seret during the night of September 6/7. We spent the day hidden in the forest along the riverbank. By some miracle we escaped detection by the Red Army troops combing the forest. We swam across the Seret after dark on the evening of September 7. We were able to take our uniforms and everything else we had with us to the west bank. Undetected, we crossed the Bucau-Adjud road, which was heavily travelled by the Soviets. Once again we came to a heavily wooded area, the western edge of which we reached during the night of September 8/9. Here the Russians had set up a strong blocking line to catch the groups of Germans who had broken out. We were unable to get through. During the following nights we therefore veered more to the north. As before we hid in the woods during daylight hours. Once we were surprised by the Russians, but most of us escaped with a fright. Finally, during the night of September 10/11, we broke through. We turned back toward the southwest and crossed the Bucau-Onesti road unhindered. Daybreak on September 12 found us on a hill near the village of Caractaul. Far and wide there were no forests, and the village was heavily occupied; they must see us. In order to make pursuit more difficult, the General decided to split up our group, which still numbered twenty-five men, once more. My group consisted of nine men. There was no time for discussion and deliberation. We had to move if we were to get away. *General* Buschenhagen planned to make his way northwest with his group. My people and I maintained a west-southwesterly direction . . ."[20]

Hauptmann Platz (258th Infantry Division):
"After we had broken through the Russian blocking position (August 29), we quickly made our way to the Barladul, which we crossed over a still-intact bridge. There was no resistance. A great mass of soldiers, most on foot and only a few with vehicles, were heading west. As I had a *Schwimmwagen*, I was able to negotiate the terrain quite easily. At a marshy area I took the Ic of the 370th Division, who was wounded, into our vehicle. At about 1000 we reached Foltesti. Outside the village I met the Ia of the 258th Division, who was likewise driving west. He had just spoken with the commander of the 376th Division. The two agreed to rest for two hours then strike out west in the direction of Kronstadt. After the rest stop, while soldiers were still coming out of the pocket from Vutcani, I drove out of the village in a westerly direction with the Ia of the 258th Division and about eight other vehicles to Silistea. There we learned from the inhabitants that the Russians had been on the road west of Silistea, but that the area was now free of the enemy.
We drove on along the road which led south from Silistea. Suddenly, we were attacked by Russians. This resulted in a brief firefight,

during which our group, which was about thirty men strong, was able to drive away the enemy and then continue on its way. In the melee the Ic of the 370th Division was shot in the back, this being the eighth time he had been wounded. We drove on. In the meantime it had become dark, and we had to cross the Par Tutopa. The Russian sentries near the village of Pogana failed to notice us and the bridge over the river was unguarded. As a result, we were able to turn west again just outside the village of Bogesti. We spent the night in a wood.

The enemy maintained a constant watch on the elements which had broken out of the pocket at Vutcani from the air and launched air attacks against the larger groups.

On the morning of August 30 we resumed our journey. We obtained food from the local civilians, who were relatively friendly. The Rumanian soldiers we encountered along the way, some with weapons and some without, did not exhibit any hostility towards us.

For us everything depended on getting out of this area as quickly as possible, so as to escape the search being carried out by the Russians in the area. In the forest north of Tavadaresti we encountered various Rumanian civilians, and questioned them about the condition of the bridges at the Seret. We learned that there was supposed to be a good and intact road bridge near Bogoaza. We waited for dusk. During this time we met a group of approximately thirteen men from the 10th Panzergrenadier Division, who were making their way west under the leadership of an *Oberleutnant*. We gave them a 1:300,000 map.

At about 2000 we drove to the Seret, but were unable to find the bridge in question. We therefore set out along a very good road running along the east side of the Seret from northwest to southeast and came to an intact and unguarded bridge, which we crossed. We encountered no enemy traffic in the Seret Valley. Just before the rail bridge, however, the vehicle in front of me – I was the fourth in line – stopped. We turned off our engines and listened. We could hear Russians celebrating about 150 meters away. There was no trace of our first vehicle. It turned out that the second vehicle had run out of fuel. Its crew set out to the west on foot. We were not far from the rail bridge and quite close to the Bucau-Adjud highway. Where our road joined the highway there was a Russian sentry. He spotted us and opened fire on the vehicle in front of me. I drove away at high speed, overtaking enemy artillery as I fled, finally becoming stuck in a corn field. We were also out of gas. We rendered our vehicle unusable and set out on foot in a westerly direction. I had a march compass and a 1:300,000 map, which made orientation relatively difficult. Later in the mountains the map was as good as useless. We had not eaten properly for some time and our nourishment was primarily grapes and water. We spent the night in a forest northeast of Borsani.

t dawn on August 31 we resumed our march in a southeasterly on. Our progress was slow as the seriously wounded Ic of the Division could move only with great difficulty and at times had to be carried. The use of roads was out of the question, we had to trek 'cross-country' to avoid encounters with the Russians. At about 1700 we reached the edge of the forest and the bank of the Trotusul, about three kilometers east of Borsani. Here we observed traffic on the highway until darkness fell. It was mostly supply traffic, isolated trucks and horse-drawn vehicles, now and then a tank. The villages didn't appear to be particularly heavily occupied, so I decided to cross the Trotusul, the railroad tracks and the highway after dark, in order to reach the forest south of Borsani-Balca.

We waded the Trotusul by moonlight – I had scouted a shallow place during the afternoon – and reached the railroad tracks. The waters of the Trotusul were hip deep and the current was quite strong. We crossed the railroad tracks and highway unnoticed and were soon in the forest south of Borsani. Sometime about morning there were loud tank noises. We ran in a westerly direction and then laid down in a thicket to sleep. The Ic from the 370th Division lay moaning in great pain. As evening fell we moved on in a westerly direction. By the time morning came we suspected that we were quite close to the southern section of Balca. We observed a house off to one side for about an hour and saw no Russians. As we had no food we decided to approach the house. We received a friendly reception from the inhabitants and were given corn and fruit. The Ic of the 370th Division decided to stay there until his wounds had healed somewhat. The inhabitants of the house placed him in a potato cellar located off to the side and cared for him. There were no Russians in the village. From the population we learned that they were using the Adjud-Onesti road only as a supply route.

After dark the three of us, *Oberwachtmeister* Gzyl, *Obergefreiter* Birke and I, set out again, in a westerly direction as before. We continued to avoid the roads. We spent the night of September 1/2 in the forest southeast of Marinesti. After walking until noon the next day, we came to a small train station. There we were warmly received by former Rumanian soldiers and other inhabitants, who provided us with food. Some Rumanians, who had apparently escaped from a pocket, promised to guide us into the Ousoro area. We followed the two Rumanians all day, and about evening arrived in the correct area. Along the way we repeatedly encountered small groups of Rumanian soldiers, who were without weapons. They all readily gave us information and told us that other groups of German soldiers were on the run. We had suspected this, because Russian aircraft were constantly patrolling the area, primarily old, slow biplanes.

Once again we spent the night in the forest and on the morning of September 3 came to a village. After determining that it was free of the enemy, we went up to a house. The people motioned us away, but soon afterward came with corn bread and bacon. They told us that the whole area was being patrolled by the Russians, who were severely punishing any inhabitants helping German soldiers. The village was called Gura-Vai. We moved on from there and along the way met the occasional herdsman.

After another evening in the forest we moved on, using only the march compass. There were no villages in this area, so that orientation from our map was impossible. After walking uphill and down through thickets until noon without finding a path, it began

to rain. The rain was so heavy that we were soon soaked to our skins in spite of our tent squares. In the evening, after a long walk through undergrowth and over hills and through valleys, we came to a group of houses which appeared to be inhabited. It turned out that this was a Hungarian border station, where about fifty German soldiers had stopped, all escapees from the Vutcani pocket.

We spent the night here, dried our uniforms, cooked some potatoes and ate some apples. The next morning we went on our way, and another group of about twenty men marched along with us. Soon it began to rain again. At about midday we came to another Hungarian border house on an old pass road in the Carpathians. It was abandoned and there was no food present. After another hour we came upon two riderless horses in the pouring rain. We shot one of the horses and started a fire with the aid of a box of matches. Soon everyone was enjoying a piece of roast horse flesh. Afterward we continued along the pass road. In the hills we met numerous small groups of soldiers. Since early morning we had been hearing battle noises, especially artillery, from the west. The front was obviously not far away. In the afternoon we met a group returning from that direction. They reported that the pass road led directly to the Russians. I therefore decided to head south to, if possible, go around the front. We spent the night in an empty house.

On September 6 we resumed our march, initially in a southerly direction. After about an hour we turned west again. On the way we scaled an unwooded hilltop. Below us we saw a plateau with several villages. We could still hear the sounds of battle to our right, and we believed that we had successfully skirted the Russian lines to the south. We hurried down into the valley and still had several small hills to cross before reaching the plateau. Suddenly we heard the sound of marching men and engines not far away. There was a column on the road about 100 meters from us. It was not, as we had hoped, German soldiers, rather we found ourselves right beside a Russian advance road. Since crossing the road unseen in broad daylight with a group of twenty men seemed unlikely, we split up into various groups. About ten men stayed with me.

When a gap developed in the column I decided to dash across the road with my people as quickly as possible. Another swing to the south did not seem advisable, primarily because we were no longer up to it physically. We managed to cross the road without being spotted by the Russians. As we did not know where we were in the Russian rear we moved only by night and passed close by a Russian artillery position. As it was pitch black and we had made a great deal of noise passing through a thicket, we waited until the moon rose at about 2400. Suddenly we found ourselves facing a Russian sentry, who was guarding a group of horses about twenty meters away. Once again we had to disappear quickly and once again we spent the night in a wood.

On the morning of September 7 we saw a village ahead of us in which fighting was going on. We met a shepherd who told us that the village of Gelencs, about six kilometers away, was still occupied by German troops. We walked south at first then veered southwest. After crossing a hill we came to a small Hungarian refugee camp where we were given some food. Soon, however, the call went up that the Russians were coming and we were chased away. An old man, who spoke some German, described the way to the German lines. He also maintained that the village of Gelencs was still occupied by German and Hungarian troops.

We walked down the mountain toward the road which led to Gelencs. We could see the village ahead. The sound of fighting and air attacks could be heard and seen to the north. We reached Gelencs at about 1900. In the village we met two German pioneers who had orders to blow the bridge, as our troops had just withdrawn.

We had made it to our lines and were saved . . ."[21]

Oberleutnant Steinmeyer (161st Infantry Division):

"August 28 – Following the breakout from the marshy Prut lowlands I assembled a group of about 400 men and with these reached the wooded area south of Husi. We surprised and overpowered a Russian Major. On him we found a map covering the area to the Seret, which later proved to be very useful. In the forest I ran into *Major* Schwammberger, whom I knew from my division. He had broken through with a handful of people the previous night. We now decided to stay together and try and make our way to the new German lines.

Suspecting a threat, we resumed our march to the southwest that same evening, and the next morning found us at the major Vaslui-Barlad road, east of Deleni. *General* Müller had earlier specified a general direction of southwest. But as we observed a very heavy flow of traffic in that direction – tanks, motorized and horse-drawn columns and marching Russian units –, and concluded that the enemy advance south from Jassy was aimed toward Galatz and Foscani, we reached the decision to strike out toward the west in an attempt to reach our troops at the Seret. The next morning we heard the sound of combat in our rear, especially heavy weapons, and assumed that the Russians had surrounded the entire forest and were now advancing against our troops inside to finish them off.

˙On August 30 we were chased by enemy search parties for the first time and were split up. In the period that followed we had almost daily contact with the enemy, most often by night, so that our group was soon reduced to fifty, and later eleven, men. This was partly due to combat losses and partly to individual groups becoming separated. They lost contact with my group, which was leading the way, in the dark nights and in the extensive forests and corn fields, and in spite of our efforts we were unable to find them again. On September 5 we swam across the Seret. We were disappointed not to find our troops there, but we did not lose our courage or energy, nor did we give up hope that our plans would succeed.

The next day we were fired on and surrounded by Rumanian soldiers in the Carpathian foothills. After an hour long battle seven of us managed to break out of the encirclement. From then on we suspected that the Rumanians had turned against us. On one occasion we captured two Russians as well as two rifles and a large quantity of ammunition.

Our diet consisted mainly of fruit, cucumbers, corn and raw or hastily-cooked potatoes. Now and then we approached villages looking for food, which we received from the more or less friendly villagers. After being betrayed several times to Russian patrols and search parties we avoided any further contact with the Rumanian population.

Once we found a German leaflet from army headquarters with an appeal to the soldiers of the Sixth Army and a sketch of the situation of the front in the Carpathians. It was somewhat dated but gave us some important clues. Sometimes we heard the thunder of guns in the distance. We celebrated too soon, however, as for days we got no closer to the front as our troops appeared to be withdrawing.

In about mid-September the Soviets began a prepared campaign to influence the civil population against us with the usual lies and slander. It urged them to 'soften up' any German soldiers trying to escape by refusing them assistance and thus force them to give up. When we reached the area near the front we found that a story had been spread among the population that there was no longer a front, rather a large, new pocket which was about to be destroyed. In spite of all their clumsy efforts, the Soviets failed to break our will to reach our lines – in spite of the effects of physical exhaustion, the reduction in the pace of our trek caused by the numbers of wounded, the festering sores on our feet and in spite of the mental strain and disappointment when we neared the German front only to have it withdraw again. We were discovered and pursued almost daily. Again and again, however, we succeeded in evading the Russian search parties, and after crossing the Carpathians disappeared into the forests of southern Hungary.

On September 23, following a thirty-two-day trek of over 570 kilometers, we – Schwammberger, an *Obergefreiter* from another division and I – reached our own lines, a Hungarian regiment in the Adrian area in Transylvania, west of Saxon Regen."

This handful of men were not the only ones to have escaped destruction. About 10,000 men of the rear-echelon units of the Sixth and Eighth Armies escaped through Galatz and via Ploesti to Transylvania, including 500 men of the 257th Infantry Division's field workshop company.

The Sixth Army had been completely destroyed.

The Eighth Army was left with the three German divisions making up its left wing, which had not been attacked.

This was all that remained of the two German corps on the Rumanian front following the total collapse of Army Group South Ukraine, which had tried to defend Rumania according to Hitler's will. Twenty-one numerically strong German divisions had been obliterated within nine days.

Once again the Soviet Command had carried out a tremendous operation with great force and speed, employing huge numbers of troops, tanks, artillery and aircraft, and had brought about the total collapse and complete destruction of the German-Rumanian front.

At the end of the battle on September 5, 1944, the war diary of Army Group South Ukraine observed:

"The surrounded corps and divisions of the Sixth Army must now be considered as lost. There is no longer any hope that some cohesive units will fight their way through. It is the greatest catastrophe ever suffered by the army group."

Lost were:

6 corps headquarters (IV, VII, XXIX, XXX, XXXXIV and LII Army Corps); from these two Commanding Generals were killed, three were captured and one was able to break through.

18 infantry divisions (9th, 15th, 62nd, 76th, 79th, 106th, 161st, 257th, 258th, 282nd, 294th, 302nd, 306th, 320th, 355th, 370th, 376th and 380th), as well as the 153rd Field Training Division, 10th Panzergrenadier Division, 13th Panzer Division and *Panzerverband* Braun. Of the division commanders five Generals were killed, twelve were captured. Of the remaining thirteen Generals only one was able to escape.

7 assault gun brigades and many army and corps units, in addition to all of the war materiel of the above units.

The previously quoted officer from the 62nd Infantry Division wrote of Soviet captivity:

> "After being taken prisoner we stayed three days in a collection camp near Hancesti, then about 20,000 prisoners were marched about 120 kilometers to Tiraspol. We had to cover this distance in seventy-two hours, driven on by escorting Russian soldiers. The less-seriously wounded were also forced to walk, there were no vehicles for those with foot injuries. All those who could not keep up were shot with submachine-guns by the Red soldiers. In Thigina we were forced to pass through the village as a "show march" for the population, who stood in the doorways and watched silently and depressed as we passed by.
>
> In Tiraspol about 60,000 of us prisoners were forced to live in the open along the Dnestr. On September 13 about 800 German and 300 Rumanian officers were loaded into wagons and on October 1 arrived at Jelabuga, where the largest POW camp for officers in the Soviet Union was located. Convicted of alleged war crimes I was sent to various prisons and punishment camps, among them Workuta on the Polar Sea coast and several in Siberia. In 1955, after ten years in Soviet captivity, I returned home."

Here, too, exact German losses are unknown. About 125,000 were estimated to have been killed. 80,000 prisoners are said to have died in Rumanian collection camps, which have become known as starvation camps, during transport by rail to Russia and in Soviet camps. The number of returnees from Russian captivity is given as 70,000.

According to an official Soviet report from September 13, 1944, German losses were 256,000 men, of these 150,000 killed and 106,000 captured. In addition to vast quantities of war materiel of every kind, the German forces lost destroyed or captured: 830 tanks and armored vehicles, 330 aircraft, 3,500 guns and mortars and 35,000 vehicles.

Extracts from Wehrmacht Communiques:

August 26:
... In the Rumanian part of the Eastern Front our divisions are continuing to withdraw into the assigned areas while fighting off numerous enemy attacks ...

August 27:
... In Rumania the enemy continues to advance southward with motorized units and powerful armored forces. German battle groups are in the process of breaking through Soviet blocking positions on both sides of the Lower Prut in heavy fighting ...

August 28:
... In Rumania our troops are engaged in heavy fighting on both sides of the Lower Prut in an effort to break through. Continuing his advance to the south and west, the enemy has crossed the Seret and has taken Foscani in spite of bitter opposition from our troops. The enemy has lost many tanks in the fighting there ...

August 29:
... In Rumania our units continue to fight on both sides of the Lower Prut against the enemy forces attacking from all sides. Southwest of the Lower Seret, Buzau fell into the hands of the Soviets after a major battle. 27 enemy tanks were destroyed. In the southern part of the eastern Carpathians heavy fighting is under way in the Hungarian frontier area between German and Hungarian troops and advancing Soviet battle groups ...

Disposition of Army Group South Ukraine

(from West to East)
Army Group Headquarters (*Generaloberst* Frießner)

Command Reserves:
10th Panzergrenadier Division
153rd Field Training Division
959th Artillery Brigade

German Eighth Army (*General der Infanterie* Wöhler)

Command Reserves:
Rumanian "Greater Rumania" Armored Division
Rumanian 8th Infantry Division
Rumanian 18th Mountain Infantry Division
905th Assault Gun Brigade

XVII Army Corps: (*General der Gebirgstruppen* Kreysing)
8th Jäger Division
3rd Mountain Infantry Division
Rumanian Border Patrol Units

Rumanian VII Army Corps
Rumanian 103rd Mountain Infantry Brigade
Rumanian 104th Mountain Infantry Brigade

Rumanian I Army Corps
Rumanian 20th Infantry Division
Rumanian 6th Infantry Division

Rumanian V Army Corps
Rumanian 1st Guards Infantry Division
Rumanian 4th Infantry Division

LVII Army Corps: (*General der Panzertruppen* Kirchner)
46th Infantry Division
Rumanian 1st Infantry Division
Rumanian 13th Infantry Division
286th Assault Gun Brigade

Rumanian Fourth Army: (General Avramescu)
Rumanian VI Army Corps
Rumanian 5th Infantry Division
Rumanian 101st Mountain Infantry Division
76th Infantry Division
325th Assault Gun Brigade

Rumanian IV Army Corps
Rumanian 7th Infantry Division

Rumanian 3rd Infantry Division
Rumanian 5th Cavalry Division
Rumanian 102nd Mountain Infantry Brigade

IV Army Corps: (*General der Infanterie* Mieth)
79th Infantry Division
Rumanian 11th Infantry Division
376th Infantry Division
228th Assault Gun Brigade

Rumanian Army Group (General Dumitrescu)
Command Reserves:
13th Panzer Division
Rumanian 1st Cavalry Division

German Sixth Army: (*General der Artillerie* Fretter-Pico)

VII Army Corps: (*General der Artillerie* Hell)
370th Infantry Division
106th Infantry Division
Rumanian 14th Infantry Division
236th Assault Gun Brigade

XXXXIV Army Corps: (*Generalleutnant* Müller)
62nd Infantry Division
258th Infantry Division
282nd Infantry Division
335th Infantry Division
911th Assault Gun Brigade

LII Army Corps: (*General der Infanterie* Buschenhagen)
161st Infantry Division
294th Infantry Division
320th Infantry Division

243rd Assault Gun Brigade

XXX Army Corps: (*Generalleutnant* Postel)

384th Infantry Division
302nd Infantry Division
257th Infantry Division
15th Infantry Division
306th Infantry Division
239th Assault Gun Brigade (in process of being removed)

Rumanian Third Army:

XXIX Army Corps: (*Generalleutnant* Freiherr von Bechtoldsheim)
Rumanian 4th Mountain Infantry Brigade
Rumanian 21st Infantry Division
9th Infantry Division
278th Assault Gun Brigade

Rumanian III Army Corps
Rumanian 15th Infantry Division
Rumanian 2nd Infantry Division
Rumanian 110th Infantry Division

Rumanian II Army Corps
Rumanian 9th Infantry Division

Security and coastal protection battalions on the Black Sea coast.

Luftwaffe

Luftwaffenkommando 4 (*Generalleutnant* Deichmann)

Headquarters I Fliegerkorps
15th Flak Division with four anti-aircraft regiments.

In total I Fliegerkorps had at its disposal 7 reconnaissance *Staffeln*, 1 bomber *Gruppe*, 1 close-support *Gruppe*, 1 anti-tank *Staffel*, 2 night close-support *Staffeln* and 3 fighter *Gruppen* with a total of 318 aircraft.

Of this total 232 aircraft were serviceable on August 20: 60 reconnaissance aircraft, 43 bombers, 57 close-support and night close-support aircraft, 41 fighters and 31 night-fighters.

Notes:

[1] The first German Sixth Army had been destroyed at Stalingrad.
[2] For example, actual strength of the 15th Infantry Division on August 19: 336 officers, 12,697 NCOs and men, 6,355 horses, 419 vehicles
[3] Since the end of July
[4] 200-220 guns per kilometer of front
[5] From the outline of a division history by retired *Brigadegeneral* Willemer in *Die Katastrophe in Rumänien 1944* by Hans Kissel.
[6] Excerpt from a report by an officer of the division.
[7] Focke-Wulf Fw 189
[8] Excerpt from H.F. Reck: *Gehetzt, geflohen, gefangen* . . .
[9] 21st Panzergrenadier Regiment (Commander *Oberst* Feschl)
[10] Belonging to XXXXIV Army Corps
[11] 79th, 258th, 370th and 376th Infantry Divisions
[12] Unaware of the failed surprise attack by the 282nd Division and the enemy situation
[13] Taken from notes
[14] Probably a Russian in German uniform in a captured vehicle
[15] Commanding General of XXXXIV Army Corps
[16] Excerpt from: W. Rehm: *Jassy*
[17] *General* Mieth
[18] Leading to the Carpathians
[19] Not proved
[20] Excerpt from: H. Kissel: *Die Katastrophe in Rumänien 1944*
[21] Excerpt from: H. Kissel: *Die Katastrophe in Rumänien 1944*

Bibliography

Bibliography

Bader, Andreas (Pseudonym "Hausen"): *Von Gott verlassen?*, EOS Verlag, St. Ottilien, 1955

Bauer, Eddy: *Der Panzerkrieg*, Volumes I and II, Verlag Offene Wort, Bonn

Dahms, Helmut, Günther: *Geschichte des Zweiten Weltkrieges*, Wunderlich Verlag, Tübingen, 1965

Degrelle, Léon: *Die verlorene Legion*, Verlag K. W. Schütz KG, Preuss, Oldenburg, 1972 (New edition)

Fricke, Gert: *Fester Platz Tarnopol*, Rombach Verlag, Freiburg, 1969

Frießner, Hans: *Verratene Schlachten*, Holsten Verlag, Freiburg, 1969

Fuller, John F.: *Der Zweite Weltkrieg 1939-45*, Humboldt Verlag, Vienna-Stuttgart, 1952

Gackenholz, Hermann: *Der Zusammenbruch der Heeresgruppe Mitte* in "Entscheidungsschlachten des Zweiten Weltkriegs", Bernard and Graefe Verlag, Frankfurt/Main, 1960

Gareis, Martin: *Kampf und Ende der 98. Infanteriedivision*, Podzun-Verlag, 1956

Görlitz, Walter: *Der Zweite Weltkrieg 1939-1945* Volumes I and II, Steingrüben Verlag, Stuttgart, 1951 and 1952

Großmann, Horst: *Geschichte der rheinisch-westfälischen 6. Infanteriedivision 1939-1945*, Verlag Hans-Henning Podzun, Bad Nauheim

Gschöpf, Rudolf: *Mein Weg mit der 45. Infanteriedivision*, Oberösterreichischer Landesverlag, Linz, 1955

Haupt, Werner: *Heeresgruppe Mitte*, Verlag Hans-Henning Podzun, Dorheim, 1968

Haupt, Werner: *Die 8. Panzerdivision in 2. Weltkrieg*, Podzun-Pallas Verlag, Friedberg, 1987

Heidkämper, Wilhelm: *Witebsk*, Kurt Vowinckel Verlag, Heidelberg, 1954

Hillgruber, Andreas: *Die Räumung der Krim 1944*, Special Edition of the "Wehrwissenschaftlichen Rundschau" No. 9, 1959

Hinze, Rolf: *Der Zusammenbruch der Heeresgruppe Mitte im Osten 1944*, Motorbuch Verlag, Stuttgart, 1980

Jacobsen, Hans-Adolf: *Der Zweite Weltkrieg in Chroniken und Dokumenten*, Wehr und Wissenschaft Verlag, Darmstadt, 1959/60

Kameradenhilfswerk der 78. Sturmdivision (Merker, Ludwig): *Das Buch der 78. Sturmdivision*, Tübingen, 1955

Kissel, Hans: *Die Katsatrophe in Rumänien 1944*, Wehr und Wissen-Verlagsgesellschaft, Darmstadt, 1964

Lange, Wolfgang: *Korpsabteilung C*, Scharnhorst-Buchkameradschaft, Neckargemünd, 1961

Manstein, Erich von: *Verlorene Siege*, Athenäum Verlag, Bonn, 1955

Ploetz, A.G.: *Geschichte des Zweiten Weltkriegs*, Ploetz Verlag, Würzburg, 1960

Reck, Hans, Friedrich: *Gehetzt, gefangen, geflohen . . .*, Kurt Vowinckel Verlag, Berg am See, 1986

Rehm, Walther: *Jassy*, Scharnhorst-Buchkameradschaft, Neckargemünd, 1959

Riecker, Karlheinrich: *Ein Mann verliert einen Weltkrieg*, Friedericus Verlag, Frankfurt/Main, 1955

Röhricht, Edgar: *Probleme der Kesselschlacht*, Condor Verlag, Karlsruhe, 1958

Shilin: *Die wichtigsten Operationen des Großen Vaterländischen Krieges 1941-1945*, Verlag des Ministeriums für Nat. Verteidigung, Berlin, 1958

Stoves, Rolf: *1. Panzerdivision*, Podzun Verlag, Bad Nauheim, 1962

Telpuchowski, Boris S.: *Die sowjetische Geschichte des Großen Vaterländischen Krieg 1941-1945*, Bernard und Graefe Verlag für Wehrwesen, Frankfurt/Main, 1961

Tippelskirch, Kurt von: *Geschichte des Zweiten Weltkriegs*, Athenäum Verlag, Bonn, 1951

Vormann, Nikolaus von: *Tscherkassy*, Kurt Vowinckel Verlag, Heidelberg, 1954

Wagener, Carl: *Heeresgruppe Süd*, Podzun Verlag, Bad Nauheim

Werthen, Wolfgang: *Geschichte der 16. Panzerdivision*, Verlag Hans-Henning Podzun, Bad Nauheim

Winckler, Walter: *Der Kampf um Sewastopol*, Kurt Vowinckel Verlag, Berg am See, 1984

Documents, reports, magazines and other sources from the author's archives.

Rank Equivalent Charts

Ranks of the Waffen-SS, Heer and U.S. Army

Waffen-SS	Heer	U.S. Army
General Officers		
- No equivalent -	Generalfeldmarschall	General of the Army
Oberstgruppenführer	Generaloberst	General
Obergruppenführer	General	Lieutenant General
Gruppenführer	Generalleutnant	Major General
Brigadeführer	Generalmajor	Brigadier General
Staff Officers		
Oberführer	- No Equivalent -	- No Equivalent -
(Wore the shoulder strap of a Colonel)		
Standartenführer	Oberst	Colonel
Obersturmführer	Oberstleutnant	Lieutenant Colonel
Sturmbannführer	Major	Major
Company Officers		
Hauptsturmführer	Hauptmann	Captain
Obersturmbannführer	Oberleutnant	1st Lieutenant
Untersturmführer	Leutnant	2nd Lieutenant
Officer Candidates (Basically equal to Oberfeldwebel & Unterfeldwebel)		
Oberjunker	Oberfähnrich	- No Equivalent -
Junker	Fähnrich	- No Equivalent -
Non-commissioned Officers		
Sturmscharführer	Stabsfeldwebel	Sergeant Major
Hauptscharführer	Oberfeldwebel	Master Sergeant
Oberscharführer	Feldwebel	Technical Sergeant
Scharführer	Unterfeldwebel	Staff Sergeant
Unterscharführer	Unteroffizier	Sergeant
Enlisted Men		
- No Equivalent -	Stabsagefreiter	Admin. Corporal
Rottenführer	Obergefreiter	Corporal
Sturmmann	Gefreiter	Acting Corporal
SS-Obersoldat*	Obersoldat*	Private 1st Class
SS-Soldat*	Soldat*	Private

*Note: Soldat is a general term. Other words here are Schütze, Grenadier, Füsilier, depending upon the combat arm to which the soldier belonged.

Source of U.S. World War II army equivalents: War Department Technical Manual TM-E 30-451, *Handbook on German Military Forces*, 15 March 1945.

Ranks of the Luftwaffe, RAF and USAAF

Luftwaffe	Royal Air Force	US Army Air Force
Generalfeldmarschall	Marshall of the Royal Air Force	General (Five Star)
Generaloberst	Air Chief Marshall	General (Four Star)
General der Flieger	Air Marshall	Lieutenant General
Generalleutnant	Air Vice Marshall	Major General
Generalmajor	Air Commodore	Brigadier General
Oberst	Group Captain	Colonel
Oberstleutnant	Wing Commander	Lieutenant Colonel
Major	Squadron Leader	Major
Hauptmann	Flight Lieutenant	Captain
Oberleutnant	Flying Officer	First Lieutenant
Leutnant	Pilot Officer	Lieutenant
Stabsfeldwebel	Warrant Officer	Warrant Officer
Oberfeldwebel	Flight Sergeant	Master Sergeant
Feldwebel	Sergeant	Technical Sergeant
Unterfeldwebel	- No Equivalent -	- No Equivalent -
Unteroffizier	Corporal	Staff Sergeant
Hauptgefreiter	- No Equivalent -	Sergeant
Obergefreiter	Leading Aircraftsman	Corporal
Gefreiter	Aircraftsman First Class	Private First Class
Flieger	Aircraftsman Second Class	Private Second Class

Schiffer Military History
Additional Hard Cover Titles

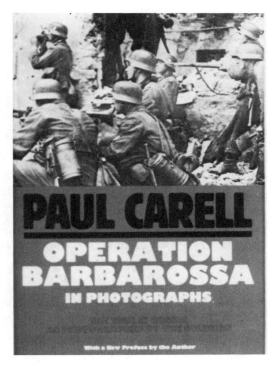

Paul Carell's

OPERATION
BARBAROSSA
in Photographs

Size: 7" x 10"   460 pp.   Over 570 b/w & color photographs, maps, charts, listings $44.95

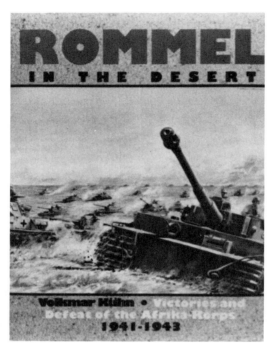

Volkmar Kühn's

ROMMEL
IN THE DESERT

Size: 8 1/2" x 11"   224 pp.   Over 150 b/w photographs, maps, charts, listings $35.00

Holger Nauroth's

THE LUFTWAFFE
From the North Cape to Tobruk
1939-1945 • An Illustrated History

Size: 7" x 10"   236 pp.   Over 500 b/w photographs $29.95

LUFTWAFFE RUDDER MARKINGS
1936-1945

Karl Ries/Ernst Obermaier

Karl Ries & Ernst Obermaier's

LUFTWAFFE RUDDER MARKINGS

1936-1945

Size: 7" x 10"   192 pp.   312 b/w & 12 color photographs $29.95